Information Technology for Schools

Second Edition

Katherine Toth Bucher

Linworth
PUBLISHING, INC.

PROFESSIONAL
GROWTH
SERIES®

Linworth Publishing, Inc.
Worthington, Ohio

Library of Congress Cataloging-in-Publication Data

Bucher, Katherine Toth, 1947-
    Information technology for schools / by Katherine Toth Bucher. -- 2nd ed.
      p.   cm. -- (Professional growth series)
    Includes bibliographical references.
    ISBN 0-938865-65-X (perfect bound)
    1. School libraries--United States--Data processing.
  2. Instructional materials centers--United States--Data processing.
  3. Computer-assisted instruction--United States. 4. Media programs
(Education)--United States. I. Title. II. Series.
Z675.S3B773   1998
027.8'0285--dc21

                                                97-41032
                                                   CIP

Published by Linworth Publishing, Inc.
480 East Wilson Bridge Road, Suite L
Worthington, Ohio 43085

Copyright © 1998 by Linworth Publishing, Inc.

Series Information:
   From the Professional Growth Series

ISBN 0-938865-65-X

5 4 3 2 1

Table of Contents

Acknowledgments

My deepest thanks go to the following people: Francis Clark and Elizabeth (Betsy) Davis, two Norfolk, Virginia, school library media specialists, for their continued support and advice; Lesley S. J. Farmer and Mary Alice Anderson for their review of the manuscript for the second edition; Patti Lane and Jeri Orlando, for checking mail addresses, Internet URLs, and telephone numbers; and Kaye Alsbrooks for scanning documents.

About the Author

Katherine Toth Bucher is coordinator of the graduate program for school library media specialists in the Department of Curriculum and Instruction, Darden College of Education, Old Dominion University, Norfolk, Virginia. She also holds the position of graduate program director for elementary and middle school education. While she has worked in school library media centers, public libraries, and academic libraries, her true love is the school library.

Introduction

When the first edition of this book was written, technology was beginning to arrive in school libraries in unprecedented quantities. The flood has continued in some schools with the updating of microcomputer hardware, the installation of T-1 lines for Internet access, and the purchasing of CD-ROM electronic reference sources. Other schools have only recently begun the process of developing online catalogs and circulation systems or providing electronic reference sources. Still other schools have found that the initial flood of technology has slowed to a trickle and once state-of the art technology falls behind while manufacturers continue to produce faster computers and more powerful software.

The constant in all of this change has been the need for school library media specialists (SLMS) to become technology literate. No matter what type or form of technology arrives in a school library media center, the school library media specialist must be prepared to work with it and to show students and teachers how to use it. With the emphasis on technological information systems, librarians have become "Cybrarians." Technology is also changing what librarians stress in the teaching of library skills. No longer is the emphasis on how to use an index, card catalog, or other reference tool to locate information. Rather, the focus is on how to evaluate and use the information that technology locates or retrieves. The teaching of library skills to students has been expanded to include teaching technology skills to teachers as well.

Why was this book written?

Most SLMSs agree that technology is wonderful. They talk about the benefits of automated library systems and electronic reference sources, the excitement of students using CD-ROM for research, and the enthusiasm of teachers incorporating videodiscs into their lessons.

But, more and more librarians also seem to be talking about stress, specifically "technostress." There are more types of technology arriving everyday in the library, but no one has put more hours in the day, provided more staff, or offered to take any responsibilities off the shoulders of the school librarian. Added to that are the pressures that many librarians feel as they have to cope with the impact of decisions that are made by others. As one high school librarian said, "Anything that comes into the school with a plug automatically goes in the library media center."

This is probably not going to change. Everyone seems to be asking for more from an education system that is often already stretched to the limit. Shrinking budgets on the state and local levels limit the funds available to many schools. In addition, as long as staffing standards are made according to the number of students in a school and not to the jobs performed by the librarian, there will be little hope of additional staff in many libraries. However, if the school library media center is to be the instructional heart of the school, school library media specialists need help coping with the new technologies.

As librarians tune the satellite dish, instruct teachers in the use of videodiscs, teach students to use CD-ROM, plan cooperative lessons with teachers, maintain the automated library management system, and select materials for the collection, their jobs become more complex.

If you are feeling technostress in the library and have turned to this book for help, you must keep several things in mind. First, no one can ever feel completely up-to-date with technology, and an anxious feeling is perfectly normal. Realize that with the rate of change in the modern world, even if you were up-to-date this morning at 9:00 a.m., by noon you would be falling behind.

Next, neither this book nor any other single book will resolve all your technology problems. Technology is changing too rapidly for anyone to know everything. But remember, the job of a librarian is not to know everything, but to know how to find information. You need enough information about the technology to understand the questions and to know where to locate the answers. Also, you do not have to understand the finer points of how a particular machine works in order to use it. Just as you can drive a car without understanding the engineering of the internal combustion engine, you can use technology without being a computer scientist.

Finally, you need to hone your public relations skills and let others in the school and the community know about the wonderful technology found in today's school library media center and about the many things that a school librarian does in the technology age.

What will this book do?

This book was written to help school library media specialists cope with and, hopefully, enjoy technology. Along with explaining each technology, this book will suggest ways to set it up, use it, manage it, troubleshoot it, and introduce it to students, teachers and staff.

Written for the SLMS with varying levels of technical knowledge, it contains practical, easy-to-locate information. In addition to the index, the table of contents provides an outline of each section, and the glossary contains definitions of a variety of terms. At the end of each chapter you will find an annotated bibliography for that chapter. New to this edition is a special Resources section with addresses, Internet addresses, and other frequently needed information about technology.

The intent of this book is to provide you, the school library media specialist, with enough information about modern technology so you feel comfortable about the technology and have basic knowledge that will help you explore individual topics in more depth. This book does not have to be read from cover to cover. Use the index and table of contents to select the parts that interest you and use the glossary to define unfamiliar terms.

Coverage will begin in this section with some terms and information on instructional technologies in general. The first chapter will give suggestions for planning, purchasing, using, and maintaining technology. The following chapters will each present one particular technology in more detail.

Throughout, the emphasis will be on purchasing and using quality equipment. However, since many school libraries cannot upgrade all equipment and often have to "make do" with existing technologies, this book will try to provide practical suggestions and resources for further exploration for a range of technologies.

What won't this book do?

There are, however, things that this book will not accomplish. First, it will not teach you to use specific programs, nor will it teach you to connect every brand of hardware. It also will not give you specific prices for hardware or software since these prices would be out-dated in three to six months. For example, when the first edition of this book was written, a particular fax/modem cost $189. Only nine months later, the cost of that fax/modem dropped to $39.95 and newer, faster modems were on the market.

What this book will try to do is give you enough basic information so that you can have the confidence to talk to a technician or vendor or to read a more technically in-depth book on a specialized topic. You should also know the basic terminology to read and understand the software manual or the hardware set-up instructions. This book will also provide lists of resources with names of sources, products, and vendors that you can consult for up-to-date pricing information. In addition, this book will provide practical tips and suggestions for using technology in a school library, instructing students in information skills, and planning staff development programs for teachers.

Technology is changing rapidly. You are probably reading about or using things in your library that were not commercially available when this book was written. The challenge of technology can really be exciting for you, your students, and your teachers. But, it does require continuing work to keep in touch with trends and new advances. To keep up-to-date, you must attend conferences; visit vendor exhibits; talk to other librarians; read library, education, and general technology periodicals; and take classes and workshops.

Basic Terminology

Below are some basic terms and some abbreviations you should know as you begin to read about technology. Others will be introduced throughout the book.

SLMS. School library media specialist or school librarian. All three will be used interchangeably.

Instructional technology. The hardware and software used in an educational setting. Often referred to simply as technology.

Hardware. Equipment consisting of its physical components and electronic parts.

Software. Programs or the information and instructions used by the equipment to do something. This includes traditional audiovisual software as well as computer programs, videodiscs, CD-ROM discs, and so forth.

Data. Information.

Database. A collection of data or information. A shelf list is a print database with one card (one record) for each item in the library.

PC. An abbreviation used to refer to IBM personal computers and to microcomputers that act like those made by IBM.

Mac. An abbreviation used to refer to the Macintosh series of micro-computers made by the Apple Corporation.

Types of Technology Arriving in School Libraries

While each of these technologies is discussed in detail in later sections, here is an overview of the most common types:

Microcomputer. First used for basic tasks such as word processing, computers are now used to automate circulation systems and control online catalogs. Microcomputers also are the basis for multimedia systems that combine other technologies such as CD-ROM with computers.

There are two major types or platforms of microcomputers commonly found in school libraries today. One centers around IBM PCS and IBM-compatible hardware that use operating systems such as DOS, Windows 95, or Windows NT. The other is based on Apple products such as the original Apple II and the Macintosh. In addition, some schools use Amiga and Commodore systems. Look for a complete discussion of these in the section on computers.

Multimedia. The use of a computer to integrate and control graphics, video, audio, and text information.

CD-ROM (Compact Disc-Read Only Memory). In addition to containing animation, video, and audio information, a single CD-ROM disc can store between 250,000 and 2.5 million pages of information that can be accessed quickly by a computer. More recent developments in disc technology include the DVD (Digital Video/Versatile Disc).

Networks. Two or more computers that are connected electronically and can exchange data. LANs (local area networks) connect computers, printers, CD-ROM drives and other electronic equipment within a room, building, or several buildings and allow sharing of information. Other sharing arrangements or networks such as WANs (wide area networks) exist to connect computers over greater distances to form statewide networks and even national and international networks.

Telecommunications. A term applied to a method of communicating over a distance. In most cases, a computer, communications program, and a modem are all that is needed to reach the world outside the walls of a school via a telephone line. Electronic mail (E-mail), electronic bulletin boards, online search services, facsimile transmission (fax), and teleconferencing are a few of the options.

Internet and World Wide Web. This network of interconnected networks provides access to information throughout the world in print, audio, and video formats.

Cable and satellite television transmission. Cable television is a network for transmitting television signals from a source to members of the network. One familiar example is the commercial cable television system found in many cities and towns. Satellite television relies on satellite senders and receivers such as satellite dishes to transmit the television signal over larger distances.

Interactive video or laser videodisc or videodisc. A single videodisc the size of a 33 rpm record can hold more than 100,000 still pictures, each of which can be accessed by the player in one second. Videodiscs can also store text and video data. A level I videodisc player stands alone. On levels II and III, CAVI (computer-assisted videodisc instruction) allows a computer to control the videodisc.

Desktop video. The use of a computer and special video software and accessories such as the Video Toaster to generate video, to add graphics, titles, and special effects to videotapes, and to function as a video editing system.

Hypermedia. Most frequently associated with Macintosh computers, hypermedia can link text, audio, and video information so that it can be accessed in different ways by different users.

Emerging technologies. Currently, this refers to such technologies as virtual reality, 3-D animation, video information systems (VIS), artificial intelligence, and expert systems.

Chapter 1

Working with Instructional Technology

Technology is changing the work in school library media centers. Book cards are giving way to barcodes, while card catalogs are being replaced by automated online catalogs or OPACs (online public access catalogs). Online searches and CD-ROM databases replace volumes of periodical indexes and sets of encyclopedias. Film clips and slide collections are now stored on laser videodiscs and CD-ROMs. As fax machines receive copies of articles requested from other libraries, computers with Internet connections bring information from resources throughout the world into homes and libraries. Technology is even changing the way in which students take notes and prepare reports as hypermedia stacks replace or supplement the term paper.

This chapter discusses suggestions for becoming technologically literate, and some ideas for planning for technology, maintaining it, using it safely, and training others to use it.

How can you become technology literate?

There is no need to know everything about technology before you purchase it. However, do plan to spend some time gaining basic information about technology. Begin by educating yourself and by keeping current on the changes in the field. Remember, your goal is not to know everything but to have a general idea about what is happening and where to find additional information.

Read general publications. Read articles in general magazines as well as basic books on technology. Even general newsmagazines such as *Newsweek* have features on the changes in technology. One of the simplest and best overviews of computers, printers, and fax machines appeared in the September 1997 issue of *Consumer Reports*.

Read professional publications. Reading professional journals such as THE BOOK REPORT, LIBRARY TALK, TECHNOLOGY CONNECTION, *School Library Media Quarterly, School Library Journal, MultiMedia Schools, School Library Media Activities Monthly, Media and Methods, Computers and Libraries, Information Searcher*, and *Emergency Librarian* will let you see what is happening in other school libraries. Also look at the general technology and computer magazines that are published for schools. Addresses and titles are listed under Resources at the end of this section.

Read a technical publication. While many school librarians benefit from technology magazines written on an advanced level, some technology magazines are available for beginners. My favorite for computers is *Smart*

Computing in Plain English (formerly *PC Novice*). A similar title for Apple computers is *Mac Addict*. There are also special technology magazines available for specific computer platforms, for special applications such as multimedia design, and general software packages such as popular word processing or office programs. Go to a bookstore or magazine stand that stocks a good selection of periodicals and look at a few, especially those designed for home use of computers. Often these are easier to read and less technical.

Use technology. Play with technology. Try it out at a computer show or at a retail sales outlet. Run all the demo programs at the local technology superstore.

Visit others. Visit schools that have a certain type of technology and talk to the people about it. Try it yourself. If your state has a demonstration center where vendors place copies of their materials, schedule a visit.

Team with others. Find a colleague to talk to about technology. If your district has a library supervisor, turn to him or her for assistance. If there is no one in the central office to ask, encourage other librarians in your district to form a library support group. If you are the only elementary SLMS in your system, look at neighboring districts. If you have access to a modem, you can even find someone to answer questions online.

Perhaps you could organize a system of cooperation. Geraldine Andrews, library supervisor in the Chesapeake Public Schools in Virginia, offered a summer with software. Each Wednesday morning during the summer, librarians could drop in at one of the schools for an informal practice session with a new program. A different program was featured each week, and the emphasis was on librarians helping librarians.

Ask teachers for help. Talk to the teachers in your school about technology. Have they seen things at conferences that they liked?

Attend meetings. Take advantage of the programs and workshops offered by state associations or by the state department of education.

Take classes. Computer stores offer a variety of classes as do some school districts in their adult education programs. Find out what your school district offers as staff development. Enroll in a class at a community college or check with surrounding districts to see what they offer.

Seek out experts. Find a friendly expert to adopt you and your library. Parents and students can be a great help. You might even be able to find a clerk in a computer store to help. Finding an expert you can trust takes time. Go slowly and get referrals from friends and other educators. Before you follow an "expert's" suggestion for a major system purchase, try their advice on a small, less costly item.

Check your volunteers. Ask parent volunteers or other friends of the school library for assistance. Perhaps someone in the group could provide some one-on-one training for you.

Request demos and approvals. Arrange for vendors to place materials in your library on an approval basis. That way, you can try out potential purchases. While a demonstration program does not show you the full features of the original, it can still give you the feel of the program.

These ideas will not only help you learn about technology, they will also help you keep current with the major changes in the field and with new products as they are being announced.

What are the myths about purchasing technology?

In some instances, technology will appear in the school library as a gift of an administrator, or as part of a technology package developed by the central administrative office. In those cases, the individual SLMS may not have any input into the selection of the hardware or software. In other cases, it may be up to the individual SLMS to formulate a plan for the purchase of technology and then to find the necessary funds or to convince an administrator to fund the purchase. How should you go about planning for technology?

Begin by being aware of four technology myths.

Myth one: Wait. Technology will stabilize. Don't get caught in this trap. Change in the field of technology is inevitable and new developments are happening every day. Decide what it is that you want technology to help you do, find the technology to do it, and buy it. Yes, new models will come along. But, if you made your purchase based on what the technology would do for you, your original purchase will keep doing its job for years to come.

When *The Electronic Bookshelf* first came out, we purchased two Apple IIe computers, the program, and four titles disks to use with our children's literature classes for pre-service teachers. Our goal was to allow our students to experience what it would be like to take simple comprehension tests on a computer and to prepare tests for a computer database. Each semester, we ask each of our college students who are taking children's literature to take ten electronic tests and write questions for one book which is not already in our database. Now, almost ten years later, we are still using that original program on Apple IIe computers, although we now have over twenty-five disks of questions on hundreds of books. Yes, there have been many upgrades to the original program, but we do not need them. Our original purchase still does the job and our students seem to enjoy seeing the use that can be made of "old technology." Another plus is that we do not have to worry about computers breaking down. Every time a department in our University replaced their old Apple IIe computers, we grabbed a few spares. If something goes wrong with a piece of hardware, we simply replace it.

Myth two: Wait. Prices will fall. Waiting for prices of technology to fall can be a false economy. While experts do not advocate buying technology as soon as a new innovation is announced, they also do not recommend waiting for the price to hit rock bottom. One problem with that approach is the question of how low is low? While you are waiting for the price to fall another hundred dollars, new models with new features may be announced. So you wait for the price of the new model to fall. The result: the technology never gets purchased.

Myth three: It's cheap. We'll find something to do with this hardware. Don't buy technology simply because it seems like the thing to do, or because it's cheap, or because you want to keep up with a neighboring school district.

Here's an example of what can happen to bargain hunters: It sounded like a great deal and an inexpensive way to get the hardware for a computer lab. A friend of mine found 15 monitors and keyboards and two big "towers." But they were being sold at auction and she had to buy them immediately before they were snatched up by someone else. After making a "real steal," she knew she was in trouble when she called the original manufacturer and was asked "do you have U.S. Navy security clearance?" The super deal turned out to be government surplus equipment developed for a special Navy project. The towers were stripped inside, and she never did figure out what to do with the hardware.

Myth four: Technology will solve all your problems. Unfortunately it won't. You will probably find that you have traded your old set of problems for some new ones. Equipment will break. If you install an online catalog, eventually the computer will go down and, at those times, you will wonder why you ever threw out the card catalog. But, in spite of its problems, all of the librarians that I talked to in researching this book agreed that they would never give up technology.

What should you do before you purchase?

Before you rush out to buy technology or sign a contract for a major purchase, there are some things you will want to keep in mind. Planning ahead of time is very important when purchasing technology.

Determine outcomes first. Begin by identifying the things that you hope to happen because of technology. Identify why you want technology and what you expect to do with it. Relate your purchases to the curriculum. Remember that technology is not an end in itself. Rather, it is a means to accomplish something such as faster retrieval of information or better access to the information in the card catalog. If possible, illustrate how technology will save time or money for you, the faculty, and the students. Explain how it will provide new or improved services in the library.

Educate yourself. Gather as much information as you can about the technology, both the hardware and the software that you are considering. Read about the technology. Talk to others, especially to other librarians and to teachers who have had experience using the technology. Visit other schools where the technology is working. Chat on electronic networks about the technology (more about this later). Form an informal professional support group with others who are planning to purchase technology.

Look at both sides. Become familiar with the advantages and the disadvantages of the technology you wish to purchase. In most instances, technology allows things to be done faster (inventory in two days instead of two weeks). In other cases, technology allows you to do things that you might not be able to do otherwise without spending a great deal of time (locate all science books in the library published before 1985).

But you also need to keep your eyes and ears open to the drawbacks to technology. There are some things that can be done just as well without technology, and in some cases you may be trading one set of problems for an even bigger set. Try to profit from experiences that other people have had.

Select software before hardware. If possible, first decide on the software or programs that you want. Then identify the hardware that will run those programs or use that software. There are lots of horror stories about people buying one of the two major platforms of computers only to find that the software they wanted was not available for that system.

Link technology to learning. One selling point of technology is that many of the newer technologies provide information for students with a variety of learning styles and are especially useful with cooperative learning groups. Keep this in mind as you select software.

Consider a consultant. If you are thinking about a major purchase, you might want to hire a consultant with experience in the technology field. Be sure that the person has worked with a similar situation before; request and check references. Don't rely on a resume. Beware of the person who has lots of experience but none of it in education or with school libraries. Also be skeptical of the consultant who is sold, in advance, on one brand of computers. This person usually has on blinders that prevent him or her from seeing the advantages of any other hardware or of systems that do not run on their pet system.

Prevent failure. There are two major reasons that technology fails: (1) when it is not accepted by the user, and (2) when there is inadequate support after the purchase for training, maintenance, and user assistance.

What is a technology plan?

Many schools and school districts have begun to develop formal technology plans to guide the purchase and use of technology. While producing a useful plan is a major undertaking, a well thought-out and unilaterally supported plan is well worth the effort involved. One source that provides information and sample technology plans both in print and via the World Wide Web is the National Center for Technology Planning. See the resources section at the end of this section for complete information on this and other planning aids.

The planning team. While the final plan is important, the procedure used in developing that plan can help assure its success or its failure. Ideally, a technology plan is created by a team representing all individuals who have an interest in the outcomes. This means administrators, classroom teachers, library media specialists, other school faculty and staff, students, and parents. It also means including representatives from businesses; community institutions such as public libraries, technical schools, and colleges; and the general public.

Perhaps representatives from neighboring school districts or from the state department of education belong on the committee. In some cases, a consultant might be hired. Together, these individuals should have expertise in technology, libraries, administration, curriculum, and instruction. In addition, they should be able to articulate the needs and concerns of their respective constituencies.

The planning process. Developing a technology plan is similar to planning a school curriculum.

- A goal is developed or a mission statement is created.
- A timeline for the planning process itself is created.
- Information about the existing technology is gathered and a needs assessment is done.
- Classroom, library, administrative, and other instructional needs are all considered.
- After the data is collected and evaluated, a plan is prepared. Critical issues such as curriculum changes, technical support, budget considerations, training and staff development, student access, the role of the library media center, changes to the physical plant, plan administration and evaluation, and equity are addressed.
- A timeline for implementation, evaluation, and revision is developed and the final report is written.
- The report must be presented to the community in order to gain public support.
- The revised or amended plan is implemented and the ongoing evaluation and revision process begins.

The contents of the plan. While any technology plan should be unique and personalized to fit the needs of the school or district that created it, there are some broad categories of information that should be considered for inclusion. The nature, extent, and degree of formality of the plan will be factors in the degree and the order in which the items are addressed.

- Introduction to the plan: Why was this plan developed? Who does it serve?
- Mission Statement (Vision Statement): What will this plan do? What will the school(s)/library(ies) look like as it is being implemented? When will implementation be completed? Is technology shown to be an investment for the future rather than an expenditure for present use only?
- Development of the plan: Who was involved in developing the plan? How was the plan created? Who supports the completed plan?
- Specific goals of the plan: What are the specific goals and how do they relate to each stakeholder? In what ways is technology being used to support the overall goals of the school and school district? Have uses of technology for technology's sake only been avoided?

- Critical Issues: How does the plan address each of the following critical issues?

  Uses of technology
  - Curriculum
  - Library Media Center
  - Administration
  - Students (including equity issues)
  - Community

  Staff development
  - Hiring
  - Training
  - Evaluation and rewards

  Physical plant/Facilities
  - Maintenance
  - Construction and renovations
  - Security

  Technical support
  - In-house
  - Off-site

  Technology
  - Standards
  - Upgrades
  - Supplies
  - Telephone lines
  - Networks

  Administration of the plan
  - Funding
  - Purchasing
  - Evaluation
  - Modification

- Timeline for Implementation: When will the plan begin? What will happen and when? What will be evaluated? Who will do the evaluation? How will the evaluation be done? When will evaluation occur? Is there ongoing evaluation?

- Budget: What funding is required? How will the funds be acquired? Who is responsible for administering the budget? What cost saving and cost-control measures have been considered and implemented? How does this budget relate to the entire budget of the school or district?

Appendixes, bibliographies, and other items can be added to the end of the plan as needed. In addition, be sure to include an executive summary or abstract with your plan. Geared to those people who will not read the entire plan, the summary should be no longer than one single-spaced page and should include the important points.

What are the hard questions?

In preparing for technology, many librarians are shaken not by questions about the technology itself but by questions about their role after technology comes. Prepare yourself to answer questions similar to these based on your unique situation:

- If technology will make everything so fast and easy, why will we still need a SLMS? Won't clerks do just as well to run the hardware? Why don't we just hire a computer technician?
- If we have a network with access to information in all of the classrooms, why will we need a library media center? Can't the librarian just have an office and go to the classrooms to teach library (information) skills?
- If we have all of this technology and all of these ways to access information, why will we still need to buy books for the library?
- Why are we spending money on machinery when there is nothing wrong with the way we do things now?

Once you get technology, be prepared to answer questions from students and teachers beyond the obvious questions about how to use it.

- How do I make a reference/bibliography citation on an electronic encyclopedia?
- Why do I have to make note cards when I can download information from the CD-ROM and organize it right on the computer?
- Why do I have to write a 700-word paper when I could make a much more interesting multimedia presentation?
- Why should I change my way of teaching just to use this new technology?

You might not know all the answers or even all the questions that will arise because of technology, but be prepared. Read some of the articles in the Resources sections at the end of the chapters in this book and talk to other SLMSs. But beware, there are no pat, easy answers to any of these questions. You really have to think about them and about your changing role. Technology in your library will not only make you a technology manager, but it will also change the way you work with students and teachers as an instructional consultant and information specialist.

How should you purchase software?

It always helps if you know what you want technology to do or what services you want it to help you provide before you make a major purchase. One of the worst misuses of technology is when educators use it to do a non-technology job and then believe they are using technology. I cringe when I see students completing the same old ditto pages, but now they are doing on a computer what they used to complete on paper.

While the following sections include ideas on purchasing various types of software, here are some general suggestions of places to turn for assistance:

Journal Reviews. Certainly, when making any software purchases you want to rely on something other than the producer's catalog. Many of the professional journals such as THE BOOK REPORT, LIBRARY TALK, TECHNOLOGY CONNECTION, *Emergency Librarian, MultiMedia Schools, Booklist*, and *School Library Journal* provide reviews of software including computer programs, CD-ROM programs, and videodiscs. Don't forget to look for reviews in technical journals, computer magazines, and general education periodicals.

Review Guides. Only the Best, an annual guide to recommended educational software, contains reviews of materials for Commodore, Amiga, Apple II series, IBM PC and compatible, Macintosh, Tandy, and TRS-80 Model III. It is available in hard copy, in a disk version for Microsoft Works on IBM or Macintosh, and on many educational electronic bulletin boards. Other guides are listed at the end of this book.

Peer Recommendations. Sometimes the best review comes from an actual user. Teachers and other librarians will often tell you about materials that they have seen or used at conferences and workshops. If you have access to an electronic bulletin board with an educational emphasis, post questions about potential software purchases there.

Articles. Professional journals often contain articles in which librarians write about their experiences with specific software programs or where they share hints for purchasing software.

Preview software. Sometimes the only thing to do is to look at a piece of software yourself or to ask teachers or students for assistance. Figure 1.1 shows a sample software evaluation guide that you can use or modifiy to fit your situation.

What about purchasing hardware?

Software should be the main driving force in any hardware purchase and the curriculum should be the driving force behind the software. However, once you have selected the initial software, you will need to make decisions about the hardware. When purchasing hardware, there are several general principles to keep in mind. Specific tips for individual types of hardware are included in later sections.

Price versus quality. In purchasing hardware, price should not be the first consideration. While no one wants to pay too much, don't sacrifice quality. Obviously cost is a factor, but other things to look for are the capabilities of the machine, its speed in doing those things, and its ease of use. Determine if the hardware will run the current software and have something in reserve for future updates.

If you are worried about the price falling, try the investment strategy of dollar cost averaging. If your plan is to buy six videodisc players, buy two now, two later after the price has fallen somewhat, and two after a further price decline. One disadvantage of this is that you may miss out on quantity discounts. Another is that there will be a lack of standardization of hardware if the

Software Evaluation Guide

Title _____ Type of Software _____

Manufacturer/Vendor_____

Hardware required _____

_____

Date Produced _____ Grade(s) _____ Price _____

Purpose/Instructional Objectives of the software: _____

_____

Key: R - Recommended   A - Acceptable   M - Marginal   NR - Not Recommended

Content Is Appropriate for Intended Audience

	R	A	M	NR		R	A	M	NR
Accuracy	—	—	—	—	Organization	—	—	—	—
Currency	—	—	—	—	Scope	—	—	—	—
Vocabulary level	—	—	—	—	Ease of use	—	—	—	—
Appeal to students	—	—	—	—	Creative	—	—	—	—
Pacing	—	—	—	—					

Physical Features Are Appropriate for Intended Audience

	R	A	M	NR		R	A	M	NR
Clear colors	—	—	—	—	Readable print	—	—	—	—
Pleasing sound	—	—	—	—	Attractive pictures	—	—	—	—

Other physical features: _____

Special Features Are Appropriate for Intended Audience

	R	A	M	NR		R	A	M	NR
Support Materials (Students)	—	—	—	—	Support Materials (Teachers)	—	—	—	—
Warranty	—	—	—	—	Flexible	—	—	—	—

Comment: _____

Potential Use:

____ Curriculum tie-in ____ Personal development ____ Professional development

Comparison to similar titles: _____

Recommendation: _____

Evaluated by: _____

*Figure 1.1 An evaluation form adapted from forms
developed by Linworth Publishing*

models change drastically over the years. On the other hand, all of your hardware will not die at the same time.

Don't buy more than you need or will grow into soon because technology will always be improving. Plan your system for expandability and look for components that can be upgraded.

Always buy the best equipment you can afford. Yes, you can sometimes "make do" with less than the best, but you should plan on your equipment having a useful life of at least five to seven years. Cheap equipment may be close to becoming obsolete when you buy it.

Vaporware. Sometimes it pays to be a skeptic. Just like "the check is in the mail," the words "our newest model is due any day" should wave a red flag in front of your eyes. Selling "vaporware" or products (hardware and software) that, while planned, do not really exist is a problem within the technology business. If you can't see it, don't buy it. If you can't try out the program, be suspicious. If you are told "that problem is fixed in our latest model," demand to try out the latest model.

Problems of new models. Do not assume that newer models are always more reliable. The upgrade of the model that everyone raved about may have its own set of problems. For example, programs written for Windows 3.1 may not run under Windows NT. Likewise, current Macintosh software will not run under NEXT, the new operating system that Apple recently purchased for use on future Macintosh models. While some people may advocate installing two operating systems (such as DOS and Windows NT) on the same machine, technical requirements such as installing software overlays and building partitions on the hard drive for the different systems make this an option only for those who have advanced technical skills.

Hands-on test drive. In deciding on hardware, have the vendors bring their products to your school. Then, let everyone who will use that equipment try it out. That includes the students if it is for their use too. The salesperson may be able to make everything work, but can you?

Technical support. Before you make a decision, call the technical support number for the hardware. Is it a toll-free number? Do you constantly get a busy signal? How long does it take until you get through? Are you put on hold? (IBM estimates that an average call to its technical support has to wait less than 30 seconds. But that wait time increases to several hours in the two weeks after the Christmas holidays.) Does a human answer the telephone? Does a machine tell you to leave a number so that a technician can call you back later? Later in some cases can mean several days.

Clones. Clones, compatibles, or act-like machines are part of the technology business, especially in the microcomputer field. Many manufacturers make machines that act like IBM microcomputers and there are even a few Apple clones. Some modem manufacturers claim that their hardware is compatible or the same as Hayes or U.S. Robotics. While clones can be great, some clones may not always work exactly the same way as the original. Also, some clone manufacturers use specialized parts so that repairs can only be made by using the clone manufacturer's parts.

Check a company's track record. Small manufacturers may go out of business, which makes getting parts and service a major problem. Since you are going to purchase the hardware to run specific software, try the software on the clone. Don't take a salesperson's word that it works. Try it or find other schools and school libraries that successfully use the combination. Unless a clone is 100% compatible, Murphy's law says it will not run the one program you forgot to check or the most important program you bought the computer to run. For example, a friend bought an IBM clone computer. It could do everything the original could do with one major exception. It could not run any of the programs with graphics, such as *Print Shop*.

Bid specifications. If you do not want a clone machine and if your school must send purchases out on bid, be sure to write very tight, specific bid specifications. Ideally, if you decide on a clone, try to get a contract that states that if the software does not work properly, the hardware can be returned at no charge for a full refund.

The exact information that needs to be included in bid specifications varies with the type of equipment. Check your state and local guidelines for complete information on bid specifications. Also, look at some of the resources suggested at the end of this book.

Test site. Some vendors may be willing to offer a special deal if your school is willing to be a test site (sometimes called a "beta site") for new hardware or software. While this may sound enticing and may be cheap in the beginning, it may end up being expensive. If you spend a great deal of time putting your entire card catalog on the microcomputer in the unique format used only by company A, and company A goes out of business, you may be faced with re-entering all of your catalog information for a new system. Or what if you get three new untested CD-ROM drives and all three break the week that the tenth grade starts to research term papers?

Before you become a test site, be sure you know exactly what is involved including any record keeping you will need to do. The bottom line is to determine how much you and your library users will benefit. Remember that "the cutting edge is often the bleeding edge."

Manufacturer and vendor. While many hardware salespersons are excellent, others may not know very much about the technology they are selling or about schools and school libraries. Investigate the experience and track record of the manufacturer and vendor. Check with others about the technical support provided to users. Also check with system users about the repair records of the equipment and about the knowledge of the company representative who will work with you.

What are the hidden costs of technology?

As you spend your money on hardware, remember that hardware is just one of the expenses involved.

Software. Be sure you are aware of all the software requirements of the hardware you are purchasing. For example, an inexpensive purchase such as a modem requires telecommunications software that may add to the price. Are there special site licenses?

Hardware. In addition to the major hardware, will you need items such as network cards and special cabling? Will current hardware need special modifications to work with the new technology?

Training. Factor in the cost of training. Who will set up and maintain the system? Will that person need training? If the hardware includes a network, how will the manager of the network be trained? If the school district is purchasing a large amount of one type of hardware, it might be wise to pay to have one person from the district attend a training school for operation and maintenance of the equipment.

Staff development. Consider the cost of training the teachers, LMS, administrators, and staff, who will use the technology. This is the most overlooked cost of technology. However, unless the people in the schools are trained to use the technology, it will go unused or be under used.

Consumables. Ribbons, paper, disks, and telephone charges can take a sizable portion of the budget. In fact, before buying a printer, you might want to check on the cost of ribbons or ink cartridges. A cheap printer may use expensive cartridges. The usefulness of an online search service is limited if there is no money to pay the telecommunications charges. Shop reputable mail order suppliers, discount office supply stores, and merchandise warehouses for bargains. Be sure to check their refund policies in advance.

Maintenance. The cost of maintenance of the hardware must be considered. In addition to the cost of necessary repairs because of accidents, there is also the cost of maintenance of the equipment because of normal use. Should you purchase a service contract or extended warranty from the vendor? Will the vendor make on-site repairs or provide a free "loaner" for your use? Can a local computer specialist provide the maintenance the technology requires? Do you need a network-certified technician?

Accessories. Another expense is the cost of any accessories such as new furniture, keyboard rests, copyholders, or electricity controls. Surge suppressors are a cheap form of insurance but need to be matched to your equipment to work properly. In some instances, continuous power sources may be necessary if you suffer frequent power blackouts or brownouts.

Dedicated telephone lines. Having at least one phone line to the library is a must. The alternative is talking to a technician on the principal's phone as you discuss a problem about the computer in the library down the hall. The ideal is a dedicated phone line that you can use for telecommunications and a separate phone line for voice calls.

Insurance. Technology is a frequent target of thieves. Nothing is worse than purchasing a new multimedia computer with a CD-ROM drive and find it gone the next Monday morning, the victim of a weekend robbery. Find out the type of insurance held by the school district. Is there any special procedure for adding new equipment to the policy? If the district is self-insured, how long will it take to replace stolen items? Do you need or want special insurance for your technology?

Our department worked hard to get a new Macintosh computer with CD-ROM only to find that, when it was stolen, its value was less than the policy's deductible, and the school did not have the money to replace it.

How can you find funding for technology?

Getting money for technology can be a challenge. However, there are some things that you can do to overcome even this obstacle.

Relate purchases to goals. Justify your requests and explain how this technology will affect student learning. If the administrator has yearly objectives for the school, relate your requests to those goals. For example, if you do not need to spend three hours every Friday doing overdues, you can spend that time in developing instructional partnerships with teachers and planning cooperative lessons.

Team with others. Know who has the money in your school and team-up with them. If the science teachers have some funds to spend, be sure that they know about recommended programs that will match their curriculum. Convince them that by putting their new CD-ROM purchase on the network everyone will have access to it.

Sell the teachers first. Get technology on approval from a vendor for a month. After you show your teachers how they can use it, let them convince the principal that it's a necessary purchase.

Identify local groups. Request money from parent groups. Show them how technology will help their children. Let students demonstrate and explain how technology can help students with different learning styles. Approach your school business partners with your requests.

Try fund raising activities. Try a special book fair or see if the athletic department would donate the proceeds from one sporting event (such as one football game) toward the purchase of technology for the school. Be sure to check with the administration before planning any fund raising event in case there are special school policies that need to be followed.

Negotiate discounts. If you are purchasing a variety of hardware items from one vendor, try to get a volume discount on the entire purchase rather than a price on individual items.

Take advantage of school discounts. The December 1996 issue of *American Libraries* reported that the FCC (Federal Communications Commission) voted in favor of 20% to 90% discounts on a number of telecommunications services for schools and libraries. Follow these and similar developments to take advantage of reduced rates.

Be prepared at all times. Be aware of unspent money and of spending deadlines. Always have your consideration/request file ready. Be especially alert at the end of the fiscal year. For example, although there was no money in the budget for hardware, one June there were suddenly some unspent funds. My request for a modem was successful because the request was accompanied by detailed specifications and the name of a local vendor who could deliver the item the next day.

Standardize and economize. Look for ways to trim expenses. Try to standardize consumable supplies such as printer ribbons or cartridges and purchase in bulk.

Be creative. Look for alternatives on accessories. You do not need a special accessory to hide all the cables on the back of a multimedia computer set-up. A slit piece of pipe insulation will do the job at a fraction of the cost. Watch journals for helpful hints and create a file for future reference.

Consider used equipment. Everybody wants the newest and the fastest technology. However, there are many things that can be done perfectly well with older equipment. While schools tend to keep computers for seven to 10 years, large corporations turn their equipment over more frequently. A three-year-old computer may be out-of-date in some businesses but may be just what you need for word processing stations in the library. Check your local computer dealers for used equipment. When you consider the price, don't forget to consider the costs involved in maintaining older equipment.

Consider upgrades to existing equipment. Sometimes computers can be upgraded or individual parts replaced. Just be sure the upgrades will really improve the performance of your present hardware.

Apply for grants. Individual school districts sometimes provide competitive grants for technology. In addition, some manufacturers, producers, and vendors have special grants programs.

How can you get grants?

Grant writing is not for everyone. In addition to taking time, there is no guarantee of the results. But if you are willing to try, there are a few hints that might help. (Full citations are in the Resources Section.)

Locate grant sources early. Regularly check the grants listings in periodicals such as *Electronic Learning, Technology & Learning, Media & Methods*, and *T.H.E. Journal*.

Subscribe to specialized publications. Order the *Aid for Education* newsletter. Scan copies of *Funding Resources Bulletin* and *Education Technology News* as soon as they are published.

Use electronic resources. Monitor educational online discussion groups such as LM_NET and K12ADMIN. Check the Internet for Web sites and online listings.

Check books for grant sources. Use some of the books listed in the Bibliogrpahy section of this chapter to identify agencies and foundations that provide grants for technology. Contact them directly to find out about upcoming grants.

Attend grants seminars. Attend one of the sessions on grant writing that are held at many educational conferences.

Focus on the goals of the grantor. Read the call for proposals carefully. When writing the grant, provide the information requested in the guidelines. Match the rationale, outcome, timeline, and budget to the stated goals of the individual or institution providing the grant.

How should you plan facilities for technology?

While some schools are built with technology in mind, in most instances technology has to fit into an existing facility. In either case, there are some things to keep in mind.

Wiring. Older schools frequently do not have enough outlets and circuits to handle the demands of power-hungry technology. In most cases, if you put a photocopy machine and a circulation computer on the same circuit, you are asking for trouble. Stringing multiple extension cords and power strips is not the answer. Check with the school electrician about the proper total power loads on circuits. If necessary, plan for rewiring parts of the room or the school.

Cables. If you are building a new school, plan for the electrical loads technology will use and install the cables for networking. Even if you do not have the money now to run the cables for networking, at least include conduit with pullwires through which cables can be fed at a later date.

Asbestos. Your plan may be to network an older school by running cables through the ceiling. If your school was built with asbestos, that might not be possible without the added costs of professional asbestos removal.

Climate Control. Computers and some other types of hardware like temperatures between 68° and 74° with a humidity of 45% to 55%. This does not mean that the equipment will not operate at higher or lower temperatures, but it means that this range is their ideal operating temperature.

Most equipment generates heat as it works, thus raising the temperature of its environment. When computers get too warm, they may begin to do strange things. One computer I own puts numbers in the middle of words when it is getting too warm. If air conditioning is not a possibility, fans do provide some relief.

Hardware space. Technology takes space. Plan new facilities with that in mind. A circulation desk may need to be modified for an automated circulation system. Include work space beside computers for materials. If the computer has a mouse, the mouse will need a space at least 10" by 12" on the right side of the computer for right-handed users and space on the left side for left-handed ones. If that space is not available, try a trackball (a pointing device where only the ball moves).

Tables work well to hold computers since teams of students can work together at them. Carrels tend to limit space too much unless the computer will be used by only one person at a time. Computers attract kids so be sure to have the space for active, involved learning.

Storage space. Try to locate storage space for supplies near the point that they are used. Remember, the printer will need paper and ribbons or ink cartridges.

Convenience. Locate equipment as close as possible to the technology that it serves. Ideally, a student printing from a CD-ROM should be able to see the printout without having to walk across a room. The CD-ROM indexes should be near the periodical storage area.

Visibility. Consider placing computers with Internet access in areas where they can be monitored. Knowing that the screen can be seen by other library patrons and the staff will keep most students on task. One SLMS reported that a problem with computer crashes on computers whose monitors faced a wall was dramatically decreased when those computers were turned another way.

Lighting. Monitors should be located so that the users do not face a bright light and so that glare on the screen is minimized. Inexpensive hoods to shade monitors can be made with black mat board or heavy posterboard, and filters can be purchased to cut down on the glare.

Accessibility. Make sure that technology is located where it is accessible to handicapped users. For example, having high tables where students stand to search the online catalog keeps the catalog from being used by students in wheelchairs. For wheelchair use, the tables should be between 28 and 34 inches high. Check your library for other modifications that may be necessary to assure accessibility for all users.

What are some inservice or staff development ideas?

It is not enough simply to have the newest technology; the technology must be used if it is to justify its purchase. One of the two major reasons that technology fails is that it is not accepted by the user. Two factors contributing to the lack of use are, first, that many people are afraid of technology and, second, that many people do not know how to use it and do not want to appear stupid by asking for help. While there is an entire chapter on this subject later in this book, here are a few general ideas.

What can you do on a limited budget? First, learn to use the technology yourself. Then teach others how to use it. In some cases you will be teaching the use of the hardware and the software. In other cases, you may just be introducing new software.

Think big, start small. I have what I jokingly call the termite theory of librarianship. When librarians complain that they will never get their teachers to use the new technologies, I remind them to think about the termite. I assume that a termite does not walk up to a wooden building and say, "That's too big. There's no way that I can eat that." He just starts chewing, and then he gets his friends to help. And we all know what happens after that. The same thing applies to staff development. Get one teacher, hook him or her on the technology, and success will breed success. Since no one likes doing grades, you might "sell" a computer grade book program. That teacher will sell others, and you are on your way.

Insure success. Do not set yourself up for failure by trying first to sell the teacher who has boasted that he or she will never turn on a computer. The termite does not waste energy chewing on a steel beam. Start your training with a willing learner.

Provide peer tutors. Just as you use cooperative learning groups and peer tutors with students, try them with teachers. Train a core of teachers to use a certain technology and let them show others. You might want to select one key teacher on each grade level or in each department to train first. This person then becomes your expert to help teach others.

Offer before or after school specials. Try an ongoing series of informal workshops for teachers before or after school with a different focus each week. Refreshments help, as can a door prize. This could be donated by a local business or could be something as simple as summer checkout of equipment. (Check with your administrators regarding your school's regulations.) For each workshop attended, a teacher can put his or her name in the hat for a drawing to take place during the last workshop.

Give rewards. To create interest, you might provide some incentives for teachers to attend one of your workshops. These might include recertification points, the first chance to use a new piece of equipment, one hour of special planning time with the SLMS when the teacher's class is covered by an instructional aide, or a perk from the principal such as special equipment checkout.

Keep it short and simple. If you do have large-group inservice meetings, try to keep the sessions short with time for hands-on practice. If you have a lot of technology to cover, have several short sessions rather than one long one.

Provide access. After a teacher learns about a new technology, be sure that he or she has access to it.

Consider administrators. You might want to include building level or central office administrators in some of your workshops. There are really two opinions about the wisdom of this. One side holds that including administrators will help them learn the teachers' needs and problems. On the other hand, it can backfire. Some administrators like to appear "all knowing" in front of their teachers and may be reluctant to participate if they do not already know how to operate the equipment.

Consider self-instruction materials. While some people can learn by reading a manual, others learn best by seeing or listening and then doing.

Prepare a short videotape or audiotape on the operation of a new piece of equipment and let teachers use the tape before working with the hardware. Purchase step-by-step instruction books that you can loan to teachers.

Publicize programs. Stay up-to-date about workshops that are offered by your state department of education or by professional associations. Share this information with your faculty.

Cooperate with others. Build relationships with other schools, both public and private, and work with them to offer staff development programs. Together, you may be able to invite an expert in for some special training such as a session on advanced Boolean searching tips.

Provide temptation. Put the new technology (hardware and software) in the teacher's lounge for a few hours each day and see what happens. You might want to insure success by making arrangements with a teacher or an instructional aide who will be in the lounge during that time. If a teacher has a student teacher who is ready to be left alone in the classroom, that teacher might be willing to "play" with some technology in the lounge. The idea is to tempt others to use it.

Prepare newsletters. Short, interesting newsletters can be used to tell others about technology and to advertise what's available.

How can you keep technology secure?

When you think of security and technology, there are really two separate issues involved. The first issue is the security of the hardware and software from theft. The second issue is the security of the information that is stored on the hardware and the protection of systems from destructive programs called viruses. This second type of security is discussed in the chapter on computers. What follows here are some suggestions for keeping technology hardware from walking out of your building.

Statistics show that most thefts are committed by amateurs and most stolen equipment is never recovered. Even if the case of the equipment is marked with identification numbers, equipment can be broken down and sold for parts.

It is likely that the people stealing school equipment are those who have seen the equipment in the school. They are not on a fishing expedition to see what they can find. As amateurs, they are not well-equipped with tools such as hacksaws and bolt cutters. You can use these facts to prevent losses.

Store equipment in a secure place. If your equipment is on rolling carts, put it in a secure room, especially over the weekend and during the summer. Be sure the room is completely secure. If the ceiling has suspended tiles, a thief will usually have no problem going through the ceiling into the secure room. If you have this type of ceiling, be sure the lock on the secure room door is a dead bolt that requires a key on each side. Make sure the door to your secure room does not have a glass window that can easily be knocked out.

Store hardware and software separately. Do not store your software, especially your computer backups, beside the hardware where, if the hardware is stolen, the software will be taken too. A friend faithfully made backups of her online catalog system. Of course, when the thieves stole the computers from the library, they also took all the disks that were sitting beside the computer, including the backups. For additional safety, make two sets of backups of your data and take one set home.

Protect software. The theft of software, like the theft of other library materials, is something that can happen at any time. Following the copyright guidelines, you can keep your original in a safe place and use your backup on a day-to-day basis. I also recommend making a copy of every hardware manual. As with the software, keep the original in a safe place and circulate the copy with the equipment if needed.

Cover equipment that can easily be seen from outside the building. If equipment is stored in a first floor library or classroom with lots of windows, be sure to put a cover over it at the end of the day to hide it from prying eyes. While this might not work for an entire lab, it is an effective way to hide stand-alone units.

Use bolts. Lockdown products secure hardware to some fixed or large object such as a desk or table. The simplest kinds are bolts that run from the equipment into the furniture. While ordinary bolts from the hardware store may do the trick, even better are those that require a special tool to remove. Do not store this tool near the equipment you are trying to protect. If bolts are not feasible, try the security plates that can be attached to hardware with industrial strength glue. Yes, they come off, but not easily. Some security manufacturers provide a limited warranty that may cover some of your expenses if a thief defeats their system.

Install baseplates. If you have equipment that you sometimes need to move, baseplates may be the answer. One part of the plate is attached to the equipment's normal home or storage place. The other part is attached to the hardware itself. Normally the two parts of the baseplate are locked together to secure the equipment, but they can be separated by using a special key if you need to move the equipment for a short time.

Purchase cables. Cables can be run through several pieces of equipment and then secured with a lock to a large piece of furniture. While they will deter the amateur thief, most cables are easily defeated with bolt cutters.

Lock part of the hardware. A power lockup, a locked cover for the internal expansion cards, a keyboard lock, a disk drive lockout, and locks for CD-ROM drives are all commercially available products that will make your hardware less attractive to thieves. A disk drive lockout also is useful in preventing unwanted disks from being used in a particular computer.

Prevent computer cases from being opened. No part of a computer is immune from theft. Thieves in California stole only the microchips from library computers. The solution is to install special CPU screws that can only be opened with a custom screwdriver.

Mark all hardware. Don't rely solely on visible stickers to mark equipment. Engrave the school name and/or some other ID in at least one place on all equipment.

Create a database. Record information about your technology in a computer database. Include identification information such as the purchase order number, date of purchase, cost, and serial number, along with a description of each item. In addition to being useful in case of theft, this database will be useful when you need warranty information. You can even create a MARC record for each piece of equipment that you own and store the information in your circulation system.

Try technology. A service called Compu-Trace can be used in computers with modems. Developed primarily for use with portable computers, this software program is loaded on the hard drive where it remains undetected by antivirus programs and unaffected by drive formats. Once a week, the program activates the computer's modem to call the Compu-Trace center where its ID number and the telephone number that it is calling from are shown. These are matched against a list of stolen computers and authorities are notified.

Make others aware of any theft. In addition to contacting your local authorities, call the Stolen Computer Registry. It's also a place to check when buying used computers.

How can you use technology safely?

Of course, use of electric equipment brings its own set of safety concerns. Look for potential problems and try to solve them before they become major disasters.

Check for adequate wiring. Whether you are building a new facility or putting technology in an existing one, an adequate power supply is necessary for equipment to operate correctly. Give the specifications for your hardware (all of your hardware) to the local school or government safety officers to check. Be sure that they know which hardware will be on a given circuit.

Do not overload circuits. Do not put too much equipment on any one circuit. Even a coffee maker can present a problem if it is on the same line as a computer.

Limit the use of power strips. Resist the temptation to create more outlets by plugging one multiple power strip into another. While a wall outlet meant for two plugs can suddenly become the home for two power strips with six outlets on each, this creates an overload and is only asking for problems.

Be careful with extension cords and grounding. Use extension cords only if they are rated to handle the load of the equipment. This means at least 14 gauge wire for most equipment, not the common household extension cords. When purchasing extension cords, look for the UL (Underwriters Laboratory) label, a rating of 15A/125V, and a notice such as "this indoor cord works with any appliance that needs up to 15 amps." Many are sold as "major appliance cords."

Do not break off the round grounding prong on the electrical plug. Try not to use adapters to change a three-prong plug into a two-prong plug. Proper grounding and electrical cord ratings are two safety features that should not be ignored.

Power up equipment slowly. Equipment draws a major load when it is first turned on. Thus, if you have several pieces of equipment on a single circuit, power them up one at a time.

Watch for symptoms of power problems. If any of the following happen frequently, you need to have the wiring in your school checked:

- Circuit breakers open or fuses blow.
- Lights dim when equipment comes on.
- The image on a monitor wiggles or shrinks.
- Power cords are very hot to the touch.
- Things smell hot.
- You see smoke. Do Not Wait. Turn everything off.

Consider alternative power supplies. Have you watched the lights dim when a photocopier or air conditioner on the same circuit as the lights started to draw power? This is a power draw-down that you can see. To compensate for these and other instances of low power on a circuit, you can use battery-backup devices or a standby power supply which, at times of low power, will switch to battery. The faster the switch occurs the better, 50 milliseconds being the maximum time delay. An uninterruptible power supply, or UPS, is the most expensive type but is the best way to insure constant power.

Purchase surge suppressors. At the other extreme from power supplies are surge suppressors, which compensate for power surges or spikes. It is estimated that 90% of the power-line problems result from surges and spikes.

Talk to a technician before purchasing a surge suppressor since the suppressor must be rated to break the circuit before the hardware is damaged. After purchasing a suppressor, be sure not to plug more equipment into the suppressor than it can handle. Even with a suppressor, pull the main plug when the equipment is not being used. A nearby lightning strike can cause damage even with a surge suppressor on the line. An unpredicted weekend thunderstorm wiped out three computers in our building because the plugs had not been pulled when school closed on Friday.

Check surge suppressor ratings. Simple but effective power bars, power strips, and multiple outlet surge suppressors are available in a wide price range. Look for the UL label and an indication that the device meets UL 1449 Surge Suppressor specs. Read the box the device comes in to be sure the rating is at least 15 amps. You can get adequate protection on all three wires (hot, neutral, ground), and shielding from radio frequency (RFI) and electromagnetic interference (EMI) for less than $30.

Buy telephone surge suppressors too. Lightning hits telephone lines too. Look for a UL telephone listing of 497A on the device. Telephone and electric surge suppressors are often included on the same device.

Turn equipment on and off slowly. Avoid turning equipment on and off frequently or quickly. To prevent power surges, allow at least five to ten seconds after turning equipment off before you turn it on again.

Unplug equipment. If you are not using equipment or if you are cleaning or repairing it, be sure that you unplug it first. One exception is a disk drive that must be operating to be cleaned. Pull the plug by pulling on the plug itself, not on the cord. Remember, some electronic components such as capacitors and video tubes can store a charge after the power is disconnected. And, while you are pulling the plug, always be alert for frayed cords and loose plugs.

Do not mix technology and water. Keep food and drink away from hardware. If you have a sprinkler system near the equipment, be sure that your circuit has a Ground Fault Circuit Interrupter (GFCI). The GFCI will cut the current if any electricity leakage is detected and will prevent shock if the equipment comes in contact with water. Clean the outside case of equipment with a damp, never wet, rag and unplug it first.

Be persistent with electrical problems. If you note a safety problem, contact the proper administrators and/or local officials. If no one claims responsibility for the problem, follow up your verbal concern with a letter. Document what you do and be persistent.

A SLMS reported problems with her circulation computer. The wiring in her 25-year-old school building could not handle the power necessary to run the technology in the library. After lots of finger-pointing by vendors and the school district, the problem was solved. Only the librarian's persistence solved the problem before there was a fire.

Be careful of magnetic fields. Much of the new technology is sensitive to magnetic fields. Data found on audiotapes, videotapes, and computer disks can be changed or erased by strong magnetism. Even decorative refrigerator door magnets can cause problems. Never place computer software on top of a disk drive, by the telephone, or under a computer keyboard where magnetic fields are present.

Even unshielded power cords have their own magnetic field. Be sure to keep power cords away from the cables that connect pieces of equipment. If the cords and cables need to cross, to avoid interference, they should do so at right angles.

Keep the environment clean. Hardware is sensitive to smoke, ashes, static electricity, humidity, and dust (including chalk dust), and should be covered when not in use. Static electricity is an enemy of electronic equipment. Take your sweater off by the computer on a dry winter day, and you might erase everything from the computer screen. To prevent this and other potential disasters, use properly grounded antistatic mats under the hardware and/or under the chair. Then teach everyone to touch the mat before touching the equipment.

Protect cords. Clips or pipe insulation can be used to keep cords together and out of a user's way. If you must walk or push equipment over cords, use cord protectors that lie flat. Duct tape should be used for a short time only.

Watch cords and carts. If the equipment is on a moveable cart, wrap the cord around the leg of the cart before plugging it to the wall outlet. This will help prevent accidentally pulling the equipment off the cart if someone moves the cart without unplugging the equipment. Perhaps the best thing to do with equipment on carts is to mount a power bar on the cart and plug everything in to it. Then there is only one cord going from the cart to the outlet.

Check your carts. Carts have been used in school libraries for years, but a few basic precautions bear repeating. Keep carts short; they should be no higher than 48 inches to keep the center of gravity low. Use flared bottom carts that are at least four inches wider at the bottom to cut down on a cart's tendency to tip. Rubber, not plastic, wheels at least six to eight inches in diameter are best. Use straps to secure the equipment to the cart, but remember that these straps are not a replacement for an anti-theft device. Set up a regular schedule to check carts for loose shelves, broken or weak welds or joints, and loose or broken wheels.

Remove batteries. If you have equipment that takes batteries, remove them when the equipment is stored over the summer. This prevents battery leakage and corrosion from ruining the equipment. Then, in the fall, use all new batteries or use a battery tester to determine the amount of life left in the old ones. Do not mix new and used batteries since this will drain the new batteries and decrease their life. Partially used batteries can be marked as such and stored in the refrigerator.

Read the disaster plan. Find out if your school has a disaster recovery plan that spells out what should be done in case of a major emergency such as a flood or a fire. If there is no plan, develop your own for the school library. When the fire department is pouring water into a smoldering library, it is too late to remember that you should keep a backup list of all the serial numbers from your hardware in a separate secure place outside the school building.

Establish a maintenance schedule. Set up a schedule for doing cleaning and maintenance of individual pieces of hardware. In some instances, simple cleaning and checking for loose cables can be done by student assistants. Watch professional journals, computer publications, and even general magazines such as *Home Mechanics* for maintenance tips and guidelines.

Record Error Messages. When using a computer, keep a log of error messages that appear on the computer screen. While many of these indicate minor problems, an ongoing problem list is useful for diagnosing chronic problems and/or discussing problems with a technician. Remember to keep a record of all equipment maintenance and record this in a database. Figure 1.2 provides a sample record form that can be used to keep information in a computer or a print database.

```
┌─────────────────────────────────────────────────────────────┐
│                     Hardware Record                         │
│                                                             │
│  Item:_____  Serial No.:_____   │
│                                                             │
│  Purchase Order:_____  Purchase Date:_____   │
│                                                             │
│  Description:_____    │
│  _____   │
│                                                             │
│  General Cleaning Date:_____  Done by:_____   │
│  Procedure:_____    │
│  _____   │
│  _____   │
│                                                             │
│  Special Cleaning Date:_____  Done by:_____   │
│  Procedure:_____    │
│  _____   │
│  _____   │
│                                                             │
│  Problems noted: _____    │
│  _____   │
│  _____   │
│  _____   │
│                                                             │
│  Repairs: _____    │
│  _____   │
└─────────────────────────────────────────────────────────────┘
```

Figure 1.2 Hardware record

What are the health problems related to technology?

With the growth of computers and related technologies in the workplace, home, and school, people have become concerned about possible health problems caused by technology. Two common problems are repetitive stress injuries (RSIs) and cumulative trauma disorders (CRDs). Unlike a broken bone, these injuries do not happen all at once. Instead they build up over time as the result of improper work habits or working conditions. Today, the U.S. Department of Labor ranks RSIs as the number one cause of job related illnesses. The science of ergonomics considers both the comfort and the health of the person using technology and attempts to prevent injuries.

While the most typical RSI is carpal tunnel syndrome, which is caused by stress on the nerves and tissues in the wrists, other RSIs and CRDs affect the neck, shoulders, and upper back. Pain, numbness, tingling, and hands "going to sleep" are all signs of possible problems. Eyestrain can result in headaches, double vision, and difficulty focusing. However, there are some things that can be done to help prevent these problems.

Maintain proper posture. Sit with both feet on the floor and with the keyboard at the same height as your elbows. Keep the monitor slightly at or slightly below the line of sight. Your hip, knee, and elbow joints should be at 90 degree angles.

Maintain proper wrist position when typing. The best position for the wrist is flat, with a straight line drawn from elbow to knuckles. While there are experts on both sides of the issue, enough advocate the use of wrist rests to make them worth trying. Another approach is to wear a wrist brace. While simple ones can be purchased at most office and computer supply stores, inexpensive braces with a metal insert can be found in many drug and general discount stores. Obviously, if you experience a lot of pain or continued numbness, a visit to a doctor is best before lasting damage is done.

Use an ergonomically correct mouse. Some manufacturers have developed a rounded mouse that fits the contours of the hand. Others make a mouse with built-in wrist support.

Try an ergonomic keyboard. Ergonomically designed keyboards are angled and allow the hands to stay in a more natural position.

Tilt the keyboard away from the user. Instead of using the height adjusters on the back edge of the keyboard to tilt it toward the user, try elevating the front edge instead.

Purchase appropriate furniture. Chairs should supply good upper back support, have adjustable seat height, and be curved to fit the lower back. If the chair has arm rests, they should allow the forearms to rest easily without causing the shoulders to slouch or hunch. Tables and/or desks should keep the monitor at eye level or slightly below. Tests done by *Consumer Reports* show that first impressions are an accurate measure of how comfortable furniture will feel by the end of the school week.

Eliminate glare on the monitor. If possible, move the light or the monitor. Be sure that sunlight does not create a glare during certain times of the day. If moving or adjusting the monitor is not possible, try glare guards or filters. As a last resort, use a pair of lightly tinted sunglasses.

Use protective filters. Most computer monitors made today meet MPR11 standards and have low or no emission. With older models, be sure the monitor is at least 18" away from the user and that users sit in front of and not to the side of the monitor. If you are still concerned about the effects of electromagnetic field radiation from monitors, you can use glare filters that will shield users from almost all of the VLF (very low field) and the ELV (extra low field) radiation. Some filters also reduce static electricity, cut glare, improve image contrast, and prevent eye strain. Be sure to remove these filters before cleaning the monitor.

Take breaks. Overuse problems tend to develop when people spend a long time at a computer as can happen if you are entering all of your shelf list information on the computer yourself. Every 10 minutes, rest your eyes for five to 10 seconds. Focus on things farther away or close your eyes and let your body relax. To relieve tension, shrug your shoulders and put your hands at your sides and shake them. Every 20 to 30 minutes, get up from the computer and walk around.

Reduce noise. While much hardware operates silently, printers, especially inexpensive ones, are known for the noise that they make. You can purchase acoustic covers to reduce printer noise. Using a special stand or mat will cut down on the impact noises produced by dot matrix printers.

How can you troubleshoot and repair equipment?

Following safety procedures can help prevent some equipment malfunctions. However, equipment will fail. While specific recommendations for individual pieces of equipment are made in the sections that follow, there are a few things that you can do before you call the technical or repair service.

Refer to your records. Try to keep good records on your equipment by creating a maintenance and repair file for each piece. This can ideally be done on a database program on a microcomputer. But if you are not ready for that yet, keep your records on file cards. Whether you use cards or computer, write the information down. Do not rely on your memory. Figure 1.3 is a sample of the type of information that should be included for repairs. Ideally, this information would be added to your general hardware database.

Hardware Repair Record

Item: _____ Serial No.:_____

Purchase Order:_____ Purchase Date:_____
Description:_____
_____

Symptoms: _____
_____
_____

Noticed by:_____

Repair service called:
    Name:_____
    Date:_____ Time:_____

Action taken:
_____
_____
_____

Figure 1.3 Hardware repair record

After the item has been repaired, file the information or add it to your database to maintain a repair history for your equipment. Arrange your file by the item name and its serial number to keep all the information on a single item together. If you have a problem with some hardware, check your file for helpful information based on what has happened in the past.

Also, keep in the same file a record of the maintenance given to each piece of hardware. Sometimes equipment will malfunction simply because it needs a good cleaning. Remember, always disconnect the power supply before you clean.

Create a tool kit. As you work with technology, you will begin to accumulate items for your own personal tool kit. These items are not expensive and can usually be found at your local discount store. Some suggestions of things to include:

- A can of compressed air like that used to clean cameras.
- A set of small screwdrivers.
- Assorted regular sized screwdrivers including flat-head, Phillips, and Torx (star-shaped).
- Tweezers
- Needle-nosed pliers
- Nut driver (a six-sided driver)
- A bottle of isopropyl alcohol.
- Some cotton swabs. Get some of both the flexible and nonflexible kind if you can.
- Antistatic spray and cloth.
- A pencil or ink eraser that you use only with equipment to clean the connections.
- A computer vacuum cleaner. It is a luxury but it is nice. In a pinch, you can use a regular vacuum if you decrease the suction (use the drapes setting) and put several layers of nylon fabric (like panty hose) over the end.
- System disks and the software you often need to reinstall such as printer and network drivers.

Develop a troubleshooting checklist. Compile a simple checklist of things to try before you call the repair service. By writing things down and keeping the list up-to-date you will not forget things that worked in the past. Simple ideas to try include:

- Check all electrical and cable connections to see that everything is plugged in tight and in the proper place.
- Turn everything off, wait ten seconds, and turn it on.
- If lack of power seems to be a problem, try another piece of equipment in that electrical outlet.
- Try another piece of software that you know works in that machine.
- Refer to a troubleshooting chart for that special piece of equipment.
- Check your repair and maintenance records for similar problems.
- One at a time, beginning with the power cord, try replacing the cords and cables of the nonfunctioning unit with cords and cables of a working unit.

- Try switching equipment components. If a monitor is not working on a certain computer, switch with a working monitor on a similar unit. In some instances, you can switch both external components and internal components. Keep a record of what you switch and do only one switch at a time.

Use a standardized report form. Develop a standardized form that can be used to report problems with computers and related technologies. An excellent form appeared in an article by Mary Alice Anderson in TECHNOLOGY CONNECTION (June 1996).

Use an out-of-order card. Create and use a card that you can quickly place on equipment that is not working. This lets people know that there is a problem before they begin to work and suggests an alternative for them to use if one is available. A simple card includes the information shown in Figure 1.4.

Out of Order

Item:

Date:

Alternatives:

Figure 1.4 Out of Order

The "out of order" card in Figure 1.5 is a modification of one used by the librarians at Kellam High School in Virginia Beach, Virginia. It adds a little humor to what is often a maddening situation.

The _____ is out of order!

No	☹	We cannot fix it.
Yes	☺	We have called the repair service.
No	☹	They are not here yet.
Yes	☺	They will be in today.
No	☹	We do NOT know how long it will take.
Yes	☺	We are keeping it.
No	☹	We do not know what caused it.
No	☹	We do not know who broke it.
Yes	☺	We are searching for the culprit
No	☹	We do not know what you are going to do now
No	☹	School has not been closed.

Have a Nice Day !! ☺

Figure 1.5

Develop a local "damage control" or "first response" team. Identify and provide training for a team to respond to technology problems. Use local expertise and consider putting teachers, students and volunteers on the team. You might want to consult an attorney about a liability release statement absolving team members from any financial responsibility for damages they cause in good faith.

Compile a repair manual. When something works to fix a problem, write it down! That way, if the one person who could repair the XYZ machine moves, his or her notes will remain for others to use.

Consider diagnostic software. There are now programs that provide hardware and software diagnostics, check installed peripherals, and more. Check the Resources section for a few suggested titles.

Prioritize problems. Develop a priority list of problems. For example, a problem with the school's network to classrooms takes precedence over a problem with the LCD panel in the science room, no matter which happened first.

Know when to call for help. Know the limits of your expertise and know when you need help.

Should you circulate technology?

Since the arrival of filmstrips and filmstrip projectors in the school library, there have been questions about the circulation of hardware and software to both teachers and students. Major questions arise over deciding who will be allowed to check out these items and what to do if you do not get things back.

With more and more technology showing up in the homes of some but not all students, there are pressures of a different type. Researchers have shown that there are socioeconomic and ethnic differences in access to technology. While these differences may be decreasing at school, they still exist at home. Special needs students may also have difficulty using technology because of physical access problems. Some schools have dealt with the equity issue by keeping labs and libraries open after school, providing funds for special programs, and working with the community to provide mentors and role models for students.

However, the issue of circulating software, if not hardware, remains. There really is no pat answer to this question. Your procedures will depend in part on the policies that have been established by your school district in the past. Following are some items that you may want to consider if you do decide to checkout software and/or hardware. For additional information, consult Lesley Farmer's article in the September/October 1990 issue of THE BOOK REPORT.

Request forms. For students to checkout hardware or software, some librarians report using a request form that has been approved by the school district's legal counsel and that must be signed by the student's parent or guardian.

Licenses. To be sure that the person can actually use the technology, some librarians have developed a license procedure. When students (or even teachers) demonstrate that they can actually use a certain type of technology, they are given a license by the SLMS that allows the use of that technology in the library or for checkout.

To teach patrons the skills that they need for a "license," set up stations or learning centers in the library, each with a different type of technology. Train a few students to act as "driving instructors" (peer tutors) and let them be responsible for teaching others. Keep a checklist or a computer database record of each student and the technology that he or she has mastered. Then issue a "technology driver's license" (Figure 1.6) and use a special stamp or hole punch to indicate the technology the student has mastered.

Technology Driver's License

Issued to: _____

Driving instructor:_____

License issued by:_____

Date: _____

PC	MAC	CD-ROM	VCR	VIDEO-DISC	INTERNET

Figure 1.6

Manuals. When a piece of equipment leaves the library, whether with a student or a teacher, many librarians also send a copy (keep the original on file) of the operation manual.

Copyright. When circulating any software, be sure the copyright notice is attached to each item. Refer to chapter 2 of this book for samples and additional information.

What's in the future?

No one has a crystal ball that can foretell the future. But there are things that can be predicted about technology. While machines get more usable power, speed, and memory capacity there will also be more combinations of technology (including telephone and television), made possible by advances in technologies such as fiber optics.

As technology becomes more prevalent in every part of society, demands will be placed on schools to use this technology in instruction and support services. Just as 16mm films replaced filmstrips and videotapes replaced 16mm films, new technologies will replace those we regard as "high tech" today.

Technology will bring its own set of problems and will add to some of the existing ones. If teachers continue to assign the traditional term paper, plagiarism may become an even more serious problem since technology makes it even easier to copy information. Copyright violations will continue to be a problem since technology provides the temptation and the means to copy. With the reliance on technology, the words "the computer is down" will put even more stress on the SLMS.

The challenge for school librarians today is to become even more involved in the curriculum, planning with teachers and working with students. School librarians will find that technology will be indispensable to their efforts to manage libraries and to help students and teachers become efficient and effective users of information.

Bibliography

Anderson, M. A. (1996). Forms for streamlined media management. TECHNOLOGY CONNECTION, 3 (4), 16-17. Includes forms for budgeting and for reporting technology problems.

Anderson, M. A. (1992). Resources team math teachers and librarians. THE BOOK REPORT, 11 (1), 35-36. Lists technology projects to use with middle school students.

Angle, M. See entry for Hooked on Technology below.

Boardman, E. M. (1996). Managing a constantly changing array of machines, programs and processes. TECHNOLOGY CONNECTION, 3 (4), 11-22. Discusses the day-to-day activity in an automated school library.

Bushweller, K. (1993). Warning: Protected by copyright. *The Executive Educator,* 15 (7), 12-13+. Cites recent cases in which schools have been sued for copyright violations and makes suggestions for inclusion in a copyright policy.

Cope, J. (1997). A buyer's guide to virus protection. *HomePC,* 4 (2), 85-94. Reviews six protection packages for Windows 95.

Farmer, L. S. J. (1990). Getting their grubby hands on it; questions to consider in circulating software. THE BOOK REPORT, 9 (2), 39. The title says it all!

Farmer, L. S. J. (1995). Hard talk about hardware; the care and repair of equipment. TECHNOLOGY CONNECTION, 2 (9), 27-28. From basic repairs to upgrading a system, this article has advice on a variety of topics.

Freedman, A. (1994). *The Computer Glossary, Complete Illustrated Desk Reference.* New York: AMACOM. A very readable computer dictionary. Available from ISTE.

Hamilton, B. (1995). So you need more money...? TECHNOLOGY CONNECTION, 2 (5), 51. Based on an Internet survey, this article provides a variety of ideas for obtaining funds.

Home office guide; Advice on buying the equipment you need to work at home. (1997, September). *Consumer Reports*, 62, 24-40. Although written for the home-based business, this feature article has excellent information on computers, monitors, fax machines, printers, and copiers.

Hooked on Technology. (1992). Roundtable discussion, THE BOOK REPORT, 11 (3), 20-23. Melanie Angle reports on her three-step process for luring teachers to computer use. In addition, other librarians provide their favorite technology tips.

Jordahl, G. & A. Orwig (1995). Getting equipped and staying equipped, part 2: finding the funds. *Technology & Learning,* 15 (7), 28-37. Covers everything from fund raising to developing business partnerships and leasing equipment.

Kuthlthau, C. C. (1996). *The virtual school library: Gateway to the information superhighway.* Englewood, Co: Libraries Unlimited. The 14 essays in this book provide an overview of a variety of technologies and their impact on school libraries, both now and in the future.

Lankford, M. D. (1994). Design for change: how to plan the school library you really need. *School Library Journal,* 40 (2), 20-24. Library technology is one of the topics discussed in planning or remodeling a school library.

Mather, B. R. (1996). Now that you have the technology, how do you keep it up and running? TECHNOLOGY CONNECTION, 3 (4), 9-10. Describes a priority chart for repairs and how to develop a first response team.

Milone, M. N., & J. Salpeter (1996). Technology and equity issues. *Technology and Learning* ,16 (4), 38-47. The authors address economic and gender equity issues.

Novelli, J. (1993). There's never been a better time to use technology. *Instructor,* 103 (3), 37-40. Teachers explain how the use of National Geographic Kids Network, computerized learning centers, and CD-ROM changed their classrooms.

Pappas, M. L. (1996). Electronic learning in 2002. *School Library Media Activities Monthly* 13, (1), 37-38. Looks at the trends in technology and how they will change school libraries.

Pereleman, L. (1992). *Schools' out: hyperlearning, the new technology and the end of education.* New York: Morrow. A look at what's wrong with American education and some suggestions. Highly recommended in a review in THE BOOK REPORT, September/October 1993, p. 64.

VanMeter, V. L. (1990, September/October) Selection & evaluation forms for print and nonprint materials. THE BOOK REPORT, 9 (2), 28-32. Contains a selection guide for curriculum-related computer software.

Whiting, R. & R. S. Kuchta. (1989). *Safety in the library media program: A handbook.* Wisconsin Educational Media Association and the Arkansas Association of Instructional Media.

Young, J. (1996). Your guide to safe computing; prevent computer-lab health hazards for your students—and yourself. *Electronic Learning,* 16 (2), 42-44.

<u>Notes</u>

Chapter 2
Computer Basics

Computers are the driving force behind most of the technologies found in school library media centers. Thus a logical place to start any discussion of technology is with the basic computer. Whether desktop or portable, notebook or palmtop, they all have the same components. This section presents a basic overview of computer hardware and software and provides information on care and copyright. The following sections will examine, in more detail, the use of computers for telecommunications, the Internet/World Wide Web, video, and multimedia productions, as well as CD-ROM and videodisc.

There are two major groups or platforms of computers widely used in schools today: the PCS, which consist of IBM machines and the clones that are "IBM compatible," and Apple Corporation's Macintosh or Mac and its clones. In addition, other computers such as Amiga, Commodore, TRS-80, and older Apple Series II computers are still in use.

Although each brand has its own supporters, there are commonalities among all microcomputers. While it is not necessary to understand everything about how a computer works, it is helpful to know a little about hardware before proceeding to a discussion of software and computer care. Even if you do not purchase the hardware, you need to understand what it can and cannot do so that you can understand the relationship between the hardware and the software that you want to use on it.

What are the hardware basics?

The most important part of a microcomputer system is the software. It is the software which tells the hardware what to do. Of course, the two must work together, and the hardware must have the capability of doing the things that the software requires.

Most software packages list the hardware requirements, and you need to be able to understand those requirements. Also, if you are going to be involved in recommending specific computer equipment, you need to know basic information about the microcomputer and its parts. You also have to be able to use the terminology that describes computer parts and functions. The descriptions that follow might make a computer scientist cringe since they take a few liberties and tend to simplify things a bit, but they should give you the information that you need.

No matter what brand of computer you work with, all of them have the same basic types of components. The computer must have a processor that will actually do something with information, some storage devices, some ways to put information into the computer, and some ways to get information out of it. Let's look at what each part of the system does.

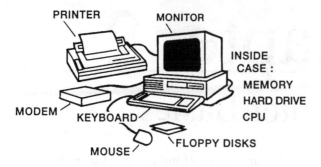

Figure 2.1 A generic computer system

Processor

All computers have a central processing unit (CPU) which is also called a microprocessor, a microchip, or simply a chip. This is the "brain" of the computer. In PCS, the chips made by Intel have numbers such as 8088/8086 (sometimes called an XT), 80286 (called a 286 or an AT), 80386 (a 386), 80486 (a 486), the Pentium, and the P6 or Pentium Pro/Pentium II. Other PC chip manufacturers have chips similar to the Pentium but are known as the 6x86 chip (Cyrix System) and the K5 (Advanced Micro Devices).

Chips differ in their ability to process different amounts of information measured in bits per second. Think of a bit as a chunk of information. The 486 chip processes more information (32 bits) at a time than the 286 (16 bits) but not as much as the Pentium (64 bits). Obviously, the larger the chunk of information (number of bits) that the computer can work with at one time, the faster it will do things. In addition to the amount of information that a certain type of chip can process at one time, chips within the same type can also process that information at different speeds. This operating speed or clock speed is usually measured in megahertz (MHZ). That is why you may see a description of a CPU with a corresponding speed such as 133MHz. The higher the clock speed, the faster the chip is at doing the things your program tells it to do. Why worry about speed? A PC with a 286 chip (16 bit chip with a speed between 8 and 12 MHZ with a 16 bit bus; a normal configuration) hooked to a CD-ROM drive will scan a disk containing a multi volume encyclopedia in 45 seconds. But, if you hook that encyclopedia to a computer with a 486 chip (32 bit chip with a speed between 25 and 50 MHZ with a 32 bit bus), the scan will only take 2 seconds. Put the CD-ROM on a Pentium and the result is even faster.

New in 1997 is Intel's P55C chip commonly called the Pentium with MMX or multimedia extensions. Built directly into the microprocessor, MMX works at speeds of 166MHz to 200MHz and affects a PC's ability to work with 3-D images as well as sound, video, and graphics by providing higher resolution and faster processing. Using SIMD (single instruction, multiple data) technology, MMX can run multiple audio channels and high quality video over the Internet. Computers with MMX are specifically designed to work with videos, games, and graphics applications. It is estimated that the Pentium Pro chip with MMX will run at 300MHz by the end of 1997.

While PCS use Intel's microprocessors, the Macintosh from Apple uses Motorola and PowerPC chips. The Motorola chips range in order of power from the 68000 to the 68040 with the higher numbered chips processing information faster than lower numbered chips. Competing with Intel's Pentium and Pentium Pro, the PowerPC microprocessors are found on computers such as the Performa 6360 and the 6400, the PowerMac 7200 and 7600, and the high performance PowerMac 8500 and 9500. The 6360 has a 603e chip which runs at 160 MHZ, while the 604e chip in the 6400, 8500, and 9500 runs at 200MHz to 225MHz.

On the horizon for the Macintosh is a chip by Exponential Technology known as the X^{704}. A PowerPC compatible chip, the X^{704} is said to have double the speed of the Pentium Pro with a potential speed of 1GHz by the year 2000.

Until recently, there were few Macintosh clones. Apple considered its system a proprietary one versus the open system found in PCS. Unlike the PC with its customizing add-ons, the Mac has traditionally offered an "all-in-one" machine with different features in different models. However, Motorola, who made the first microprocessor for the Mac, sells compatible machines under the name StarMax. With both a horizontal case and a tower configuration, Power Computing calls its Mac clones the Power Base and the Power Tower and features a customization service, allowing a purchaser to have a Mac clone built to his/her specification.

With the difference in processors, can you use the same software on both a Mac and a PC? Yes and no. You cannot always put an IBM program in a Mac and expect it to run. However there are Mac/PC translator programs that allow this kind of switching. These programs include *MacLink Plus/PC*, *Macintosh PC Exchange*, *DOS Mounter*, and *Soft PC*. In addition, Apple worked with Intel and IBM to develop the PowerPC chip, which will run PC software. Also, PCI-based PC compatibility cards allow PC programs to run on a Mac.

Bus

There is one more major controller of speed in your computer. It is the data bus, which links the chip to the other parts of the computer and its peripherals. If the bus's capacity to transfer information is less than that of the chip (a 16 bit bus and 32 bit chip), the machine will be slower than another machine with the same chip but a faster bus (32 bit bus and 32 bit chip). A fast bus will not speed up a slow chip. If this sounds confusing, think of people waiting to board a plane. If there are only 16 seats on the plane (the data bus), even if 32 people are waiting to go somewhere, the plane can carry only 16 people at a time.

The old ISA (Industry Standard Architecture) bus with only a 16 bit path was replaced by the VESA (Video Electronic Standards Association) local bus that uses a 32 bit path. Intel's PCI (Peripheral Component Interconnect) bus also uses a 32 bit path and is the basis for its Plug-and-Play or PnP standard. Announced in 1996, a new bus called the USB or Universal Serial Bus is designed to automatically configure new hardware to work with the computer. Developed for computers running Windows 95 and Windows NT operating systems, the USB has its own ports for attaching peripherals. Replacing the traditional serial and parallel ports, the USB ports allow several USB-compatible devices (scanners, printers, etc.) to be daisy chained to one USB port. Gone will be the days when it was necessary to open a computer case to change driver settings or move dip switches. You can keep track of new advances with USB on the World Wide Web at http://www.teleport.com~usb.

Complementary to the USB is the new IEEE 1394 bus known as FireWire. This high speed bus was designed for video devices such as camcorders, digital cameras, and the new DVD (digital video discs or digital versatile discs). It is predicted that both FireWire and USB will be found in PCS in the future with the USB being used for printers, modems, and scanners while FireWire is used for digitized video. The result is predicted to be an all-in-one digital home entertainment and productivity center.

Memory

The memory of a computer is where the microchip does the work of processing information. There are many types of computer memory, including upper memory, extended memory, cache memory, and expanded memory, as well as memory management software programs. However, there are two basic types: ROM (Read Only Memory) and RAM (Random Access Memory).

ROM is a permanent memory that remains even when the machine is turned off, the electric plug pulled, and the battery disconnected. It contains instructions to make the computer do basic things.

RAM is often called volatile or temporary memory because, when the computer is turned off, what is in RAM vanishes. There are some portable machines that contain batteries to keep things in the RAM after the computer is turned off, but remove those batteries, and that RAM is gone too.

The RAM memory size is measured by the units of information (byte) that it can hold. One thousand bytes are roughly one kilobyte or "1K." If the memory size is one million bytes, the computer is said to have one megabyte (1MB) or one "meg" of RAM. While some older Apple II series computers only have a RAM of 128K or 128 thousand bytes, newer computers are limited only by their operating system and the amount of money that a user wants to spend. New Macs typically have between 16MB and 32MB of RAM. In a PC, the amount of RAM to purchase with a new machine should be a factor of the operating system (minimum 8MB for Windows 95) and the type of work to be done with the computer (minimum 4MB for word processing on Windows 3.x; 16MB for multimedia on Windows 95). Heavy users of computer videos and computer-assisted design (CAD) programs regularly purchase 64MB of RAM.

RAM is important when you are selecting software, since different programs can require different amounts of RAM. Although memory chips for RAM (do not confuse them with the processing chips) can be added to some computers, certain CPUs can only work with a limited amount of RAM. For example, you would not buy a program that required 4 megabytes of RAM if you had an 8088 microprocessor since that microprocessor cannot work with that amount of RAM. To use 4MB (4 megabytes) of RAM in a PC you need at least a 286 microprocessor, preferably a 386.

The computer's main RAM is sometimes called the DRAM (Dynamic Random Access Memory). DRAM usually comes in memory modules and is sold as DIMMs (dual in-line memory modules) or SIMMs (single in-line memory modules). SIMMs come in two sizes; a 30 pin and a 72 pin. There are a few proprietary computers that will only accept their own SIMMs. Inserting

SIMMs in a computer is fairly easy if you remember that, with 30 pin SIMMs, all modules in a bank or group must be the same. In addition, new SIMMs must match the parity (parity vs. nonparity) of the original modules. Check a technician or the computer specifications if you are unsure. Incompatible SIMMS will not destroy a computer, but they will prevent it from working.

In addition to the general RAM, there are several additional types of memory. VRAM or Video RAM is a special video memory found in later computers. Designed to increase the computer's ability to work with video clips, a VRAM of 2MB is a good choice. Cache memory, fast RAM or SRAM (Static Random Access Memory) comes in two types. Internal (or L1) cache is built into the CPU itself and is designed for high speed retrieval. It's where the CPU looks first to find things. The Pentium chips with MMX have 32KB L1 cache. External cache or L2 cache is inside the computer case but not on the microprocessor. L2 cache varies from 64 KB to 1MB and is also designed for fast access. In comparison to regular RAM, cache memory costs six to eight times more.

The Motorola series of chips for the Mac can use from 16MB of RAM for the 68000 chip to 256MB of RAM for the 68040. An Apple Power Mac 9500/200 has 512 L2 cache while Power Computing's Power Tower Pro 225/RAID has 1MB L2 cache. That is more than is needed for instructional programs. In a school setting, the minimum RAM for a Mac with the System 7 operating system is 4MB. To run "memory-hungry" programs, be sure you have at least 8MB to 16MB of RAM.

Instead of adding more RAM to increase performance, some people have tried RAM boosting software. Unfortunately, these programs, which claimed to produce the same increase in performance as adding more RAM, do not perform as claimed. A better solution is to physically add more RAM.

Storage on Hard Disks and Floppy Disks

Some people confuse computer storage and memory. RAM memory is temporary; storage is more permanent. In general, there currently are two places on most computer systems to store information so that you can retrieve it later. One place is on a floppy disk (removable storage) and the other is on a hard disk (nonremovable or fixed). In addition, there are other forms of removable storage such as tape drives, optical disks, magneto-optical (MO) disks, phase change disks, and other types of magnetic disks.

The floppy disk, sometimes called a diskette, is usually one of two types: a 5.25" disk and the flexible plastic cover that it comes in, or a 3.5" disk that has its own hard plastic cover. Currently, 99.8% of new computers use 3.5" drives and the 5.25" disks are becoming harder to find. Because of this, people with the older 5.25" drives may have difficulty installing new software which is often available only on 3.5" disks. Even if you are able to locate a computer with both size floppy drives, it is often difficult to transfer from 3.5" to 5.25" disk since the smaller disk actually contains more information. An article by Cindy Kruchenisky in the Resources section has information on solving this problem.

To prevent accidental erasures of information by the drive, floppy disks have write-protect features which, when used, keep a computer from writing information on the disk. The write protect feature on the 3.5" disk is a hole in the hard plastic case with a plastic tab that can be moved to cover and uncover it. When the hole is open, the disk cannot be written on.

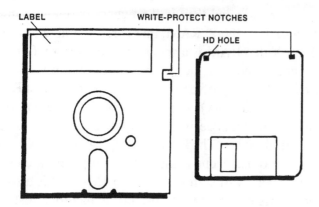

Figure 2.2 5.25" floppy disk and 3.5" floppy disk

Floppy disks can have several characteristics and need to correspond to the drive where they will be used. While older disks were sometimes single sided (SS), today's disks are double sided (DS). Another feature is the density or spacing of information on the disk. With storage hungry graphics and video clips, manufacturers are looking for ways to have more storage. The most common drives use high density (HD) disks. Usually HD drives can use and read both double density (DD) and HD disks. However, there are problems with this among PCS. When making backups of the information on the hard drive or of programs that take several disks, be sure the backup disks are all the same density. Do not try to do a single backup on a mixture of DD and HD disks. The stylized HD on the slider and the presence of two holes on the hard case indicate a HD disk.

The other major type of storage device is the hard disk. While this disk may also be either internal (inside the microcomputer) or external, most hard disks are internal. A hard disk differs from a floppy disk in that it is a sealed unit. What it offers is more space for the storage of information than floppies and a faster time to find that information and get it to the microprocessor. Even though a hard disk can hold a large amount of information, it can become full, especially if video and graphics are stored on it. When some new programs are installed on a hard drive, they may take up 60 to 120MB of storage. That's why a minimum 1 Gigabyte (1GB or 1000MB) hard disk is recommended for most computers today. Older computers such as those with 386 or 486 processors cannot work with hard disks larger than 528MB. In those machines, it might be possible to install a second hard drive if additional storage is needed.

Both floppy disks and hard disks need to be formatted before they can be used. In the past, most floppy disks were sold unformatted and the purchaser had to use the computer's operating system to format them. Today, disks are usually sold as formatted for either the PC or the Macintosh platform.

Other Removable Storage

With floppy disks currently holding 1.44MB of information and with the growing need for more space to store bigger video and text files and to transport those files easily between computers, other forms of removable storage have developed. Tape drives, similar to those used for audiotape but with a holding capacity of up to 4.4GB provide linear, not random, access to information and are best used to backup systems for security. Recordable and rewritable CD-ROM (Compact Disc, Read Only Memory) discs have recently been introduced and are discussed in a later chapter.

For a long time, the magnetic removable storage market has been dominated by SyQuest and Iomega. Gaining popularity as a removable storage device is Iomega's Zip drive and cartridge system. The Zip drive can be installed internally, connected to SCSI port, or can share a parallel port with a printer. While programs can be run directly from the Zip drive, its main use is to transport text and video data among machines. With its 100MB removable cartridge, the Zip drive provides fast access to a large quantity of information. A competitor to the Zip drive is the LS-120 system, a 120MB removable storage device that can also read and write to the standard 3.5" floppy disk and the SyQuest EZFlyer which stores 230MB. Iomega also makes the Jaz Drive which can store up to 1GB. Its competitors include the SyQuest SyJet 1.3GB cartridge.

Marketed as a "removable plug-and-play hard disk," the KanguruDisk is a "dock" that can be installed internally or connected to the computer's parallel port. Kdisks containing between 850MB and 1.6GB of information are then placed in the dock. These Kdisks are ideal for transporting large quantities of data or for backing up a hard drive.

A problem with all of these is that the cartridges are proprietary. That means they cannot be used in a competitor's disk drive. In some cases, such as that of SyQuest drives, other vendors have started to make compatible products. Market factors may help determine which of these formats survives. However, all of them may be replaced by newer technologies such as digital video discs.

A portable hard drive, modem, or a network connection can all be found on a PC Card developed by the Personal Computer Memory Card International Association (PCMCIA). This credit card sized hard disk varies in thickness and can hold between 40MB and 200MB. In addition, it can assume the functions of some hardware peripherals.

Other portable storage devices such as compact discs are continually being developed. As with other technologies, initially their prices may be high but, as the public accepts them, prices will fall. Those not accepted by the public will be driven from the marketplace by newer technologies. DVD (digital video discs or digital versatile discs) hold great promise with the ability to store between 4.7GB and 17GB of information. Although the first will be read-only, writeable discs are sure to follow. While CD-ROM discs are read only, the new CD-Recordable are write once and can store 650MB. However, they are expensive and are not rewritable. Although CD-Erasable discs holding 650MB are available, their cost prohibits their use in most schools.

Keyboard

Along with floppy and hard disk drives, a keyboard serves as a way to put information into the computer. Today's standard keyboard contains 101 keys with the function keys at the top and a number pad at the side. For the PC, the newest keyboards have a special "Windows" key near the space bar.

Try out the feel of any keyboard before you buy it, and be sure the arrangement of the keys is in the QWERTY pattern (starting at the top left row of letters). There are a few keyboards with strange letter arrangements that are designed to speed up typing. Be sure you want that arrangement before you buy it.

Mouse or Trackball

People who do not type have historically been at a disadvantage when using a computer. Therefore, most computers today use a pointing device such as a mouse or trackball to select items shown on the screen, and thus, give instructions to the computer. (Touch screens are another option and are discussed in the section under monitors.)   In the mouse, the ball on the bottom of the device must be rolled on a firm surface or on a special "mouse pad" near the computer. In comparison, in the trackball the ball is on the top and is rolled by the fingers or the palm of the hand.

With either one of these pointing devices, check the ease of removing the ball from the device since kids love to take them. Some models require a special tool to open them. Anyone, other than "authorized personnel," caught with one of those tools should lose privileges in a hurry. Also beware, the entire mouse or trackball device is frequently stolen.

Scanner

A scanner allows you to transfer an image from a printed page into a computer. While most scanners that fall in a school's price range were originally limited to transferring pictures and graphics or text which was stored as a graphic, this has changed. New scanners come close to 100% accuracy reading text when used with the appropriate OCR (Optical Character Recognition) software. Documents read into a computer's storage as text take up less space than if they were stored as graphics. A 1KB text file can be a 75KB graphic file. In addition, text files can be edited by a word processing program.

There are flatbed scanners which look like small photocopy machines, sheetfed scanners which only scan flat sheets, and smaller hand-held ones. If you use a hand-held scanner, a portable alignment guide will minimize hand motions and will help you align sections of a full-page scan. In purchasing a scanner, consider the size and type of the items you will want to scan. Books will not fit on a sheetfed scanner. Resolution is a factor with popularly priced scanners ranging from 150dpi (dots per inch) to 400dpi. While higher resolution provides better quality, it comes at a higher price and requires more storage space and a slower scan rate. Some scanners use file compression to decrease the storage space. There are photograph scanners and even slide scanners to use with 35mm slides and photographic negatives.

No matter what type of scanner you use, you also need scanning software to make the transfer. Be sure to check if it is included with the scanner and if it provides OCR and editing capabilities. If you plan to use a scanner for text, check a variety of scanned documents with your wordprocessor.

Most scanners are easy to install on either a SCSI, parallel, or serial port. However, if you are hooking one up on the same port as a printer, be sure the scanner uses the same bi-directional interface used by most modern printers. Any PC scanner and its software should be TWAIN (a protocol agreed upon by both hardware and software manufacturers) compliant for compatibility. Mac scanners and software should support the Adobe Photoshop protocols.

Monitor

While all monitors allow you to see information, there are features that affect your comfort in using one. Resolution refers to the sharpness of the image as measured in dots called pixels and is written as the number of pixels horizontally by the number of pixels vertically as in 320 x 200. Another measurement is the dots per square inch or dpi. The more dots or pixels, the higher the resolution and the better the detail.

While monochrome monitors display things in black and another color (usually white, orange or green), color monitors fit into one of several categories. Each monitor in a PC system is controlled by a graphics adapter board or video adapter card inside the computer.

The first generation of IBM color monitors, a CGA monitor, displayed up to 16 colors, but now both VGA and SVGA monitors are capable of 256 colors with the VGA having a resolution of 640 x 480 and the SVGA, a resolution from 800 x 600 up to 1024 x 768.

It is important to match your monitor to your computer to get the best display. If a computer has a video graphics array board and a VGA monitor, buying an SVGA monitor will not improve the on-screen display unless you also upgrade the video adapter board inside your computer.

While there are many other characteristics of monitors such as dot pitch, there are only two other major features that you really need to know. One is the screen size and layout. IBM monitors come in the traditional layout that has a viewing area that is wider than it is tall. Macintosh monitors can be purchased in the traditional layout or in either the portrait or full-page layout, or in the two-page layout that shows two pages at a time.

Screen size is measured on the diagonal before the cabinet is put on. A 14" screen is the most common, with each inch usually adding nine percent to the viewing area. Beware that with some brands a 13" and 14" monitor may actually have the same screen size. While more expensive, a 15" to 17" screen can make a big difference if you use the computer a lot, especially for applications such as desktop publishing and developing Web pages. A last monitor characteristic is scanning frequency or refresh rate, which describes how fast the image forms on the screen. Some monitors require several scans to form an image, which results in a distracting screen flicker. The best way to select a monitor is to comparison shop. Set up several monitors side by side and, feeding off the same computer, run the software that you will use.

For primary children as well as special-needs students, touch screen monitors may be necessary. With these, the mouse or pointing device is replaced by the touch screen. Unfortunately, these cost between three and four times as much as a regular monitor. A touch screen panel which is added in front of a regular monitor brings down the cost. Even less expensive is a product called TouchMate which sits under the monitor but provides touch screen capabilities.

Newer monitors are not susceptible to the damage from "burn-in" that plagued older models. While screen saver software programs can be a lot of fun, they are no longer necessary. In response to the decreased need for the screen savers, some companies have tried new approaches such as a news headline screen saver for computers that are hooked to the Internet.

With the success of thin monitors on notebook computers, this technology is predicted to move stand-alone monitors for use with desktop computers. Although the price for the "skinny" monitors will initially be high, it should drop as the lightweight monitors become more popular.

Printer

Printers range from the low-cost impact dot matrix printers to the non-impact ink jet (it actually squirts ink on the page) and the top-of-the-line non-impact laser printers. While dot matrix printers are the cheapest for drafts and printouts of searches, non-impact printers are quiet and produce sharp images.

The laser printer produces professional quality results, but it cannot match the dot matrix for speed and quality at a reasonable price since the cost of supplies as well as the hardware must be considered. Only dot matrix printers can handle carbons and NCR forms because the pins in a dot matrix printer actually hit the ribbon against the page of paper.

To increase the quality of a dot matrix printer, look for one with 18 or 24 pins in the print head. Some nine-pin dot matrix printers can also produce good looking documents. By increasing the passes that the print head makes over the paper, NLQ (near letter quality) and LQ (letter quality) documents can be printed.

A newer trend is toward color printers. Here, the ink jet shines because of its reasonable cost in comparison to the laser printer. Originally ink jet printers had problems with the accuracy and permanency of the ink. While newer models have eliminated these problems, a document printed with an ink jet printer will not retain its color the way a document printed with a laser printer will. In about a year, the ink jet document will begin to fade. Before purchasing a color printer, be sure to consider the speed of printing, clarity/ sharpness of the images and text, the accuracy of the color, and the cost of the ink cartridges.

An ideal situation is to have at least one laser printer, which is used when the quality of the printing really matters, and an ink jet for color documents. Dot matrix printers can then be used for routine printing and for draft copies.

Some types of printers have fallen out of favor. Daisywheel printers, a type of impact printer, originally were used to produce letter-quality documents, but they were slow and have been replaced by the laser and ink jet. Use of non-impact thermal printers has declined because of the high cost of supplies and the poor quality of the document produced.

When selecting a printer, keep in mind the speed of printing and the noise produced, two major factors in library settings. Laser printers produce little or no noise. Commercial printer covers can cut down on noise made by dot matrix printers. Since printers are slower than computers, waiting for the printer may tie up the computer, especially when printing graphics, which generally take longer to print than text. Printer buffers can free up the computer faster by taking the information from the computer, storing it, and sending it to the printer gradually. Some printers even have their own internal buffer.

Another consideration is the type of paper and paper feed that the printer can use. Most dot matrix printers allow both tractor feed (be sure it is located so that the paper goes through it before it goes through the print head) of computer paper (with the holes on the margins) and friction feed of single sheets inserted one at a time. Still others allow for friction feed of single sheets off a large stack placed in a paper tray.

A final cost factor in printer selection is the price of the ribbons that the dot matrix printer uses and the ink cartridges or toner of the non-impact printers. Laser printers cost about two to three times as much to operate as dot matrix printers. Obviously, using a dot matrix printer in draft mode instead of NLQ mode or LQ mode will increase the life of the ribbon by cutting down on the number of passes the print head makes for each line.

When shopping for a printer, several other items might be important. First is the ability of the hardware to print on transparency film. Be sure to check to see if special film is required or if off-the-shelf brands will do. Also, if the printer is to be used on a network, check for network connectivity. Be sure the printer you are considering can be used with the computer platform you have. If not, you may need to purchase a cross-platform adapter. Finally, look to see if any software programs come bundled with the printer. It is not uncommon to find draw programs, color enhancing tools, and even T-shirt transfer programs.

There are multiuse printers that can also serve as fax machine, scanner, copier, and telephone. While these are great space savers, these machines present several problems. First, when the hardware breaks, you not only lose the use of your printer but you also lose the use of all of its components: copier, scanner and fax. In addition, while combination hardware devices can do a number of things, they usually do each of them with only mediocre results.

Modem and Fax

The section on telecommunications discusses the modem and the fax modem in detail. For purposes of this discussion, note that the modem allows your computer to use a telephone line to communicate with other computers and that a fax modem allows it to send and receive telefacsimile (fax) messages. Unlike regular modems which convert the computer's digital signal to analog before transmission, special ISDN (Integrated Services Digital Network) modems transmit digital information over the telephone lines.

Communication Ports

Many of the external devices such as the monitor, external drive, mouse, and modem are attached with cables to the communication ports (sometimes just called ports) or connectors on the back of the computer. Of the two basic types, parallel ports are used to connect printers while serial ports are used for the modem and the mouse. In some cases, a serial printer may be connected to a serial port, but serial printers are slower and are used less frequently.

The newest type of port is the SCSI (Small Computer System Interface) or "scuzzy" port. With much faster speeds than serial or parallel ports or the IDE (Integrated Drive Electronics) interface for the hard disk, it is used to connect hardware such as scanners and CD-ROM drives to the computer. When using a SCSI interface, be sure to match the cable to the device.

The most common types of ports and the connectors on the cables found on both PCS and Macs are shown in Figure 2.3. The arrangement of the ports for these connectors will vary according to the brand and model of computer. Check your computer manufacturer's manual for specifications.

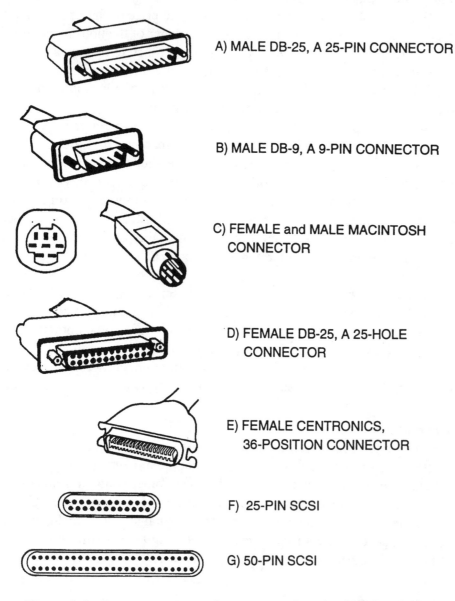

A) MALE DB-25, A 25-PIN CONNECTOR

B) MALE DB-9, A 9-PIN CONNECTOR

C) FEMALE and MALE MACINTOSH CONNECTOR

D) FEMALE DB-25, A 25-HOLE CONNECTOR

E) FEMALE CENTRONICS, 36-POSITION CONNECTOR

F) 25-PIN SCSI

G) 50-PIN SCSI

Figure 2.3 Common ports and connectors found on PCs and Macs

Motherboard

If you looked inside a computer and saw a green piece of fiberglass with silver or gold colored lines all over it, you would be looking at the motherboard, the piece of electronics that holds the microprocessor, RAM chips and ROM chips, and contains the electronic pathways between the components.

The motherboard can also hold slots or places to add more memory (RAM chips) or to add expansion cards such as the internal modem. Obviously, a computer that does not have any vacant or available slots on its motherboard would be hard to expand. One new trend is to replace the motherboard on an older model computer to give it new life. Another option may be to use a daughter board which plugs into the motherboard.

Other Components

New features and peripherals for computers are constantly being designed. Wavetable synthesis sound cards offer more realistic sound. Remote controls for computers allow a teacher to control a point and click program from anywhere in the room. New SVGA color active matrix projectors can deliver images as sharp and colorful as those seen on an SVGA monitor. There are even MFPs or multi functional peripherals which combine the capabilities of fax, modem, scanner, printer, and copier into one piece of hardware. While these MFPs are compact and very cost effective, unfortunately a problem with one component often means a problem with the others.

Specialized technologies have received a lot of publicity. CTI or computer telephony integration allows computers to function as answering machines, voice mail, fax, speed dialer, CD-ROM interface and telephone. With a Voice-View modem, you can talk to a technician at a remote site while he or she is using the same phone line to receive and send data to your computer.

Highly specialized are the computer "appliances" which are replacing the traditional multipurpose computer for some functions. Designed to perform only one function, such as assisting with reading instruction or providing Internet access, these inexpensive machines are being marketed by major manufacturers such as Apple and U.S. Robotics. The main selling point of the "appliances" is their low cost when compared to a full-functioning traditional computer.

Assistive technologies allow students with special needs to use computers. Along with touchscreens and interactive books on CD-ROM with sign language added to the visuals, there are computers with alternative keyboards and pointing devices. A special interface known as Ke:NX allows a student with limited motor skills and no speech capabilities to use a computer with a switch that is activated by head or foot movements. Voice recognition and word prediction software are available to assist students who have difficulty typing. For visually challenged students, braille displays, speech synthesis, and text-to-speech software are alternatives to large screen monitors. In Boston, WGBH, a public television station, is experimenting with a Web site for blind individuals. Check the resources section for their Web address and for other adaptive technology information sources on the Internet.

Finally, there are the new video/television cards. Once installed on your computer, they turn it into a complete education system with both television and computer capabilities. The television picture can be shown on the full computer screen or in a small window while you use your computer for other purposes. However, *Consumer Reports* (1996) indicated that their tests on current models showed that some of the combinations produced "fuzzy" full-screen images and "on-screen objects [which] suffered from jagged edges when seen from a normal computer viewing distance." Compare models closely before purchasing one of these combinations.

What are the software basics?

While there are lots of variations, for the sake of this discussion we will divide software into three basic types.

In the first category are the operating systems (OS) that direct the computer. Next are the utility programs that help the manager software function and help you prevent or solve problems. Finally there are the applications programs that are used to play games, type letters, figure grades, circulate materials in a library, and even regulate the temperature in buildings. Let's look at each of these three types.

Operating Systems

The computer's operating system manages and controls the working of the computer, including the way in which the CPU works with the floppy and hard disks to store and locate information. Programs to format a disk, copy a program, and erase information from a disk are usually part of the operating system. Although there are many operating systems for various types of computers, we will look at those used most frequently on PCS and on Macs.

Microsoft DOS (commonly referred to as MS-DOS or just DOS) was invented by Microsoft Corporation for IBM microcomputers and compatibles. A 16 bit operating system (processes 16 bits of information at a time), the first versions were what is called command driven OS and were very structured. To use it, you needed to type a command exactly with spaces and symbols in precise places. About the only advantage of a command-driven is that it requires the least amount of RAM (512KB) and storage (6.1MB on a hard drive), leaving more storage and memory free for other programs. Versions 4.0 and later of MS-DOS are menu driven. Using a menu called a DOS shell, these versions allow you to select many commands from a menu rather than having to type them.

The Macintosh uses a system finder screen to show its icon-driven operating system. An icon-driven operating system is also called a GUI or graphic user interface because it uses pictures (called icons) instead of words to move the user into the programs. The current Mac GUI operating system is called System 7 and is very easy to use.

Although the Macintosh computers were the first major group to use a GUI, a similar system called Windows was developed by the Microsoft Corporation for IBM computers. In its first versions, Windows was an environment, not an operating system, because it was installed on top of the operating system and worked with MS-DOS to make it appear as if there were an icon-driven operating system. Windows 3.x is used to refer to the Windows 3.1 and Windows for Work Groups (a Windows version with built-in networking capabilities) environments. Both work best on a 386 or higher chip with 8MB of RAM.

Finally, in 1995, Microsoft released its Windows 95 (Win95). Unlike Windows 3.x, Win95 is not an overlay to DOS but rather a combination 16 bit and 32 bit operating system. Requiring 16MB of RAM for best operation, Windows 95 still runs most DOS and Windows 3.x software; however, software written to take advantage of the newer 32 bit processing runs faster. A new feature (for the PC world) of Windows 95 is PnP or Plug and Play. With PnP, the operating system automatically configures the software to work with any PnP peripherals that are added to the system. Microsoft is also expected to release a set of standards for Windows computers known as PC98 to improve convenience and compatability.

Microsoft has also introduced Windows NT, a true 32 bit operating system. However, NT requires a high power PC with 64MB RAM, 90MB to 120MB of hard disk space, and even dual microprocessors. While Windows 95 certified applications are supposed to work on NT (some do not), applications that were written for the 16 bit DOS and Windows 3.x will not run. That eliminates a lot of educational software. Trying to use both DOS and NT operating systems on the same computer requires fairly sophisticated partitioning of the hard drive and special management software.

Competing with Windows 3.x is IBM's own OS/2 and OS/2 Warp, its 32 bit counterpart to Windows 95. Both are designed to be compatible with Windows and to run the same applications that run under the Windows operating system. Since IBM has targeted OS/2 to home office and small business customers, OS/2 is not generally used in schools.

Today, all major operating systems use a GUI: the Macintosh, Windows 3.x, Windows 95, Windows NT, and IBM's own GUI called OS/2. All of these GUI systems need more RAM (4MB to 64MB), large hard drive space (35MB to 110MB), and a high resolution video display. They are also multitasking operating systems, which means that they manage the computer so that it can actually run several applications programs at the same time, such as a word processing program, grammar check, and encyclopedia.

What lies ahead is uncertain. Apple has purchased *Next* to serve as a base for its new operating system, which should be OS 8. The system, with its 3-D look, is still in development; but, in its current form, it is not compatible with the current Apple software and will be based on a new hardware specification called the Common Hardware Reference Platform. Predicted in 1997 or 1998 from Microsoft is a new operating system which is code named Memphis but often referred to as Windows 97.

Utility Programs
The best way to explain utility programs is to list a few of them and explain what they do. Names of some programs and addresses of producers are in the Resources sections of this book.

Hard drive back-up programs. This software will make a copy of all the information on your hard drive. This is particularly important if you have the library's circulation information or all of your card catalog information on hard drive where it may be vulnerable to a mechanical failure or other disaster. You should regularly make a backup or copy of the information that you have stored on your hard drive. This copy can be made on floppy disks that you then store in a safe place.

Virus protection. A computer virus can be spread when computers are in contact with each other through networks and modems, when an infected disk is used in a machine, and when other users of a computer intentionally give it a virus. To prevent a virus, limit the disks that are used with a given computer and do not download information from the Internet or a computer bulletin board. If those precautions are not possible, use anti-virus software.

A virus can be benign and display a smiley face on your monitor, or be destructive and destroy the data on your hard drive. Most common viruses affect the boot-sector and start-up or infect files by working on executable files. In contrast, macro viruses do not attack executable files. Instead, they hide in a file and attack the application that opens that file. Similar to viruses and just as deadly, worms, Trojan horses, and logic bombs lack the ability of a virus to duplicate itself.

Virus protection utility programs can check disks (both hard and floppy) for viruses, try to "heal" any infections, and work invisibly behind your other programs to protect against any future infection. While basic virus protection is included as part of some operating systems, independent commercial virus software offers the safety of frequent updates for new viruses. They are often involved with Web sites where you can check for bogus virus alerts and download new virus definitions for your protection software.

Data compression. If you are running out of space on your hard drive, a data compression utility program will squeeze things together to make more room.

Hard disk maintenance. Some programs will check the drive and will then stay in the background while the computer is running to detect potential hard drive failures. Other programs will read hard-to-read data, find lost files, restrict access to your hard drive, and reformat hard drives.

Data recovery. If you press the delete key by mistake, your data is gone, isn't it? Well, that's not exactly true. There are data recovery programs that attempt to find lost data for you if you use them right away.

Applications Programs

Applications programs allow the computer to perform the tasks that you really bought the computer to do: type catalog cards and reports, file circulation records, calculate purchase orders, average student grades, and provide library instruction. Generically, they are divided into groups such as word processing programs, database programs, spreadsheet programs (number crunchers), and integrated packages that combine from all three general types and allow you to transfer information easily between them. In addition, there are graphics programs that allow you to draw, design, and become an artist. Library circulation, computerized library catalog, instructional tutorials, and desktop publishing are really specialized programs that combine the features from general word processing, database, spreadsheet, and graphics programs to perform specific functions.

Applications programs aid in library management. Word processing programs are great for typing letters, forms, handouts, and flyers. Add a general purpose graphics print/draw program to produce banners, signs, and transparencies and to make your handouts more attractive. With a database program compile reading lists, other booklists, a community resource file, a volunteer directory, or mailing lists. Newsletters are easy and fun with the help of one of the many newsletter programs.

Gone are the days when each application program stood alone. Integrated software packages or "suites" of software from a single publisher provide a family of programs that are designed specifically to work together to provide word processing, database, spreadsheet and even presentation applications. Applications programs from different software publishers can even share and use the same documents because of OLE (Object Linking and Embedding). This protocol, which was developed by Microsoft, allows documents created by different PC applications programs to be shared or combined. Thus a spreadsheet created with software from one company can be placed or embedded in a word processing document created by a program sold by another company.

What if the programs are on two different computers; one on a PC and one on a Mac? Several options permit what is called cross-platform use. Many software developers, including Microsoft, Claris, Corel, and Adobe, now include cross-platform compatibility in their programs. This allows a PC to read a file that was created by a Mac and vice-versa. System 7.5 for the Mac includes a utility called PC Exchange that lets a Mac read a disk which was formatted on a PC. Separate software programs such as Here & Now allow PCS to read from and write to Mac disks. In switching between programs, save files as ASCII for basic text or RTF (rich text format) to retain many formatting commands. Some programs have "export filters" that allow a document created with one program to be saved in the format used by another. A program called *Word for Word* by Adobe can even transfer files from one program to another (such as *WordPerfect* to *ClarisWorks*) and retain the complete formatting and the graphics.

Terminate and stay resident programs (sometimes called memory resident software or TSRs) stay in the background in RAM, behind other working programs. One example is a virus checking program that runs automatically every time you turn the computer on. It stays in the background and keeps working each time files are brought into the computer from the floppy disk or the modem.

Another type of TSR, such as a "personal information manager" or PIM, may stay in RAM until you summon it. For example, you may be using a word processing program to type a flyer for the upcoming book fair when you remember that you need to add the dates to your schedule book. You hit a hotkey or previously defined series of keys (such as control-alt-B), and your weekly planner pops up on the screen. After you enter the date of the book fair, you close the planner, and you are back working on the flyer. While TRS programs have lots of advantages, they can cause problems and use too much

RAM if too many of them are running in the background at the same time. The multitasking features of Macintosh computers and Windows 95 have helped eliminate most of the problems.

What about computer software requirements?

Why do computer users need to know about things like RAM, SVGA, and processors in order to use computer software? In addition to helping you troubleshoot computer problems, knowing about hardware will help your software work better. Basically, hardware and software need to work together. When you select software or try to use a particular program on a given computer, it is important to know a little about the hardware and software requirements. Not even the best software will work if the hardware does not have the capability of doing the things that the program wants it to do or if the hardware is too slow for the demands of the software.

Below are the listings of requirements for two pieces of software. Look at each and try to make some decisions about the hardware that is needed to use it. A similar listing is usually found on the software box, in the review of the program, or in the producer's catalog.

Software listing #1: IBM or compatible PC with 486 or higher microprocessor, Windows 3.1 or later, DOS 4.0 or higher, 4MB of RAM, sound card, SVGA display, 3.5" disk drive, 2.5MB to 5.5MB hard disk space; any graphics adapter card; mouse. Modem for communication module.

Explanation: To use this program, you must have an IBM or compatible with a 486 or Pentium microprocessor and at least 4MB of memory. The operating system must be Windows 3.x running over DOS 4.0 or higher, or Windows 95. There should be a 3.5" floppy disk drive and between 2.5MB and 5.5MB of space free on the hard disk to install the program. In addition, you need an SVGA monitor, a sound card, graphics adapter card (the specifications are broad enough to let you use any one), and a mouse. If you plan on using the communications module, you need a modem and a telephone hookup.

Software listing #2: Macintosh 68030 or PowerPC, 12MB of RAM with System 7.1 or earlier; 16MB RAM with System 7.5 or later; hard disk with 7MB free. Includes program on both CD-ROM and 3.5" disks

Explanation: This program requires a 68030 or PowerPC Macintosh computer. The amount of RAM required depends on the operating system that you are using. Your hard drive should have 7MB of storage free. You must have either a 3.5" disk drive or a CD-ROM drive to load the program onto your hard disk.

How can you keep track of what you have?

Computer specifications can be confusing, and many school librarians have many different computers to work with. To help you keep track, create a card file or a computer database with the specifications of each computer or ask the

```
                          PC Card

Computer brand _____
         Operating system _____
Processor type _____ Speed _____ MHz
         RAM memory size _____
Floppy disk drives
         Size: _____   Number: _____

                 Density: _____
         Size: _____   Number: _____

                 Density: _____
Hard Drive
         Size: _____ MB
Monitor
         Color: _____ Monochrome: _____
         Graphics: _____
Printer
         Brand: _____
         Model: _____
```

```
                   Sample Completed PC Card

Computer brand  XYZ Brand_____
         Operating system  DOS 6 ___._____
Processor type  486_____ Speed  25____ MHz
         RAM memory size  4 MB_____
Floppy disk drives
         Size:  3.5"_____   Number:  1_____

                 Density: HD_____
         Size:  3.5"_____   Number:  1_____

                 Density: HD_____
Hard Drive
         Size:  ____80_____ MB
Monitor
         Color:  X_____ Monochrome: _____
         Graphics: SVGA_____
Printer
         Brand:  ABC Brand_____
         Model:  F-93, 18 pin NLO_____
```

```
                    Macintosh Card
Computer Model _____
         Operating system _____
Processor _____
         RAM memory size _____
Hard Drive
         Size: _____ MB
Monitor
         Shape: _____
         Color:
                 B&W _____
                 Gray Scale_____
                 Color _____
Printer
         Brand: _____
         Model: _____
```

```
                 Sample Macintosh Card
Computer Model __Performa 200_____
         Operating system _System 7_____
Processor ___68030_____
         RAM memory size ___4 MB_____
Hard Drive
         Size: ____40_____ MB
Monitor
         Shape: __full page_____
         Color:
                 B&W _____
                 Gray Scale_____
                 Color __X_____
Printer
         Brand: ___Apple_____
         Model: ___Imagewriter_____
```

Figure 2.4 Computer Specification Cards

technology person in your school to make them for you. Keep this information handy whenever you purchase software or when you are trying to talk to someone about your system. While figure 2.4 shows sample specification cards, this same information can easily be kept in a computer database.

How should you use hardware and software information?

What do you need to keep in mind when you purchase hardware and software? Some of the major considerations are the following:

- Know the size of the floppy disks you will use. If your existing data is on 5.25" disks, you should have at least one machine that has both a 3.5" and 5.25" disk drive.

- Be sure the hard disk has enough storage space for now and for the near future. Graphics programs are especially memory hungry.

- While the cost of large hard drives has decreased, the amount of storage space required by newer versions of programs has increased.

- Buy as much RAM as your microprocessor can use or, with newer hardware, as much as you can afford. More can be added later.

- Be sure your keyboard is comfortable to use and that it has a number pad, especially if it will be used for mathematical operations.

- Check the type of monitor required by your software and be sure that you have the graphics board necessary for the monitor type. If not, be sure your microprocessor will let you upgrade to that board.

- Match the resolution of the monitor to the type of software you will use.

- Look at the communication ports on the computer. Are they adequate for the types of input and output devices that you want to use?

- If you are considering adding internal devices such as an internal fax modem to the computer, be sure that a sufficient number of expansion slots are available on the motherboard and that there is space inside the case.

- Look for any built-in security devices such as locks for the keyboard or the hard drive that are standard with the computer.

- Check the warranties. Most last from one to three years. Some, but not all, include a specified amount of free technical support either on-site or via the telephone. Find out the hours that technical support is available and what the cost is if you exceed the free hours.

- Determine the reliability of hardware and software. Use computer bulletin boards to check with other teachers and librarians.

What computer should you buy?

The best advice is to buy the computer that will suit your needs. First determine what software you will be using with the computer. Will you primarily type library reports with a wordprocessor and keep track of expenditures with a spreadsheet? Or will you publish a library newsletter, create computer slide shows to enhance your information skills lessons, develop multimedia presentations to be shown to community and business groups, and surf the World Wide Web? Will it be used by students with a CD-ROM encyclopedia or periodical database to search for information? The applications that you use will help dictate the hardware that you need. Remember, too, that better hardware will become available, so look for a system that can be upgraded.

Consider also where you will buy the computer. Options include direct from the manufacturer, through the mail, in a retail store, from a discount store, at a computer speciality store, or from a value added retailer who can build a custom system to your exact specifications. Check with the Better Business Bureau. Then look at the technical support provided, the warranty, bundled software, and brands sold by each. Maintenance, assistance after the sale, and training are other factors to consider.

As this book is being written, a good system to meet almost any need (except high-end video production which needs a Pentium II with MMX) and to run the application software used in a school library would look like the following:

	PC	Macintosh
Processor	166MHz to 100 MhzPentium or Pentium II	160MHz to 180MHz PowerPC
Memory	16MB to 32MB RAM; 64MB for graphics intensive systems	16MB to 64MB RAM
Video RAM	1MB to 2MB with appropriate video acceleration card	1MB to 2MB
Storage	2GB to 3.2GB hard drive	1.6GB to 2GB hard drive
Monitor	15" to 17" SVGA Noninterlaced dpi .28 or less 75Hz refresh rate	built-in
Audio	Wavetable synthesis 16 bit sound	built-in
CD-ROM	6x to 8x	6X to 8X
Modem	33.6KBps fax modem	33.6KBps fax modem
Extra	Zip drive, scanner, color printer, Plug N Play	Zip drive, scanner, color printer

What can you do if you have an old computer?

Old is a relative term when dealing with computers. While businesses may consider a four-year-old computer obsolete, many schools have to make do with much older models. The thing to remember is that as long as a computer is doing the job it was purchased to do, and that job is still an appropriate one, the computer is fine.

However, there are times when software is upgraded and the old hardware is discarded. If the hardware is still in working order, there are a variety of uses for it. Linda Skeele of Western Elementary in Georgetown, Kentucky, reports using old computers in keyboarding labs, as teleprompters for school news shows, and as loaners to students who do not have any computer access at home.

Businesses sometimes donate older computers to schools. Try not to accept ones with a processor older than a 386 unless you have a specific use in mind. To locate software to use with older computers, try pawn shops, garage sales and auctions, second-hand software dealers such as Surplus Software, and direct from the software manufacturer.

Some old equipment can be upgraded. However, beware. In some instances, the cost of the upgrade may be more than the purchase of new hardware. Problems often occur in trying to fit new components into old cases or trying to locate proprietary parts if the original computer did allow for the use of other brands of parts. Upgrading a graphics card or disk controller can be easily done, but to upgrade a motherboard, go to a reliable source.

What accessories are available?

Computer supply catalogs offer an amazing number of accessories and gadgets ranging from monitor arms that let the user move the monitor to a comfortable position to a CPU holder that will hold large CPU units sideways to save space. Described below are some gadgets that are nice but not necessary, including several of my personal favorites.

Do you tear the paper when you remove the tractor feed edges on continuous feed paper? Then you might like an inexpensive margin remover that leaves a smooth edge with a minimum of effort. If you have lots of different disks for different areas of the curriculum, try colored disks and holders. Plastic pages that hold disks allow you to keep paper copies and disks together. Cut eye strain with filters, and eliminate paper shuffling with copyholders in the form of stands and even clips. If you have other problems, for a price you will probably find the answers in computer supply catalogs.

How should you care for a computer and its software?

In addition to the general tips for caring for technology included in Section 1, consider the following as you begin to work with computers in the library.

Learn basic information. Start caring for your computer by reading the manual that came with it. Individual systems have their own quirks, such as when to power up an external hard drive or how to turn the system off correctly. Determine if there are any test programs that will troubleshoot minor problems for you.

Keep records. Keep a journal of all of the procedures that you do including backups, printer ribbon or toner cartridge changes, and so forth. Be sure to include a date. Whenever something unusual happens with a computer, list what happened, who was involved, and what software was being used.

Educate your users. Have an orientation session for everyone who will use a computer and keep a list of do's and don'ts posted near the computer. One idea would be to laminate an instruction card with simple start-up instructions and other important information and put it on the power cord or the security cord of each machine or on a stand by the computer.

Create and use passwords. Passwords provide protection against unauthorized use of a computer or a network. However, they work only if they are used and are kept secret. Do not write your passwords down and leave them by the computer. If you cannot remember your passwords, use clues. For example, only you might know that "first dog's name and mother's birthday" on a clue sheet translate to the password "Caesar825."

Mark connections. Look at the cords and connectors on the back of the computer and the accessories. If necessary make a chart of where each plug goes. One hint is to color code the cords and connections with permanent markers, paint, or colored electrical tape.

Check the power supply. Erratic performance of a computer can be caused by power problems. Electronic noise or interference can be caused by things such as radios or small motors. Do not put the computer on the same circuit as a photocopier, vacuum cleaner, or coffee maker. In fact, dedicated circuits are a good idea for computers. Voltage spikes (sharp and brief increases in power) and voltage surges (longer increases) can be caused by turning off a heavy power load on the same line or by surges in the line caused by things such as lightning. Voltage sags occur when a heavy power load is added to a line.

A surge suppressor costing between $10 and $100 will divert excess power from the line. A line conditioner or voltage regulator costing in excess of $100.00 will control surges, spikes and sags. An uninterruptible power source or UPS will provide battery backup for a system.

Do not turn a computer off and on repeatedly. Also do not turn the power on and off in rapid succession. When shutting down a computer at the end of the day, be sure to close all applications and follow the computer's shutdown procedure.

Turn a computer off before moving it. A little jolt can destroy the hard drive by sending the head crashing onto the surface.

Watch magnets. Because computers store information in magnetic form on floppy disks and hard disks, the magnets in TV tubes, telephone receivers, screwdrivers, and so forth can damage that information. Remember, a computer monitor can also give off an electromagnetic field that can create problems for disk drives. Do not place disks and disk drives on the monitor and keep all disks away from telephones. Do not use magnetized screwdrivers around computers.

Use anti-static devices. Static electricity can be a shock to both you and your computer. Anti-static mats that you stand on or touch before using the computer or anti-static sprays can cut down on the amount of static electricity transferred from your body to the computer.

Save data regularly. While you are working with a program, such as a word processing program, remember to save your work regularly. Many word processing programs allow you to set an automatic backup feature that saves your work at regular intervals. The automatic backup does not take the place of saving your work when you are done, but it does prevent the problem of spending two hours typing a 10-page report only to see it vanish when the power goes off.

Make backups. Be faithful in making copies (backups) of your data by scheduling backups and keeping to the schedule. They can be made on a floppy disk, a tape drive, Zip drive, CD-R disc, or other types of removable storage. No matter what the medium you use for the backup, keep two sets of backups and alternate between them. For example, if you backup your catalog on a weekly basis, this week use Backup A and next week backup on Backup B. Then, should a problem arise while you are making your backup copy, you will have lost only one week's worth of work.

One librarian was making her weekly backup of the hard disk when, unknown to her, something went wrong with the hard disk. Not only did it begin to fail, but it wrote gibberish on the backup floppy. If she had alternated between two floppies, she would only have lost one week's worth of work. As it was, both her hard drive and her single backup were worthless.

When making backups, be sure the disks that you use for the backups are all the same density.

Prepare a bootable disk. For each computer, prepare a bootable diskette to use if the hard drive will not start up or if someone deletes (by error or by mischief) a start-up file. Each operating system has its own required files that enable the computer to function and its own procedure for making a bootable disk. Read and follow it! If you change your system start-up files, make a new bootable disk, but save the old one just in case problems occur.

Keep equipment clean. Computers are vulnerable to dust, dirt, hair, smoke, and food. Do not eat, drink, or smoke near the computer. Keep the work space by the computer clean, with cables and cords tucked away. Dust in floppy drives can cause problems and can even bridge circuits. Keep monitors clean with special cleaning cloths, which can be washed and used again. Cans of compressed air can be used to blow dirt out of computers. Clean the mouse by wiping the ball with a soft cloth and thoroughly cleaning the inside of its case. Regular isopropyl alcohol on a lint-free cloth is a good cleaner, but be careful. It can remove the lettering on some keyboards.

Clean drives. Use commercially available disk drive cleaners to remove residue in the drives and help cut the static. Follow the recommendations that come with the cleaner, and you will save on disk repairs.

Clean the mouse. Use a commercial mouse pad under the mouse and use the pad only with a mouse. This will prevent the mouse from picking up dirt from a table or desk. However some cloth-type mouse pads can actually leave lint on the mouseball.

If the mouse gets dirty, you can purchase a special mouse cleaner and a plastic pocket that can be placed on the monitor to hold the mouse or trackball when it is not being used. Other options include a mouse or trackball cover.

Keep a cleaning kit. In it store isopropyl alcohol, non-lint tissues, a soft one-inch artists brush, and tweezers.

Cover equipment. Anti-static plastic is a good choice for covers for computers and accessories. Many brands have been designed to fit specific types of computers, monitors, modems, printers, and so forth. In a pinch, old bedsheets work well when you need to cover equipment. Clear, flexible keyboard covers will protect keyboards from spills, dirt, and paper clips, and still allow full use of the keyboard.

Watch temperature extremes. Too hot or too cold an environment can cause problems with computers and with computer disks. The best temperature range is 50° to 75° with low humidity. Maintain a six-inch space around the computer so heat can escape when the computer is on. A Styrofoam cooler in your car is cheap insurance if you frequently transport software. Keep disks off car dashboards and out of car trunks.

Develop a cleaning schedule and a checklist for each machine. Regular cleaning can prevent problems if you follow a schedule. At a minimum, give each computer a thorough cleaning once a year. That involves opening the case and carefully cleaning dust, especially from the fan blades.

Develop a care and maintenance schedule.

Daily
Make backups of heavily used files.
Scan all disks for viruses the first time they are used in a computer and each time after they have been used in another computer.

Weekly
Make system backups. (May be done more frequently if necessary.)
Scan all computers for viruses.
Clean exterior surfaces including the monitor and keyboard.

Monthly
Defragment the hard drive. Can be done more or less frequently depending on the use made of the hard drive.
Clean the fan on computers that are used in dusty areas. (This can be done without removing the case by using a vacuum cleaner on the fan intake.)
Check power cords and connectors.

Yearly
Thoroughly clean the computer, inside and out.

Preserve 5.25" floppies. If you have data on the older floppy format, be sure to keep the 5.25" floppies in their paper envelopes and do not touch the exposed shiny plastic disk itself. Write the label before attaching it to a 5.25" floppy or use a felt tip pen. Do not stack this type of floppy; store them vertically in a protective case. Above all, do not bend, fold, crease, jam, or force them into a drive. If possible, back these disks up on the 3.5" floppies.

Pamper the hard disk. Electronic equipment does eventually wear out, and a hard disk can "crash" or die, usually without warning. Problems include mechanical failures, surface defects, head alignment drift, and low-level format aging. A microscopic particle of dust or smoke can also cause a hard disk to crash. Even too many TSR (terminate and stay resident) programs such as anti-virus software that runs in the background behind the main program can cause problems.

If you rely on a hard disk, consider purchasing a hard drive maintenance utility program. If you are using a computer for word processing, spreadsheets, or databases, consider storing the program on the hard drive and keeping all the data on floppy disks. Should something happen to the hard drive, the data will still be accessible on the floppy disks, which can be used on another compatible computer.

Take care of the printer. Printers have many of the same care requirements as computers: check cables, keep clean, use power protection, cover when not in use. In addition, use a good quality ribbon, since the fibers from worn cloth ribbons can cause printing problems.

Cleaning is important, so check the manual to see exactly what is required. In most cases (check for exceptions in the manual) the carrier rod for a print head can be oiled with a drop or two of light, high-quality oil. The print head itself on impact printers can be cleaned with alcohol on a non-lint cloth. Clean the paper guide, platen, and the print shield with alcohol too.

Some printers have setting switches called "dip switches." Make a chart showing the normal setting (up or down) that you use with programs. Then if someone accidentally plays with them, you can check them first if there is a printing problem. If all your software requires the same settings, mark them with a permanent marking pen.

Prevent phosphor burn-in on monitors built before 1995. Leaving an image unchanged for a long time can etch or burn the image into older monitors. It may then appear as a fuzzy image behind any other program that you run. In a library where people may constantly interrupt your work at a computer or where you have an automated catalog program running, this can be a serious problem. Prevent this in one of the following ways:

- Turn the monitor off (not the computer itself) when it is not being used.

- Turn down the brightness control on the monitor when you leave.

- Use a screen saver or screen blanker program. When there has not been any activity at a computer for a set period, this program either blanks the screen or puts a special moving design on it. Many operating systems now include a screen saver.

What should you do before you call for help?

If you are having a problem with a computer system, there are a few basic things that you can do before you call the repair technician. As you go through the following procedures, also listen for strange noises.

- Try the procedure again.
- Turn everything off, wait 30 seconds, and start over.
- Check all cords, cables and plugs. Be sure the connections are tight, and cords and cables are not pulled out.
- If there is no power, try another outlet, check the powerstrip, and examine the circuit breakers.
- If there is no picture on the monitor, check the settings for contrast and brightness.
- Try the software you were using in another machine.
- Try another program on the problem machine.
- If another program works, try the backup of the program that you were using.
- Try other peripherals (monitor, drive, mouse). If your disk drive does not stop spinning, try replacing that drive with one that you know works.
- Record what you did and the results.
- As a last resort, open the computer case to check for loose cards and connections.

Refer back to the troubleshooting checklist in chapter one for more advice.

Many schools still have Apple IIs. While these machines have handled a tremendous load of use for years, many of these workhorses are wearing out and are now suffering power supply failures. If there is no beep when you turn on an Apple II, check the power supply first.

If you do decide you need to call for help, be sure you have the following information noted in the problem report form shown here:

```
┌────────────────────────────────────────────────────────────────┐
│                   Computer Problem Report                      │
│                                                                │
│  Computer (brand)_____ │
│                                                                │
│        Model _____  │
│        Serial number or other ID _____   │
│           Stand alone_____ Networked _____   │
│           Operating system _____   │
│                                                                │
│        Applications running when problem started:              │
│                                                                │
│                                                                │
│        Error message displayed:                                │
│                                                                │
│                                                                │
│                                                                │
│        Peripherals connected to the computer:                  │
│                                                                │
│                                                                │
│                                                                │
│        Description of the problem:                             │
│                                                                │
│                                                                │
│                                                                │
│                                                                │
│                                                                │
│        Recent changes (new software, etc.) to that computer.   │
│                                                                │
│                                                                │
│                                                                │
└────────────────────────────────────────────────────────────────┘
```

What's involved in complying with the copyright laws?

With the ease of duplicating computer programs, library collections of computer software are frequent targets for people who want to build large software collections without spending any money. Thus it is no surprise that software manufactures are concerned about copyright laws and with educating (and sometimes scaring) users about the legal restrictions regarding the purchase and use of computer programs. Yet, as soon as companies began to put special anti-copying codes in programs, other companies began to sell programs that would "unlock" the protected program and aid in the violation of the copyright law.

Copyright protection is provided in the United States by a series of laws including the 1978 Copyright Law, the 1980 Computer Software Copyright Act, and the Computer Software Rental Amendment of 1990. To be sure that you are abiding by these laws, there are some basics about computer copyright that every SLMS needs to know and do. In addition, there are guidelines which have been agreed upon by software vendors and education users that, while they do not cover the weight of law, do serve as a guide for the proper use of copyrighted software. Some of those guidelines related to multimedia are discussed later in this book.

Is that program copyrighted?

According to the rules of copyright, computer software that is available today can be divided into three basic types: public domain, shareware and commercial. Public domain software is essentially available free of any charge. True public domain software can be copied without worrying about copyright. Shareware may initially be acquired without cost, but the idea behind it is to allow you to try the product. If you like the shareware program, you are to send a fee to the originator of the program, according to the specific directions included with the shareware. If you do not like it, you pay nothing. However, should you decide to use the shareware program, ethically you should pay for it.

Shareware fees (sometimes called registration fees) are usually quite modest and will register you as a user. You may then receive special manuals and notices of updates to the program. You may freely pass copies of the program on to others with the understanding that, if they use it, they should send in their own registration fee. Shareware programs include programs such as screen savers or specialized applications programs.

Unlike public domain programs and shareware, commercial computer programs are governed by the copyright laws and present legal problems in many libraries. These problems center in three areas: the reproduction, distribution, and preparation of a derivative work. While you really need a lawyer to interpret the fine points of the law, there is one question you should ask whenever the question of copyright violation arises: Am I depriving the copyright holder of money? Notice, the question does not involve the issue of whether you have the money, as in the frequent excuse of "we couldn't afford to buy it." And it does not address the excuse that making illegal copies is "for the good of the children."

Exactly what are you buying?

Today, schools and school libraries purchase computer software in many ways. Traditionally, they would buy single copies of computer programs or several copies of a much-used program. Perhaps there were even purchases of class sets of multiple copies. More recently, software companies have been selling a variety of licenses.

According to the Software Publishers Association (SPA), there are four basic types of licenses. These types are discussed in detail in an article by Sue Kamp that is listed in the Resources section.

Designed for use on one specific computer, but by any number of people using that one machine in person, is the machine license. A similar restrictive license is the individual license which is given to one specific individual. This permits the individual to use a program on any number of machines, but, depending on the wording of the license, the individual can use the program on only one machine at a time.

A concurrent license permits the use of a program by a number of people at the same time up to the amount specified on the license. For example, there may be 20 computers on a network. However, a concurrent license with a limit of eight would allow only eight of the users of the network to run the program at a single time. A concurrent license requires software to monitor the users.

Finally, there are site licenses. Originally, purchasing a site license allowed a school to make an unlimited number of copies for use in that school building or campus. Recently, however, software publishers have gone to site licenses which are more like "volume discount agreements" in which the price per copy of a program decreases as more copies are purchased. In 1996, Apple Computer announced its own version of a site license for its operating system software. If a school buys one copy of the latest system software for each type of Macintosh computer that it owns, it can then install that operating system on all compatible computers at no additional cost.

Purchasing software and making multiple copies without a site license is illegal. Purchasing a single copy of a program and putting it on a network when a networked version is available is also a violation of copyright. In both instances, the copyright holder has been deprived of income.

In some instances, it is possible to take one program, put it in the disk drive of one computer, load the program into RAM, then repeat the procedure for other computers. This is called simultaneous or multiple machine loading. In essence, no copy is made since the program will be erased when the computer is turned off. Another variation is to run one copy on a server computer on a network and to allow several people to use it at one time.

Determining if this is a copyright violation is a gray area because of the definition of copy. However, when this procedure is used to allow an entire class of students to use one copy of a program, the intent of copyright violation is present since multiple copies could be purchased. The lack of money is not an excuse for breaking the law. Using one copy of a program to install the program on the hard disk of a number of computers is a clear violation of copyright.

An issue in the copyright of computer software has been the shrink-wrap license which is often similar to a machine license or an individual license. Commercial software producers have sought to control the use of their programs by saying that when you purchase a program, you are really only buying a license to use the program. Since a notice of this appears on the plastic wrap on the software package, it has been called a shrink-wrap license.

A problem is that in many cases this license allows you only to use the program on the computer for which it was purchased. "No problem," you say until you realize that you have five computers in the school library. Can you really be expected to remember which programs you bought for which computer? And what happens if that program is running on a network? Although at least one state backs the shrink-wrap law, experts doubt that it would stand up to a legal challenge if a purchaser were only using one purchased copy of a program on one computer at a time.

Should you tell vendors of programs that have shrink-wrap licenses how you will use a program? Some experts believe that if you are buying a copy to circulate, even if only to teachers, you should include a statement of intended use on your purchase order. Other experts say don't tell if you're not asked. In any case, be very careful if you are asked to sign any software license agreement that restricts the use of software.

Can you legally make any copies?

The copyright laws do not mean that all copying of computer software is illegal. When training teachers to use a particular program that they will then use individually or with their students, simultaneous machine loading is permissible for a brief training session.

Copying commercial computer software is also legal when you are making an archive copy. Experts suggest making an archival copy of all software. When a commercial program arrives in the school library, one archival copy can be made to keep in a secure place while the original program is being used.

But the archival copy is just that—a spare to use in case you have a problem with the working copy of the program. It is not to be used to give you two working copies of the program. The bottom line is that you should use only the number of copies that you purchased and paid to use.

Can you legally lend software?

The 1990 Computer Software Rental Amendment stated that computer programs could not be rented, leased, or loaned commercially, but it exempted nonprofit libraries and educational institutions. In addition, it stated that libraries cannot be held responsible if patrons illegally copy library computer software.

However, all copies of software loaned by libraries are required to have a warning attached to them stating that unauthorized copying may violate copyright laws. To be safe, attach a warning to all the computer programs that you purchase, even if the programs are only used in the school library.

According to the copyright Software Rental Amendments Act, computer software can be circulated provided the following copyright notice is permanently affixed to all circulating copies or the container holding the software:

Notice: Warning of Copyright Restrictions

The copyright law of the United States (Title 17, United States Code) governs the reproduction, distribution, adaptation, public performance, and public display of copyrighted material.

Under certain conditions specified in law, nonprofit libraries are authorized to lend, lease, or rent copies of computer programs to patrons on a nonprofit basis and for nonprofit purposes. Any person who makes an unauthorized copy or adaptation of the computer program, or redistributes the loan copy, or publicly performs or displays the computer program, except as permitted by Title 17 of the United States Code, may be liable for copyright infringement. This institution reserves the right to refuse to fulfill a loan request if, in its judgment, fulfillment of the request would lead to violation of the copyright law.

How can you protect yourself?

First be sure that you have posted copyright notices by copy machines, printers, computers and scanners, and on computer software, even if the software does not circulate. On smaller items which may be copied, such as computer software, the following notice can be placed:

NOTICE: This material may be protected by Copyright Law
(Title 17, U.S. Code)

The following notice should be placed in a prominent position near each photocopier, scanner, printer, computer, or any other place were copies can be made. It should be legible and no smaller than 8 point type.

Warning Concerning Copyright Restrictions

The copyright law of the United States (Title 17, United States Code) governs the making of photocopies or other reproductions of copyrighted material.
Under certain conditions specified in the law, libraries and archives are authorized to furnish a photocopy or other reproduction. One of these specified conditions is that the photocopy or reproduction is not to be "used for any purpose other than private study, scholarship, or research." If a user makes a request for, or later uses, a photocopy or reproduction for purposes in excess of "fair use," that user may be liable for copyright infringement. This institution reserves the right to refuse to accept a copying order if, in its judgement, fulfillment of the order would involve violation of the copyright law.

Make sure that information on computer copyright is part of your school library media center's general copyright statement. If you do not have a copyright statement, check with your central school office for a district-wide policy. If there is none, work with the technology staff to write one for your school, inform the administration and faculty, and educate the students. Be sure your policy is approved by the administrator or by the library supervisor. Sample policy statements are available in a number of books on copyright and from professional organizations. (Check the Resources section for additional information.)

How can you stay up-to-date with technology?

What will computers look like in the future? Will processors run at a speed of 4 Gigahertz and handle 100,000,000,000 instructions per second? Will there be holographic storage, molecular memory, and quantum computers? These are only a few of the predictions made about technology in the future.
The only sure thing in the computer world is change. There will always be newer machines and software. There will be all kinds of extras that we cannot even imagine. Unless you devote all of your time to computers, you cannot really stay on top of the new products in the computer field. But there are resources which will help you find out about the major events and latest products. You will find some listed in this book. By reading journals, attending conferences, and talking to other librarians, you will be able to stay informed about the latest inventions in the computer world.

Bibliography

Copyright Books and Articles

Bruwelheide, J. H. (1995). *The copyright primer for librarians & educators*. 2nd ed. Chicago, IL: American Library Association.

Simpson, C. M. (1997). *Copyright for school libraries: A practical guide*. 2nd ed. Worthington, OH: Linworth Publishing.

Sinofsky, E. R. (1994). *A Copyright primer for educational and industrial media producers*. 2nd ed. Washington, DC: Association for Educational Communications and Technology.

Sivin, J. P. And E. R. Bialo. (1992). *Ethical use of information technologies in education: Important issues for America's schools*. Washington, DC: U.S. Dept. of Justice.

Vlcek, C. (1992). *Adoptable copyright policy: Copyright and manuals designed for adoption by schools, colleges, and universities*. Washington, DC: Association for Educational Communications and Technology. Note: Includes a computer disk with policies you can adopt or revise.

General Books and Articles on Computers

Black, B. R. (1989). *Troubleshooting micro's*. Bartow, FL: Polk County board of Public Instruction. Contains suggestions for working with older computers such as Apple IIC, IIe, IIGS, and ImageWriter printers.

Borman, J. L. (1995). *Computer dictionary for kids—and their parents*. New York: Barron's Educ. A complete review of this easy-to-understand, user-friendly dictionary appeared in the March 1, 1996 edition of *Booklist*.

Computer resources for people with disabilities (1994). New York: Hunter House. The August 1994 issue of *Booklist* called this "a veritable clearinghouse for the different technologies" available for people with disabilities.

Davis, F. (1994). *Windows Bible combo*. Berkeley, CA: Peachpit Press. Friends of mine claim this is "the best" book on Windows 3.1! With over 1000 pages, it covers everything.

Desktop computers: what's new? (1996, December) *Consumer Reports, 61,* 21-22. This article includes ratings for some high performance computers for desktop publishing, games, and video.

Desmond, M. (1996). Windows 95, the essential guide. *Multimedia World*, 3 (2), 82-88. Contains a list of "tips and tricks" for using Windows 95.

Gookin, D. (1995). *Windows 95 for Dummies* San Mateo, CA: IDG Books. This popular title is part of a whole series of books on computers written for the true beginner. Other titles in the series include: *Macs For Dummies*, *PC's For Dummies*, and *Windows For Dummies*, and *DOS for Dummies* game book.

Graf, N. (1995). Windows 95, the hands-on lowdown. *Technology Connection*, 2 (8), 10-12. A Macintosh user, Graf examines the new PC operating system.

Holzberg, C. S. (1995). Windows tools for diagnosing PC illnesses. *PC Novice,* 6 (10), 28-30. Looks at software packages to " troubleshoot hardware, resolve software glitches" and help things run more smoothly.

Home office guide; Advice on buying the equipment you need to work at home. (1997, September). *Consumer Reports,* 62, 24-40. Although written for the home-based business, this feature article has excellent information on computers, monitors, fax machines, printers, and copiers.

Kamp, S. (1996). Publishers listen to educators about software license needs. TECHNOLOGY CONNECTION, 3 (2), 32. A discussion of the major types of software licenses.

Krushenisky, C. (1997). Dealing with 5.25 inch diskettes. *PC Novice,* 8 (1), 87-89. Discusses solutions to problems in working with computers which only have the older sized drives.

Lamb, A. (1990, May/June) You and your computer: a new PR team. THE BOOK REPORT, 9 (1), 18. Suggests some computer programs to help you promote the school library.

Macintosh Bible. (1996). Berkeley, CA: Peachpit Press. Everything you ever wanted to know about Macintosh computers is in this book. Includes an extensive list of companies and their products for the Macintosh. If you have a Mac, buy this!

Meeldijk, V. (1993, June). Rx for PC troubles. *Home Mechanic* 89, 32-34. Lists diagnostic software and includes solutions to typical problems.

Miller, M. (1993). *Oops! What to do when things go wrong.* Carmel, IN: Que. Easy-to-read explanations of how to fix common PC problems. Chapters have titles such as "Computer basics for the technically timid" and "Why bad things happen to good computer users." Also *Oops! Windows.*

Moore, J. (1997). Pick a card. *Mobile Computing and Communications,* 8 (2), 97-104. A buyer's guide to PC Card modems and ISDN adaptors for telecommunications.

Paulson, L. D. (1995). How to buy a database. *PC Novice,* 6 (5), 52-53. Information on the types of database programs available and suggestions for making a decision about the type to purchase.

Scott, P. B. And R. D. Howell. (1984). Troubleshooting: dealing with a misbehaving Apple. *Computing Teacher,* 11 (6), 29-30. Presents troubleshooting suggestions for Apple II computers.

Smith, R. (1996). Sleep better at night...back up your data. *MultiMedia Schools,* 3 (1), 67-70.

Thibodeaux, A. (1995). A new network with secondhand computers. THE BOOK REPORT, 14 (Nov./Dec), 23. Thibodeaux describes her experience in a high school library.

Thompson, T. (1996). When silicon hits its limits, what's next? *Byte,* 21 (4), 45-54. Explores devices that may replace the computer chip.

Troubleshooting hardware and software problems; Apple II series computers. (1987). *The Computing Teacher,* 15 (Nov.), 27-28. Having trouble with your old Apple IIs? Check this article for possible answers.

Weingarten, F. W. (1996). Technological change and the evolution of information policy. *American Libraries,* 27 (11), 45-47. A look at formal and informal policies dealing with information and the impact that technology is having on how libraries provide access to that information.

Wright, G. (1996). Storage solutions. *Interactivity*, 2 (5), 26-36. Examines some of the newer types of storage and includes a list of suppliers.

Wright, G. (1996). The Truth about Windows NT. *Interactivity*, 2 (9), 27-32. Includes a review of five workstations and a partial list of compatible software.

Chapter 3

Library Management with a Computer

While computers and related technologies are causing changes in all aspects of the school library media program from the indexing of periodicals to the delivery of information skill instruction, one of the areas of greatest impact has been in the management of the school library itself. This chapter begins with an overview of the library procedures that are most frequently managed with the aid of a computer, continues with a more detailed discussion of the automation of circulation and cataloging, and ends with an overview of information retrieval systems.

Specific programs and systems are not discussed. They are changing too rapidly to be covered in a book and are best reviewed in magazine articles and discussed in user groups or via the Internet. What this chapter does contain is some general information to guide you and make you a more informed shopper. The Resources list has additional information on specific programs.

Why use computers for management?

Do the following situations sound familiar? Do students ask when *Catherine, Called Birdy* (or any popular title) is due back in the library? Do they wonder if you have any short books on ...(pick a topic)? Is a teacher looking for a book that has "mustard jelly" somewhere in the title? Do you wish you knew (without going card-by-card through the shelf list) how many of the books in the 500s were published before 1980? Have you been asked, on a hectic day, to sign a release form stating that a student has no materials checked out of the library so that she may withdraw from school right now (Dad's waiting in the principal's office)? Does it take you 30 minutes to find the cards to check-in 50 books? Are you spending two hours every Friday typing overdue notices? Do you wish you had an easy way to prepare subject bibliographies for teachers? Have you been meaning to find the time to pull the cards from the card catalog for all those books that have been lost or discarded? Do you dread typing catalog cards for all those videocassettes that arrive in the library without processing kits? Automated library systems can solve these problems and many others.

Also driving the push toward automation of school libraries is the increased emphasis on resource sharing. Modern technology such as computers, modems, CD-ROMs, and the Internet allows access to the catalogs of other libraries. This could not be provided as long as library catalogs were still on printed cards filed in drawers.

Obviously, one of the major stumbling blocks to complete automation is money, not only the cost of the hardware and software, but also the cost in dollars and time to make the system operational and to maintain it. However, there are less costly programs that can help you with some of the routine library duties while you are waiting for total automation.

How difficult will the switch be?

The process of automating (using a computer to help manage certain library procedures or systems) involves work. In fact, depending on the system, as you make the switch to a computer-managed or assisted system, you may be overwhelmed by the amount of work involved.

However, most librarians agree that the work involved in automating is, in the end, worth the effort involved—provided the change was well planned and the resulting system does what it is supposed to do. Planning is a must! Know what you want a system to do. Talk to others who use the system you are considering to be sure that it will indeed meet your needs.

What are the computer management options?

While many people equate library automation with putting the circulation system or card catalog on a computer, computers can assist with many other library routines. Older computers such as the Apple IIe can even help with some of the simpler options such as catalog card and overdue notice production. All library management does not have to cost thousands of dollars.

General Applications Software
The previous chapter included some ideas for using general applications software packages for library procedures. You can take a commercial, nonlibrary program and use it in the library.

A database can store:
- circulation records and overdues
- bibliographies, lists of special collections
- lists of community resources
- indexes to local newspapers and the vertical file
- order and consideration files
- equipment inventories and projector lamp information
- equipment warranty, maintenance and repair files
- lists of favorite Internet sites

A spreadsheet can calculate:
- circulation statistics
- budget figures and special library accounts
- book fair tallies
- grades

A word processing program can produce:

- forms for the consideration file, purchase orders and requisitions
- memos, reports, letters, lesson plans, and handouts
- newsletters, brochures and bookmarks for public relations
- reading lists, instructional aids, and research guides
- banners, posters, and signs

Check the articles by Anne Clyde and Pat Burns in the Resources section for other ideas.

Specialized Programs for Collection Management

Catalog cards. For most people, typing catalog cards is such a chore that they are tempted to drastically cut back on the number of subject headings assigned to an item to decrease the number of cards to type. Many librarians claim that they will never order an item unless it comes complete with catalog cards. But the sad fact is that many audiovisual items (including computer software) do not come with catalog card sets, nor do gift books or purchases from the local book fair. Catalog card programs are fairly inexpensive and will produce sets of cards to your specifications following the rules of AACR2R, the latest cataloging code. They can add the ISBD punctuation now used on catalog cards, produce labels, and let you print bibliographies of new materials.

Overdue notices. A computerized overdue system is an inexpensive purchase that will save time. You will still need to type the basic information into the computer for each overdue item, but you will be able to store that information and use it to produce a variety of reports and forms such as individual notices, grade or homeroom notices, a list by the titles of the overdue materials, or a list by authors. Sending second and third notices is much easier since the information is already in the computer.

Order systems. Computerized order or acquisition systems can stand alone or be part of the circulation or catalog system. Designed to manage orders, they can speed up the ordering process and keep a record of expenditures. Some are designed to be used for specific vendors, while others are more generic.

Instead of typing purchase orders or individual order cards, you may be able to type only the ISBN or LCCN on the computer using a special program. Then your order is transmitted electronically over the telephone via a modem to a vendor. Depending on the system, the vendor may be able to respond immediately or within a few hours, and provide a verification complete with a listing of the titles available to be shipped, those on back order, and those the vendor is unable to supply. The vendor should also be able to tell you the current prices, discounts, and other expenses related to your order.

Serials systems. Do you use cards to check-in each magazine as it arrives in the library? A computerized periodicals system allows you to check in the magazines on a computer. If a magazine is late or missing, the system will inform you and will even type letters automatically to request the missing issues from the jobber or publisher.

Interlibrary loans. School libraries can borrow from other libraries if both have computerized systems that allow them to send requests electronically.

Circulation systems. An automated circulation system ideally will monitor circulation, aid in inventory, prepare circulation reports, type overdues, and generate monthly statistics and annual reports. Some systems place holds or reserves on items in circulation and on order, and may even prepare simple bibliographies.

In most circulation systems, you enter information about the collection items and patrons into a computer. Barcodes or unique identification numbers are assigned to each item and to each person. You also enter information about your library such as your check-out periods for students and faculty, and for special items such as reference books and magazines. Once all the information has been entered, items are circulated by scanning the barcode or typing in the identification number of the item and the borrower. Using the information that you entered about your library, the program will usually calculate the due date, provide an alert if the patron has any overdues, determine fines, print overdue notices, produce circulation reports, and take an inventory.

There are many ways to enter the information about your collection into the computer for your circulation system. Some are much faster than others. In fact, with some systems, you do not even have to enter information about your entire collection before you start using the system. You just enter information as the materials are checked out. Then, as time allows, you go back and enter the information about the titles that have not circulated.

One word of caution about a topic that is discussed in more detail later in this section: if you hope to move from a computerized circulation system to a computerized or online catalog, be sure that the information put in the circulation system is complete or that it contains enough information so it will be easy to upgrade to a catalog program. Some circulation systems ask you to enter only a few items of basic information about each item, not enough to suffice as a catalog entry.

Online catalogs. An online catalog, computerized card catalog, or OPAC (online public access catalog) uses a computer to locate information in a library catalog that is stored on a hard disk or a CD-ROM disc. Some systems provide not only information about the materials currently in the collection but may also contain information about the materials that are on order.

Searching the OPAC catalog is a little different from looking in the drawers of a card catalog. In addition to the usual author, title, or subject searches, keyword searches are possible. If set up on the system, searches can also be done by categories such as reading level, state curriculum objective, and book awards. Students and teachers are no longer limited to the subject terms thought up by a cataloger, and words within a title or subtitle can be located.

You may also be able to do Boolean or logic searches that let you combine concepts, such as looking for all science books published before 1980, or all materials that discuss the subjects of immigration or naturalization or emigration. Some online catalogs go beyond the usual card catalog and also include journal indexes. A student searching for information on Bosnia would find a list of books as well as a list of periodical articles. Some of the new systems allow users to create a bibliography directly from their search results. While an online catalog can be housed in one computer, most OPACs are networked to provide access for a number of patrons. (There's more information about networking in a later chapter.) Not only can there be several computers in the library providing access to the library's automated catalog, but there can also be computers throughout a single school or in several schools that can access the same catalog. A further step would be to allow faculty, staff, and students with a modem to access the catalog no matter where they are. Imagine a teacher planning a unit at home on the weekend and being able to find out how many items the library had on a given subject simply by calling up the library's OPAC.

Integrated systems. The OPAC can be an independent system, but it is usually part of an integrated system that also includes circulation. This means that users of the OPAC may also be able to see if the item they want is checked out, on the shelf, missing, or at the bindery. As these systems become more popular, special features are added to the programs. Things to look for include history features for tracking individual fines and circulation records, media booking modules, serials check-in, graphical interfaces, and even Internet access, as well as the management utilities listed next. Many libraries are installing computer networks that allow access to the library catalog and CD-ROM databases from computers throughout the library, the school, and even the community.

Management utilities. With the increased use of integrated circulation and catalog software has come the development of specialized products that can work with those systems.

Young children frequently have problems trying to use a card catalog. Unfortunately, their reading, thinking, spelling and typing abilities can also prevent them from successfully searching many OPACs. However, new graphical interfaces (such as *Kid's Catalog*) with plenty of pictures and point-and-click features are being designed to eliminate some of those problems.

"What's a good book to read?" is a common question in school libraries. Programs such as *Book Wizard* provide book reviews and help students locate books about their interests and on their reading levels. Some of these can interface with or act as a front-end to an OPAC, providing the call numbers for materials in the collection.

No one had ever had time to enter all of the subject cross-references into the card catalog. With an OPAC, there are databases with cross-references for subject headings. Once loaded into the system, they provide all the necessary "see" and "see also" links for the system.

With some utility programs, it is now possible for a user to enter one set of search terms and have a computer search the library catalog and a number of periodical databases. A further extension of this is to provide an Internet link through the automated system — a true library without walls.

Networked information systems. Many libraries are installing computer networks that allow access to the library catalog and CD-ROM databases from computers throughout the library, the school, and even the community. These systems are discussed later in this book in the chapters on CD-ROM and networks.

What should you consider before buying a collection management system?

Before you embark on a major automation project or decide to update an existing system, take some time to decide what you want and, more importantly, what you need.

First, realize that every system will bring some additional work for the library staff until the system is operational. If you are computerizing the circulation system, the information about your collection and your patrons has to get into the computer. This means that either the library staff enters the data, volunteers do the work, or you pay an outside person or a company to do it for you. Accuracy is important and checking of volunteers' work may be necessary. One library reported four different spellings of the word dinosaur. Know your own limitations.

After the system is operational, someone must take the responsibility for its maintenance. You will find yourself cleaning up records, changing subject headings or adding "see" and "see also" references. Disks of information received from vendors with orders will need to be checked. You will need to anticipate problems. When the electricity goes off, the circulation system and online catalog go off too, unless you install an uninterruptible power supply. In many ways when you automate a school library, you will trade one set of problems for another. The problems may be smaller and less frequent, but you will need to anticipate and plan for them. With an automated system, card drawers cannot be hidden or dumped, but hard drives can crash and systems can go down when the power goes out.

Know the features you want. Before you begin to look at programs, identify the reports that you make with your current system. Also list the important features of your current manual system. Does the eighth-grade English teacher want a list of all the books that each of her students checks out? Will your new system take care of that or will you still need to keep those special cards?

Do not assume that an automated system will contain the reports you want or offer the services you need. Make your list first, then compare it to the reports and services of automated systems. You may change your want list as you go along, but have some basic ideas first.

Many times one automated system is selected for all of the schools in a system. In that case, volunteer to serve on the selection committee if one is being formed. If that is not an option, provide your want list to the individuals involved in the selection.

Plan for the future. If you are planning to purchase an automated circulation system, think about the future as you do so. Maybe an online catalog is not in the plans for your library yet, but plan ahead. If you are going to the trouble of entering your entire collection into a computer database, it makes sense to input basic information that will allow you to use that database or to easily upgrade it to a format that can be used for a catalog.

In planning for future developments also keep the requirements of networking in mind. Will the system that you select allow access to the catalog from the entire school or from any place in the community? Will you be sharing your catalog via a network with other schools or libraries? Will your system (hardware and software) be easy to upgrade?

Consider the needs of your school. Match the expertise of your patrons to the technology. Who will use the system? Will it be library staff only? Teachers? Students? Once you know the system users and their skills, try to select a system that they can use.

If your patrons are not very technologically literate, lots of menus (lists of choices) and explanations may be needed. However, if your patrons are experienced, menus and explanations may frustrate them and slow them down. Some systems allow you to adjust the level of the explanations and menus as the patrons learn the system.

Also consider the effect of the system on library services and the instructional program. What changes will you need to make as you are trying to get the system operational after the system is in place? What impact will the system have on both services and instruction?

The technological and architectural limitations of your library are also an important consideration. Is the current wiring in your library adequate for a computer system? Is there an electrical outlet near the circulation desk? Will the circulation desk need to be modified for a computer and printer? What are your chances of getting a dedicated telephone line in the library to use with the telecommunications feature of your program and to receive technical support?

Be realistic about how technology will work in your library. You may think that you will only need one computer to run your circulation system, and that may be true. However, will your system allow you to keep circulating materials and run overdue notices or print reports at the same time? In most cases, circulation stops while overdue notices are being printed. Is there a time when you can print those overdues or can you plan an alternative check-out procedure (such as writing down the student and item barcode number and entering them later) while the overdues are being printed?

Weed before you automate. Do not put unwanted, out-of-date, worn out materials into the new system. Doing so will cost time and money. Each item must be barcoded or numbered and entered into the system.

One word of caution. Weeding can present a public relations problem. Let people know what you are doing and why. Several years ago, a local newspaper ran a story about school libraries that, in the process of automation, were throwing away the "classics." It seems that a reporter found copies of some classics in a school dumpster. It did not matter that these books were duplicates, worn out, or titles that were no longer studied in the curriculum. What did matter was that these were books, and they were being thrown away. It took a while to overcome the negative publicity generated by the story.

See Chapter 1 of this book for more purchase considerations.

What is available?

You need to ask some hard questions when you begin to search for automated circulation and catalog systems:

- What are the major systems of this type?
- Who makes them and what is the track record of each company? How long has the company been in business?
- What guarantees and warranties do they provide?
- Who uses each system and what are their feelings about it?
- Is it a "turnkey" system with all hardware and software provided as a single package by one vendor?
- What features does each system have?
- How do these features compare to your "needs-and-wants" list?
- How friendly is each system? Does it have:
    - menus?
    - on-screen directions?
    - manuals?
    - tutorials?
    - free or low cost training sessions?
    - technical support (at what cost and for how long)?
- What equipment is required to run it? Do you have this equipment? If not, can you get it?
- Is this the same equipment used in other schools in the district? If not, is there someone locally who can help troubleshoot the equipment?
- Can the system be expanded later to add other features?
- If applicable, can the system be networked to the whole school? To the community?
- How secure will the system be? Can you limit access by passwords to certain features?

Many vendors have free detailed handbooks on their automated library systems and many also offer free demonstration disks. Get the handbooks and read them. Order the demo disks and use them. While these are not substitutes for actually using the programs, you will get a feel for each system and you will see the reports that are generated.

Ask other librarians for their input. Attend the meetings of people who use the system that you are considering. These "users groups" often meet at state and national conferences. Use a telecommunications network to ask other librarians for advice.

What should be in your purchasing plan?

Prepare a purchasing plan in which you identify and plan for the obvious and the hidden costs of automation. The plan will also be beneficial as you look at sources outside the school such as the community, business and industry, the state department of education, and other grant-giving agencies for support.

Develop a budget for all expenditures. Hardware and software will take a major portion of the budget for any automated circulation or catalog system, but there are other major expenditures that will need to be made throughout the purchasing cycle. These expenditures may occur over a period of several years but need to be considered when making an initial purchase. While automation can be done with some older computers, such as a 386 PC, speed and some program features will need to be sacrificed. A major cost may be for the labor involved in entering information into the computer about the collection and patrons.

Include staff training. With the installation of any major circulation or catalog system, staff members need to be trained. Consider where the training will take place, how long it will be, who will take part, and how much it will cost. Try to get the vendor to promise in writing that the company will set up the system and provide local training.

Remember maintenance. In major school library management systems, hardware is used constantly and will need basic cleaning and maintenance. Data will need to be backed up on a regular basis. Decide who will do this and what the costs will be.

Identify sources of technical support. Most systems come with a set number of days of free technical support, but 30 or 60 days of free support is not enough. By then you are just beginning to find out what your problems are! Sometimes it seems that the free support runs out on the day the system will hang up or freeze, or someone will enter the wrong code or hit the wrong key.

Before this happens, determine whom you will turn to for help. Is there someone in the school district who can handle the problems? Will you turn to the company? Will you purchase a technical support contract or will you pay as you go? Remember, too, to have a backup person in mind in the event "your person" quits or moves.

Budget for a telephone. To assist you when you need technical help, locate a telephone near the computer or buy a long cord for the handset. Telephone wire is cheap and easy to string, and a phone near the computer will cut down on frustrations when you try to work with a technician to solve a problem over the phone. If running telephone wires is not possible, purchase a portable telephone.

Determine the costs of networking. If you are thinking about networking your system now or in the future, don't forget to determine if the system can be networked and how much it will cost. Be sure to see if the network suggested by the automation software producer is a common network system (see the network section for more information) or if it requires a special network available only from the automation software producer. Will you be charged a fee for the automation software or a per-workstation fee determined by the total number of computers connected to the network?

Determine the costs of updates. Most programs are issued in versions with each higher numbered version containing additional features or solutions to problems in existing software. In the past, what have been the costs (if any) to upgrade to a new version of the program? Is this likely to be true with future updates? How much work has been required in the past to use the updated versions? Was it necessary to make major changes to the information about the collection or the patrons that was in the library's computer? What upgrades are planned for the future?

Remember that software should dictate the hardware selection. The computer must be able to use the software that you purchase. (Chapter 2 contains a discussion of general hardware specifications.) In addition, your computer must have the space in hard disk storage to contain the information on the collection.

One popular online catalog program requires at least K or one thousand bytes of storage for every item in your collection. Thus a collection with 10,000 individual items requires a minimum of 10MB of available memory on the hard disk just to store the information.

Prepare a purchasing timeline. Outline your plan of action. A sample timeline is provided in Figure 3.1. As with any timeline, some of the events are relative. For example, if you have access to computers in your library, you can begin the local data entry before your complete system arrives.

What are some practical problems of automation?

Automating a circulation or cataloging system presents special challenges for school librarians. In other words, there are potential problems that need to be considered.

Initial Decisions

Part of a group or independent. In some school divisions, a decision might be made at the division level to order a specific brand of automation software and hardware for all school libraries. A large group order could mean discounts or other incentives from vendors. In other school divisions, the decision might be made by individual schools as money becomes available. In the later case, each SLMS must decide on the system that is best for his or her library.

However, everyone must keep in mind that if, in the future, there is to be sharing of information among the schools in the division, the information in the computer catalog must be in some standard form that everyone can use. Also, if everyone selects a different automated system, local and company technical support can be a problem.

Integrated vs. stand-alone systems. Today, it is possible to purchase an integrated circulation and catalog system or to purchase separate circulation and OPAC programs. A minor benefit of separate systems is that if something happens to one system, the other can still work.

However, separate systems may present problems if each system requires that you enter information about your collection in different ways. Does anyone with a 10,000-volume collection really want to type information into

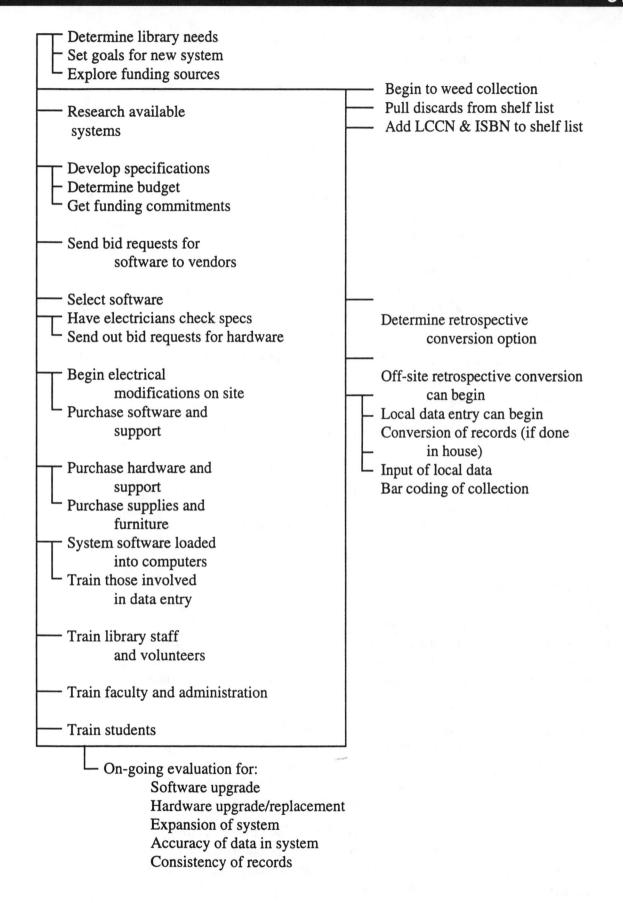

Determine library needs
Set goals for new system
Explore funding sources

Begin to weed collection
Pull discards from shelf list
Add LCCN & ISBN to shelf list

Research available
   systems

Develop specifications
Determine budget
Get funding commitments

Send bid requests for
   software to vendors

Select software
Have electricians check specs
Send out bid requests for hardware

Determine retrospective
   conversion option

Begin electrical
   modifications on site
Purchase software and
   support

Off-site retrospective conversion
   can begin
Local data entry can begin
Conversion of records (if done
   in house)
Input of local data
Bar coding of collection

Purchase hardware and
   support
Purchase supplies and
   furniture
System software loaded
   into computers
Train those involved
   in data entry

Train library staff
   and volunteers

Train faculty and administration

Train students

On-going evaluation for:
   Software upgrade
   Hardware upgrade/replacement
   Expansion of system
   Accuracy of data in system
   Consistency of records

Figure 3.1 Sample timeline

the computer one way for the circulation system and then retype that same information in another format for an online catalog?

Standardized record format. Many vendors of library automation systems have standardized the format for the information about the items in a collection that is entered into the computer. But this is not always the case, so beware.

MARC (machine readable cataloging) was developed and accepted by the library community as a standard format into which cataloging information could be put so that it could be read by computers. A version of the MARC format was developed for microcomputers and was named MicroLIF (Micro-computer Library Interchange Format). Since 1992, the full name of this standard is USMARC/MicroLIF Protocol.

Along with a shipment of new books, most jobbers now can send MicroLIF information on a computer disk so that the information can easily be added to your library's circulation system or to the online catalog, provided the system can understand the MicroLIF format.

Off the shelf vs. "customized" program. Purchasing a commercial circulation or online catalog program can be expensive. However, beware of the "free" offer of a concerned parent or school business partner to take a commercial database and turn it into a library circulation program. Most things in libraries are a little more complex than they seem at first glance; while circulation appears easy, it has enough options and exceptions to make it a programmer's challenge.

A programmer really needs to understand library operations to write a good circulation or catalog program. Yes, some parents could write a circulation program, but do you really want to go that route? And what happens if that parent (the only person who understands how the program operates) moves to Labrador?

Conversion of Records

No matter how you decide to automate circulation or the card catalog, the information about each item in the collection must be entered into the computer system. This process of putting the existing paper circulation or catalog information into the computer is called retrospective conversion. There are several different ways to go about this, but of course, care is required with each option.

Enter as you go. If you are just automating circulation, you may be able to enter the items as they are circulated and new materials as they are purchased. If you are entering a minimum amount of information for each item into your circulation system this may be an option. However, if you use the "enter as you go" option to establish an online catalog, you will need to use both the old print and the new computer version until the process is complete.

Librarian enters everything in advance. This option involves sitting down with the shelf list and typing the information into the computer in a standard format (hopefully MicroLIF compatible) used by the program. While some argue that this saves money, staff time has value.

If the SLMS is sitting in front of a computer for hours entering information, who is working with the students, helping the teachers, planning public relations activities? What image of librarianship is being presented to students, faculty, staff, and administrators? If there is a capable staff or great volunteers, it may be possible for the librarian to delegate this. People who do this job will need keyboarding skills and must be capable of accurate work.

Remember, the catalog will only be as good as the information that is entered into it. It's the GIGO (garbage in, garbage out) idea. Be sure to use reliable people (staff, volunteers, or outside agency) for data entry. Bad data leads to frustration by the users and the library staff.

Vendor converts everything off-site. With this option, you make sure that your shelf-list cards (or a special computer disk supplied by the vendor) contain the LCCN or ISBN for each item in the library. Send the shelf list or the disk to the vendor.

For a fee, the vendor will match the collection against its master collection of thousands of titles. Every match is called a "hit" and the title is "claimed" for your collection. You then get computer disks from the vendor with the information about the claimed titles as well as an indication of the titles that it could not match. Loading the disks of matched titles into the library's computer provides the beginning of your database. Then you have to decide how to put the unmatched or missed titles into your computer. Sometimes supplying additional information to the vendor can result in more hits.

Remember, you cannot expect a large number of hits if you send an incomplete shelf list or one with missing data. Librarians report that including the LCCN on each shelf-list card greatly increases the number of hits on the first try.

Obviously if you select this option, you want to choose a vendor who has a large database that contains titles similar to those in your library. Choose a vendor whose database has mainly secondary school titles and you will have a low hit rate or few matches of titles from your elementary collection. If your collection contains a lot of audiovisual titles and computer software, be sure that the vendor's database contains the NICEM A-V MARC database, the A/V ACCESS database, or something similar with these types of materials.

If a vendor prepares your database, you also need to be concerned about the quality of the records that are being searched and those that become part of your library's database. Ideally, these records should be in MicroLIF format and should contain complete information. You might also want to determine the types and completeness of the subject headings that are used in the database being searched by the vendor. How easy will it be for you to add additional subjects later?

Some vendors charge by the hit, while others charge a flat fee based on the size of your collection or a fee per item searched. A flat rate or a charge per record searched is not cost effective when there are few hits. Check with other librarians who have used the vendors that you are considering. Are their library collections similar to yours? Use their advice and hit rate to determine your probable cost.

One last word about vendors' databases. Be sure you consider in advance what to do with classification problems such as the placement of biographies in the 920s or with the specific subjects throughout Dewey.

Librarian works with commercial database. This option is similar to allowing the vendor to convert off-site, except that the SLMS, clerk, or volunteers in the local library match information from the shelf list against a database (such as *Precision One* by Brodart or *Alliance* by Follett) supplied by the vendor or other company on computer disks or on CD-ROM. Each "hit" or match is then added to the local library's own database.

The same suggestions governing the selection of a vendor apply here. This method is a good compromise, and you have better control of the accuracy of your database. In some cases, you can add local information to that supplied on the commercial database. This might include items such as reading level or special subject headings.

Librarians use combinations. Librarians have successfully used combinations of these major options to develop the library's database. Vicki M. Sherouse, librarian at the Lakehill Preparatory School in Dallas, Texas, reported using a commercial database to enter all her fiction. She then started to use the system for circulation. If an item of nonfiction was checked out, she used a short title and a temporary number until the complete record could be entered. Her rationale was that this was a morale booster for both the library staff and the volunteers assisting in the project.

Barcodes

Mention placement of barcodes on materials to a group of librarians and get set to hear some strong opinions. There seem to be pros and cons to all possible placements. Should it be inside or outside the cover? On the front or on the back? Where should it be on software? Try to locate the barcode in a place where it will not come off easily, can readily be located for checkout and check-in, and can easily be read during inventory.

You can also barcode the equipment that you circulate to students and teachers. Then you can check it out through your automated circulation system.

What you do with patron barcodes will depend on the procedures in your own library. However, be sure to talk to other librarians and learn from their experiences. Some librarians give all students library cards with barcodes. If students have school ID cards, the barcodes could be placed on them. Other librarians prefer to keep the student barcodes in the library on cards in a Rolodex, sheets in a notebook, or cards kept by the classroom teacher.

Access Points

With a card catalog, there were usually enough drawers for several students to search at a time. With an OPAC, a major concern surrounds the number of computers that are needed for students, teachers, and staff to access the catalog. In addition, with an integrated system, there need to be computers for circulation functions and management.

In a recent article, Edward P. Caffarella used queue management principles from the business world to look at the lines at a library's OPAC. He noted that, in addition to the number of people expected to use the OPAC at a single time, a key factor is the time for each search. This is a factor of the following: the size of the library's database, the type of search (simple author search vs. a complex keyword or Boolean search), whether the user sits or stands, the user's familiarity with searching and with the system, and the availability of printers to print the results or disks to save the results of the search. Caffarella found that the average time for a search was two minutes and fifty seconds.

System Failures and Maintenance

The words "the computer's down" or "the power's out" will take on new meaning when you have an automated library. Be sure you read and follow any instructions that came with the hardware and review the guidelines discussed in Chapter 1.

To prepare for power outages or computer problems, develop a procedure that will allow you to continue to circulate materials for a short time without the computer. Some librarians keep the cards in the books and put the barcode number on the cards. Then, when the system is down, the borrower can put his name and patron ID number on the card, and the information can be entered into the computer later. Other librarians list the book title and patron barcode on a sheet of paper. There are also some portable devices that, while they are used primarily for inventory, can hold up to 1,000 transactions if the computer is down or busy printing reports.

Computers, especially hard drives, will malfunction. Always make regular backups of the system. Be sure to make two sets of the backups and keep one of those sets in a separate building from the library. Discover how to restore data to your system before you have hard disk problems.

When problems do arise, keep a log book. In it you should list the following: date, description of the problem, person who noted the problem, action taken to solve the problem including the name of the persons contacted about the problem and the names of the persons who solved it, and the solution. This log book will prove invaluable with recurring problems and with helping you describe a problem to someone over the telephone. You will also have a record of the individuals who are most successful in solving your problems. See Figure 3.2 for a sample form.

The vendor of your library automation system should be available to help you with problems as they arise. However, user groups are a very important part of the solution to the problems of automation. There are local, state, and national groups of librarians sharing the same library automation systems. These groups meet informally, at conferences and on telecommunications networks, to share problems and solutions. When you automate, become active in a user group.

What will the effects of automation be?

Training will be necessary for everyone who uses the system. Use lots of visuals to explain the system. If you are beginning an OPAC, be sure to provide charts or lists of procedures near each computer on the system. This is especially true if your system is different from the OPAC in the local public library.

System Solution Form

Date	Noted by	Problem	Action taken	Persons contacted	Solved by	Solution

Figure 3.2 System Solution Form

Students will usually welcome the new technology, and knowledgeable students can serve as tutors to teach faculty and other students. With an OPAC, the students might need instruction in the Boolean or logic searches used in electronic searching. Introduce them to this searching gradually; do not wait until their first major project is due.

There will probably be increased demands on the collection. The OPAC may allow students and teachers to discover materials that might have been unused or lost with the card catalog. There might even be requests for more technology in the library as patrons see the benefits of electronic searching.

A study by the Computer Services Section of the North Carolina Department of Pubic Instruction found that, when the catalog was automated, there was:

- increased use of both the automated and the paper catalog
- less reliance on the SLMS for assistance
- better understanding of the research process
- use of a wider variety of resources
- better organization and use of information
- use of higher level thinking skills to evaluate information
- more student interest in the collection

Provide plenty of training for library staff, volunteers, faculty, students and administrators. Use brochures, posters, and signs to promote the new services and to provide directions for using it. Since students often take to computers faster than adults, use students to help design tutorials and to act as peer tutors. Trained student aides can wear "Ask Me" buttons to indicate that they can assist with the new system.

With any new system, problems will arise. Be up front with users about the problems that occur with the new system. When something goes wrong, do not be afraid to say "I don't know" but be sure to write everything down to discuss with the technician or the vendor's technical support staff.

What is a media retrieval system?

Another technology-based library management tool is what is called a media access system, media distribution system, or media retrieval system (MRS). Basically, it is a combination of hardware and software that allows teachers to access the audio-visual resources of the library from the classrooms of the school by remote control. The usual set-up of a MRS is that the media (including videotapes, videodiscs, audio tapes, slides, CD-I, and even television) and the hub of the electronic delivery system are housed in or near the library. Some or all of the classrooms in the school have television monitors that are hooked up to the central system. Using MRS software programs, teachers schedule media delivery in advance. At the beginning of the day, the SLMS or an aide loads the appropriate media into the electronic delivery system. When the media is needed, the teacher uses a classroom control device (a panel, touch pad, remote control, or computer) to contact the central distribution system which then delivers the requested media directly to the classroom television.

What are the advantages and disadvantages of a media retrieval system?

Like any other technology, there are pros and cons to using a media retrieval system. An immediate benefit is that teachers and library staff no longer have to push carts through the halls and arrange for the sharing of equipment. Scheduling by the MRS software takes the burden off the SLMS. (Ms. Watson cannot erase Mr. Pesapane's name off the scheduling form when there are no VCRs left on Friday.) Because equipment is not moved and is used only by trained staff, maintenance on videotape recorders and other equipment may decrease. In addition, most systems keep records and statistics on the use of the media and act as an index to the library's audio-visual collection. The systems also provide more administrative control over the use of videos in the classroom and cut down on the use of inappropriate rented videos or illegal home or off-air tapes brought to school by teachers and students.

Unfortunately, some of the advantages to an MRS may be disadvantages. Since the library staff loads all media on the system, the staff members become the copyright enforcers. At times this can place the librarian in the difficult situation of having to refuse to allow the use of some materials over the system. Obviously, this is an area where the full support of the principal is necessary. Other problems in using an MRS occur because someone on the library staff must be accessible to take care of problems with the system. Also, a backup plan must be in place in case the entire system goes down. Finally, a major drawback to an MRS is the cost involved in setting up the system. Depending on the type of installation, an average MRS will run over $100,000.

What types of media retrieval systems are available?

There are several types of systems. However, these are changing as the technology evolves. The primary systems today are broadband and baseband. Although both use coaxial or fiber optic cable, they differ in the way that they send out signals. Several signals are carried on the broadband systems, which use a cable layout of one main line leading from the central hub with branches to each room in the school. In contrast, a baseband system requires a direct independent link from the central hub to each room. While baseband provides better visual quality, it does so at a much higher cost because of the need for more wiring. Other systems use video broadband of baseband over level 5 twisted pair wire. Unfortunately, there is a great loss of picture quality if the wires are over 300 feet in length. While the newer ATM (asynchronous transfer mode) technology promises baseband quality on a cheaper broadband network, its cost is prohibitive. For a more complete discussion of these systems and a rating chart for the primary vendors of MRSs, read the article by Joe Huber that is listed in the Bibliography section of this chapter.

What factors should be considered in selecting a media retrieval system?

Cost is a primary factor in selecting a retrieval system and depends a great deal on the type of delivery system selected and the cost of wiring the school. The physical layout of the school may be a factor in determining where the central hub should be and which classrooms will be wired. In most cases, the same cables or wires that deliver the media can handle the control functions. But it is important to check first to be sure.

The software for the system is another important component. A decision must be made if the scheduling computer will be a standalone system or part of the school's network. If it is part of the network, it should have cross platform technology that supports input from any of the types of computers on the network, both PCs and Macs. If it is not part of the network, there must be a convenient way for teachers to access the system to schedule media. Other items to look for are scheduling modules that check for conflicts as the media is being scheduled (not just at the end of the day), and built-in presentation software that permits the teacher to control playback in the classroom.

What does this mean for librarians?

Computers are changing the way librarians manage libraries. Catalog card files are replaced by OPACs and media carts give way to media retrieval systems. At times it seems that one set of problems is just exchanged for another. But as all this change occurs, it is important not to lose sight of why this is being done. Hopefully it is not for the sake of technology itself, but to free school librarians from mundane tasks and to allow them to improve the ways that they provide services for the students and teachers of their schools.

Bibliography

Bishoff, L. (1997). *Coping with the electronic library; Strategies for service & collection development*. New York: Neal-Schuman.

Buckhalter, J. (1993). Help! I just bought a library automation system...Now what do I do? Library Talk, 12 (2), 7-9. Gives nine hints for getting started once the equipment and barcodes arrive in the library.

Burns, P. (1992). Using a database in library management. The Book Report, 11(3), 28. Describes the use of a general database to track circulation, compile statistics, develop a consideration file, and more.

Caffarella, E. P. (1996). Techniques for increasing the efficiency of automation systems in school library media centers. *School Library Media Quarterly,* 24 (3), 151-154.

Clyde, A. (1996). Generic software packages in school libraries. *Emergency Librarian*, 23 (5), 51-53.

Clyde, A. (1996). Update on automated library systems. *Emergency Librarian* 23 (3): 50-52. A look at Athena, KidsCatalog, and Book Wizard.

Day, T. T., B. Flanders, and G. Zuck. (1994). *Automation for school libraries; How to do it from those who have done it*. Chicago: American Library Association. In this collection of essays, school librarians describe their experiences. Contains a detailed sample request for proposal (RFP).

Dewey, P. R. (1994). *202+ Software packages to use in your library: descriptions, evaluations, and practical advice*. Chicago: American Library Association.

Ekhaml, L. (1993). Some common myths about library automation. *School Library Media Activities Monthly,* 9 (9), 40-41. Explores myths such as "automation saves time," "computers always have the right answers," and "the computer is very sensitive and I might break it."

Huber, J. (1995). How to choose a media retrieval system. Technology Connection, 2 (8), 14-17. This in-depth look at the technical side of media retrieval systems includes a comparison chart for several major systems.

Macciocca, J. (1996). Approaches to media management. *Media & Methods*, 32 (5), 6-8. Describes methods to "organize and monitor" media resources including the use of media retrieval systems.

Moe, L. (1995). Grantwriting on the run. Technology Connection, 2 (2), 17-20. When a library automation grant became available, a consortium of SLMS sprang into action. Moe goes through the process they used to win over $250,000.

Sherouse, V. M. (1995). Automate your library in two years for under $4,000. Technology Connection, 2 (6), 18-20. Sherouse explains how she automated a 10,000 volume collection on a shoestring.

Swan, J. (1996). *Automating small libraries*. Fort Atkinson: Highsmith Press. This short but fact-filled book is part of the Highsmith Press Handbook Series.

Van Deist, R. (1991). Crazy to automate? THE BOOK REPORT, 10 (3), 32-33. When you need to laugh during the process of automating a library, read this.

Woodard, M. (1995). Singing the praises of media retrieval systems. TECHNOLOGY CONNECTION, 2 (5), 26-27.

Chapter 4

CD-ROM and Other Types of Compact Discs

Computers are only as effective as the software that is developed to work with them. One of the important developments of the 1990s has been the introduction of CD-ROM (compact disc-read only memory) and related technologies. Studies show that, by the end of 1996, approximately 45% of the schools in the United States have installed CD-ROM technology. This chapter looks at CD-ROM software and hardware and their use in the school library. In addition, the new competitors for CD-ROM are explained.

What is CD-ROM?

Like the audio CDs that have replaced records, CD-ROM is an optical media that uses light for the storage and retrieval of information. This is unlike the computer floppy and hard disks, which rely on magnetism. (As part of that distinction, computer disks are spelled with a "k" while CD-ROM discs are spelled with a "c.") Both the audio CD and the CD-ROM are "read only," meaning that once they are manufactured, information can only be read from them; it cannot be written to them as is possible with magnetic disks. Because of this, the CD-ROM discs are considered a technology of publication, not a storage medium. There are, however, other types of compact discs including CD-R (writable or recordable), CD-RW (erasable or rewritable), CD-I (interactive), and the new DVD (digital video discs or digital versatile discs) which are all discussed later in this section.

One thing that is impressive about the small 5" CD-ROM disc is the amount of information that can be stored on it. While exact figures vary, in general, one disc can store about 300,000 typewritten pages, 74 minutes of audio, 5,000 color pictures, 60 minutes of full-motion video, or a combination of these formats. That's as much information as 1,900 floppy disks.

Because of the CD-ROM's ability to store text, sound, animation, graphics, and even video, the term "multimedia" is frequently used to describe it. While true "multimedia" includes more than just CD-ROM, there is no doubt that CD-ROM, with its combination of sound, text, and graphics controlled by a computer, is a modern multimedia technology.

Indexes, curriculum information, bilingual dictionaries with sound, union library catalogs, encyclopedias, specialized reference books, test banks, picture books, maps, and more are currently available in a CD-ROM format. One company has even released CD-ROM titles that are legally available for rent from video rental stores. To use CD-ROM, you put the disc into a CD-ROM drive attached (external) to a computer or housed within (internal) the computer case. Then you use a CD-ROM control software program in the computer to access the information on the disc and display it on the computer screen. The data can also be sent to the printer or saved on the computer's hard disk or floppy disk. Some CD-ROM programs even have a note taking function built in.

Before you buy this powerful technology, there are a few other things you might want to know about it.

What are the advantages of using CD-ROM technology?

Provides a variety of information formats. Text, illustrations, animation, video, music, and other sounds can be on the same disc. This means a dictionary can contain the text of definitions as well as a recording of the correct pronunciation of the words. An encyclopedia article on jazz can contain a brief selection from a well-known jazz artist. Children reading a picture book can have an animated story character talk to them.

Is a durable disc. Because the information on a CD-ROM is read by a light, there is little wear on the discs. They are projected to last up to 100 years with normal use.

Is not magnetic. Unlike data on computer disks, the information on a CD-ROM is not affected by magnetic fields.

Has a large storage capacity. With a large amount of information contained on a single disc, CD-ROMs are an ideal medium on which to publish large collections of information (databases). Imagine years of a periodical index on one small disc.

Saves space. CD-ROM discs take up much less space than print reference sources and are easy to carry.

Provides fast access. Information can be rapidly located on the disc and shown to the user by a computer. While a CD-ROM disc cannot be searched as fast as a computer hard drive, it can be searched much faster than a print copy. Compared to text versions, large databases can be scanned in a short amount of time.

Allows easy information transfer. Most information that is retrieved from a CD-ROM disc can be transferred to a floppy disk or hard disk for storage or to a printer when a hard copy is desired.

Contains helpful features. When you use a print reference book and come to a word that you do not know, you need a dictionary for help. With many of the CD-ROM titles, you have a feature known as "hypertext." Using a mouse, you can point to the word that you do not know, and click. If the word that you have clicked on is a "hot spot," the definition will display on your screen. Thus, the CD-ROM has a hidden dictionary that is accessed by a point and a click. The same principal applies to other explanatory devices including music and video clips.

Permits sophisticated searching. No longer is it necessary to know the exact terms used by the producer of an index. The computer can use sophisticated searching techniques to find information. This includes keyword searching and the technique known as Boolean or logic searching, which can link and exclude topics in a single search.

Is a local resource. In comparison to an online database that is located away from the library and must be searched over the telephone lines, a CD-ROM is part of a local library's collection. There are no telephone charges, no database users fees, and no per item printing charges.

Can be shared. Each CD-ROM does not necessarily need its own computer since it is easy to change the discs as needed. In addition, while a single or multiple CD-ROM drive may be attached to an individual computer, it may also be part of a network. In that case the CD-ROM may be used by a number of computers on the network. If you plan to use a CD-ROM title on a network, be sure that you purchase the network version and indicate "for network use" on your purchase order.

Is easy to use. The GUI (Graphical User Interface) on the Macintosh computer makes it easy to use CD-ROM. With Windows 3.x and Windows 95 (the GUIs for PCs), the PC world is not far behind. This ease of use of CD-ROMs on both platforms means that many formerly reluctant library users will want to do CD-ROM research themselves. Students like to act as peer tutors for each other, freeing the SLMS for other responsibilities.

Is often less expensive than other formats. With rising printing costs, a CD-ROM encyclopedia may be much cheaper than a print copy. If it is used frequently, a CD-ROM index is probably cheaper than online search costs. In addition, if an index provides the full text of articles, the cost for periodical subscriptions may decrease.

Provides indexes for specific age groups. With the development of computerized databases, vendors are able to produce periodical indexes which are geared for specific ages of school children. Middle schoolers do not have to use an index geared to adults or to high school students.

What are the disadvantages of CD-ROM?

While CD-ROM technology has a lot to recommend its immediate purchase, there are some negatives to consider.

Can be initially expensive. The initial cost of getting a CD-ROM system up and running can be expensive. Not only is there the purchase of the CD-ROM software and hardware, but there is also the possibility that older computer hardware will need to be modified or upgraded in order to work with the CD-ROM. The upgrade might include a sound card, speakers, a mouse, and a printer. Fortunately, most newer computers come with an internal CD-ROM drive.

Provides limited access. Unless it is on a network, a single CD-ROM can only be used by one person or small group at a time. This is in contrast to a set of encyclopedias that several people can use at one time.

Is stationary during a search. When students are searching for information, it is easy for them to take a reference book to a teacher or SLMS when they need help. With a CD-ROM, however, the help has to come to the students' workstation.

May require headphones. Loud sounds can be a distraction in a library. Even though the sounds (voice or music) being played by a computer from a CD-ROM can be adjusted with the volume control, it may be easier to use headphones with CD-ROMs.

Offers limited storage of video. Storing video with full motion on a CD-ROM disc takes a lot of space. Therefore, the videodisc, not the CD-ROM, is the first-choice medium to store video. Newer technologies, however, such as the DVD may change this.

Cannot easily be updated. Unlike the online database, CD-ROM discs cannot be updated; a new disc must be produced. Quickly changing databases that are updated daily or weekly, such as stock market prices, might best be accessed online. In contrast, some indexes are updated monthly in both CD-ROM and online versions.

May require a printer. In many instances, users will want to print information from CD-ROMs to use later. Students copying information by hand and those who read slowly will tie up the CD-ROM workstation unless a printer is available on the system. One other option is to teach students to save data to their own disks. It can then be read or edited at another computer.

May be stolen. Because the CD-ROMs are so popular, the hardware and software are often the target of thieves. Be sure to use security cables or base plates to secure external drives. To protect the discs, some "locking" software programs or CD-ROM drives with actual locks prohibit unauthorized removal of the discs from the drives.

What is available in CD-ROM format?

A wide variety of CD-ROM discs are available. Some are strictly for pleasure such as games, while others are designed for library and school use. There are even swimsuit and X-rated CD-ROM discs. It seems as if everyone from the CIA to the Library of Congress has joined with commercial producers to issue a vast number of titles. Marketing sources predict that the number of CD-ROM titles will grow at a rate of about 48% per year until the end of this decade.

Reference sources. Traditional library reference materials including encyclopedias, dictionaries, bibliographies, almanacs, atlases, and indexes have been issued on CD-ROM.

Collections of materials. Collections that might be impossible to obtain otherwise are now readily available on CD-ROM. The Library of Congress is gress is putting American speeches and documents from its vast collection onto discs in its American Memory series. One publisher is issuing a series of discs each containing the works of a well-known author, while another is issuing discs containing the text and illustrations from 450 literary classics. History discs can contain actual news footage and interviews along with the text. Art libraries and clip art for computer use are also available.

Teaching tools. In addition to the curriculum guides and materials that some states are now issuing on CD-ROM discs, commercial vendors are publishing materials for teachers. Primary teachers can find discs about colors and concepts, while high school teachers and students can find collections of literary criticism or science materials.

Electronic books. Books for children and adults are being published on CD-ROM. While some are text only, others are true multimedia with sound, text, and animation. Especially interesting are the illustrated story books for children. In these, the "pages" can be turned and the child can read the story or have it read by the voice on the disc. As the voice reads, phrases or paragraphs are highlighted on the screen.

By using a mouse to point and click on highlighted words, the child can see a definition and hear the pronunciation. A click on other words shows the dictionary entry. In the illustrations, there are even hidden surprises that can be found with a point and click of the mouse. The surprises can include music, animation, or even another visual.

So many materials are available on CD-ROM that there is now a CD-ROM Directory and a CD-ROMs in Print. Of course, they are available in hard copy or on CD-ROM. (See the Resources section for full information.) Specialized periodicals such as *CD-ROM World* and *CD-ROM Today* are also published.

Some CD-ROM discs can be used on either a PC or Macintosh computer. In other cases, there are separate discs for each platform. When you see that a disc is available for both the IBM and Macintosh computers, remember that the two versions may not be the same! Because each may contain different features, be sure the features that you want are actually on the version that you purchase. Also be sure that you check the software requirements against the hardware that you currently have.

Why add CD-ROM to the library collection?

With CD-ROM, it is not necessary to teach about alphabetical order or guide words. Thus CD-ROM technology makes us think about the skills that we are teaching in the library. Are we more concerned with teaching the thinking process of research or in showing students how to use all the indexes and tables in a particular reference source? Is it better for students to spend time searching for information or to spend time working with the information once they have found it?

With information increasing so rapidly, electronic publishing and searching are becoming the preferred methods of keeping up. As CD-ROMs find more use in the home and in the business world, students need opportunities to gain the skills they will need to use these resources. A school library is one place that students can have an opportunity to work with CD-ROMs as a form of electronic information retrieval.

CD-ROM searches can quickly make students feel as if they are experienced researchers and can give them positive feelings about doing "library research." Elementary school children as well as high school students find that they can be successful doing research with CD-ROM. Just remember that the emphasis now needs to be on teaching students how to develop a search strategy and how to use the information that they find.

A single CD-ROM disc can give students a variety of searching options that fit the learning preferences or styles of the individual student. One student may be more focused and may begin searching by key words or by a phrase. Another may browse through the information on the disc by looking at a list of topics or by using a topic outline that shows relationships between subjects. In the same way that you fan through a book to look at the pictures, a student may take a picture tour that consists of a random display of the pictures on the disc. When an interesting picture is shown, a click on a mouse or the touch of a key can let the student see more information. Still other search options include maps, timeliness, and feature articles with sound and video.

Remember, too, CD-ROM is not just for research. Picture book CD-ROM discs for younger children can provide hours of pleasure and reading instruction. Some CD-ROM discs are fun to explore just for the pleasure of learning or the experience of playing a game on a computer.

What selection criteria should be used for CD-ROM discs?

Because CD-ROM is a publication technology, you can use many of the same criteria that you use in evaluating other library materials. For example, if you are thinking of buying a periodical index on CD-ROM, check whether your students will have access to the periodicals or whether you will need to purchase additional materials with abstracts or full-text (the complete article). Perhaps you can buy the index on CD-ROM and the full-text on microfiche. If you are thinking about purchasing CD-ROM titles to replace online search services or hard copy indexes, compare the frequency of use and the method of updating the data as well as the costs. The CD-ROM should enhance, enrich, or optimize the use of the resource over the print version.

The old library term "special features" takes on a whole new meaning in multimedia. You will need to look at the quality of the audio, graphics, and animation/video. Don't assume that every CD-ROM program will have all the new features. Some are nothing more than text on a computer. On electronic books, look for text highlighting, as well as the quality of the reading voice.

In many cases, you will want to see the CD-ROM disc in use, try it yourself, or talk to others who use it. Ask about the search capabilities, the ease of use, and the ease of installation. Also, unless you are purchasing new equipment, you need to be sure that the disc is available for your current hardware.

As with any of the other new technologies, try to match the software to your users. Can you or the users change the searching levels of the software from novice to advanced or experienced? Do your students and teachers need color-coded keys, help keys, and lots of menus and prompts? Or can you get by with some special instruction cards that are kept by the computers?

The specific things that you look for in a CD-ROM program and the best programs for your school will vary, based on the curriculum of the school and the needs of your students and teachers. However, the following is a starting point for developing a review checklist that you can use.

General CD-ROM Software Checklist

Content
What would be the primary use? Instructional? Informational? Recreational?

How does it differ from other materials in the library? In the classroom? On the market?

Is the information accurate? Up-to-date?

How is the information organized and accessed?

How in-depth is the information?

Is the content free from bias?

For what age(s) is it intended?

Educational Suitability
Is it curriculum related?

What curriculum objectives does it meet?

How might it be used in instruction? Introduction? Direct teaching? Reinforcement?

Does the program follow accepted learning theories?

What levels of thinking skills are involved?

How does it keep the student engaged? On-screen questions? On-screen manipulatives? Accompanying workbook?

How much time is needed to use this CD-ROM effectively in the classroom or library? Preparation? Actual use?

Are there guides for the teacher?

Is there any other supporting material?

Does the CD-ROM show both genders and various cultural groups while avoiding stereotypes?

Ease of Use
How easy is it to use?

Are there menus? Icons?

Are there levels of interaction (novice, advanced, etc.)?

If applicable, can searches be done by keyword? Boolean logic?

How clear are the on-screen instructions?

Is there on-screen help?

Is there documentation for the program? Is it helpful? Readable?

Technical Qualities

Is text readable?

How is the audio quality? Can any "reading voice" be easily understood?

If there is video, how long does it take to run? How does it look? How large is the video image on the monitor?

Can it be used on a network?

Special Features

What are the special features? Is it interactive?

Are there "hot links" between parts of the CD-ROM?

Are there video clips? Audio clips? Combinations?

Is there a built-in dictionary?

What does each add to the CD-ROM? Are they integral to the program or are they fluff?

Can you print text? Graphics? Pictures?

Can you mark passages/portions for printing?

Can you limit the amount printed?

Can information be saved to a disk for editing or printing?

Does the CD-ROM use built-in recording tools?

Installation and Maintenance

Can the CD-ROM be used with existing hardware?

Will it run on an existing network?

How difficult will it be to install?

Is technical support available? Cost?

Cost

What will the CD-ROM cost?

Will there be an additional costs (supplies, hardware, etc.)?

How do the benefits of the CD-ROM compare to the costs?

Other

Is the vendor reliable?

The number of reference works on CD-ROM has grown rapidly with some schools having several encyclopedias and two or more indexes available for students. This is a constantly evolving field especially for the periodical indexes with the lists of periodicals included in each index just beginning to stabilize. While no one is ready to eliminate the periodical collection, these indexes have made searching easier and have increased the number of periodicals available to many students by offering options ranging from abstracts to the full text of some magazines. The result has been that most students now look forward to searching for information. The vendors of several of these indexes are listed in the Resources section along with the references to articles which compare them.

Just as the selection of other CD-ROMs depends on the individual school and its curriculum, the selection of CD-ROM periodical indexes depends on the individual library where it will be placed and the existing periodical collection of that library. However, the following checklist contains some of the important features to consider in selecting a CD-ROM periodical index:

Checklist for Periodical Indexes

Total number of periodicals indexed?
    Number of full-text periodicals
    Number of abstracted periodicals
    Number with citation only

Total number of student periodicals?
    Number of full-text periodicals
    Number of abstracted periodicals
    Number with citation only

Total number of professional periodicals?
    Number of full-text periodicals
    Number of abstracted periodicals
    Number with citation only

Additional sources included?
    Types? Newspapers? Special Reports? Pamphlets?

Searching options?
    Title
    Subject
    Keyword
    Boolean
    Limiting options
        Date
        Language
        Type of record (full-text, abstract, citation)

Years of coverage?
    (Does the content vary throughout the years?)

Appropriate age levels?

Number of disks?

Hardware required?

Networking capable? Requirements?

Annual Cost?

Updates per year?
    (Does the cost vary with the number of updates received?)

Special features?
    Local holdings indicated?
    Variety of print options? (Librarian controlled?)
        Citation only
        Full record (abstract, full text, citation)
        Selections from full text
    Search history maintained?

In comparing any reference tools, perform several searches on each. For each search, begin with a topic. Make some topics broad and others narrow. Then take the print source, use the index, locate the topic, check each page referenced in the index, and record the results of your search. Now, do the same search on the CD-ROM, starting with the same topic. How much information did you find in each and were you satisfied with it? How long did each search take? How easy was it to expand or limit your search?

Some companies are offering preview discs and inexpensive (but still good) shareware discs. These contain everything from sampler discs with short demos to discs with complete programs. With many of the sampler discs, if, after viewing the demo, you decide you would like the entire program, you call a telephone number and become a "registered user." For a fee you will be given the commands needed to unlock the entire program.

If you do not have time to review the CD-ROMs yourself, look for reviews. Many of the library periodicals such as *School Library Journal*, TECHNOLOGY CONNECTION, *MultiMedia Schools* and *Library Journal* review CD-ROMs as do general computer magazines. In addition, there is a Web page at the University of Texas Graduate School of Library and Information Science (http://volvo. gslis.utexas.edu/~reviews) where you can find reviews done by graduate students.

What hardware is needed?

How do you go about selecting the hardware that you will need to run the CD-ROM discs? First, begin with the software. Use your library literature, including CD-ROM lists and directories, to determine the types of discs that would be best in your library. Then, look at the computer hardware that you already have. You will need to make decisions about whether you will be able to use this hardware, upgrade its components, or perhaps even change to a new computer. To make those decisions, you need to know something about CD-ROM drives and industry standards.

CD-ROM Drive Types

Like floppy disk drives, there are both internal and external CD-ROM drives. An internal CD-ROM drive can be mounted inside a computer if there is available space. Called a half-height unit, a CD-ROM drive takes up about the same space as a 5.25" floppy disk drive. It gets its power from the computer and requires no external cables. Many PCs and Macintosh computers are sold with internal CD-ROM drives.

CD-ROM DRIVE

Figure 4.1 An internal CD-ROM drive has been installed next to a floppy disk drive on this computer. Speakers and headphones could be added to this system if desired.

Installing an internal drive is usually not hard. If there is a vacant half-height bay in a PC, you should be able to add an internal drive and should find a color coded pigtail connector inside your computer. The sockets on the connector fit the pins on the internal drive. Slanted corners on the connector help you make the right connection. Be sure to check your computer and drive manuals for complete information.

An external CD-ROM drive can be attached to a computer by cables. While it does not take up any space inside the computer, it does require desk space and its own electrical connection. The advantages of portability and not having to open the computer case are offset by the external unit's higher cost. Of course, it is easier to send an external drive to the shop for repairs. If you do purchase an external drive, check the set of drive identification switches. They should be accessible without opening the drive itself. Mark your settings just in case they get changed by accident.

Figure 4.2 An external CD-ROM drive as well as a speaker and headphones have been added to this computer.

While the instructions for using the new drive will vary with the type of computer, once the drive is attached to the computer, using a CD-ROM disc is fairly straightforward. First the driver software is loaded into the computer and the system is checked to be sure it recognizes the new drive. Then the CD-ROM disc is placed in the drive and the CD-ROM software is loaded.

If you want to use different discs on a single drive, the drive should be located where it is easy to insert and remove the CD-ROM discs. Easy access may, however, be a problem in some libraries. If you think people might remove the discs from easily accessible drives, you might want to consider using only external drives that can be located away from the computer or using special software with passwords to "lock" the disc in the drive.

To aid in security, Susan Kallok, a school librarian in Los Angeles, California, suggested building a bottomless and backless box that fits over the computer. Large enough to permit air to circulate, the wooden box provides a platform for the monitor and covers the CD-ROM drive.

CD-ROM Drive Features

Three of the main features to look at when selecting a CD-ROM drive are transfer speed, buffer size, and access (or seek) time. All are important factors in determining how well a given drive will work. Access time is the average amount of time that it takes for the drive to locate information on the disc. The access time for a computer hard disk can run between 9 and 30 milliseconds (10ms to 30ms). With CD-ROM drives, access time can range from 1,000ms to less than 100ms. The lower the access time number, the faster you will see your information on the computer screen. When given a choice, select a drive with an access time of no more than 200ms. One word of caution: the times stated on the vendor's literature were measured under optimum conditions. Independent testing has shown that the actual times during normal use will be slower.

Transfer speed refers to the amount of information per second that the drive can transfer to your computer. Drives are rated as 2X, 4X, etc. by their transfer speeds. The greater the data transfer speed, the faster information will come to your computer. For smooth audio and video playback, you need a fast transfer speed. The chart below shows some common transfer speeds and access times. If there is a choice between fast transfer rate or fast access, select the drive with the faster transfer rate. Remember that much of the educational software does not take full advantage of drive transfer speeds over 6X. In the face of the threat of DVD technology, current advances in CD-ROM technology are focusing on CD-R and CD-RW capabilities rather than on increasing the speeds of CD-ROM drives.

CD-ROM Speed Comparisons

CD-ROM Drive	Transfer speed	Access time
2X	300KBps	280-500ms
4X	600KBps	150-400ms
6X	900KBps	120-300ms
8X	1200KBps	110-200ms
10X	1500KBps	100-200ms
12X	1800KBps	100-150ms

The buffer is a holding area for information. Because some CD-ROM drives can find the information faster than they can send it to the computer, many drives have a buffer or reservoir where the information is stored until the computer can use it. With a large buffer (up to 1MB) the reservoir is never empty until the last piece of information is sent. This feature is necessary for the smooth flow of sound and motion from a CD-ROM disc. Sometimes you will hear CD-ROM drives with a buffer referred to as continuous read drives.

As a general rule of thumb, look for a low access time, a high transfer speed, and a large buffer.

One other feature divides CD-ROM drives into two camps: caddy and caddyless drives. A caddy is a hinged plastic carrier into which the CD-ROM disc is placed. The entire caddy is inserted into the drive. Additional caddies can be purchased for $10 to $12 each so that the CD-ROM discs can be stored in the caddy when they are not being used. This protects the CD-ROM from handling. With caddyless drives, the disc is placed directly in the drive. Besides the protection feature, one advantage of the caddy drives is that they tend to have faster access times than the caddyless drives. However, most of the newer drives do not have caddies.

In addition to single CD-ROM drives, there are multiple CD-ROM drives and CD-ROM changers. With some of the changer drives, you can load several CD-ROM discs at a time. After reading the contents of each disc into its memory, the drive can access any of the discs. Units exist to load between two and twelve discs; however, the drive can read only one disc at a time. In contrast, multiple CD-ROM drives can run two CD's at once.

Should you upgrade an older CD-ROM drive to take advantage of increased speed of the new ones? The answer depends upon your use of the drive. For use with programs having video or animation, the higher speeds are better. With simple text, a 2X or 4X can do the job and an upgrade might not be worth the cost.

CD-ROM Interfaces

The CD-ROM drive must be linked to the computer by something called an interface. Some drives have what is known as a proprietary interface that is hardware dependent and is designed to be used only with a certain brand of CD-ROM drive. In addition to the drive, an internal interface card is needed to let the computer and drive communicate. To use a proprietary interface CD-ROM drive, you must have an expansion slot to accept the internal interface card. In upgrading with a proprietary interface, be sure the new drive will work with the existing interface.

On the other hand, there is what is called a SCSI (pronounced scuzzy) or Small Computer System Interface. Drives that work with a SCSI interface are usually more expensive than those with a proprietary interface but are best in the long run. The SCSI controls the peripherals of the computer with one SCSI card handling up to seven peripherals. SCSI-1 supports transfer rates of 5MBps on an 8 bit interface while SCSI-2 or "fast SCSI" can transfer 10 MBps on an 8 bit interface or 20MBps on a 16 bit interface. SCSI has become a common communication standard for computers and peripherals. SCSI CD-ROM drives can be used with any Macintosh or PC that has a SCSI port or that permits the use of an internal SCSI expansion card.

Some computers do not come with a SCSI port on the back. Others may not have any internal expansion slots (for example, notebook computers), or they may have all of their expansion slots full. Even these computers can be modified to work with a SCSI CD-ROM drive because of a device known as a parallel to SCSI interface. You do not even need to open your computer's case to install one. Just plug it into the parallel printer port on the back of the computer. The best of these devices is transparent, which allows you to use the single printer port for both a printer and a SCSI device. The interface is called transparent because you can use your printer as if the SCSI was not even there.

There is a disadvantage in using the parallel to SCSI interface. Because it slows down the data transfer speed more than an internal SCSI interface, there can be problems in playing sound or motion. But, if you want a CD-ROM drive and you don't have a SCSI port or any available internal expansion slots, the parallel to SCSI interface is your only practical choice.

Like SCSI, IDE (integrated drive electronics) is another interface. A problem is that the IDE interface is a little slower and is not backwards compatible with its earlier versions. If the IDE interfaces do not match, a new interface card must be installed.

Sound from a CD-ROM

One advantage of CD-ROM programs is that many include sound. Thus CD-ROM drives include audio output jacks so that you can use headphones or run sound to speakers. Base your decision on where the CD-ROMs will be used. While headphones provide the least distraction for other people, some librarians have reported problems monitoring students.

For your computer to take full advantage of the sound data that is stored on a CD-ROM, you need a sound card or sound board. This device comes with Macintosh computers. Although many PCs now come with a sound card, others need to have a card installed internally in one of the expansion slots. To use your card with audio other than CD-ROM, make sure it is ADLib and Sound Blaster compatible and that it has 16 bit sound and 16 bit SCSI.

MIDI, or Musical Instrument Digital Interface, is a standard for storing music in a digital format so that it can be read by a computer. Synthesizers use the MIDI standard and composers who write music on a computer rely on it too. To play MIDI music files from a CD-ROM disc, be sure that your computer's sound card supports MIDI.

A Computer for CD-ROM

Some CD-ROM drives can work with older PCs such as the XTs and compatibles. However, these less powerful (slower) computers are best used for text only since they do not allow you to take advantage of the sound and video of CD-ROM.

While some CD-ROMs will run on less powerful computers, the minimum practical requirements for a PC to take advantage of the multimedia features of CD-ROM would meet the requirements for MPC (Multimedia PC Marketing Council) Level 1 shown in the chart below. An ideal PC to use the full features of a multimedia CD-ROM would meet MPC Level 3. If your system does not meet these specifications, you may be able to upgrade. But shop around. In some cases, it's just as cost effective to purchase a new computer.

Connect a CD-ROM drive to a Macintosh computer with a SCSI port, and you're ready to go. But even on a Macintosh computer, the final performance will depend on the CPU (chip) and the clock speed of the computer. Anything above a Mac Plus, SE, or Series II should give you acceptable results.

A good multimedia Macintosh would be a Power Mac 7200 or 7600. For top performance try a Power Mac 8500 or 9500 or a Performa 6360 or 6400.

MPC and MPEG Standards

CD-ROM was one of the first technologies to work with the computer to create a truly multimedia environment: the combination of text, audio, graphics, animation, and video in a single working unit. But how well the parts work together depends on things such as the transfer rate, access speed, and the specifications of the computer.

An attempt was made to help computer purchasers know the minimum hardware requirements for using multimedia. One standard for CD-ROM is ISO 9660, or the High Sierra standard, set up by the International Standards Organization (ISO). Basically, it is a standard for organizing information on the CD-ROM so that it can be accessed by any computer with an ISO software program in its operating system. Unfortunately, while many Macintosh computers and PCs meet this standard, it does not mean that computers from both groups can read the same disc. They can locate the information, but they might not be able to read it. This is especially true of graphics and other visual information.

In an effort to provide some degree of standardization for PCs, the Multimedia PC Marketing Council, part of the Software Publishers Association, set technical specifications for multimedia CD-ROM software and the hardware to run it. All approved products receive the MPC logo. To use MPC rated CD-ROM software, the PC must have the specifications shown in the following table:

Specifications for Multimedia PCs

	MPC1 (1991)	MPC2 (1993)	MPC3 (1996)
Processor	368SX, 16MHz	486SX, 25MHz	Pentium, 75MHz
RAM	2MB	4MB	8MB
Hard drive	30MB	160MB	540MB
Monitor/video	VGA, 16 colors	VGA, 65,536 colors	VGA, full-motion video, MPEG1
CD-ROM	1X (150KBps)	2X (300Kpbs)	4X (600KBps)
CD-ROM access time	1 second	400ms	250ms
Sound board with MIDI	8 bit	16 bit	16 bit wavetable
Audio output	Speakers or headphones	Speakers or headphones	Speakers (3 watts/channel) or headphones
Operating system	Windows 3.0	Windows 3.0	Windows 3.11 with DOS 6.0
Other		Multisession CD-ROM drive	Multisession CD-ROM drive

The term multisession CD-ROM drive refers to a technology developed when Kodak's Photo-CD allowed an individual to have photographs "printed" on a photo-CD and then later to add more photographs to the same photo-CD. A multisession drive is required to access these various "sessions" of photographs. In addition, a multisession photo CD-ROM requires appropriate software such as Kodak *Access Plus*, Adobe *Photoshop*, or Corel *Photo CD Lab* to view the photos.

In selecting CD-ROM drives for a computer group, look for the following:

- Macintosh: Drive reads ISO-9660 format and Mac HFS (Hierarchial File System)
- PC: Drive reads IS0-9660 format and is MPC compatible.

Beware of buying the minimum. While you can upgrade some components later, this may prove to be more expensive than buying a good system in the beginning. The rule of thumb with technology purchases is to try to purchase a system that will be useful for at least five to seven years.

Storing video requires large amounts of space on CD-ROM discs or on a computer's floppy disc or hard drive. MPEG (Motion Picture Expert Group) is a video compression standard which is designed to save storage space but to deliver full-motion, full screen digital video. The MPEG standard does this by looking primarily at the changes from one frame to another of a video. This is like looking at the individual frames of an old 16mm film and recording only the items that change from frame to frame. The resulting playback with MPEG is VHS quality video.

Recommended hardware for MPEG1 playback with a PC is 386 or higher, 16 bit ISA bus, 2MB RAM, 2MB free on hard disk, VGA or SVGA monitor, sound card, CD-ROM with a transfer rate of at least 150KBps, Windows 3.1 or higher, DOS 5.0 or higher, and MPEG card. Mac users need at least a PowerMac. MPEG playback software is included in later versions of Windows 95. MPC3 supports MPEG1. The result is that more manufacturers are selling systems set up to meet MPEG requirements. In addition, more software producers are including MPEG video clips on their CD-ROMs.

Emerging Technologies

Standardization is great, but it takes time. Like audio and video technology several years ago, CD-ROM technology is currently an "emerging" or "changing" technology. Currently there are technologies known as CD-Audio, CD-ROM, CD-I, VideoCD, PhotoCD, CD-R, and CD-RW. On the horizon is DVD. Below are descriptions of some of these. Read the professional journals to keep current in this rapidly changing field.

Kodak sells a Photo-CD that takes film shot with a regular 35mm camera and "develops" the images on a photo-CD disc. About 100 pictures can be placed on each gold-colored disc. This disc can be viewed on a regular television with a special portable Photo-CD player or a five-disc carousel Photo-CD player. The portable Photo-CD player lets you show the images on any television set. A Photo-CD can also be used with a computer and CD-ROM drive as part of multimedia slide shows or in desktop publishing. With the help of software programs such as Micrografax's *PhotoMagic* and *Picture Publisher*, Adobe *Photoshop*, Corel *PhotoPaint*, Kodak's *PhotoEdge* or *Renaissance*, or *PageMaker*, a computer can change the order of the images; zoom, edit, and manipulate the images; and even add sound. But, beware. At present, several rolls of film (up to 100 images) can be put on one CD-ROM disc, but you need a "multisession" CD-ROM drive to access all the pictures. Some CD-ROM drives will access only the first set of images. Check to be sure your CD-ROM drive is multisession capable.

CD-I (compact disc-interactive) has been developed to work directly with a television set without a computer. The only hardware needed is a CD-I player and a TV or AV monitor. Excellent for storing video, CD-I has found its niche in some areas of education and training and in the kiosk market. Around 35% of the electronic kiosks are now using the non-linear CD-I technology.

CD-R (CD-Recordable) or CD-WORM (write once, read many) technology has been developed, and prices are falling. For less than $1,000, you can purchase a recordable CD-ROM drive to store information on 650MB CD-ROM discs that cost about $10 each. Most CD-R discs can be read in a regular multisession CD-ROM drive. Experts agree that you definitely need to purchase the recording/authoring software first since there are programs on a great range of levels from novice to expert. For CD-R, you need to have a minimum of a fast 486 PC or 6830 Macintosh, 16MB RAM, SCSI interface, and a large hard drive with a fast access (15ms average; 800KBps sustained transfer). The CD-R drive should be at least 2X or 4X with multisession capability if necessary. For the blank discs, follow the hardware manufacturer's recommendations. One safe choice would seem to be Kodak's gold-colored discs with their 100-year guarantee. Right now, a major use for CD-R discs is for backups of large databases and for storage of multimedia.

Also available, but at a little higher price, is CD-RW (CD-Rewritable) or CD-E (CD-Erasable) technology. With CD-RW discs, you can write, erase, and rewrite information just like on a floppy disk. Most manufacturers claim that, once written on, a CD-RW disk can be used in regular CD-ROM drives but there have been some problems reported with this. Just how reusable the discs are varies with quotes ranging from 1,000 to 10,000 times.

DVD (digital video disc or digital versatile disc) technology is being touted as the successor to CD-ROM. It was developed when manufacturers were trying to identify a way to store large amounts of high quality video on a compact disc, in part to cut down on the illegal pirating of videos/movies. Originally two technologies were developed. HDCD (high density compact disc) had 3.7BG of storage on each side of a disc while MMCD (multimedia compact disc) had 7.4GB on a side of a "multi-layered" disc. Eventually a compromise was reached to produce a single or double layer disc with up to 4.7GB per layer. In addition, the disc can be flipped over and another 4.7GB per layer can be stored on the other side. The layered effect is created not by actual physical layers, but by the use of a process that focuses a laser on two different focal points. The total of 19GB of storage would allow a 4.5 hour video to be placed on one disc which would be played at a transfer speed of

1,350KBps. In addition, it appears that there will be two versions of DVD; DVD-ROM for use with computers, and DVD-Video for use with TVs and AV monitors. Although manufacturers of the DVD-ROM drives claim that their drives will play the current CD-ROM discs at 4X speed, it appears that not all of the first drives will be compatible with existing CD-ROMs.

Whether or when DVD technology will replace CD-ROM is an unanswered question. Announcements in late 1996 skimmed over still unresolved issues such as copy protection and regional control that were keeping manufacturers from releasing the DVD technology. Some market analysts believe the takeover will be complete by the year 2000. But don't throw away those CD-ROM drives yet. Other surveys show that, in 2000, CD-ROM will outsell DVD two to one. If DVD technology is successful, DVD-R (recordable) and DVD-E (erasable) are sure to follow.

Hardware is changing to take advantage of the capabilities of the current CD-ROMs. There are self-contained multimedia players including one 11-pound model with a speaker, keyboard and screen that you can use with the new electronic books. Another system includes a CD-ROM drive, microprocessor, screen, speaker, and keyboard in a two-pound package.

How do you put it together?

How do you go about setting up CD-ROM hardware and software in a library? While it is impossible to give the specifics for each brand of computers and accessories, it is possible to walk you through the general process.

Let's begin by saying that you have a dot matrix printer and a PC that meets MPC1 standards, has three available expansion slots, but does not have Windows. Now you need to decide on a CD-ROM drive that can play your new CD-ROM disc which contains primarily text with only a few audio or video clips.

Here are the specifications for a drive: External, access time 250ms, MPC1 compliant, 64KB buffer, SCSI, 300KBps data transfer rate.

Will this meet your needs? If you check back to the hardware explanations in this section, you will see that this external drive meets Multimedia PC Marketing Council standards, has a fast access time, a double speed transfer rate, and a large buffer. In addition, it uses a SCSI interface. It should do everything you need. Remember, however, that a CD-ROM with more video would require a faster access time and transfer rate.

Read the instructions. To begin the installation, read the instructions in the manuals or guides that come with the computer and the CD-ROM drive. If you jump right in without reading the instructions, don't blame the computer if something goes wrong.

Pull the plug. Make sure that the computer is turned off and that the electrical plug is pulled. If accessories get their power directly from an outlet instead of through the computer, be sure that their plugs are pulled, too. One nice thing about plugging everything from one computer into a single powerbar is that you can then pull the plug for the powerbar and be sure that there is no current coming into anything in the system.

Ground yourself. Before you handle any electronic components, be sure you have touched an antistatic device or a metal surface to remove static electricity from your body.

Install the sound board. If your PC meets MPC standards, you know that it has a sound board or card already installed. If it didn't, you would need to add a sound card by taking off the computer case and plugging the card into an available expansion slot.

Install the interface card. If you already have the sound board, begin by opening the computer case, installing the SCSI interface card in the PC, and closing the computer case.

Connect and check cables. Next connect the CD-ROM drive to the PC with a cable and check to be sure that the mouse, printer, monitor, and speakers are all connected.

Reconnect the power. Once the computer case is closed and the cables are connected, plug all system components into the electrical supply.

Turn on the CD-ROM drive and insert the CD-ROM disc. Install the CD-ROM drive setup software. If your computer does not have Windows 3.1, which includes multimedia software, install the setup software that comes with the CD-ROM drive by following the instructions in the drive's manual. This software tells the computer about the new CD-ROM drive and allows the computer to access the drive just like it accesses a hard disk. The only difference is that the computer is not able to write information to the CD-ROM disc.

Install the CD-ROM program retrieval software. We also will need to install the retrieval software that comes with each disc. Sometimes this is on the CD-ROM disc itself, while other times it is on a floppy disk. Follow the directions included in the CD-ROM package.

Run the CD-ROM program. As technologies have evolved, they generally become easier to use. CD-ROMs are no exception. Most newer CD-ROMs now install and run with a click of a mouse on an icon on the screen. However, older systems may require more steps. The exact steps to follow to run your CD-ROM program will depend on your computer and its operating system. Betsy Davis, a middle school LMS in Norfolk, Virginia, provides the following instructions for her teachers using a DOS-based circulating computer. These could be modified for computers running Windows, a Macintosh, or a computer with an internal CD-ROM drive.

Using the External CD-ROM

First, you must be sure the equipment is all connected; the CD-ROM, speakers, mouse and printer are plugged into the computer; and all electrical plugs are plugged in.

Second, turn on the CD-ROM unit. This must be turned on before the computer is so when the computer searches the information on the CD-ROM drive, something is out there.

Open the door on the CD-ROM drive, insert the disk right side up, and close the door. Don't force it. Give it a little push, and it will close on its own.

Next, turn on the computer. The driver software, the information the computer needs to access the CD-ROM, has already been loaded onto the computer's hard drive. When you turn the CPU on, it will run through its start-up procedures until it displays a C> on the monitor.

When you see the C>, you must key in the access code for the program on your CD-ROM. This code is in the documentation for each program. All the codes are listed on the back of these instructions.

After you have typed in the code, press Enter and wait. The introduction of the program will be displayed and the main menu will appear on the screen.

Using the mouse (on the mousepad), select the menu item you want and click the left button. Instructions are displayed on the screen to walk you through any procedures you may desire. If you shut the system down, you should always go back to the Main Menu and exit until you return to the C>. Then it is OK to turn off the computer, CD-ROM and printer.

One final word of advice when buying hardware for your CD-ROM. Beware of bundled software. Drives often come with a few CD-ROM discs and even a sound card and speakers. Sometimes these are great bargains. In other instances, these "free" goodies are older versions of software and accessories that the vendor is trying to get rid of. Look carefully at the titles and copyright dates. Then check for updates or newer versions before you purchase a "bargain."

How can you care for CD-ROM discs?

Manufacturers estimate that CD-ROM discs will last 100 years under proper conditions. For stability, the core of the disc is made of the same material that is used to make bulletproof windows. On top of that are placed layers of reflective and nonreflective metal with a sealer to protect the metal. Finally a label is screened on the top.

CD-ROM discs are designed to last, while CD-R and CD-RW are more susceptible to damage. Kodak photo CDs are more durable than CD-ROM. However, none of the compact discs are indestructible. If you want your current discs to be around for the turn of the 21st century, just follow the suggestions on this checklist:

- Handle discs by the edges only; fingerprints can prohibit the reading of data from the disc.

- Store the discs in their case or in the drive caddy.

- Keep disks away from the sunlight to avoid fading on photo CDs and CD-R discs.

- Keep the temperature below 120° to avoid warping.
- Keep the humidity between 10% and 90%.
- Do not scratch or mark on the disc with a pen or pencil.
- Do not put an adhesive label on the disc.
- Clean with a soft lint-free cloth.
- Wipe a disc in a straight line from the inner hole to the outer edge; never wipe in a circular motion.
- Do not use abrasive cleaners or chemical cleaners on a disc; they can eat the sealer.
- Do not use water to clean a disc.
- Clean dirty discs with isopropyl alcohol.
- Clean caddies with compressed air.

Can your CD-ROM drives be linked?

Before you think seriously about networking or linking together several CD-ROM drives, look at some basics. You can have one CD-ROM drive per computer or you can have several drives attached to a single computer. The most sophisticated system is to link many computers and CD-ROM drives. In that case, all computers on the network should have the ability to access all of the CD-ROM drives. While networks are discussed in a later section, the following brief information provides an overview of the options.

A simple way to allow a single computer to use several CD-ROM discs is to use a changer drive. This CD-ROM drive can hold between two and 12 discs depending on the brand, but can access only one disc at a time.

A jukebox (also called an "auto changer" or "disclibrary") is like the old-fashioned record jukebox. A robotic mechanism locates an individual disc from the many stored in the jukebox and places the disc in a CD-ROM drive within the jukebox. Originally sold to libraries as security devices that would keep valuable CDs away from patrons while allowing their use, jukeboxes have limited use in school libraries. While they can hold up to 1400 CD-ROM discs, only two to four of the discs (depending on the actual number of players within the jukebox) can be accessed at a given time. Students needing access to CD-ROMs for an extended amount of time will keep others from using the other discs in the jukebox.

It is possible to daisy chain or connect up to seven or eight CD-ROM drives to a single computer by linking one drive to the computer, another drive to the first drive, and so on. To do this, the drives must all have SCSI interfaces, or they must have the same proprietary interface.

Another solution is a tower (think of drives stacked on top of each other) that can hold up to 21 CD-ROM discs. The network in a Carrollton, Georgia, school can have up to 240 towers. That means that there could be a total of more than 5,000 CD-ROM discs available for use by the computers in the network.

There are several types of networks. In a peer-to-peer network, all computers are equal and all can share programs and data with each other. Thus, a CD-ROM loaded on a single drive can be shared by others on the network. A problem of a peer-to-peer network is that it provides slow access and works best with less than five computers on it.

More typically found in schools are server networks. In these instances, it may be possible to add a CD-ROM drive or tower to an existing server. This locates all the CD-ROM drives in one place and provides faster access than the peer-to-peer network. One problem is that of compatability of CD-ROM drives if several are to be daisy chained together. In addition, heavy CD-ROM usage on the network can slow it down.

Perhaps the ideal is to add a dedicated CD-ROM file server on a server network. Hooked up like another node on the network, this powerful computer with a fast processor (such as a Pentium 133MHz with 16MB-32MB RAM or a Power Mac 8500) can take a burden off the main server and provide CD-ROM access without slowing down the network. The CD-ROM drives themselves should be SCSI compatible and can be daisy chained externally, located in a separate tower, or installed internally in a tower/server combination.

There is no one "right" way to configure a network for CD-ROM usage. Nancy Graf reports successfully using a 486DX file server with 1GB hard disk space and 24MB of RAM to run a 14 CD-ROM tower on a network with 14 Windows 3.x workstations. Melanie J. Angle, an elementary librarian in Georgia, reports running 29 computers on a network where the file server has two 3X daisy-chained CD-ROM drives each running a different periodical index. In addition, nine of the computers on the network also have CD-ROM drives. The number of drives that you will be able to hook to the server depends on the software and the hardware that you have and the use that you expect the system to get. For information about building your own CD-ROM network, consult the article by Arne Almquist in the Resources section.

Before you decide to link or network your CD-ROM drives, take several things into consideration.

- The costs for computers, drives, software, cables, wiring, interface cards, and maintenance of equipment.
- The installation cost and technical support fees.
- The network licenses available for each CD-ROM disc that you own. Check Chapter 2 of this book for more details on copyright. Some CD-ROMs are not licensed for networks.
- The compatibility of currently owned and "to-be-purchased" CD-ROM discs and hardware.
- The data security problems that may arise if a network is used.
- The ability of the network software to run CD-ROMs and other programs such as online catalogs.
- The number of stations that will be available for student and teacher access.
- The number of people who will need to use the CD-ROMs at one time.
- The number and placement of printers.

Check the Bibliography for this chapter and the chapter on LANs for more information on networking CD-ROMs.

How can CD-ROMs be used in instruction?

CD-ROM technology and the ways in which it stores and retrieves information affects the library skills that you teach. Instead of teaching students how to physically hunt for information, you can now stress the critical thinking skills needed to evaluate, select, and organize the pertinent information on a topic. This is not to say that you will be ignoring such basics as determining a topic or narrowing an idea. You will be showing students and teachers how to develop search strategies and how to use the technology to do research.

As additional CD-ROM titles are purchased for school libraries, more is being written about the skills needed to use them. In the November/December 1991 issue of THE BOOK REPORT, Connie Pawlowski and Patsy Troutman discussed how technology changed their library skills instruction. Included in their article is a sample topic attack and search strategy. The North Carolina Department of Public Instruction has worked to identify the skills that students need to use technology such as CD-ROM to locate information. Professional journals and conferences will help you keep up-to-date.

Practicing librarians report that students seem to profit in many ways from using CD-ROM reference sources. They

- use the CD-ROM technologies more frequently than they used print sources
- are more successful searchers
- spend time working with the information rather than just looking for it
- become peer tutors
- work cooperatively in groups

To help students use CD-ROM, try some of the following ideas.

Set and publicize guidelines. Since searching on CD-ROM can be addicting, you may need to develop guidelines about the amount of time that a student can spend searching. Some librarians use a sign-up sheet with 10-or 15-minute blocks. The sheet can be kept beside the computer or at the circulation desk, and students can sign-up in advance to use the CD-ROM. This system will help you be consistent and fair to all CD-ROM users.

Use CD-ROM and print. Some librarians use a combination of print and CD-ROM materials. For example, a team of students might use the CD-ROM version of a reference source to identify a topic, narrow their search, and determine specific articles that they want. To free the CD-ROM for others to use, these students might then use the hard copy of that source to read the articles.

Use CD-ROM and microform. Students can take advantage of the searching capabilities of CD-ROM by using a CD-ROM index to periodicals. Then they can locate the articles in hard copy or in a microform (microfilm or microfiche) collection. Microfiche collections of journal articles are often sold with CD-ROM indexes.

Have students print information. A student's slow reading speed may tie up a CD-ROM reference source. An alternative is to have the student print out information and read it later. This solution has both its pros and cons. While it frees the CD-ROM for others to use, it also can use a great deal of paper. In an effort to conserve paper, some librarians limit the number of pages that an individual student can print. This has the side effect of forcing a student to evaluate the information before printing it. Another option is to encourage students to save information to their own disks for use later.

Prepare search guides. You could probably list the topics that students frequently research in your library. For a few of the most popular, prepare a guide or "pathfinder" showing how to use CD-ROM sources. You might list synonyms, related words, technical terms, and some limitations that students need to be aware of.

Develop trivia questions. Encourage the use of the CD-ROM sources and develop your students' and teachers' searching skills by keeping a list of trivia questions near the CD-ROM sources.

Train students to serve as assistants. In a large class, you can train a few students in the use of the CD-ROM. They can serve as peer tutors. This can be expanded to a core of trained students who are available to help others. If you use the "license" idea mentioned in Chapter 1, these students can become your "driving instructors."

Ask your students for feedback. Let your students give you suggestions to help them become better library users.

Borrow ideas from others. Many library periodicals are now including sample lesson plans and ideas for using CD-ROM with students and faculty. Look in the Resources section for some listings.

Use CD-ROM with disabled students. Disabled students who have difficulty using the heavy, cumbersome reference sources found in most libraries may have a much easier time using the computer's keyboard to find information on CD-ROM.

Will teachers need special help?

Some teachers will welcome the new technology while others will be reluctant to use it. Try one of the following and then review the suggestions in Chapter 1 and consult the section on staff development for some additional inservice ideas.

Develop special searches. In the November/December 1992 issue of THE BOOK REPORT, Nancy Smith describes how she developed a series of special "technology search" workshops for teachers. At these workshops, which (with the principal's permission) took the place of a faculty meeting, teachers worked through a series of searches that taught them the features of the CD-ROM resources.

Circulate CD-ROMs. Cathy Cheeley, a Virginia high school LMS, reports that she has had success putting multimedia computers with internal CD-ROM drives on carts. She then circulates the cart and software to teachers just like any other piece of equipment.

What lies ahead?

Some of the newer technologies receive a lot of hype in the media before they fade from view. This is not the case with CD-ROM. While businesses have been slow to purchase CD-ROMs, the greatest market has been for home and school use. Its growing acceptance has led to the inclusion of columns on CD-ROM in the mainstream computer magazines and to the production and sale of more multimedia PCs and Macintosh computers. With increased demand, prices are falling and even the CD-R and CD-RW drives are becoming affordable. Even with the rise of DVD technology, CD-ROM discs will continue to meet the needs of teachers and librarians.

Bibliography

Angle, M. J. (1996). From zero to 123 in 5.2. TECHNOLOGY CONNECTION, 2 (10), 25-26. Angle explains how the number of CD-ROM discs in her library grew from zero to 123 in five months and how she coped with that growth.

Almquist, A. J. (1996). How to purchase, set up, & safeguard a CD-ROM network. TECHNOLOGY CONNECTION, 3 (2), 14-17. A technical discussion about networks.

Bennett, H. (1993). Photo CD: a Macintosh primer. *CD-ROM Professional,* 6 (4), 93-98. Describes Photo CDs and the software needed to view them on the Macintosh.

Bennett, H. (1994). To instruct and delight: children's and young adults' literature on CD-ROM. *CD-ROM Professional,* 7 (4), 84-94. Reviews seven publishers of multimedia books on CD-ROM.

Berger, P. and S. Kinnell (1994). *CD-ROM for schools: a directory and practical handbook for media specialists.* Wilton, CT: Eight Bit Books.

Bonime, A. (1994). Kodak's new Photo CD portfolio. *CD-ROM Professional,* 7 (4), 16-26. Along with a discussion of Photo CDS is a description of a simple authoring system to use with it.

Bowers, R. (1994). Welcome to the second computer revolution: A beginner's guide to CD-ROM. *CD-ROM Professional,* 7 (1), 20-32. A detailed discussion of CD-ROM.

CDi: A dead horse rides again. (1996). *Interactivity,* 2 (5), 48. Although a success in Europe, CD-I has not been a big seller in the U.S. This article looks at its few successes.

Dearman, M. (1993). Kids teaching kids to use CD-ROM programs. *School Library Media Activities Monthly,* 9 (10) 41-43. Describes a project at a middle magnet school and includes kid-designed instructions for using Grolier's *Electronic Encyclopedia* and *Microsoft Bookshelf.*

Ekhaml, L. and C. Brown. (1993). CD-ROM and the curriculum. *School Library Media Activities Monthly,* 10 (3), 41-44. Discussion of some titles as well as some ideas for using CD-ROM with a variety of students. Includes a CD-ROM network exercise.

Ekhaml, L. and P. Ekhaml. (1993). Implementing CD-ROM? Do it right! *School Library Media Activities Monthly,* 10 (2), 38-40. Lots of tips for using CD-ROM, including 12 steps for implementation.

Elshami, A. M. (1996). *Networking CD-ROMs: the decision maker's guide to local area network solutions.* Chicago: American Library Association. This 339-page book covers everything from the basics of CD-ROMs to developing peer-to-peer networks, sharing on Novell networks, using Macs on networks, and network standards and specifications.

Fahey, K. (1995). Practical advice on circulating CD-ROMs. Technology Connection, 2 (8), 13, 37. Fahey explains how she circulates CD-ROM discs to her students.

Glass, B. (1994, March). Buyer's guide: 31 multispeed CD-ROM drives. *Multimedia World,* 74-79. A comparison of multispeed drives.

Glatzer, H. (1994). CD-ROM jukeboxes improve access and secure CD-ROMs. *Computers in Libraries,* 14 (8), 22-24. Glatzer discusses the use of jukeboxes in a college library.

Graf, N. (1996). MPEG: Videos on CD-ROM. Technology Connection, 3 (2), 26. A brief description of MPEG.

Hurtig, B. and R. Trubitt. (1997). Burning your own gets easier...And more complex. *New Media* 7 (2): 53-69. A complete discussion of CD recording plus reviews of recording software.

Jacso, P. (1996). Hardware helper. *School Library Journal,* 42 (11), 30-33. Discusses the hardware necessary to use multimedia CD-ROMs, both "budget" and "power" versions.

Jizba, L. (1994). *Guidelines for bibliographic description of interactive multimedia.* Chicago: American Library Association. If you need to catalog CD-ROM discs, this is the book for you.

Martin, R. (1992). SIRS on CD-ROM. *School Library Media Activities Monthly,* 9 (1), 45-47. Detailed description of the use of SIRS on CD-ROM with middle school students.

McClanahan, G. (1996). CD-ROM network configurations: Good, better, best. *MultiMedia Schools,* 3 (1) ,75-77.

Nicholls, P. and J. Ridley. (1996). A context for evaluating multimedia. *Computers in Libraries,* 16 (4), 34-39. Places the evaluation of multimedia within the context of evaluation and the history of multimedia and presents a "general evaluation framework for electronic materials."

Pawlowski, C. and P. Troutman. (1991). Blending print & electronic sources. The Book Report 10 (3): 14-17. Search strategies and "topic attacks" help student learn how to use CD-ROM reference sources.

Perone, K. (1996). Networking CD-ROMs: a tutorial introduction. *Computers in Libraries,* 16 (2), 71-77. Provides an introduction to networking CD-ROMs.

Phillips, M. (1996). Beyond the "best CDS" list. *Electronic Learning,* 15 (16), 16. Discusses the things to look for in evaluating CD-ROMs.

Shields, D. (1995). How to install two CD-ROMs. TECHNOLOGY CONNECTION, 2 (3), 6.

Shoemaker, J. (1995). The bottom line: Are CD-ROM encyclopedias worth the cost? *School Library Journal*, 41 (2), 28-31. After examining the cost effectiveness of both CD-ROM and print encyclopedias, the author suggests that both have their place in school libraries.

Singer, L. A. (1994). Tips for success: CD-ROM technology in school libraries. *CD-ROM Professional*, 7 (Jan.), 158. Lists some tips developed by a committee of Fairfax County (Virginia) Public School librarians.

Smith, N. (1992). Teaching teachers to search electronically. THE BOOK REPORT, 11 (3) 23-24. Describes a series of workshops to help teachers learn to use several CD-ROM resources. Includes a sample worksheet.

Sparrow, S. F. (1994, March). Easy connections. *CD-ROM World*, 52-55. Directions, tips, and tools for installing a CD-ROM drive with a SCSI adapter.

Troselius, R., B. Morris, and M. Mattson. (1996). Full-text magazine indexes & more on CD-ROMs. TECHNOLOGY CONNECTION, 15 (2), 30-34. An overview of the features of the leading magazine indexes for schools k-12.

Wade, D. (1994, Spring). Shareware salvo; 10 CD-ROMs you don't want to miss. *CD-ROM Today*, 51-54. Description of 10 CD-ROM shareware discs and discussion of myths of shareware CD-ROMs.

Wolfe, J. L. (1994). Special considerations for networking multimedia CD-ROM titles. *CD-ROM Professional,* 7 (1), 55-57. Addresses the issues of licenses, SCSI devices, workstations, and minimum system requirements for some popular titles.

Wright, G. (1996). Burn your own. *Interactivity*, 2 (12), 44-51. "Everything you need to know" about recordable compact disc technology.

Wright, G. (1996). Digital versatile delirium. *Interactivity*, 2 (11), 53-55. Details some of the problems facing DVD technology, including patent and license issues, that may affect costs and the acceptance of this new technology by software developers.

<u>Notes</u>

Chapter 5

Videodiscs in the Library

Imagine that you have just finished a Red Cross first aid course. Driving home through the country, you come upon the scene of a major accident. As you stop your car and jump out, someone cries "I think we're losing this one! Does anyone know first aid?" Running over, you notice that the victim is bleeding profusely and does not seem to be breathing. What should you do first? Stop the bleeding? Begin CPR? Wait until trained emergency personnel arrive? The wrong decision could be fatal!

If you were viewing that scene on a videodisc, you could respond to the situation, knowing that your response (A, B, or C) would be evaluated and you would be able to see the results of your actions without the fear that you would feel in a real situation. Programs such as this medical training simulation use all of the features of a videodisc: video clips, audio information, and the ability to go to another part of the disc automatically depending on your answer to a problem.

Why should you use videodiscs?

Videodiscs are true visual reference sources for the school library, teaching tools for teachers, and presentation tools for everyone. With full-screen and full-motion video capabilities, videodiscs are excellent for viewing by individuals or by entire classes on large monitors. Students and teachers can do a little planning and easily integrate videodiscs into lessons, reports, and presentations. This process of customizing a videodisc to fit individual needs, called repurposing a videodisc, will be discussed in more detail later in this section.

In kindergarten through high school, teachers, librarians, and students report success in using simple setups consisting of videodiscs, videodisc players, and television monitors.

> In the October, 1993, issue of *Teaching K-8*, Janis Lowe reports how she used Optical Data's *Encyclopedia of Animals* and Apple's *Visual Almanac* on videodiscs and a software program called *LessonMaker* to help first grade students create their own illustrated books on China. As students wrote their books, they made and inserted barcodes to identify specific pictures on a videodisc. Then, when they read their books, they scanned the barcodes to view the pictures on the videodisc monitor.

> At Hunters Woods Elementary School in Reston, Virginia, a teacher/librarian team of Anne McCracken and Linda Hamilton have used videodiscs to take kindergarten and first grade students on "field trips" to national parks and to explore great works of art without ever leaving the school.

> In the Metropolitan School District of Perry Township, Indiana, high school U.S. history teachers and ethnic literature teachers

developed an interdisciplinary civil rights unit using videodiscs including one of Martin Luther King, Jr.

The Fairfax (Virginia) Public Schools are using videodisc players, IBM computers and Linkway software to help students and teachers use a videodisc encyclopedia to create their own presentations. These presentations are then saved on videotape for later use.

The state of Florida has created a set of Florida Science Videodiscs and has trained teachers to use the videodiscs to make science come alive in their classrooms.

For high school students and literature teachers, the Literature Navigator combines a videodisc and a Macintosh computer to provide an interactive exploration of classics such as *The Great Gatsby*.

These are just a few examples of uses that should win videodiscs a place in your library and your school.

What is a videodisc?

A videodiscs (with a "c" in disc), also called laserdisc, optical videodisc, or laser videodisc, is designed to contain a large amount of visual and audio information on a shiny silver disc about the size of a phonograph record. The visual images can be in either individual stills (similar to slides), motion video segments, or a combination of both. The videodisc is read when a laser light reflects off the disc.

While videodiscs are available in 8" or 12" sizes, 12" discs are the most common. The 8" discs can contain over 25,000 images while the 12" discs store over 108,000 images. Exactly how many images the disc contains depends on the format used to store the images, but the most common number of images found on a disc is about 54,000.

One way to picture this amount of visual information is to compare each image to a slide. Put the slides in a carousel slide tray and you would need a stack as high as a seven-story building to hold the same number of images that are on one videodisc. Each of the individual images can be accessed by the videodisc player and shown on a TV monitor in less than one second.

In addition to the visual information, each videodisc can have two or more audio tracks. Stereo sound can be stored on the tracks, or each track can contain different information. Computer programs can even be placed with the images on the videodiscs.

Formats of Videodiscs

Discs with either format can be played on the same videodisc player, but one format has an advantage over the other. Videodiscs in the CAV (Constant Angular Velocity) format store information in concentric rings with about 30 minutes of motion video and the audio tracks on each side of the videodisc. Each ring on the disc has all of the information needed to show a single still image or frame and contains a unique frame number. Thus, in addition to playing full motion video, a CAV format disc allows a user to access and show each individual still image or single frame of motion video on the disc by its frame number.

In contrast, videodiscs in the CLV (Constant Linear Velocity) format store information in a continuous spiral like the groove on a record. A CLV format disc usually has 60 minutes of motion video and two 60-minute audio tracks per side. The disadvantage of this format is that only expensive videodisc players can display single still images from CLV videodiscs or can access a single image on a CLV format disc by its frame number with 100% accuracy. CLV format discs are best used to store movies or complete motion video programs where it is not necessary to find individual images or frames of the video. Keep these two formats straight by remembering CAV has the advantage while CLV goes in a continuous line.

Levels of Interactivity

The advantage that a videodisc has over videotape is that the user can interact with and accurately control the images on the videodisc. In addition to playing a videodisc through from start to finish, you can use only portions of it, change the sequence of the images, or produce customized lessons and student reports. You will hear people refer to three levels of videodisc interactivity. Each level is determined by the amount of control you have over the disc and by the hardware and software that give you that control. The following discussion briefly describes each of these levels. More complete information along with a detailed description of the hardware is found later in this section.

Level I. In the first level of interactivity, the videodisc is controlled in one of three ways. One way is to use the buttons on the front panel of the videodisc player itself. These buttons are similar to those found on a VCR.

Another Level I way of controlling a videodisc is through the use of a remote control device similar to the one used with a VCR. With the use of the remote control, you can eject the disc, play, pause, step forward and backward by individual frame, scan, and turn the audio off and on.

The third Level I method to control a videodisc is to use a barcode reader or bar wand to "read" frame information. Barcodes often are found on the printed materials that accompany the videodisc. You can also make your own. A single barcode can instruct the videodisc player to go to a specific frame, play the audio and video of the segment ending at a specific frame, and then stop.

Let's say you are developing a lesson and want to use several still images and a motion segment from a videodisc in your lesson. Begin by viewing the videodisc or by using the printed information that came with the videodisc to determine the frame numbers of the still images and the beginning and ending frame numbers of the video segment that you wish to use. Note those numbers in the appropriate place in your lesson plan. Then, when you teach the lesson, key in those numbers at the appropriate time using the remote control.

If you prefer to use the barcode reader, you may be able to copy the barcodes for each frame that came as part of the videodisc disc documentation. The copies can then be taped to your lesson plan at the appropriate place. Teach the lesson and use the bar wand to access the appropriate information on the videodisc.

If the videodisc did not come with barcodes or if the documentation has been lost, you can use a special computer program to print barcodes of the frame numbers that you want. Attach those barcodes to your lesson and you are ready to go. (Specific barcode programs are mentioned later in this section and in the Resources list.)

Figure 5.1 Level I videodisc setup with player and monitor

Level II. This level of interactivity is not currently used in many schools. It requires a special videodisc player containing a microchip that allows the user to interact directly with the player. Level II takes advantage of the videodisc's ability to store computer programs directly on the videodisc along with the audio and video information. This program drives the videodisc through a lesson or series of lessons.

The problem with Level II is that you cannot modify or change the program on the disc. In addition, certain brands of discs can only be used on certain brands of players. You cannot successfully use a videodisc which was produced for Level II on a Level III player.

Level III. The most interactive use of videodiscs is found at Level III. Here a videodisc player is connected to a microcomputer. Some people refer to Level III as an interactive multimedia videodisc system or simply interactive videodisc. Software programs on the computer control the videodisc player.

Sometimes commercially prepared software is sold with videodiscs for use on Level III. In other cases, there are "authoring" programs that allow you to create your own programs to control the videodisc. For the most part, the authoring programs are fairly easy to learn to use; all of the difficult programming has been done for you. Many authoring programs are as simple as filling in the blanks with frame numbers and providing multiple choice questions. Each answer on a multiple choice question sends the user to a different frame on the videodisc.

Suppose you were authoring the program on first aid that is used in our opening paragraph. An incorrect answer to the question of what to do first leads to frames showing the result of that incorrect answer (for example, the victim dies) or to additional information to help the user make the correct choice the next time. A correct response takes the user further into the program. (Now that the victim is stabilized, what should be done next?) Or the correct response could lead to some additional information about the topic.

Because Level II videodisc players are not widely found in school libraries, our discussion will focus on Level I and Level III uses of videodiscs. Later in this chapter, you will find more complete information on the hardware you will need to use a videodisc on either one of these levels.

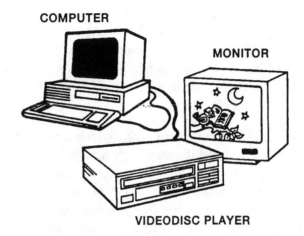

Figure 5.2 Level III videodisc setup with videodisc player, monitor, and microcomputer

What are the advantages of using videodiscs?

There are several advantages to using videodisc technology in the school and in the library.

Easy to handle, use, and store. The hard plastic coating on the videodisc helps protect it from damage. The videodisc loads easily in the videodisc player in a manner similar to an audio CD or CD-ROM. When not in use, the videodisc can be stored upright like a 33rpm record.

Little wear and tear. Since the videodisc is "read" by a laser, there is a minimum amount of wear on the disc itself. Compare this to film and videotape, which are "threaded" automatically or manually and are worn as they travel through the projector or VCR.

Better images than videotape. Videodiscs have a higher quality image of both still and motion video than videotapes. In addition, it is possible to locate an exact frame or image quickly and easily on a videodisc and to display that single frame with excellent image quality, much better than the image shown with the "pause" or "still" control on a VCR.

Better, faster control than videotape. With the use of the remote control, barcodes, or a computer program, the videodisc player provides fast access to any individual frame or segment of the videodisc. Compare that to the "fast forward-play-rewind" cycle you often have to use with a videotape. Furthermore, it takes almost 40 seconds to search the full length of a 30-minute videotape and less than 1 second to search a 30-minute videodisc.

Random access and resequencing of information. Using the frame numbers, you can determine the order of the images and segments that you show to fit your own individual needs. This can be done with the use of the remote control, a barcode reader, or a computer.

More options. A single videodisc can store motion and still visuals, sound, text, and graphics. Producers can currently provide up to four audio tracks on each videodisc. Two of these tracks can be digital audio (a form that can be used by a computer) while the other two can store analog audio, giving the user some choices. There may be narration in different languages or on both a simple and advanced level. There can also be a choice of narration or just music to accompany the visuals. And remember, you also have the option of turning the audio off entirely.

Ideal for use in interactive multimedia systems. The ability to access an exact frame on the videodisc and the ease with which the videodisc player can be connected to a computer makes this technology ideal for use with computers in interactive multimedia systems (Level III). A normal counter-based VCR needs to have a port to interface with a computer in order to be used on a level similar to the videodisc's Level III. However, even with the right hardware and the necessary software and cables, few VCRs are accurate enough to find an exact frame on a tape with any degree of consistency.

Yes, there are time code-based 1/2" VCRs which, unlike the counter-based VCRs, record a time code on the tape and search by this code. However time-code based VCRs are not generally found in schools since they are two to three times more expensive than counter-based VCRs. Any VCR must still have a serial port or special hardware to allow it to be connected to a computer for use in an interactive multimedia system. Cables and software are also needed to complete the system.

Individualized instruction. With Level III use of a videodisc and a computer, it is possible to produce programs that can be controlled by the individual learner. A student can move at his own pace through the program and can review things as many times as necessary.

Decreasing cost. As more videodiscs are produced and sold, the costs for the discs and the players are falling. Call your equipment vendors or the sources listed in the resource list for the latest price information.

Are there any disadvantages?

While there are many advantages to using videodiscs in a school, there are still some disadvantages that you need to keep in mind.

Lack of standards. When using a videodisc player with a computer, you must be sure that the player has the appropriate connections, that you have the proper cables, and that the software is appropriate for your system so that your computer and videodisc player can work together. Some Level III commercial programs are available either for a PC or a Macintosh while others are available for both.

Read only. Unlike videotapes, videodiscs are basically "read-only." Sony has designed a "write-once" videodisc recording system but, because of the cost, the system is currently marketed to business and industries for training and archival storage. Local production of videodiscs in schools is difficult and expensive. To produce your own videodisc, you would probably need to make a 3/4" or 1" videotape and send it to a lab for processing into a videodisc. Therefore, if local production is important, even for interactive multimedia, a videotape will probably be the least expensive choice.

Less storage than videotape. A videotape can store more motion video than a videodisc, which can only store 30 minutes of motion video on each side. To play the other side, the videodisc needs to be turned over in the player or you must have a multiside player that can automatically read both sides of the disc.

Costs of hardware. While prices are falling, videodisc players can be expensive to purchase and to maintain. If you plan to use a videodisc on Level III, you also need to consider the cost of the computer.

Necessary hard drive space. If you are planning to use Level III, you need to be sure that your computer has enough storage space on the hard drive to store the necessary software program. Programs requiring 8 to 10 megabytes of hard drive storage space are not unusual.

Time for planning. With the exception of showing a videodisc from beginning to end or using a commercial teaching package, developing your own program takes time. This has become a major stumbling block to the widespread use of videodiscs in education.

(Read the article by E. Peto in the bibliography section to find one librarian's solution.)

What is available in videodisc format?

With videodiscs, you can have the Louvre, the National Gallery of Art, the national parks, and the solar system in your library. In fact, entire visual encyclopedias can be found on videodiscs.

Recently there has been an increase in the availability of videodisc titles and a corresponding increase in the number that are written about and reviewed in educational publications. Some cable television channels are producing both Level I and Level III videodiscs for schools. Titles from a variety of producers can now be found for math, language arts, social studies, music, science, health, foreign languages, guidance, business, art, and computer science. Many of these videodiscs come with barcoded instructional materials packaged with the discs or with barcode information on the videodisc jacket.

When documentation that allows users to find specific images is supplied with the videodisc, it is important to copy it and circulate the copy with the videodisc. Keep the original as your archival copy and store it in a secure place.

Since 1991, major textbook publishers such as D.C. Heath, Glencoe, Prentice-Hall, and Holt, Rinehart & Winston, have been including barcodes for Optical Data Corporation's videodisc set *The Living Textbook* with many of their science textbook series. By including barcodes for these videodiscs on life science, earth science, and physical science with the teacher's editions, the publishers have made it easy for teachers to use the lessons directly from the teacher's guide, modify those lessons, or create their own by copying the barcodes and arranging them in the desired sequence on their lesson plans.

Another alternative is to use a computer program to print the barcodes on adhesive labels that can be attached to the lesson plans or teacher's edition. Some publishers such as Holt, Rinehart & Winston are offering sets of adhesive barcode labels that teachers can use to customize their texts.

Several videodiscs come with their own software programs for use on Level III and with repurposing utilities, which allow you to set up your own lesson. In addition, there are commercial software programs that help you create your own barcodes for Level I use or create control programs to use a videodisc with a computer on Level III. Some of these are listed later in this section.

Why add videodiscs to the library collection?

Videodiscs are becoming an important information source in schools, especially as more titles are published in videodisc format. Currently movies are being issued on videodisc instead of film and videotape. Interactive learning packages on Level III videodisc present information and test learners. There are even multimedia reference libraries on videodisc that combine video, still pictures, audio, graphics, and text. With the ability of a videodisc to provide access to thousands of still images, this medium is ideal for storing large visual reference libraries. Finally, there are a number of games and simulations available.

Some schools report that the videodiscs are used as an alternative to texts while others say that the text and videodisc are used together. Texas has classified videodiscs as curriculum materials and has permitted schools to spend textbook funds on videodiscs.

However, teachers are not the only people who can take advantage of the wide range of videodiscs available. Students can prepare their own presentations using videodiscs. Frame numbers or barcodes of appropriate segments of a videodisc can be part of a student's written report or oral presentation.

What selection criteria should be used for videodiscs?

When purchasing videodiscs, use the same criteria that you would in purchasing any materials. Be especially concerned about the following:

Quality of the visuals. Even on a videodisc, a bad picture is still a bad picture.

Content of the videodisc. In an effort to jump on the technology bandwagon, some producers are simply reissuing old films and videotapes in disc format. The content may not be accurate or up-to-date. Also, it may be impractical to use these videodiscs in any way except as a motion video. That's fine if you know in advance exactly what you are purchasing.

Quality of the documentation. When selecting a videodisc, look at the materials that accompany it. Check for things such as a listing of the contents by frame number or barcode, an alphabetical index to the images, a topic guide, and other supplementary materials. Remember, to use a videodisc interactively on Level III or to find a specific frame on Level I, you must be able to access individual images or segments of the video by the frame number. If this information is not provided on the documentation, you have to go through the videodisc to find the frame numbers of the segments that you want.

Hardware required. On Level II and on Level III, specific hardware is required in order to use videodisc packages. These requirements include the type of computer needed (Apple, IBM, Mac), the size of the memory (RAM), type of computer monitor (monochrome or color), and peripherals such as a printer or a mouse.

Type of software required. To use a videodisc with a computer on Level III, you will need a software program. Some companies are selling their own search/retrieve software packages that must be used with their programs.

Sound instructional practices. If you are purchasing interactive videodisc instructional packages for use on Level III, be sure that you evaluate the instructional strategies used in the package. An overriding concern should be to determine if the package really fits the objectives of your school's curriculum and the needs of your students and teachers. Since most vendors permit a 60 to 90 day preview, it might be best if you and some of your teachers (maybe even some of your students) try the package before purchasing it.

What hardware is needed?

The Electronic Industries Association of Japan projects a 14.9% annual growth in the sale of videodisc players over the next five years. With the variety of videodisc players currently on the market, it is important to select one that meets your needs.

As you look at the hardware, remember to ask yourself how you plan to use the videodisc software. For example, if you plan to use the videodisc with barcodes, the player must have a barcode jack.

Level I Requirements

On Level I, you will need a videodisc player and a color television monitor similar to the one used with a VCR. You might also need a remote control for the player and a barcode reader/wand.

Remember, you can control the player by the buttons on the front panel. While the buttons may vary slightly with different manufacturers, they will allow you to do things such as:

- Stop, open (eject), and close the player
- Play or start the videodisc player
- Skip or fast forward and reverse
- Scan or view the videodisc in a fast mode both forward and reverse
- Step or advance and reverse frame by frame.

The back of a videodisc player has connections similar to those on a VCR with the usual jacks for audio and video output.

Most players also have a remote control unit, sometimes called a touch pad. The remote unit has some of the same keys that are on the front of the player and allows you to play, stop/eject, scan, and step through the disc. In addition, with the remote, you can:

- Use the number pad to access an image by its frame number
- Switch audio tracks
- Set the play speed (regular, slow motion)
- Freeze frame or pause on an individual image

Some players come with their own barcode reader/wand while others allow a "third-party" or other manufacturer's barcode reader to be connected to the player. If you plan on using a barcode reader, be sure your player has the appropriate jack unless your reader is the wireless type. Then just scan the barcode reader over the barcodes in the manual that came with the videodisc or the ones you created yourself.

Multi-disc videodisc players can usually play 12" and 8" videodiscs as well as audio CDs. The barcode scanner can be used to locate passages on an audio CD as well as frames on a videodisc.

Level III Requirements
Level III requires a computer to control the videodisc player. For this level, you will probably need a color television monitor, videodisc player with an RS-232 port, computer with an RS-232 port, computer monitor, and computer/video-disc player interface cable. You will need the two different monitors unless your computer has a video interface that allows computer images and video images to be shown on the same screen. For use with groups, you may also want an amplifier and speakers.

Currently, the major brands of videodisc players include Pioneer, Panasonic and Sony. Whatever brand of player you select, it should be able to take advantage of all the applications that you plan to use with your videodiscs. Be sure to check the access speed or the time required for the player to scan the entire disc or to locate an individual frame. These may range from .5 seconds to over 3 seconds. Also check the number of audio tracks that can be played. While some players can play up to four tracks, others are limited to two.

"Autochanger" videodisc players can play both sides of up to 72 discs. A videodisc "jukebox" can hold up to 42 videodiscs and is ideal if you plan to use a multidisc set such as a videodisc encyclopedia on a single computer. But remember, while a jukebox might hold 42 discs, the number of discs that can be used at any one time is limited by the number of players (usually one or two) found in the jukebox.

A description of a videodisc player for use on either Level I or III might include the following items:

- Search speed approximately 1 second
- 2 audio channels
- Wireless remote control
- Barcode reader compatible
- RF or separate audio and video output to connect to TV
- RS-232C interface to connect to computer

What computer software is available?

Computers can assist in the use of videodiscs. There are several computer programs that can be used to create barcodes for Level I use of a videodisc. In addition, there are programs to use on Level III when you use a computer to manage videodiscs or to create your own videodisc control programs. The most popular of these two types of computer programs include the following:

- For Macintosh computers: HyperCard with Video Tool Kit, Voyager VideoStack, Bar 'n' Coder, and LessonMaker
- For IBM computers: PC Toolbook, LinkWay, LinkWay Live!
- For Apple II computers: Hyperstudio, TutorTech.

The process of using programs such as these to "repurpose" a videodisc is discussed later in this section.

How do you put it together?

Using a videodisc player is actually very simple, even on Level III. To set up the system you need to:

Read the instructions. Before you begin, read the instructions that came with your videodisc player to familiarize yourself with the steps involved and to be sure you have all the cables that you need.

Connect the videodisc player and television monitor. Some players have their own RF output, so you can cable directly from the player to the TV monitor. Others may require a special RF modulator in order to make the connection.

Connect the remote control and the barcode reader. In some cases, the remote control and the barcode readers for videodisc player are wireless. If they are not, plug the remote control and the barcode reader into the appropriate jacks on the videodisc player.

Plug in the components. Plug the videodisc player and the TV monitor into a grounded outlet.

Now, follow these instructions for using a videodisc with a remote that Betsy Davis, an elementary school LMS in Norfolk, Virginia, provides her teachers.

Using the Videodisc Player

After everything is plugged in, you must turn on the power to the videodisc player and television monitor.

To load the disc into the player, press the reject button on the player or the remote. The door will open automatically, and a drawer will slide toward you. Place the disc on the sliding drawer, right side up (the label tells which side this is), and gently push the drawer toward the closed position. Don't force it. It will close automatically.

Press "play" on the remote and the disc will cue up at the introduction.

Check your list. Press "frame," the number, then "search." The player will search for the frame you asked for and display it on the screen. If this is a video clip, press "play," and it will begin. You will notice in the manual that the entire narration for each video clip is printed beside its beginning frame number.

To go to the next frame on the disc, press "step." If you want to scan through the slides to the next video clip on the disc, press "play." The slides will go whizzing by until the video is located and will begin to play.

To search for another specific frame, press "frame," the number and "search."

To use a videodisc with a barcode reader and preprinted barcodes from the documentation that accompanies the videodisc or from a teacher's guide, follow the above instructions with a only a few minor variations. Remember, scanning the barcodes will replace the action of pressing the controls on the key pad.

Set codes. Before you begin, be sure the barcode reader is properly connected to the player and that the switches on the barcode reader and on the videodisc player are set to the same format of code. See your hardware documentation for complete information.

Scan barcodes. To use the barcodes on the printed materials, press the "read" button on the barcode reader as you slide it across the barcode. A beep signals when the code has been read. You might need to scan the barcode for a video segment of visual still and then scan the "play" barcode to start the action.

Send information. If you are using a wireless barcode reader, you will need to point the reader at the videodisc player within 60 seconds of reading the barcode and press the send key. This is not necessary with a wired barcode reader.

To use a commercially prepared Level III videodisc, connect the videodisc player and the computer using an RS-232 serial connector before you plug the hardware into a grounded electrical outlet. Follow the instructions that accompany the videodisc Level III computer software to load the program on your computer. Once that is done, the major difference in the operation of the videodisc player will be that the software program on the computer will actually control the videodisc player.

It is beyond the scope of this book to tell you how to use specific authoring programs to make your own Level III control program. But most of the software programs on the market today come with good instructions. Addresses and additional information are in the resources list.

How can you use or repurpose a videodisc?

With thousands of still images and video clips on a single videodisc, this technology has much to offer classroom teachers and school librarians. Because most people are familiar with a VCR, they seem to have few anxieties about using a videodisc to add visual impact to a lesson. In addition, videodiscs are excellent to use with hearing-impaired students and with visual learners.

Obviously, the easiest way to use a videodisc in instruction is on Level I. On this level, using a videodisc can be as simple as playing a motion videodisc or using the remote control to punch in the frame number of the image or segment on the videodisc that you want to use. Or you can scan a barcode located in the guide that comes with the videodisc.

Slightly more time consuming is the process of repurposing a videodisc. Repurposing is the term often used to describe the process of creating your own script for using a videodisc. This can be done either by using the remote control to key in the frame numbers in a different order, rearranging the frame barcodes to suit your own lesson plan, creating your own barcodes, or using an authoring program on a computer to create a program to control the videodisc.

To repurpose with the remote control, a teacher can watch the videodisc or use the documentation to determine the frame numbers of the images and video clips that will work with a particular lesson. He/she then can make a list of those frame numbers, arrange them to fit the lesson, and note the numbers on the lesson plan. During the lesson, the teacher can key in the frame numbers at the appropriate times. With the remote control, still images can be shown as long as necessary and video segments can be shown in slow motion, frame by frame, with or without audio, and even in reverse. Using a videodisc on biology, a teacher can make cells divide again and again to show the process of mitosis.

You can repurpose a videodisc with barcodes by copying existing barcodes or creating your own. To rearrange the barcodes that came with the disc, you can photocopy the codes in the videodisc's documentation and then use the old "cut and paste" routine to put the codes in the order that you want.

If you want to create your own barcodes, use a special barcode program. The program can print the appropriate barcodes on paper or on adhesive labels that can be put right on a lesson plan. Most of the commercial programs available to help you produce your barcodes provide complete instructions. In general, they allow you to produce barcodes that instruct the videodisc player to:

- respond to a command such as play, pause, stop, and so forth.
- search for a frame or the starting point of a segment on the videodisc and show the frame or the first image of the segment.
- play a segment and stop at the end.
- change audio channels or turn the audio off and on.

If you decide to make your own barcodes, select the software and printer carefully to be sure the barcodes they produce will work with the videodisc player. Check the specifications provided with your videodisc player. Try out a few "homemade" barcodes before you do the entire program to check how well your printer can produce the barcodes. Check to be sure the player is accurately finding frames and performing the actions that you indicated in the barcodes. If everything seems to be working well, produce the barcodes for the entire program. If not, you may need to use another printer or program. Laser printers are best for producing barcodes, but are not absolutely necessary. The condition of the ribbon or ink supply and the paper that you use can also affect the quality of your barcodes.

Erica Peto, a SLMS at Daniel Elementary School in the Kent (Washington) School District, faced a problem when she found that her teachers were not using the videodiscs in her collection. The primary reason for their lack of use was that teachers were reluctant to use the remote control for the player. Peto solved that problem by linking the discs to nonfiction books and creating the barcodes which would allow the books and the discs to be used together. After teaching both students and teachers to use the newly created videodisc packages, she reports great success and continues to develop more packages.

On Level III, a computer program provides the control. This program can be one that came with the videodisc, or it can be one that is created using an authoring program. On this level, simulations can offer students an opportunity to put their learning into practice as they try to solve problems and view the results of their decisions. Teachers can use the programs to develop individualized lessons, create texts, and track student progress.

Since most students know how to use a VCR, they quickly catch on to using a videodisc player with a remote control. A videodisc can be used as a reference source in the library and students can use clips from it in presentations to their class. Frame numbers or barcodes can be included in reports that students prepare. Imagine the enthusiasm of students who are able to include still and motion video in their reports. They probably will not even realize that they are using higher level thinking skills to create their presentations.

There are some similarities between the use of videodisc and CD-ROM with students. Guidelines for use must be set, and students trained as peer tutors. Refer back to the section on CD-ROM for more information on this topic.

What lies ahead?

Currently, videodiscs are an excellent storage medium for still and motion video, especially when those visuals are to be accessed and used in instruction. One drawback has been that videodiscs, unlike videotape, cannot be cheaply and easily produced. The usual production process involves making a "glass master" from a videotape at a cost beginning at $3,000.

However, an inexpensive videodisc (checkdisc format) can be produced from a 3/4" videotape for less than $500. This format does not have the quality of a regular videodisc but can be used in the same ways. In the future, costs for videodisc production will probably decrease as new technologies are developed. We can also look forward to the day when local videodisc production is possible.

Just as videodisc technology is changing, other technologies are being developed that may eventually replace videodiscs in schools. Digital Versatile Discs (DVD) techniques allow video to be compressed and stored digitally on compact discs for computer access. As DVD techniques are refined, these and other technologies may replace the videodisc as a visual storage medium in the future. But, for now, videodiscs are useful instructional tools in schools and school libraries.

Bibliography

Anderson, M. A. (1993). Videodiscs in the classroom. Book Report, 12 (2), 34-5. A SLMS reports on the use of videodiscs in a middle school.

Allen, D. (1991). Science comes alive. *Teaching K-8,* 21(5) Reprinted by Optical Data Corp. A SLMS explains how videodiscs can be used in science lessons.

Bennett, P. (1995). Videodiscs in schools: selecting essential players & videodiscs. *Media & Methods,* 31 (5), 14-16. Presents a general overview of videodiscs and their use in schools.

Brumbaugh, K. (1995). *K-12 planning guide for videodisc usage for teachers and administrators.* St. Paul: Emerging Technologies Consultants. This 56-page guide was developed for k-12 educators and includes information on hardware and software as well as on the curriculum planning issues surrounding the implementation of any new technology. Available from: Emerging Technologies Consultants, Inc., 2819 Hamline Avenue North, St. Paul, MN 55113.

Chagas, M. I. (1996). Teachers as innovators. *Journal of Computers in Mathematics and Science Teaching,* 15 (1-2), 103-18. Presents a case study of the use of videodiscs in the science program of a middle school.

Cohen, K. (1993). Can multimedia help social studies teachers? Or are videodiscs worth the expense? *Social Studies Review,* 32 (2), 35-43. Along with a list of recommended programs, this article discusses linking new teaching styles with the new technologies.

Ekhaml, L. (1995). Video disc Q & A. Technology Connection, 2 (3), 15. Answers some of the basic questions about quality, copyright, and problems of using videodiscs.

Freitag, P. K and G. L. Abegg. (1991). *Learning in the Middle School Earth Science Classroom.* Lake Geneva, WI: National Association for Research in Science Teaching. Reports on a study of the use of videodiscs with middle school students.

Lowe, J. L. (1993). Laserdiscs, pandas and the Great Wall of China. *Teaching K-8,* 24 (2), 72-73. First graders use videodiscs to write a book.

Markuson, C. A. (1996). Audiovisual media: videodiscs. *Booklist*, 92 (Feb. 1), 946-7. A review of currently released videodiscs. Markuson does a yearly review of videodiscs.

Multimedia & Videodisc Compendium for Education & Training (1997). St. Paul: Emerging Technology Consultants. A 192-page directory of over 2,800 educational titles.

O'Neil, J. P. (1996). A look at laserdisks. *Science Scope,* 19 (Jan.), 50-1. Discusses the technology of videodiscs and the preparations needed to use them in the classroom.

Peto, E. (1996). Laser discs, barcodes, and books...A great combination. TECHNOLOGY CONNECTION, 2 (10), 22-24. When her laser discs were collecting dust, this librarian found ways to entice the teachers to use them by preparing "laser disc books" they could use.

Rock, H. M. and A. Cummings. (1994). Can videodiscs improve student outcomes? *Educational Leadership*, 51 (7), 46-50. In a study conducted in biology classrooms in 15 high schools, videodisc technology was found to have a positive impact on student outcomes. However, the authors note that training for teachers is "critical to success."

Sales, G. C. (1991). Videodiscs: An exciting resource in school library media centers. *School Library Media Activities Monthly,* 8 (2), 39-42. Overview with sample lessons.

Schultz, C. B. (1996). *Master Guide to the American History Videodisc & CD-ROM.* Annapolis: Instructional Resources Corporation.

Shamp, S. A. (1993). A primer on choosing the medium for multimedia: videodisc vs. videotape. *T.H.E. Journal*, 20 (7), 81-86. Discusses videodiscs and time code-based VCRs.

Snepp, L. (1994). Creating a videodisc with fifth graders. *Computing Teacher,* 22 (Oct.), 28-9. Snepp describes her work with eight fifth-graders to plan and create a videodisc.

Ultimate laserdisc players. (1996). *Media & Methods*, 33 (Nov./Dec.), 41.

Waring, B. (1994). Laserdisc players for multimedia. *NewMedia*, 4 (5), 37-39. Comparison of videodisc players for use on Level III.

Chapter 6
Local Area Networks

What is a network?

In the technology world, the term "network" is used to describe a variety of arrangements used by computers to communicate and share information with each other. Today, when people refer to a computer network, they can be referring to a LAN or Local Area Network, to a specialized WAN or Wide Area Network, or to the public Internet/World Wide Web (WWW). As technology changes, the boundaries between these types of networks begin to blur and become less defined. But, at present, a network is considered a WAN when it uses dedicated cables (cables available only for its use) or telephone lines, modems, and sometimes microwaves to link computers over a long distance.

How long is "long?" Well, that varies. Commercial networks such as CompuServe and America On Line and public or "free" networks such as the Internet/World Wide Web use telecommunications to form national and international networks. Other WANs include networks which serve an entire community, and networks used to link all schools or all libraries in a state. Because most WANs in education rely, in part, on telephone lines, they will be discussed in the next section of this book dealing with telecommunications. The Internet/World Wide Web is discussed in its own section.

This chapter will focus on LANs. While some experts say a LAN is composed of two or more computers connected to each other or a group of computers in one room or one building, others say a LAN can link computers in several buildings on a single campus, or a number of buildings located within several miles of each other. In fact, some wireless LAN transmitters can send data up to six miles. A fairly new type of LAN is called an Intranet because it brings the benefits of the interactive, multimedia World Wide Web to a local network with the option of interfaces with the global WWW. However, for our purposes, we will think of a LAN as a network within a single school or school campus.

LANs are designed to encourage the sharing of software, hard disks, data files, printers, modems, CD-ROM drives, and other hardware; and their use is growing. When you realize that "internetworking" uses special hardware to allow different LANs to interact, you can see how the distinctions between LANs and WANs are disappearing.

What will a network do for you?

Later in this section, after a discussion of the terminology of networks, there will be a detailed discussion of the advantages and disadvantages of establishing a network. But, the most basic reason why you might want to think of putting a network in your school or library is that it will enhance your ability to make the most of your resources.

Here are a few examples of how having a network will allow you to share:

Hardware

- A variety of types of printers as well as modems, CD-ROM drives, and computers can be placed on a single network.
- You can print your draft of a document on a dot matrix printer located by your computer and then print the final document on a laser printer located in a central location without leaving your computer.
- Even though your school only has a telephone in the office and the cafeteria, you could use your network computer and the central network modem to reach an online information service.

Software

- Keeping track of software and upgrading to new versions can be simplified.
- If you do not have a site license, do you have version 5.2 of a word processing program in the library while the office has version 6.0 and the business teacher has version 4.0? Loading the network version of the software on a central computer will allow everyone on the LAN to use the same, up-to-date version. It can be used either on the server or downloaded to the hard drives of individual computers on the network.

Information

- With a network, searching an online computer catalog can be done throughout the library and throughout the school.
- If each teacher has access to the network in the classroom, or has a personal "electronic mailbox," you can "tell" the social studies teachers about the new CD-ROMs that just arrived, or let the second-grade teachers know about the big books that you just unpacked, or deliver personalized public relations messages to each teacher without leaving the library.
- With CD-ROMs on a network, students at different computers can use the same network-licensed CD-ROM disc at the same time.

LANS can be wonderful, but they are not for everyone. You may have heard that networking is a complex subject, and it is. This chapter will not make you an expert. However, it should help you understand the fundamentals of LANs; their pros, cons, and requirements; and some things to think about if you do decide to plan for a network.

What are the network basics?

Part of the confusion about networks arises because of the many terms that are used to refer to them. These terms relate to a variety of things including the cables used to connect the hardware as well as the software used to manage the network. To clear up this confusion, you need to know about:

- Main types of networks
- Methods to connect things on the network - cables and wireless
- Physical arrangement of the network - topology
- Network transfer architecture - the network interface to allow data to flow over the network to the hardware
- Management software - network operating system (NOS)

Each of these items places different demands and restrictions on how the network can be set up.

However, before you learn about these specific items, it may be helpful to know a few general network terms. Think of a simple network in which a group of computers and printers are connected by some cables.

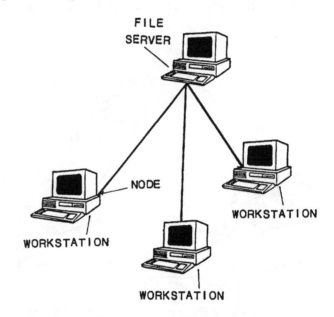

Figure 6.1 Generic network with central server

In a network, each connection of a hardware device (i.e., computer or printer) to the network is called a node. Each individual computer on the network is also called a workstation.

The exception to this is when there is one computer that is acting as a central controller to the network. In that case, the central computer is called the server or file server. A general rule is that on a server network, any device that can be accessed by anyone on the network has the name "server" added to it. For example, you can have a modem server, which is a modem that anyone on the network can use on a first-come first-served basis. Also on a server network, each computer attached to the server is sometimes referred to as a client. Thus you will sometimes hear a server network called a client-server network.

Each workstation can be either "dumb" or "smart." A smart workstation is a fully functioning computer that can stand on its own. This is useful because the computer can function on its own if the network "goes down." A dumb workstation or dumb terminal can only be used on the network since it is incapable of processing information on its own. Dumb workstations are used very infrequently in educational settings.

In addition to cables, LANs require interfaces and software to make them work. A network interface card (NIC), LAN card, network adaptor card, network interface unit (NIU), or network transfer architecture governs how the data is sent through the network. The NOS, or network operating system, acts like the operating system used on a single computer but manages the entire network.

Types of Networks

Networks can be divided into two basic types depending on how the network is controlled. A server, file server, or client-server LAN uses a computer that is dedicated to controlling the network. We will use the common term and refer to a network with a dedicated server computer as a server network and its central computer as a file server. In contrast, a peer-to-peer LAN does not need a dedicated file server.

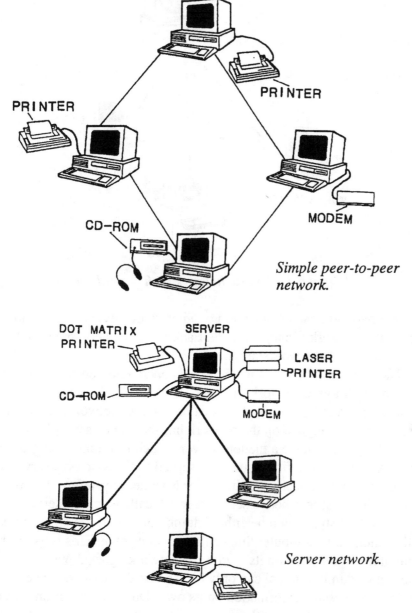

Simple peer-to-peer network.

Server network.

Figure 6.2 Two types of networks

Peer-to-peer networks. In a peer-to-peer or workgroup network, every computer on the network is equal. Using an interface card or a built-in interface, each computer can exchange information with every other one. At each node, a determination is made as to which files on that computer are private and which are shared with other computers. Peer-to-peer networks are less expensive, require less maintenance, and are simpler to change than server networks.

However, there are some tradeoffs for the ease of use. Peer-to-peer networks are slow in their transfer of data, especially when there are a number of users on the network. In addition, they provide a limited amount of security and control of access to information. Because all workstations are equal, it is difficult to keep any computer from accessing the information contained on the hard drive of any other computer on the network. Linked crashes can occur when computers are sharing data and a single computer goes down.

Server networks. In contrast to the equality of a peer-to-peer network, a server network requires a dedicated computer called a file server to control and monitor the network. With a large capacity hard disk drive, the file server provides central storage of data for the network and regulates the flow of that data to the workstations. Resources such as printers and CD-ROM drives that are connected to the server computer can be accessed by the workstations on the network. The size of the file server's hard disk and the processing speed of the file server computer itself place some limits on the speed of the network.

Using the network's operating system and security features, such as passwords, the file server can limit access to the application programs, data, and hardware on the network. Thus some users on the network may only be able to read data, others may be able to read and change data, while others may not be able to access certain data at all. For example, in a school, it might be impossible for a student to use the network to locate the schedule of another student. With a general password, the SLMS could use the computer network to find out the schedule of any student. However, only certain members of the school administration with special passwords could actually change the student's schedule.

In contrast to a peer-to-peer network, a server network is more expensive and complex to install and maintain. When the file server computer is out of operation, the whole network is down. On the positive side, one advantage of a network is the speed at which it can transmit data. In addition, special network software allows the file server to control the workstations and provide central management of the network. This includes such things as tracking usage and providing a high level of data security by monitoring and limiting access to data.

Network Connections-Cables and Wireless

No matter what type of network you have, you need to connect the components. Traditionally, this has been done through the use of wires or cables that are physically strung throughout or between buildings. The latest network technology involves the use of wireless systems.

When looking at connection methods, whether cable or wireless, you need to check the speed at which data transmission is allowed, the maximum length (cable run) of transmission allowed before signal boosters are required, and the ease of modifying the network by adding or relocating nodes. (Figure 6.6 summarizes this information later in the chapter.) You will sometimes see the term "bandwidth" used to refer to the amount of data that can be carried by a specific type of cable in a given amount of time. The following discussion will not make you a cable expert, but it will make you aware of the basic types in use today. (See Figure 6.3.)

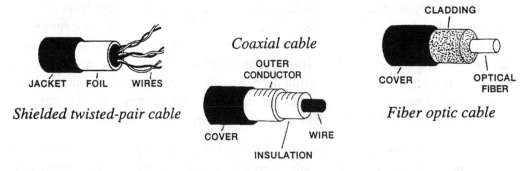

Figure 6.3 Types of cable

Twisted-pair cable. Like telephone wire, inexpensive twisted-pair cable consists of two copper wires twisted for each pair. While more than 25 pairs of unshielded twisted-pair (UTP) wires can be in each cable, most frequently used are level 3 and level 5 cables. In level or category 3 twisted pair, there is only one pair of copper wires, while in level or category 5 twisted pair cable there are four pairs of wires. Flexibility and ease of installation are two of its advantages. A disadvantage of UTP cable is that it is highly susceptible to interference from common electronic devices such as telephones.

More expensive is shielded twisted-pair (STP) wire, which has a layer of aluminum foil or copper mesh around the twisted pairs. While adding protection against electromagnetic interference, the shielding also adds to the cost of the cable.

Twisted-pair cables can transmit up to 100 megabits of data per second with STP wire transmitting over longer distances than UTP wire All twisted-pair cables are, however, limited by the distances that they can transmit a signal with a maximum distance usually being 650 feet from one end of the system to the other, or 300 feet in a single run.

300 feet   300 feet

Figure 6.4 Maximum cable runs of twisted pair cables

One solution to this problem is to decrease the size of the LAN segments through a process known as microsegmentation. With this method, the LAN is broken down into segments with wiring closets throughout the system.

These closets contain expensive relay equipment and switching hubs and are usually linked to the server by a "backbone" of fiber optic cable. Another name for a hub is a concentrator or device in which data is collected and sent to the server. Twisted-pair cables are then used from the closet to the individual computers on that section of the network. (See figure 6.5)

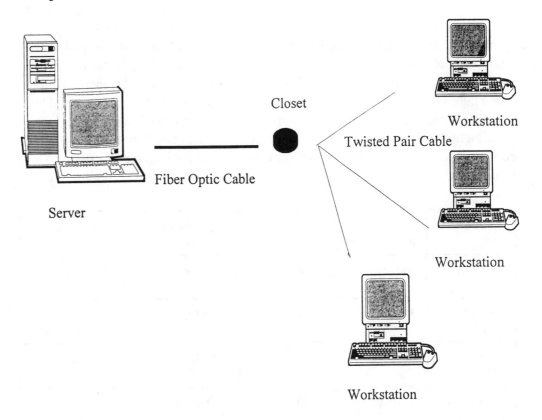

Figure 6-5 Backbone wiring of fiber optic cable
with twisted pair cable to workstations

Some people say that you can use the telephone wiring in a building as the twisted-pair cables for a computer network. While this can be done, if the wiring in your building was installed before 1988, you will probably not be satisfied with the results.

Coaxial cable. Coaxial cable, or co-ax, consists of a single conductor with shielding and insulation. It can easily transmit 10Mbps (megabits per second) and can sometimes go as high as 100Mbps. Thick co-ax or 10BASE5 coaxial cable is 1/2" to 5/8" in diameter (about the size of a garden hose) and, though bulky, maintains a strong signal over distances up to 1625 feet. Thin or 10BASE2 co-ax is about the diameter of a pencil and more flexible than thick co-ax. However, the thin co-ax limits the length of the network cables to about 600 feet and does not allow as much hardware to be connected to the network as thick co-ax.

One solution when using coaxial cable over long distances or on a network with many nodes is to use a hardware device known as a repeater to clean the signal and retransmit it. The type of system in which the coaxial cable is being used determine the number of repeaters that can be used on it.

Fiber optic cable. Glass fibers (usually 2 or 4 strands) in fiber optic cable make the cable very light in weight and allow high data transfer rates over long distances while maintaining a high resistance to interference. With fiber optic cable, a transmission speed of 100Mbps is normal. In experiments, speeds of up to 100,000Mbps have been achieved.

The tradeoff is that this cable is very expensive (about twice the cost of twisted-pair cables) and requires special installation with very precise alignment at the connection points. Adding to the cost is the need for special terminators at each end of a strand of fiber. Because of the skill needed to install fiber optic cables, all cables should be tested for continuity and transmission when they are installed even if there are no immediate plans for their use. This situation frequently occurs when a school is built or remodeled with plans to install a network a few years later. Once installed, a network with fiber optic cable is difficult to modify and problems within the cable can be difficult to find.

Type of cable	Maximum length of run	Approximate cost	Maximum speed of transmission	Special uses
Twisted pair level 3	300 feet	Low	10Mbps	Basic uses
Twisted pair level 5	300 feet	Moderate	100Mbps	Practical for most situations
Coaxial - thin	600 feet	Moderate	100Mbps	Video & backbone
Coaxial - thick	1,625 feet	High	100Mbps	Video & backbone
Fiber Optic	6,500 feet	Very High	500Mbps plus	Video & backbone

Figure 6.6 Network Cables

What cables should be used where? According to predictions made by Andrew Weiss, Technology Plan Manager for Chappaqua Central School District in Chappaqua, New York, new technologies are extending the useful life of twisted-pair cables. While fiber optic cable will be the choice for backbone wiring between servers and hubs, the individual workstations will be connected by twisted-pair cable. For video networks, he sees coaxial cable being the first choice but eventually yielding to fiber optics.

Wireless. If you do not want to string cables to connect the nodes of your network or if you need a network where the nodes are mobile, try a wireless system. A wireless system can be a big advantage in a building in which asbestos limits where cables can be strung or where computers circulate on rolling carts. Some systems provide a combination of wireless connections along with cabled access points where portable computers can be plugged into an existing wired network as needed. Usually this connection is made into a

LAN with Ethernet transfer architecture. (See the discussion later in this section.)

Some wireless systems use radio frequency (RF) transmitters, antennas and relays to send data up to five miles. These systems operate within the ISM (industrial/scientific/medical) bands and do not require broadcast licenses. Other systems that use infrared (IR) light rays require that the workstations be within sight of each other since the rays cannot penetrate a solid object such as a wall or a piece of furniture. Wireless LANs can allow communications between buildings as long as there is an unobstructed line of sight between the transmitters. There are even microcellular wireless LANs that work like cellular telephone networks so that you can actually work on your portable computer as you drive or roam throughout the school district. In late 1996, the FCC (Federal Communications Commission) allocated additional parts of the radio spectrum for unlicensed wireless digital communication through U-NII (Unlicensed National Information Infrastructure) devices with the hope that there would be a corresponding growth in the use of wireless communications by public and nonprofit organizations such as schools and libraries.

As with any network, standards are important if you expect to have the pieces work together. The IEEE (Institute of Electrical and Electronics Engineers) has issued a standard for wireless LANs that should permit interoperability or the ability of any equipment meeting the IEEE standards to be used on an IEEE standard wireless network.

While a wireless network may seem like the ideal solution in a school where running cables might create problems, a wireless network might not meet the needs of every school. Current wireless networks run at a speed of only 1Mbps to 2Mbps versus the Ethernet standard of 10Mbps and Fast Ethernet's 100Mbps. This means that current wireless LANs are too slow for multimedia and video applications.

Physical Arrangement-Topology

When people refer to a star, ring, or bus network, they are talking about the physical layout or the topology of the cables that connect the workstations and, when applicable, the file. While there are variations, there are four common network topologies. (See figure 6.7.)

In the bus layout, one cable is used and everything is connected to it. The individual connections are really plug-in connectors to which computers or other devices such as printers can be attached. Disconnecting one device does not disable the network. A ring layout connects each workstation to the ones on either side of it. The failure of any workstation can crash the network. In the centralized star layout, a separate cable is used to connect each of several workstations to a central computer or to a repeater hub. If one workstation (other than the central computer) crashes, the entire network does not go out of service. The daisychained network is an unconnected ring.

Network Transfer Architecture

A network requires a special interface that governs the flow of data over the network. This interface is often referred to as the network transport, network adaptor, network interface, or network architecture. We will simply call it the

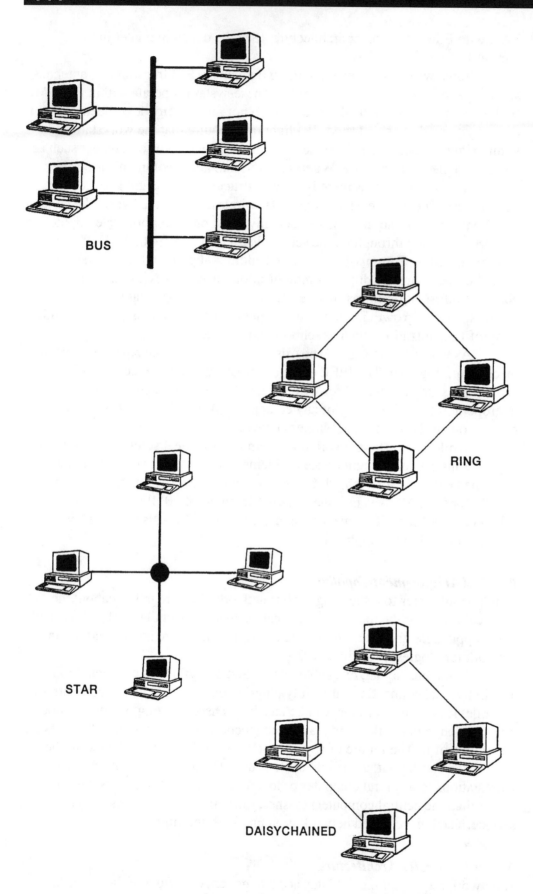

BUS

RING

STAR

DAISYCHAINED

Figure 6.7 Network topologies. Bus layout. Ring layout.
Star layout. Daisychained layout.

interface. Most often the interface is an internal card that is placed in each computer on the network or that comes from the manufacturer as a built-in interface (i.e., Apple).

Like the various network cables, the assorted interfaces have different characteristics and are capable of different speeds of data transmission. The ideal is to have an interface that will carry the most data (greatest bandwidth) across the network in the shortest amount of time with the least loss of quality or strength of the signal. The most common interfaces are Ethernet, Token Ring, LocalTalk, and ARCnet. In addition, there are networks that rely on external cards. These zero-slot networks tend to be slower and more expensive than ones using internal cards.

Why does a network need a special interface? Think about a network consisting of four computers connected to each other by cables. Computer number one is in the library, number two is in the principal's office, number three is in the guidance office, and number four is in the music teacher's room. Information can be sent from one computer to another through the cables. But each of the computers has to have some way of identifying if the information being sent along the wires is for it or for some other computer. For example, if you send a message to the music teacher, you want it to go directly to computer number four. In addition, if the principal is using computer number two to send a message to computer number three in the guidance office, you do not want your message to the music teacher to get mixed in with the principal's note. Keeping data straight is the job of the network interface.

Basic to each type of interface is the idea of information (i.e., your note to the music teacher) being sent through the cables in packets. Each packet has information about the source of its data and its destination as well as the data itself. The interfaces differ as to how they work with the information packets.

Ethernet. Approximately 55% of the LANs in use today and a large majority of those in schools use an interface called Ethernet. Adopted as a standard by the Institute of Electrical and Electronic Engineers (IEEE), an Ethernet interface can be used with both PCs and Macs and can provide good connection from a LAN into the Internet.

This system uses a Carrier Sense Multiple Access (CSMA) to keep track of information. In an Ethernet interface, information packets are sent through the network cables. To send a message, the interface checks to see if the cable is clear (no message packets on it). If the cable is clear, the computer sends its message packet. If a packet is already on the cable, the computer waits until the cable is clear to send its packet. An Ethernet interface can transmit information over the network at a speed from 10Mbps to 100 Mbps. The 100Mbps interface is called Fast Ethernet, runs on level 5 twisted pair cables, and requires compatible network cards and hardware hubs. As an example of the speed of Ethernet, a transfer rate of 10Mbps means that the contents of an entire floppy disk can be moved through the system each second. With an Ethernet interface, the topology is usually a bus configuration.

Various Ethernet interface cards made by a number of manufacturers can be purchased for both PCs and Macintosh computers. To select an Ethernet interface for a network, you need to know the types of cables and computers that will be used. For portable computers, manufacturers are producing

Ethernet and Fast Ethernet interfaces on PC Cards. This creates a problem, however, since the normal PC Card to portable PC interface runs at only 3Mbps. The solution is to replace the PC Card slot in the portable computer with a CardBus slot that maintains transfer speeds between 30Mbps and 40Mbps.

One word of caution. Some manufacturers produce 100Mbps interfaces that do not meet Fast Ethernet standards. Be sure any interfaces that you purchase meet the industry standard for the network transfer architecture that you are using.

Token Ring. A token ring is often used with IBM PCs. Costing more than Ethernet, this interface uses a ring topology and the concept of an electronic signal known as a token. This token is sent from workstation to workstation through the cables of the network. If a workstation has the token, it can send an information packet. The token goes with the information to the destination. Then, after the packet is delivered, the token goes back into circulation. A workstation cannot send data or requests for data until it has the token.

A token ring interface is slow compared with an Ethernet interface. The data transfer rate is between 4 megabits per second and 16 megabits per second.

ARCnet. Easy to install and inexpensive, the ARCnet is the interface used in 20% to 30% of the networks installed today. It also has the advantage of being able to adjust automatically to cable breaks without shutting down the entire network. Using co-ax cable, the total cable length can be up to 20,000 feet before special routers are required. Its problem is that it is slow, with a data transmission rate of 2.5 megabits per second.

AppleTalk/LocalTalk. Macintosh computers have built in networking protocol called AppleTalk that uses connections (shielded twisted-pair cabling, connectors and so forth) known as LocalTalk. AppleTalk can also work with unshielded twisted-pair cable by using connections from other manufacturers. While earlier operating systems are fine for peripheral sharing (printers, drives, etc.), file sharing requires System 7 and above and additional RAM.

Compared with an Ethernet interface, AppleTalk plods along. A 10 megabyte file that takes less than 10 seconds to send on a network with an Ethernet interface will take five minutes to send on Apple's proprietary network. AppleTalk's delivery speed is only 115 kilobits per second. While the network can theoretically have up to 255 nodes, anything over 32 nodes makes the network too slow. An alternative to LocalTalk is Farallon's PhoneNet which is less expensive and can have longer cable runs than LocalTalk.

Zero-slot. Instead of using an internal expansion slot for the interface card, a Zero-slot LAN uses serial or parallel ports to connect computers.

Asynchronous Transfer Mode (ATM). The transfer protocol used on many pure fiber optics networks is known as Asynchronous Transfer Mode or ATM. Developed as a standard by the International Telecom Union (ITU) and the ATM Forum, this interface has a transfer rate from 52Mbps to over 2.4Gbps. Useful on networks carrying video and interactive multimedia, the ATM interface is expensive and complex to install. Therefore it is often used as a "backbone" cabling to connect the server to wiring closets with hubs for further distribution over twisted-pair cables.

Other network transfer architecture. Several other interfaces are being developed as alternatives to Fast Ethernet. One of these is FDDI (Fiber Distributed Data Interface) which carries 100Mbps. The FDDI interface is used as a backbone over fiber optic cables to links. Fast Ethernet is then used over twisted-pair cables from each to its nodes. CDDI (Copper Distributed Data Interface) runs on the same principal as FDDI but uses cheaper copper twisted-pair wire as the backbone.

Other network connections. At times you might want to connect two different networks. Sometimes the networks will have the same data transmission rules and procedures, while at other times they may have entirely different protocols. You will need a good technician, but the connections can be made with devices known as bridges, gateways, and routers. Frequently used to monitor the amount and quality of the data transmitted by a network, bridges can connect similar systems or can segment a network into smaller sections. In contrast, gateways translate between dissimilar ones such as those used by PCs and Macs. Also used on networks are routers. While they can connect two independent networks, or networks with different protocols, their use slows down the data transfer rate.

Interface Ethernet	Cable Co-ax STP UTP 10BaseT	Topology Bus	Speed/sec 10-100Mbps
ARCnet	Co-ax Fiber optic Twisted pair		2.5Mbps
Token Ring LocalTalk	STP STP	Ring Daisychain	4-16Mbps 230Kbps

Figure 6.8 Sample Network Information

Network Operating Systems

The network operating system, or NOS, is the software that controls the operations on the network. Each brand of NOS has its own utilities and special features. Some are made for peer-to-peer networks while others control server networks.

In a network, part of the NOS runs on the file server and part on each of the workstations. On the file server, the NOS should provide for data security by controlling who has access to what applications and data. It should also be responsible for managing all reading from and writing to the file server's hard disk.

There have been some problems in using PCs with the Windows 95 operating system on networks. While many of these problems have been fixed by subsequent versions of Windows 95, you can still experience problems.

Check the Resources section for this chapter to find Internet sources to help with common problems.

Other functions of the NOS include checking licensing adherence for software use (more about this later in the chapter), backing up the system's hard drive, and helping diagnose problems that arise on the network. Some NOS will allow two or more people to work on the same data file at the same time. Others limit access to a single user at a time. A few of the peer-to-peer network operating systems offer various degrees of data security.

Several network operating systems are in use today and others are on the way. The most popular NOS for peer-to-peer networks are Artisoft's *LANtastic*, which can manage computers and CD-ROMs, Microsoft's *Windows for Workgroups*, which includes electronic mail and a calendar/datebook, and Novelle's *NetWare Lite*.

Server network operating systems include Novell's *NetWare for PCs* and its *NetWare for Mac*, Banyan's *VINES*, Microsoft's *LAN Manager*, IBM's own version of LAN Manager which is called *LAN Server*, and Microsoft's *Windows NT Advanced*. In the Macintosh world, programs like Apple's *AppleShare* software can govern a network using Ethernet or LocalTalk interfaces and can allow IBM compatible computers on the network to access data. With the Ethernet interface, the Macintosh NOS is called *EtherTalk* or *AppleTalk* over Ethernet. The *Digicard* NOS allows Apple II, Macintosh, and PCs to run off the same file server. This ability of PCs and Macs to operate on the same network is called cross platform technology and becomes important in schools where both types of computers are used.

The individual computer operating systems of the hardware on the network can assist in the management of the network. Beginning with the version known as System 7, the Macintosh's regular operating system has a built-in peer-to-peer NOS called *AppleTalk* that provides file sharing, a calendar, and an electronic mail system. For PCs, *Windows 95* has a "Network Neighborhood" icon for computers installed on a network. This allows you to see a picture of the entire network including all of these and aides in the easy installation of the software drivers for individual programs to be used on the network.

	Peer-to-Peer	Server
PCs	LANtastic Windows-Workgroup NetWare Lite	NetWare VINES LAN Manager LAN Server Windows NT
Mac	AppleTalk	Netware for Mac AppleShare EtherTalk

Figure 6.9 Popular Network Operating Systems

Other Network Software

In addition to the NOS, other programs can aid in the management of the network. These programs allow you to see who is using what software and hardware on the network, to sit at the file server computer and help someone at a workstation on the network by controlling his keyboard, or to troubleshoot problems on the network.

Apple sells the *Apple Network Administrator Toolkit* for networked Macintosh computers. Included is *At Ease for Workgroups* 4.0, a security and access management program; *Network Assistant*, a software and hardware management program; and *Apple User and Group Manager*, a program to create, modify and delete user accounts and groups. These programs are also found in *MacControl* by BOW software.

Network Administration

Because of the complexities of many networks, most server networks require a network administrator. His or her responsibilities include doing routine backups of the hard disk, checking the hard disk, deleting old files, installing new and upgraded software, conducting training on network use, monitoring the use of the system, keeping network statistics, setting up user (faculty and student) accounts, controlling the electronic mail system and general bulletin board, maintaining security information, and troubleshooting problems. The administrator may also be responsible for installing additional cables and interfaces for additional nodes, adding additional hardware such as disk drives, printers, and CD-ROM drives, and upgrading the NOS when new versions become available.

What are the advantages of a network?

Now that you have read about the cables, interfaces, and topologies of networks and have some understanding of the basic network terminology, you may be thinking that you will never even think about networking the computers in your school or library. But before you write off networking as something that only "techies" can cope with, realize that, for all their complexities, networks do have advantages.

Hardware sharing. In these days of budget cuts, sharing devices such as printers and CD-ROM drives may be the only solution. While not every computer can have its own laser or color printer, a LAN will allow everyone to have access to one. Less expensive dot matrix printers can be close to several computers while the laser and color printers are placed in a central location.

Concentration of power. With a server network, you place the most power in a fast CPU and a large hard disk drive for the file server computer. The other workstations can then be older or less powerful computers.

Access to information. A network allows users to access library resources from a variety of locations inside and outside the library. With a computer in the classroom hooked into the LAN, a teacher can check the online catalog before sending a student to the library to check out a particular book or even find information in a reference CD-ROM.

Electronic information system. You can post information about school events on the electronic bulletin board on the LAN or put a note in each teacher's personal electronic mailbox.

Software sharing. Purchasing an application software program that is licensed for use on a network may cost substantially less than purchasing a large number of copies of the same program for standalone computers.

Decreased installation time. If software is purchased to run on a server network, it will only need to be installed on the file server. Even if it needs to be installed on individual computers, it is faster to install a program from a server than from floppy disks. Compare this with the time needed to install the same program on a number of computers in different locations.

Increased compatibility. If an upgrade of network licensed software is purchased and placed on the network, everyone is automatically upgraded to the new version. This saves the frustration of installing a software package upgrade on your computer, using its fancy features to create a document, and then finding that all the computers with access to a printer still have the old version of the software. Without the new program, those new features you used will not print.

Data exchange between platforms. Special file exchange software programs on networks can allow PCs and Macintosh computers to exchange data. But remember, they may need their own versions of the same or similar application programs to use the data.

Security of information. A well-planned network with security software can limit access to information. Instead of many copies of data files on a number of computers in different offices, a network can keep the data in a central location and monitor access to it.

Centralized maintenance. With a server network, maintenance and procedures such as routine backups can be focused on the file server and its hard disk.

Internet connection. A LAN can serve as an Internet connection by hooking a high speed local network server to a high speed communications link such as an ISDN line which can communicate between 128Kbps and more than 2.048 Mbps with an end to end digital connection over a special phone line. In a usual phone line connection, the main telephone communications networks are digital while the local loops to homes, business, and school are usually analog. Sometimes used for an Internet connection is a T1 line which allows communication up to 1.544 Mbps and requires a NT1 (Network Termination) unit.

What are the disadvantages of a network?

Networks have many advantages, but there are also some disadvantages that you need to keep in mind when you consider networking library resources.

Susceptibility to viruses. Just as an individual computer can get a virus, so can a network. Of course, the problem with a virus on a network is that, without safeguards, the virus can infect every workstation and every user. Peer-to-peer networks are especially hard to protect.

To combat a virus infection, a network should include antivirus software, and frequent backups of the system should be made. Some network antivirus programs scan a program each time it is used. Another alternative is to scan the entire hard disk of the file server each day at a time (late night or early morning) when network use is light. If students and teachers use their own floppy disks on workstation computers, have each new user do a warm boot of the workstation (restart the computer) to clear its RAM of any virus before inserting a floppy disk.

If all computers on the network, such as those in a computer lab, should have the same software on each of them, an option is to use software that takes a master "snapshot" of the contents of the hard drive. Then, every morning when each computer is turned on, the server automatically checks each hard drive and removes anything that does not match the snapshot. Student and teacher files saved on the hard drive will be lost, but all unauthorized programs and files will also be removed and settings will be returned to normal. Setting up this system is not for a novice and requires advanced computer skills.

Attraction to hackers. Often networks offer a challenge to computer hackers who, maliciously or not, try to gain access to the file server computer. If they are successful, some will create major problems for the entire network by changing and erasing data. Other hackers will simply leave a message that tells you they were successful in breaking into your system. Good security protection is a must with a network. See the information on network protection in this section for advice on passwords.

Expense. Network cables, interfaces, a powerful file server computer and an operating system are costly in terms of purchase price and installation time. For example, installing or moving a single wired LAN connection can cost between $800 and $2,000. Network licenses for application software can be many times the cost of individual software programs. Once installed, the network (and all of its pieces) will need to be maintained and the programs running on the network will need to be updated. Don't forget to factor in the costs to upgrade the network version of your software, including your CD-ROMs, and to pay the salary of someone to troubleshoot and/or administer the network.

In some cases, it may be cheaper and may make more sense to buy additional hardware or software (a few laser printers, additional telephone lines, or several CD-ROM drives) to use with standalone computers than to install a network. It is imperative that you know what you expect a network to do and make cost comparisons with several different scenarios (network versus various standalone hardware configurations) before you purchase anything. Do not buy a network just because someone else is doing it.

Need for technical skills. With most networks, someone needs to be the network administrator to oversee the daily operation. Often this task becomes part of the job description for the SLMS, especially if the file server is located in the library media center. If you become a network administrator by design or by default (it's in the library, let the librarian do it), you will probably need to locate some reliable sources of technical support. These could be local sources or people within the company that supplied parts of the network.

Everyone involved needs to keep in mind that the network administrator is not just responsible for troubleshooting problems with the computers on the network, but also responsible for all the cables, connections, interfaces, and other hardware and software. He or she should also help people establish a plan for using the network and identify ways the network can be used and expanded. Ideally, unless the SLMS has advanced technical skills, has adequate additional staffing in the library media center, and is released from other library responsibilities, he or she should not serve as the network administrator.

Possibility of a total crash. With server networks, when the file server computer crashes, the entire network shuts down.

Reduction of speed. Depending on the number of users on the network and the demands that they are placing on the file server, the network can be much slower that an independently running computer.

License unavailability. Some software vendors do not sell network versions or licenses of their programs. This could mean that the software will not run on the network or that using a single copy on a network is a violation of the copyright law. If you are purchasing software to use on a network, be sure to note on the purchase order that it is for network use and identify the LAN on which it will be running.

How should you plan for a network?

It can be exciting to link everyone in the school in one giant information network where teachers and students will have access to the library's online catalog, CD-ROM reference sources, and applications programs from any location in the building. But before you start, planning is necessary. Refer back to the general planning guidelines in Chapter 1. In addition, consider the following:

- What cables should be used where? According to predictions made by Andrew Weiss, Technology Plan Manager for Chappaqua Central School District in Chappaqua, New York, new technologies are extending the useful life of twisted-pair cables. While fiber optic cable will be the choice for backbone wiring between servers and hubs, the individual workstations will be connected by twisted-pair cable. For video networks, he sees coaxial cable being the first choice but eventually yielding to fiber optics.
- What should the network do?
- What hardware and software should be on it?
    Online catalog?
    CD-ROM reference sources?
    Application software for faculty use?
    Application software for student use?
    Administrative software?
- On what kind of network will that hardware and software run?

- What kinds of computers will be connected?
- What existing hardware can be used?
- What hardware will need to be purchased?
- Where should the network reach?
- Can cable be strung to those locations?
- Are there structural or health (asbestos) barriers?
- How many nodes should there be?
- Where should they be located?
- Will you have a peer-to-peer or a server network?
- On a server network, where will the file server be located?
- What peripherals will be on the network?
- What kind of data will be on the network?
- Will there be video data?
- Will the network carry sound?
- Will the network need to communicate with other networks?
- Who will be the administrator?
- How will this affect the administrator's current job?
- How will the administrator and users be trained?
- Who will provide technical support?
- What data security will the network need?
- How will security be maintained on the network?
- Will you want remote access to the system by a modem?

As you begin to consider each of the types of network interfaces and operating systems, ask:

- How much will the entire installation cost?
- Does that include hardware and labor?
- What structural construction will be needed?
- How much electricity will the system draw?
- Can the present electrical system support the new demands?
- How flexible is the system?
- Can it be updated as technology changes?
- How easily can it be expanded?
- Is local technical support available? (Double check this one!)

Remember to contact others who use the networks that you are considering. Ask them:

- What general problems have you had?
- Have you had any virus infections?
- Does the system provide good security of data?
- How good is the company's technical support?
- How good is the company's telephone support?

Use these questions to brainstorm suggestions for your ideal network. Involve potential network users in this process.

Other things to consider when planning for a network include the following:

Identify all the costs. Look at the costs of the hardware, interfaces, cables, network operating system, networking software for CD-ROMs, and software licenses. Consider labor for installation as well as the actual hardware and software prices. Don't forget to include the cost of training for faculty and staff using the network as well as training for the individuals who will be responsible for keeping it running. Are technical support and training additional costs? Get written bids from a least three vendors and be sure the bids contain the answers to all of your questions. The bid should also contain a complete list of hardware and software, details of the installation, qualifications of the technical support personnel, and a description of the services before, during, and after the installation.

Determine where components will be placed. Be realistic when you locate hardware such as printers on your network. Just how far away from a workstation can a printer really be located and still be convenient for the user? Also, be aware that a printer located more than 15 feet from a computer's parallel or serial port will need a signal booster on the connecting cable.

Check software. Will the software packages that you currently use or that you want to use actually run on a network? Are the licenses affordable?

Locate sources of support. Are there people within your school district who can provide technical assistance and training? If not, who can provide them and what will it cost? Do the hardware and the software vendors provide support for their products?

Consider an ILS. There are some companies that sell Integrated Learning Systems (ILS) which combine, in one complete package, the network hardware, NOS, applications programs, and management software. Some people argue that it is better to buy the entire network (hardware, software, and installation) from one vendor. That keeps two or more vendors from passing the buck back and forth whenever a problem arises. A vendor selling a complete package should provide all necessary service after the sale. But realize that ILS are usually expensive and may not have all of the applications that your school needs. Also, adding other applications to an ILS can be a problem.

Develop a contingency plan. Identify a procedure to follow if your file server breaks down or if the entire network crashes from some unknown cause.

Consider a consultant. To help you ask the right questions and make the right choices, consider hiring an independent network consultant who has experience with a variety of networks. Do not rely on the "consultants" employed by individual vendors at this point in the process. The consultant's loyalty should be to you, not to a commercial firm that is trying to sell you a product. The time to rely on a vendor's staff is for training and installation after the selection is made.

Detail the job of the network administrator. The network administrator has the responsibility of the day-to-day operation of the network. Read the responsibilities of the network administrator listed earlier in this section. Be sure everyone understands in advance exactly what those jobs are and who will be responsible for them.

Do not rely on MIS. Many large school districts have a department with a name similar to "Management of Information Systems" (MIS) or "Data Processing." These are the people who run the mainframe computers that have all the data for the school administration. In some cases, librarians are told that people from this office will help with instructional networks. This may be true, but get that in writing beforehand.

One library supervisor/coordinator in a large technologically advanced school district reports that technicians from her district's MIS department will troubleshoot the administrative network and the computers in the principals' offices but refuse to do anything with the instructional networks in the computer labs or in the school libraries.

What hardware will you need?

Let's say you have begun the planning and are considering some of the questions posed previously. For security and management purposes, you decide to develop a server network. Look at some things you will need to consider whether you select Macintosh computers, PCs, or a combination of the two.

The File Server

Since your file server will be doing most of the work on the network, do not skimp on this computer. While you can run a network with a 386 PC, ideally you want to buy more than you think you will need for your server. In a PC, look for an upgradable, fast 150MHz to 200 MHz Pentium CPU with a 33.6Kbps modem or a 56Kbps after the new standards are set. (Check Chapter 7 for information on modems.) With the SCSI hard drives, it may be better to purchase several smaller drives than one large drive. The RAM should be expandable, and the L2 cache should be up to 256K for a large network. (If you are not familiar with this terminology, refer back to Chapter 2 of this book.)

	Processor	RAM	SCSI Hard drive(s)	Expansion slots
Large network	200 MHz Pentium	64 to 128 MB expandable	up to 27 GB	6 to 8 slots
Medium network	180 MHz Pentium	32 MB expandable	3.1-5.1 GB	4- 5 slots
Small network	150 to 166 MHz Pentium	32 MB expandable	2.1 GB	4- 5 slots

Figure 6.10 Minimum requirements for PC servers

In a Macintosh, Apple recommends at least a Mac SE (although some librarians recommend at least a Classic II). However, Apple sells Workgroup Servers such as the 6150/66, the 7250/120 and the 8550/200 with PCI (Peripheral Component Interconnect) slots. To do the network's processing, the computer should have at least 32MB of RAM and should be expandable with eight to ten expansion slots. For a large network, especially one carrying video, consider the Power Macintosh 9500 or compatible with 200 MHz 604e processor; 32 to 64MB of RAM, expandable; with up to a 9.1GB hard drive.

For storage of applications programs and data, the server should have the largest hard disk drive that you can afford to buy, with a minimum of 2.1 gigabytes. A 20 gigabyte hard disk drive is not uncommon on a large network. Because the network speed will depend, in part, on the access speed of the hard drive, buy the fastest (access to data) hard drive you can afford. In most cases, these are drives with SCSI interfaces. Some consultants recommend purchasing two identical hard drives and keeping the same information on each. That way, if one fails, you can switch to the other with a minimum amount of effort.

Surprisingly, the server does not need the best monitor since the only work that will be done at it will be some of the administration of the network, not the applications. In some cases, you may not even need a monitor for the server. If you do need one, a monochrome monitor or an older CGA or ECG monitor will be fine. Although many of the newer monitors have eliminated the need for a screen saver on the server monitor, some users feel safer if one is used to prevent any chance for phosphor burn-in. Another solution is to turn the monitor off when it is not being used. If you decide to use a screen saver for the server monitor, keep it simple. The ideal is simply to go to a blank screen. You do not want to use the server's power for cute screen saver graphics.

Up until now, we have talked about a file server as a single dedicated computer at the heart of a network. If there are heavy demands, you can place several file servers on one network. With several servers, one might manage the school's administrative information and electronic mail system, another might be used for all of the applications software, and another might function as a printer server to manage several high-use printers. In addition you might have a separate server computer to manage the CD-ROM drives.

Keep the server or servers in a secure area but be sure to allow for air circulation. Running at the current higher processing speeds, computer hardware generates heat and needs room for that heat to dissipate.

Nodes-Workstations

Workstations will usually consist of a monitor, keyboard, and CPU, with or without floppy and hard disk drives. While there may be situations (such as a workstation for the online catalog) for which you can use a dumb terminal (computer that cannot function as a standalone computer) or a "diskless" computer (computer without a floppy drive or hard drive) on your network, most schools use full-functioning computers for all workstations.

There is a new trend, however, in businesses to use what are called NC or network computers. These are marketed under several brand names including Sun Microsystems' Java Stations, Microsoft and Intel's NetPC, and IBM's Network Station. In addition to running a variety of applications, they also can provide Internet access. While some such as the NetPC have their own hard drive, these NCs place a greater burden on the server computer. The main attraction is that the target cost for NCs is between $300 and $500 each. Apple's Newton eMate 300 is a four-pound, low-cost unit that can connect to a network or to the Internet, interface with Macs and PCs, and can have its own basic productivity software including wordprocessing, spreadsheet, and drawing program. It will take some time to see if this technology becomes popular in schools.

In selecting standalone computers for use as nodes on a network, consider the following:

Monitor. The type of monitor that you select may vary from workstation to workstation and will depend on the applications that are being used at that station. While SVGA monitors at all workstations would be ideal, a monochrome monitor would be adequate for a workstation being used for text only, such as an online catalog. To use CD-ROMs, to run high powered graphics programs, or to view motion video at a workstation, you will definitely need an SVGA monitor that will provide color images. For most other applications, an EGA, CGA, or VGA monitor may suffice.

In making a decision, be sure to check the requirements of the application software that might be used at a particular workstation. If you are using older monitors, be sure that a screen saver with a moving pattern goes into action whenever the computer is turned on but not in use. This will prevent phosphor burn in or the development of a ghost image that will remain on the screen forever.

Disk drives. Whether or not to have floppy disk drives and hard disk drives on the workstations is your choice and should be based on the things that will be done at that workstation. A workstation to use the online catalog does not need a hard drive or a floppy drive. Remember, too, that people cannot use computers without disk drives to make illegal copies of the application software on your network.

However, if users will be working on projects or preparing reports at a workstation, they might need to be able to save their work on their personal floppy disk. A valid reason for putting hard drives on some of the workstations is that they can be used as standalone computers when the network goes down. But remember, these hard disks will need management including general file maintenance and virus protection.

CPU. If you need to economize, the CPUs of some of your workstations can often be older, slower models with fewer features than your file server. For example, on some workstations 640K to 1MB of RAM may be sufficient. However, on workstations running graphics or interactive multimedia you will definitely need a minimum of 8MB of RAM. You will also need to decide whether each workstation needs a mouse or a trackball as well as external speakers or headphones.

Think of the software your patrons will use at the workstations (both on and off the network) before making a decision. It goes without saying that you should buy the best hardware that your budget can afford and that will give you good service for five to seven years.

Network interface card. Each of your workstations will also need a network interface card (NIC) unless an appropriate interface is built into the machine. To use a Macintosh on an Ethernet network, you will need to purchase an Ethernet card for the Mac.

Workspace. No matter what hardware you select for your workstations, do not forget the work area around each of them and the environment in which each is placed. While the actual space needed around each workstation depends on the type of work done there, a good rule is to allow at least 30 square inches of work area per computer. Don't forget to allow room for easy access when you need to plug things into a workstation. In selecting the environment in which individual workstations will be placed, follow the rules for computer placement discussed in Chapter 1 of this book. If you are setting up a computer lab, be sure to use a white board rather than a chalkboard to eliminate a major source of dust.

Nodes-Printers

A network makes it possible to share peripheral hardware such as printers. You could place a dedicated printer-server computer with a number of printers (laser, dot matrix, and color) in a central location. Or you can place printers closer to groups of workstations. If you have printers in several locations, consider what applications will require heavy, medium or light use of printers. Then ask what workstations will most likely be used for those applications. A business standard is to provide one printer for every two to four workstations depending on the type of applications used.

When selecting a network printer, look at the following:

- Types of printing usually done (text, graphics, combination).
- Quality of printing needed (letter quality? near letter quality? draft?).
- Color or black and white?
- Rate of printing (pages per minute) for print, graphics and a combination.
- Rate of printing for color, if applicable.
- Amount of memory (RAM) in the printer.
- Size of paper input (number of sheets) for sheet-fed printers.
- Types of paper accepted (letter, legal, envelopes, transparencies, sheets, form-fed).
- Purchase price.
- Price of ink/toner, paper, etc.
- Network interface card (sometimes included as standard feature).
- Network operating system supported by the printer.
- Availability of printer driver software.

In many school situations, especially those in which students are printing out drafts of papers and information from CD-ROM resources, speed becomes important. "Spooling" is a term often used in association with network printers. It refers to the protocol or procedure for prioritizing tasks including the order in which print jobs will be handled. If you have impatient students and teachers, you will need to inform them that repeatedly hitting the print key will not get their document printed any faster and will only increase the waiting time for other people.

Other Hardware

If CD-ROMs will be used on your network, you will need to think about additional hardware at the file server location and at those workstations that are most likely to use the CD-ROM applications. If speakers are not built into the workstation computer, external ones may be required for some CD-ROM programs. There is information on networking CD-ROMs later in this chapter.

Modems and fax boards can be placed on a network either attached to individual workstations or to a server computer. Attached to a server, a fax modem will only be able to be used by one workstation at a time. However, all workstations will be able to send and receive faxes and to communicate via the modem. To allow several workstations to use a modem at once, you need several telephone lines.

The work of backing up the server's hard drive is made a little easier if you can back up on tape or cartridge rather than floppy disks. A tape backup drive uses magnetic tape to make a copy of the data on the hard disk while the cartridge drives use specially designed cartridges. Automatic tape backup systems will backup an entire system at preset times. As CD-Recordable disks and DVD recordable disks gain acceptance, it might be possible to back up to one of these. Just as you would use several sets of floppy backup disks, you need to use several tapes or cartridges. If you backup on tape number 1 today, backup on tape number 2 tomorrow and tape number 3 the next day. Store your daily or weekly backup in a place other than the building where the file server is located.

Uninterruptible power supplies (UPS) and surge suppressors should be basic purchases for your network. A UPS on an "intelligent" LAN can power the network for a brief period of time and shut it down gradually during a major power outage. Check Chapter 1 for more complete information.

Putting It Together

Putting a network together is a complex task because everything needs to be configured to work together. Switches need to be set properly, cable connections have to be correct, software must be set up properly. This is not work for the novice. You need to have good technical support lined up as one of the first steps of getting a network. Then, find a network professional to do the actual installation.

Be sure to find someone you can work with and talk to. Remember, a true expert can explain things so that a novice can understand. The expert can be someone at the company from which you are purchasing your network or a separate contractor. Be clear and concise in terms of what you expect the network to do, how large it will be, and the software that will run on it.

While most bid specifications will be quite detailed and, for a large network, best handled by a consultant or trained network expert, sometimes you can write simple specifications for a small network. When Annette

Thibodeaux, the librarian at Archbishop Chapelle High School in Metairie, Louisiana, wanted to obtain bids on a small network that would link thirteen second-hand computers, she used the following bid specifications:

- Provide a file server (486, 120MB or greater hard drive).
- Install a Novell 3.11 20-user operating system on the file server.
- Install network interface cards in the file server and workstations.
- Install the network adapter hub or concentrator.
- Install network connectors and connector cables.
- Install cabling.
- Install networking software.
- Configure the network menu.
- Set up the printers.
- Install the tape drive backup and its accompanying software.
- Provide network training.

Writing in *T.H.E. Journal*, Philip Hess, computer technician for the North Hills (Pennsylvania) School District adds these helpful hints:

- In wiring a lab, have three separate circuits; one for the monitors, one for the computers, and one for things that are never turned off, like the server.
- Be sure to keep up-to-date copies of all maintenance and start-up disks accessible and to keep backups of those same disks in a secure place.
- Keep the server secure.
- Provide temperature control for the server and for any lab computers.
- Store files for any administrative applications running on the network on an external SCSI hard drive that can be plugged into another machine if the entire network crashes.
- Have all prospective lab technicians screened by the state police or FBI.
- Provide plenty of training about what's on the network.

What can you put on the network?

Just about any electronic resource can be put on the network, including CD-ROM reference sources. Let's look at a few examples.

General Application Software. This includes word processing, database, spreadsheet, and other general computer programs.

Educational Software. Everything from tutorials to complete computer-assisted instruction packages are finding their way onto networks.

Electronic Mail. Electronic mailboxes can be established for everyone in the school, including the students. But remember, people need access to the network to read their mail.

Schedules/Calendars. Save paper and tell everyone about a school or community event by typing a brief message on the network. Set up calendars of all school meetings and events.

Groupware. Groupware programs are designed for several people to use as a group. Although at different workstations, members of the group can work together on a single project. Groupware programs can be a free-form type where participants jump in at random or a structured format where each participant takes a turn in a set order. Groupware builds on the ideas of collaborative and cooperative learning. Possible uses include collaborative simulations, discussions of topics, brainstorming ideas, and peer editing.

Library resources. The online catalog, CD-ROM periodical indexes, CD-ROM encyclopedia, specialized reference works, and other library resources can be accessed any place in the school that the network goes.

Network management software. Specialized programs allow the network administrator to keep track of network statistics and patterns of use, run system diagnostics, monitor workstation activities, and prevent virus infections.

Classroom management software. Easy-to-use programs help teachers set up projects for their classes, monitor student use, and track student progress.

As you think about the software that you might want to put on the network, realize that several things can happen when you attempt to put a program on a network.

- It works fine on your network.
- All or parts of it will not run.
- It runs on a network configuration other than the one you have.
- It runs but really is not aware of the network.
- Sometimes it runs and sometimes it doesn't.

If you have problems, take notes and call a technician or the software manufacturer for help.

How can you troubleshoot network problems?

The best way to solve network problems is to avoid them at all costs. In a perfect world, that would mean that once the network is up and running, you would not change it in any way. Of course, while "freezing" the network might be the ideal way to prevent network problems, it certainly is not realistic. Any network will need to grow and change over time. Unfortunately, those changes are often the source of network problems. In an effort to catch problems before they turn into nightmares, follow these guidelines:

- Be sure the network manager has formal training for the specific brand of network. Check for licenses or certification through training from or approved by the manufacturer of the network software.
- Keep up-to-date through workshops and Internet discussion groups.
- Keep your file server in a secure place.

- Allow only authorized people to have access to the file server.
- Follow the network operating system's guide to managing your network.
- Make regular backups of the entire network.
- Document any changes to the network so that you can reverse them. Yes, it takes time to write things down, but, unless you have an excellent memory, your notes will save you time in the long run.
- Change only one thing at a time and retest the network after each change.
- Backup all of your files before making any changes.
- Once you have a problem, try to isolate it by disconnecting pieces of the network in a systematic manner.
- Know your own limits. Realize that there may be some things that you can fix by yourself or changes to the network that you can reverse. However, also keep in mind that there are certified network technicians for a reason. Networks are complex and repairing them is best left to an expert.
- When contacting the technician, be as specific as possible about any changes made to the network and about the problem itself. Don't say "It won't work." Tell the technician that after you loaded the latest update to the CD-ROM periodical index none of the workstations could access that database.
- When you or the technician find the source of the problem and have solved it, write down the solution as well as the steps you took to find the problem.

What are some guidelines for purchasing software?

Because of the growth of LANs, a great deal of the software for sale today can be purchased with a network license. It is illegal to purchase a non-network version for use on a network if a network version is available.

In some instances, there is no special network version of a program, but the non-network version will run on a network. In that case, even when a network version is not available, be sure that you have the manufacturer's permission to use that particular software on the network. Include a statement that the software will be used on a network and provide a brief description of the network on your purchase order. If you are buying from a jobber or distributor, do not rely on their verbal assurances. Keep any written permission on file for verification.

Licenses can take one of several forms. First there is the single flat figure for a network version. Another variation is a per node cost for each node on the entire network, without regard to the likelihood of that software being used at all of the nodes. Finally, there is a per user cost that limits the number of workstations that can use the software at one time. With this option, the program can be used at any of the nodes on the network, but there is a limit on how many nodes can be actively using the program at a given time. Chapter 2 of this book contains information on the various software copyright licenses.

Purchasing a network license is not always the most economical way to obtain multiple copies of a single software title. Before you spend several times the purchase price of a single copy to obtain a network license, try to determine how many people are likely to use the program at one time. Carol Mann Simpson of the Mesquite (Texas) Independent School District reports that a CD-ROM vendor wanted to charge $41,000 per year for a full-text database because there were 35 separate schools on their LAN. Even when it was shown that only four schools would be likely to use that particular database, the vendor would not lower the price. As a result, she wound up purchasing a 24-user license of a similar database from another vendor at a much more reasonable price. Management software on the network keeps track of the number of workstations using the database at a given time. In other cases, several single user copies may be a better purchase than any network license.

Some software licenses for network use come with a variety of restrictions. In some cases, a distinction is made between the use of the software on a LAN and on a WAN. With the distinction between the two of these blurring at the edges, be sure that you and the manufacturer agree on the definition. Your LAN might extend over several miles to a number of schools in your district. On the other hand, the manufacturer might consider any use outside a single building to be a WAN.

Realize that with some software, especially CD-ROM periodical indexes, you may only be renting instead of buying the software. In those cases, you may be expected to return the old disc each time a new one is received. Be sure that you understand the terms of your license and know whether it is a rental or purchase agreement.

Explore the costs of future upgrades to your software. This is especially important when buying updates of CD-ROM indexes and other reference sources. Can you negotiate a special price if you agree to purchase a set number of updates? Will a subscription to the print version of the source decrease the cost of the electronic version? Can you arrange for a special trial period to be sure the software will work on your network and be used by your students and teachers?

What about network security?

A network provides access to hardware and access to information. This amount of access is the main reason that you need to take security measures. Be sure that your equipment is secure. Use the security measures from Chapters 1 and 2 to protect each of the workstations. Be especially protective of the file server in a LAN. Keep it in a secure place and make regular backups of the entire hard drive.

Your network operating system should provide you with levels of passwords or some means of giving different users access to different parts of the file server's hard drive. Some systems require two separate passwords for access to the system. The system administrator's passwords should provide complete access to the system. Be sure that everyone with access to the system is careful with the passwords. Remember a few rules about passwords:

- Be sure that the network software encrypts (either hides or does not print on the computer screen) your passwords. That way, no one can look over your shoulder as you type in your password.

- Never write passwords down and leave them beside the computer.

- Always change the passwords that come with the system to your own passwords.

- Do not use the initials of the school for anything but low level (general student use) passwords.

- Do not let others use your passwords.

- Do not use your initials as passwords unless they are part of a two-part password.

- Try to use a number/symbol and letter combination that might be difficult for others to guess. You can remember "1001nights," "B#today" (Be sharp today), or 10/25Max (my dog's birth date and name); but who would guess they were network passwords?

How are intranets used in education?

One way to increase the usability of a network is to offer more services on the network and make it easier for people to use those services. Corporations were the first to see the advantages of making some of the same services that are available on the global Internet and World Wide Web available on their own internal network. Thus began the rise of intranets, privately owned, secure networks based on Internet technologies with Internet-like features. Extranets are created when two or more intranets are linked for collaboration

An intranet uses the same standards as the Internet; TCP/IP (Transport Control Protocol /Internetworking Protocol) communications and, frequently, the Java programming language. With TCP/IP, you can use a "Web Browser" such as *Netscape* (more about this in the chapter on the Internet) to access, read, and display HTML (Hyper Text Markup Language) files, the same type found on the World Wide Web. This means that an intranet can provide things such as e-mail, file transfer, bulletin boards, discussion groups, home pages, and interactive applications.

Because TCP/IP is platform independent, an intranet can be used with almost any network cables, topology, transfer architecture, or NOS. Setting up an intranet on top of an existing LAN means installing TCP/IP drivers, a Web browser, and accessories such as movie viewers and authoring tools on the network. You can run your intranet on the regular network file server or you can upgrade to a Web server by installing Web server software such as Apple's *MacHTTP* or Novell's *Web Server for NetWare*.

Using an intranet can be beneficial for both students and teachers. Here are just a few of the things that can be done in an intranet networked school.

- Home pages can be created for each class with pictures or short video clips.

- Assignments and announcements can be posted on class home pages.

- Students can work cooperatively on projects by sharing files of information.

- Students and teachers can access the library catalog and CD-ROM resources.
- Student work can be displayed.
- Electronic bulletin boards can provide whole-school communications.
- Everyone can communicate privately through e-mail.
- Students can view digital movies and listen to audio files.
- Internet access may be available.
- Student work can be transmitted to teachers electronically.
- Blank forms can be set up for orders, reports, and registration.

Are there special considerations for CD-ROM?

To cut down on the cost of hardware for a number of standalone CD-ROM workstations in the library and to provide more access to CD-ROM resources, many librarians are networking their CD-ROMs. Unfortunately, not all CD-ROMs can be networked and not all networks can deliver acceptable video and sound from CD-ROMs. However, while a network will not eliminate the need to have some stand-alone computers or workstations with CD-ROM drives, networking some CD-ROM resources is a popular option in many schools.

Chief among the advantages of networked CD-ROMs are the following:

- Decreased costs when a number of high-speed multimedia workstations can be replaced by less expensive computers.
- Increased security of keeping the CD-ROM hardware and software in a nonpublic area of the library.
- The ability of several people to use one networked CD-ROM title at the same time.
- Ease of installing updates to database CD-ROMs.
- Decreased costs when less expensive software licenses replace multiple copies of CD-ROM resources. (Do not assume this is always true. Check individual programs.)

In a very simple configuration, a CD-ROM player on a computer can be shared on a peer-to-peer network such as LANtastic. In some small server networks, a CD-ROM drive or tower can be run off the file server. However, CD-ROM drive access is much slower than hard drive access and can tie up the server computer. More complex layouts include the use of a dedicated CD-ROM server computer in addition to the file server or a CD-ROM tower with its own microprocessor.

If you plan to use CD-ROMs on your network, be sure you have the proper software to run them on the network. Librarians report that many CD-ROM installation programs are not set up for network use. Running them on the network requires good technical support from a vendor.

When you are considering CD-ROM purchases for network use, ask the vendor for names of locations where their products are successfully running on a network. Then, contact those places and ask questions about the installation process, technical support, and maintenance support. You might even try running the CD-ROMs on standalone computers before you add them to the network. This will give you some experience with the hardware and software.

Just as the CD-ROM software must be able to run on the network, the network operating system must also be able to handle the CD-ROM drives. LANtastic has a good reputation for handling CD-ROMs on a peer-to-peer network. For server networks, a number of companies make special CD-ROM access programs. This is an example of a situation in which you need to network with other librarians to find out what is working for them. Contact companies and check references before you purchase.

If you are adding CD-ROM capability to a server network, you will probably want to have a computer to act as a dedicated CD-ROM server. The CD-ROM server will need enough power to direct and manage a number of CD-ROM drives, or a tower. With 70% to 75% of the educational CD-ROMs being PC based, more and more schools are installing PC CD-ROM servers. Look for a computer that has a Pentium chip, at least 16 or 32MB of RAM, a one gigabyte hard drive, monochrome monitor, and a SCSI interface. (While some argue for E-IDE drives, SCSI seems to be retaining its number one position.) Seven CD-ROMs can be daisy chained on one SCSI card. Newer SCSI cards allow two or three chains of seven drives per cards. Users report the best results with a PC using the EISA (Extended Industry Standard Architecture) or PCI (Peripheral Component Interconnect) bus rather than ISA (Industry Standard Architecture). Provide extra drive space to allow for the growth in the number of CD-ROM titles and the number of CD-ROM discs per title.

If, instead of adding a CD-ROM server, you elect to install the CD-ROM drives on the existing network server, you will need to consider redirector software for the workstation computers. This allows the network operating system to access the CD-ROMs for individual users. Keep in mind that redirector software takes up RAM on the workstation computer and may increase the amount of RAM that a workstation needs to use some CD-ROM resources.

The CD-ROM drives that you select to use on your network should have a SCSI interface and a fast transfer speed of 6X, 8X, or even 10X. While you can use external drives, cut costs by mounting several internal CD-ROM drives in a cabinet, daisy chaining them together, and then running one cable from the cabinet to the CD-ROM server.

On existing networks, you may need to upgrade the workstations where the CD-ROMs will be used. Many CD-ROMs require VGA or SVGA monitors and need at least a 486 chip (Pentium is preferred), 4MB of RAM, and a mouse or trackball in the workstations.

Computers older than a 386SX with 4MB of RAM will present problems on the network because of their speed, memory, and inability to function in a Windows environment. Because some data is downloaded from the server and stored in the workstation computer until needed, running multimedia CD-ROMs may require higher powered workstations with at least 8MB of RAM . In running CD-ROMs with sound, you need to check the compatibility of the sound card on the workstation computer and the requirements of each CD-ROM. The more CD-ROMs that you place on the network, the more workstations you will probably need to access them. With full-text databases, students will spend more time at the workstation or need access to a printer to obtain a hard copy of their information. If you charge for photocopies, you might want to have a per-page printout fee or a minimum number of free pages with a charge for anything over that amount.

Vicki Sherouse, SLMS at Lakehill Preparatory School in Dallas, Texas, has linked a server computer with CD-ROM to the computers in the school's computer lab. The lab computers function as workstations and allow her to use the lab to teach the use of CD-ROM resources.

With CD-ROMs on the network, you will probably want special network management utilities such as menu software that can either be part of the network operating system or be purchased as a separate program. Such management programs monitor the usage of the various CD-ROMs by tracking the number of users of each CD-ROM, monitoring usage, and limiting the number of users of a specific title to the number specified by that CD-ROM's copyright license. In addition, some management programs have time-out capabilities. If someone at one workstation has been using a CD-ROM program but then has no activity for a specified amount of time, the menu program disconnects that workstation's use of the CD-ROM. This prevents a particular CD-ROM resource from being tied up indefinitely when a student who has been using that CD-ROM leaves without properly exiting from the program.

Remember, networking CD-ROMs is not always cheaper than buying several copies of a CD-ROM. Compare the price of standalone computers with CD-ROM drives to the cost of a network. Be sure you consider the cables, network interface, network operating system, and the computer to act as the CD-ROM server. Don't forget to factor in security and management as well as access to the CD-ROMs.

What happens after the network is installed?

A network is something that should keep providing communications and access to information for a long time. But to make the most of the network, you need to manage it. And, just like any other school resource, the network needs to be publicized. Remember to provide training for users. Use some of the ideas in this book for implementing an automated library system or technology in general to communicate with the network's potential users. Demonstrate its benefits by using the network in your own teaching and communication with teachers and students. Don't forget to develop sample units and target specific teachers for cooperative lessons using the network resources. Then "network" and share your experiences with others.

Bibliography

Almquist, A. (1996). How to purchase, set up, & safeguard a CD-ROM network. TECHNOLOGY CONNECTION, 3 (2), 14-17. An overview of the hardware and software required to network CD-ROMs.

Axelson, M. (1996). Networking 101. *Electronic Learning,* 16 (1), 52-55. Axelson answers the nine biggest questions that educators have about networking.

Building your infrastructure: the basics of cabling and connection. (1996). *Technology & Learning*, 16 (7), 40-49. A discussion of LANS, WANS, and the cables that connect them.

Burke, D. (1994). What you need to know before networking CD-ROMs. *Computers in Libraries,* 12 (6), 16-22. In this technical article, Burke discusses selecting CD-ROMs, configuring workstations, creating or selecting a user interface, deciding on printer options, and maintaining security on a network.

Cornish, M. & Monahan, B. D. (1996). Network primer for educators. *Educational Technology*, 36 (2), 55-57. Provides a very simple overview of networks in general as well as the Internet.

D'Ignazio, F. (1996). Think intranet. *Learning and Leading with Technology,* 24 (Sept), 62-63. Discusses the growth in intranets for schools.

Ekhaml, L. & Ekhaml, P. (1995) Some questions and issues about school networking. *School Library Media Activities Monthly,* 11 (7), 37-9. The authors answer eleven important questions about networks including "what does every network administrator need to know?" "why is a basic knowledge of networks advantageous to a school library media specialist?" and What is one of the most dangerous threats to networks?"

Farmer, L. S. J. (1996). Growing your LAN piece by piece. Technology Connection, 3 (2), 29-31. Advice on how to connect a library LAN to the rest of the school.

Farmer, L.S. J. (1997). Make it accessible. Technology Connection, 3 (10), 26-67. Discusses ways that networking can support the curriculum and issues some praise for collaboration and some cautions regarding plagiarism.

Farmer, L.S. J. (1995). Networking: moving beyond sneaker net. Technology Connection, 2 (5), 37-39. Basic information about networking is presented by a librarian who recounts her own experiences. Read, learn, and laugh with her.

Graves, G. (1997). Mission control: Dawn of the strategic intranet. *NewMedia,* 7 (6), 32-38. Provides examples of the uses that businesses are making of Intranets and examines some of the products that they are using.

Hess, P. (1996). Tips & tricks for K-12 educational LANs. *T.H.E. Journal*, 23 (9), 84-87. A computer technician, Hess shares some tips he has found in his years working with an elementary school and in a district's computer labs.

Howden, N. (1996). *Local area networking for the small library*. New York: Neal-Schuman. This is the second edition of a popular title in the How-To-Do-It Manuals series.

Huber, J. (1997). Networking nuts and bolts for schools of the future. *Media & Methods,* 33 (Jan./Feb.), 67. Discusses T-1 lines and wireless LANS.

Jacobson, S. (1997). What's new in intranets? *Electronic Learning*, 16 (6), 12. Gives brief examples of several schools that have Intranets.

Lederman, T. (1995). Local area networks for k-12 schools. *ERIC Digest*, ED389277. This four page document, which provides an overview of LANs, is available free from the ERIC Clearinghouse on Information and Technology, Syracuse University, 4-194 Center for Science and Technology, Syracuse NY 13244-4100.

Lyndes, Craig. (1996). Network how-to. *American School Board Journal,* 183 (3), A18-A21. This special section includes advice on buying and installing LAN as well as a discussion of protocols, wiring, hubs, and routers.

Malkin, G. (1994). *Comprehensive networking glossary & acronym guide.* Englewood Cliffs, NJ: Prentice Hall. This 200-page book is a comprehensive guide to even the most technical networking terms.

Mastel, V. L. (1996). Building a school district's wide area network. *T.H.E. Journal,* 23 (9), 69-75. Mastel, a computer technician, explains the technical aspects of installing a WAN in the Bismark (North Dakota) Public School District with Macintosh, Apple II, DOS, and Windows operating systems.

Mather, B. R. (1995). The promised LAN: Networking resources in the media center. *School Library Journal*, 41 (10), 44-46. A librarian discusses planning and installing a LAN and provides ten tips for a successful LAN planning.

Mathias, C. J. (1996). Wireless, coming to a LAN near you. *Mobile Computing & Communications,* 7(10), 53-67. Discusses the costs and how to select components for wireless networking.

McCain, T. E. & Ekelund, M. (1996). *Computer networking for educators.* Eugene, Oregon: International Society for Technology in Education. Excellent overview of networking as well as examples of PC and Macintosh networks.

McClanahan, G. (1996). CD-ROM network configurations: Good, better, best! *MultiMedia Schools,* 3 (1), 75-77. McClanahan ranks CD-ROM networks as follows: peer-to-peer networks are "good," CD-ROM drives on the file server are "better," and a dedicated CD-ROM file server is "best."

Norman, H. (1996). *Local area networking for the small library: A how-to-do-it manual for school & public librarians.* New York: Neal-Schuman. This second edition of a popular book contains valuable information on setting up a LAN but is aimed primarily at public libraries.

November, A. C. (1995). Wired together—then what? *Electronic Learning,* 15 (Sept.), 20. Jeff Holte discusses how the St. Louis Park, Minnesota, school district established their local area network.

Perone, K. (1996). Networking CD-ROMs: a tutorial introduction. *Computers in Libraries,* 16 (Feb.), 71-77.

Pezzulo, J. (1993). Networking and the impact on school library media programs and services. *Computers in Libraries,* 13 (Feb), 46-47. Suggestions for the "proactive" librarian.

Schuyler, M. (1996). LANs, WANs, CD-ROMs, and networking. *Computers in Libraries*, 16 (April), 40-43. Discusses and evaluates the network at the Kitsap Regional Library System, Washington.

Simpson, C.M. (1992). Questions to answer before you branch out on a CD-ROM network. THE BOOK REPORT, 11(3), 25-26. "An experienced 'networker' shares many of the answers that she learned by experience."

Stokley, F. J. (1996). Creating an electronic village. *School Administrator,* 53 (April), 36. Stokley discusses his concept for an electronic village linked to the technology-rich classrooms of the local schools.

Thibodeaux, A. (1995). A new network with secondhand computers. THE BOOK REPORT, 14 (2), 23. One librarian recounts her experience setting up a small network.

Van Horn, R. (1997). Electronic messaging: growing your own WAN. *Phi Delta Kappan,* 78 (8), 662-663. Following the rule of "never install technology in a school if you can't teach someone there to run it," Van Horn describes the use of FirstClass for e-mail.

Watson, O. (1996) A networked learning environment: Toward new teaching strategies in Secondary Education. *Educational Technology,* 36 (1), 40-3. Network at the Townview Magnet Center in Dallas, Texas, provides student access to videocassettes, cable and satellite television, CD-ROMs, software applications, and the Internet.

Weinstein, P. (1996). Intranets: Time for a Web of your own? *Technology & Learning,* 17 (2), 50-57. An in-depth discussion of the use of Intranets in schools.

Weiss, A. M. (1995). What's in the walls; copper, fiber, or coaxial wiring? *MultiMedia Schools,* 2 (4), 35-39. A detailed look at wiring specifications.

Wolfe, J. L. (1994). Special considerations for networking multimedia CD-ROM titles. *CD-ROM Professional*, 7 (1), 55-57. Discusses configurations for servers and workstations, SCSI devices, data caching, and system troubleshooting.

Chapter 7

Computer Telecommunications

Ask three people what "telecommunications" means, and you will probably get three different answers. If you apply the broadest definition to the word, it refers to any communication over a distance whether by telephone, telegraph, radio, television, or computer. By that definition, e-mail, fax, Wide Area Networks (WANs), the Internet, and the World Wide Web are forms of telecommunications.

In this section, however, we will start with the narrow definition of telecommunications as "telecomputing" or communications using a modem and plain old telephone service (POTS) lines to transfer information between computers. Then, we will move beyond that definition to discuss fax machines, fax modems, and scanners as well as the growing field of telephony and video conferencing. Finally, once we know about the appropriate hardware and software, we will explore electronic bulletin boards (BBSs), look at some WANs for education, and discuss online services. All this will serve as an introduction to the next chapter of the book in which we will take a more in-depth look at the Internet and the World Wide Web.

How will telecommunications affect school libraries?

With a computer and a modem, you can figuratively knock down the walls of your library and provide your students and teachers with access to information throughout the world. You can:

- Help a class in your school participate in a joint project with a school in Australia.
- Search the online catalog of the local public library or college library to locate a book for a student.
- Help a class search reference sources that you cannot afford to purchase for your library.
- Let students correspond with electronic "pen-pals."
- Find out the news from all the other schools in your district without leaving your library.
- Read the education news section of a paper every day without having to subscribe to it.
- Place an order to a jobber and have immediate confirmation.
- Use the cataloging information in a regional, state, or national database to do your cataloging.
- Type a message to the members of a state library committee that you serve on and, with the push of a button, send everyone a copy.

- Let everyone in the state know about a special event happening in the school library.
- Help a teacher join in a discussion about special education with a group of educators from another country.

Of course, coupled with the joy of telecommunicating, there are some drawbacks. Chief among these is its popularity. As more and more people find out about telecommunications, telephone access lines become jammed and people find they have to wait to gain access to the various systems.

Before you start demanding the right to telecommunicate in your library, let's look at the hardware required. Then we can explore each of the types of communications in a little more detail.

What hardware is required?

Modem

In addition to a computer, the major hardware required for telecommunications is a modem. The modem's sole purpose is to allow computers to exchange information over regular telephone lines. It usually does this by changing the computer's digital signal into an analog signal. Why? Because we speak analog, but the computer speaks digital. Although we can speak over regular telephone lines, the computer cannot. A modem (MOdulator/ DEModulator) at one end translates the computer's digital information into analog, which is sent over the phone lines. At the other end, another modem reverses the process.

A basic model of computer telecommunications appears in figure 7.1. Later we will see how advances in technology are changing this basic model.

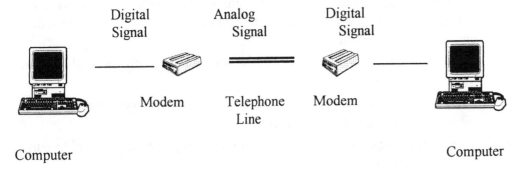

Figure 7.1 Conventional Telecommunications

Internal and external modems are available. Both do the same job, but the internal one is best if you do not have any space near your computer. It also costs less than an external modem and is more difficult to steal.

For the internal modem card, you need an empty expansion slot inside your computer. To install: pull the plug, open the computer case, insert the card, set any necessary switches on the card to tell it what communication port (COM) you will be using and close the case. In some cases, if you purchase your internal modem from a local computer store, the employees will install it free or for a nominal fee.

If you are reluctant to open the computer case or do not have a local vendor, the external modem is for you. It can be installed in five easy steps:

- Pull the plug on the computer.

- Unplug the telephone line from the phone and hook it to the modem. Then use another piece of telephone line to hook the modem to your telephone. (If you have only a telephone wall jack without a telephone, just hook the line from the modem to the wall jack.)

- Use a cable (usually an RS232) to connect the modem to the computer's serial port, usually COM1 or COM2.

- Plug in the modem and the computer.

- Turn on the modem and the computer.

If you have call waiting on your telephone, be sure to disable it before using the modem.

When you purchase your modem, be sure to tell the dealer the type of computer you have so that you can get a cable with the proper connections. (Figure 7.2 shows an external modem)

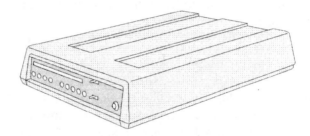

Figure 7.2 External Modem

Some people find an external modem to be very reassuring, because they can watch the lights on the panel to be sure the connections are made and the communications are really going through. If there is a problem with an external modem, you can reboot just the modem by turning it off and on without rebooting the entire computer as you would do with an internal modem. In addition, external modems are transportable from computer to computer and to the repair shop.

Modems are often referred to by their speed of sending information or rate of transmission in bits per second (bps). Some people use the term baud as a synonym; however, the baud rate is not exactly the same as the bps transmission rate and includes additional information. In general, however, when working with modems and telecommunications software, you can think of baud and bps as the same.

The modem's transmission rate can vary from 300 bps to over 56,00 bps (56K). Just use the number of bps as a means of comparison. At 2400 bps, a modem will send information eight times as fast as at 300 bps. Most modems offer a range of transmission speeds from 1200 bps or 2400 bps to their top-rated speed. Thus, a 14,400 bps (14.4K) modem can usually transmit from 1200 bps to 14,400 bps. The usual choice for a school library is a minimum of 14,400 bps while 28.8 is preferred and 33,600 bps (33.6K) is ideal.

In selecting modems, look for ones that meet industry standards for data transmission. The newer 28.8K or 33.6K modems should meet the international v.34 standard which will reduce the modem speed as low as 2400 bps automatically, depending on the transmission conditions. In addition, they should meet either or both of the following error correction and data compression standards: V.42 error correction and/or MNP (Microcom Networking Protocol). Accompanying the V.42 error control standard is the V.42bis standard for data compression.

Older PCs may not be able to work with an external fast modem. The internal chip that controls the serial port may not be able to run at 38.8 Kbps or above. To test a computer running Windows, run the Microsoft diagnostic (MSD) to check the communication ports (COM). If the UART (Universal Asynchronous Receiver/Transmitter) message says 16450 or 8250, you have a problem. The faster modems need a rating of 16550 UART. The solution is to get an internal modem with its own UART or to upgrade the serial port card on the computer.

The newest modems for regular telephone lines are the 56K modems. They take advantage of the ADC (Analog Digital Converter) used by telephone companies where signals are taken from the business and residential supply lines and changed for mainline transmission.

Promising to be twice as fast as the 28,800 bps (28.8K) modems, the 56K modems have several problems. First, no matter how great the modem, the bandwidth or carrying capacity of the telephone lines help determine the speed of transmission of data. Many old telephone lines to homes and schools will not carry data faster than 28.8K. The remedy for that is to use one of the newer telephone lines such as the ISDN (Integrated Services Digital Network) or a T1 high bandwidth telephone line that can carry up to 1.5 Mbps. Unfortunately, in many places, these higher bandwidth telephone lines come at a high price unless a special rate has been negotiated for the schools.

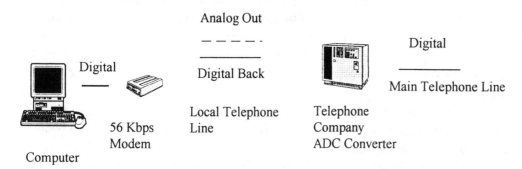

Figure 7.3 Data Transmission with 56K Modem

Another problem with the 56K modems is that there is no standard for data transmission. Unlike 28.8K or 33.6K that meet standards such as the v.34 standard or v.42 bis standard, the 56K modems use one of two incompatible technologies. K56Flex modems are supported by Lucent Technology and Rockwell, who supply components for brands such as Hayes, Compaq, and Hewlett-Packard. U.S. Robotics is selling modems known as "2x." In order to get the high-speed modems to work, both ends of the transmission have to be using the same technology. If you are using 2x and dialing into a place using K56Flex, you will not get the high speed connection. Furthermore, some people have reported that the high speed modems will not automatically drop back to a slower connection rate. Finally, even if both ends of the telecommunications link are using the same 56K technology, the higher speed works in one direction only.

What should you do? My Internet Service Provider (ISP) just issued a bulletin to all clients advising them to wait to purchase the higher speed modems until the 56K standard is released. Although modem manufacturers are promising that their 56K modems will be upgradable to the new standards, only one manufacturer, Hayes, guarantees a free upgrade. If you do want the higher 56K speed, be sure your modem will match the technology of the receiving modem.

Since modems can communicate at a variety of speeds, how do you select the right speed? There are several things to consider. First, remember that two modems can communicate only as fast as the highest rate they have in common. For example, if one modem can communicate up to 9600 bps but the other is only capable of 2400 bps, the two will communicate at 2400 bps. A modem cannot exceed its rated transmission speed. Most online services and bulletin boards will tell you the fastest speed they can accept.

Generally, select the highest transfer rate the systems will accept. However, in situations in which you pay to communicate with another computer, the amount you pay per minute or hour can vary depending on the speed of your modem. Because you can get more information in a shorter time with a fast modem, the higher transmission rates may be charged more. Check these charges before you decide that faster is cheaper.

When you select a modem, look at a few things besides the transmission rate. A universal standard for PC modems is something known as "Hayes compatible." Be sure your modem is 100% Hayes compatible. Also check to see if you can understand the documentation, including installation instructions, that comes with the modem.

In addition to standard modems, there are a variety of special ones. For portable computers, there are PCCard modems that transmit up to 33.6K and special ISDN Cards for transmissions up to 128K. On networked computers, multifunction cards combine the modem and Ethernet LAN interface.

ASVD and DSVD Modems

Since the time of Alexander Graham Bell, telephone lines were designed to transmit voice. With the advent of computers, these same lines began to carry data. For a long time, it was an either/or situation until the advent of ASVD (Analog Simultaneous Voice and Data) and DSVD (digital simultaneous voice and data) which allow "personal conferencing" or the transmission of both at the same time over telephone lines. Previously, VoiceView has allowed a user to switch between voice and data, but not both at the same time.

For simultaneous voice and data, DSVD is the best. The difference between ASVD and DSVD modems is that with the ASVD modem the voice is not converted to a digital signal. The resulting audio is inferior to the DSVD modems. If both ends of the connection have DSVD modems, voice and data can be sent together. If only one end has a DSVD modem, the transmission is data only. To use a DSVD modem, you need a computer with a sound card, speakers, and a microphone. In addition to allowing one person to "write" on the other person's monitor while talking to him/her, a DSVD modem lets a technical support person diagnose and repair a problem on a remote computer.

Wireless Modems

With the growth of portable computers (notebook and laptop size) and cellular telephones, companies developed wireless modems that can be used with cellular telecommunications. Many of these modems are found as PC Card modems and contain their own battery and antenna. Wireless telecommunications is a rapidly changing field that is currently plagued by problems of quality of the signal and distortion. If you happen to be sending data over a wireless modem from your cellular telephone and drive out of the transmission area, you break the connection and the data is lost.

Telephone Lines

For years school librarians have talked about the importance of having a telephone in the library. With the spread of computerized library systems, it became more important than ever to have a telephone to get support and technical advice about library systems, networks, and other technologies. Now, a telephone line in a library can provide a means to access the world's information superhighway.

For telecommunications, the line does not have to be dedicated (used only with the computer) and can be used for both computer and voice communications, though not at the same time. You should, however, have a direct outside line from the library (a line that makes you dial a "9" first is OK) or a line that does not go through an operator-assisted switchboard. The ideal is to have two lines; one only for computer use and one that has a cordless telephone on it so you can take it with you when you need to go to troubleshoot technical problems. If you need to carry the handset throughout a library or school building, be sure that your cordless telephone base unit has the power to transmit to it. Higher powered units cost more but are worth it.

Switches on the line can prevent unwanted interruptions. Check with your telephone equipment supplier, office supply store or computer dealer. There are also switches that automatically send an incoming call to the computer, to the telephone, or to the fax machine. While some phone systems will not accept a modem, most will. Rotary or touchtone service is fine; most software can adjust to either. If you have the "call waiting" feature on your phone, it must be turned off before a line is used for telecommunications or the transmission can be interrupted by an incoming call.

Telecommunications hardware needs special surge suppressors on any equipment that is connected to either the electric lines or the telephone lines. The integrated circuits in modems are susceptible to power spikes and surges from either line. Look for special power bars or units that have both electrical and telephone outlets.

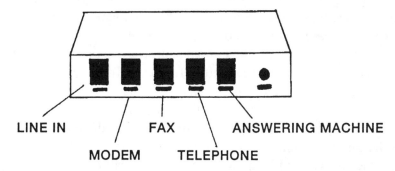

LINE IN   FAX   ANSWERING MACHINE

MODEM   TELEPHONE

Figure 7.4 A telephone line management device that will route incoming calls on a single line to a modem, fax machine, telephone, or answering machine.

ISDN Lines and T1 Links

Because most telephone lines cannot handle high-speed communications, people have looked for alternatives. One solution is ISDN or Integrated Services Digital Network. Four or five times faster than a regular modem, an ISDN transmits digital signals rather than converting the computer's digital signal to analog for transmission. ISDN technology can transmit data, voice, still graphics and video, and is usually more reliable than regular telephone lines. BRI (Basic Rate Interface) supports speeds up to 128K or 300K with data compression. PRI (Primary Rate Interface) supports speeds of 64K.

To use ISDN, you replace the conventional modem with a terminal adapter (TA) which must be configured for the telephone company's ISDN switch. In the United States, a network termination unit (NT1) is required as an interface between the TA and the ISDN phone lines. To maintain the high speed of data transmission, there must be an ISDN connection at both the sending and receiving end.

While extremely fast, ISDN technology is not cheap and not universally available. In addition to installation fees and the cost for the ISDN terminal adapter, there are usually monthly fees plus per minute charges. If you are paying for an ISDN connection, be sure that you are getting one. Monitor your connection speeds and be sure that your telephone company has made the appropriate changes in your local telephone hook-up to ensure ISDN service.

If ISDN is not fast enough, look at a T-1 link. With a transmission rate of 1.54 Mbps, ISDN earned *Smart Computing*'s title as the mother of data transmission. We'll look at it in more detail in the chapter on the Internet since its primary use in schools is to provide high-speed Internet connections.

Will you need special software?

Your computer needs special telecommunications software to communicate with the modem and to allow your modem to communicate with another computer's modem. Many modems come with software, but these programs vary in how easy they are to use.

If you are in doubt, check with the WANs or online services that you use. Do they require or recommend a particular program? In some instances, you can even download the software from that WAN or online service.

In these cases, the program is probably shareware. If you decide to use the shareware software, ethically you should send the registration fee to the shareware developer. The nice thing about shareware is that you can try it before you actually buy it, but be careful of viruses. To get you started, a few frequently used communications programs are listed in the Resources section.

Telecommunications software will help you configure or set up your computer and modem to work together. This is usually done the first time you use the program or by running a special part of the program known as "setup." Sometimes the software will autodetect or automatically determine the port to which the modem is connected. Other times, you will have to type in the name of the port, usually COM1 or COM2.

While a good telecommunications program offers many features, one of its primary functions is to help you set your communications protocols or communications parameters. In other words, the software ensures that the way your modem sends information is the way the receiving modem is expecting it. These protocols include such things as the transmission rate, the parity or error checking (odd, even, or none), stop bits to signal the end of a character, and the number of bits in a word. You really do not have to worry about the precise meaning of these. What you do need to know is that you have to use your software to specify how to communicate with the other computer. If you do not, you might wind up sending and receiving garbage.

To set the parameters to match each receiver, first learn what the computer you are connecting to expects. This information is usually contained in the literature you received when you got your passwords and telephone number to call. Somewhere you should see things such as 8 bits, 1 stop bit, and no parity. Or you might see "7E1" which translates to 7 bits, even parity, one stop bit. Another parameter you may need to set is the duplex, or the directions in which data travels over the lines. The options for this are half or full. A final parameter is what is called terminal emulation. In other words, your computer is acting like a certain type of terminal. Common terminal emulations are VT-100 and TTY.

Once you have identified the parameters expected by the telecommunications services that you call, you can use your software to enter them each time you call. If you use several services, keep a card listing the parameters of each. Some software programs will allow you to establish an electronic telephone book in which you list the number and parameters of each computer that you connect to. Then, you use your mouse to point to the number you wish to call and the software does the rest, automatically setting the parameters and dialing the number.

If you do not have a software program that sets the parameters automatically, keep a card such as that shown in Figure 7.5. Make a backup of the card to keep in a secure place in addition to the one you keep by the computer.

Your communications software will also help you after you establish communications with another computer. With a modem, it is possible to transfer complete files from one computer to another. For example, complete information on how to use a WAN may be downloaded from the network computer to yours. (Of course you have to know enough about the network in advance to establish communications with it.) Often these network manuals can be 50 or more pages long.

Service	Phone	# Bits	Parity	Stop	Duplex	Terminal
LibPen	999-9999	7	O	1	Full	VT-100
EdPen	888-8888	8	E	1	Half	TTY

Figure 7.5. Sample Card to Keep Track of Modem Parameters

There are several file transfer protocols or standards for sending data with a modem. One of the most common is what is known as Xmodem. What you need to do is read the documentation to see how the other computer likes to send information and follow the directions in your software documentation to setup that protocol. If you cannot find a listing for the protocol the sending computer likes, try Xmodem.

Besides setting protocols and keeping phone books, communication software can also serve as a very simple text editor that will allow you to edit some of the text files that you receive. This editor might also allow you to write your entire message before you connect to an electronic bulletin board or mail service. Then, with a few key strokes, you can send a long message.

One feature of some communications software programs that I do not use at school is the automatic log-on. With this feature, you enter your passwords into your computer once. Then, each time you connect to the other computer, the program automatically sends the passwords for you to log-on or gain entry to the other computer's system. This may be fine for a system that does not track its users or charge a fee. But, with this feature, anyone who uses your computer can connect with that other computer system through the modem using your identity. Unless you are 100% sure that you are the only person who has access to your computer and its software, think twice about using the automatic log-on.

What can you do with a modem?

In telecommunications, you are basically using your computer with its modem to communicate with a computer that is connected to you only through the telephone lines. You can use your computer in one of four general ways:

- To send electronic mail
- To connect to an electronic bulletin board
- To become part of a WAN
- To access online services and networks (including the Internet/World Wide Web)

The lines between these four uses are fuzzy. For example, you can access an online service and send mail through it. But, for the sake of simplicity, we will look at each of these in order.

What is e-mail?

According to an article in the February 1997 issue of *PC Novice*, the most heavily used telecommunications function either on or off the Internet is e-mail. Carrying 3.5 million messages in 1976, electronic mail grew to carry 812 billion messages in 1994 and is projected to carry 6.9 trillion messages by 2000. In 1997, it is estimated that over $25 billion dollars will be spent on e-mail systems. But for all of the money spent on it, electronic mail or e-mail is nothing more than using a computer to send a message to another person over the telephone lines. Let's look at an example to see how e-mail works.

Ben and Yolanda are both librarians in the same school district. Although they are co-chairing a special automation committee, their schools are miles apart. One morning when Yolanda arrives at work, she checks her electronic mailbox by using her computer and modem to call the school district's central computer. After entering her name and password, she is shown a list of the items in her mailbox. One is a memo from the superintendent with a schedule for the next teacher workday. The second item is from Ben. She enters the number 2 and the full text of Ben's note comes up on her screen. He is suggesting several dates for the next meeting and has sketched out an agenda.

After checking her calendar, Yolanda enters an "r" for reply. She makes a few changes to Ben's agenda, indicates the best times to meet, and sends everything electronically to Ben. Then she uses the system's downloading capability to have the district's computer send the superintendent's memo to her computer where it is stored on a floppy disk.

Yesterday, she used her word processor to write a public relations piece that she wants the district library supervisor to approve before she sends it to the local newspaper. Yolanda uses her communications software to get the news release from her hard disk and send it to her supervisor. Exiting from the electronic mail system, Yolanda uses the text editor in the communications software to print out the superintendent's memo.

After a busy day in the library, she goes back on the e-mail system. There is a note from Ben about the next committee meeting and the agenda. She knows he used a special feature of the e-mail system to send the same message to all ten committee members.

In this example, the two librarians used several features of electronic mail:

- sending and receiving messages
- downloading documents
- replying to messages
- sending one message to several people
- typing information offline and then sending it
- avoiding delays in delivering information

While electronic mail may be part of a LAN or a WAN for a school system, it may also be part of a regional or statewide network, a commercial telecommunications service, an Internet Service Provider (ISP), or a national or international network. To send a message, you must know the unique address of the person that you want to receive the message. It's the same as learning a person's address and zip code for regular mail. Sending the message is fairly simple technologically as long as you and the receiver are using the same e-mail network. If not, the message needs to go through bridges and gateways to the other network. But, as more networks are becoming interconnected and the Internet grows, the barriers are coming down. SMTP (Simple Mail Transfer Protocol) is the set of rules that most e-mail software uses to be sure that a complete message is delivered to the proper address. Data carried over the Internet must meet the TCP/IP (Transmission Control Protocol/Internet Protocol) standard. These are actually two protocols or standards for transmission of data over a network that were developed for what is now known as the Internet. When data is sent following these standards, the message that is received matches the message that is sent.

Because of a standard called the Domain Name System, reading an e-mail address can be fairly simple. Let's look at a fictitious e-mail address: catdoc@animalvet.pet.com. Reading from the @ sign to the right, we find the domain and subdomain(s), in this case the subdomain pet at the main domain animalvet. The "com" tells us that this is a commercial site. From the @ sign to the left is the user name or identification, in this case probably a nickname for a cat veterinarian. Common major domain codes are:

com	commercial site
edu	educational institution
gov	government site
int	international
mil	military site
net	a host for a network
org	private or nonprofit organization

All this does not mean that there is a uniform address system. Because of the existence of many networks, not all of them follow the same address protocol. Currently the IETF (Internet Engineering Task Force) is developing a standard address system protocol.

The growth of the Internet has been accompanied by a tremendous growth in the use of e-mail. While many people have e-mail through an Internet Service Provider, a commercial fee-based online service, or a WAN, many people without those connections have not had access to e-mail. Recently, some services have begun to offer e-mail only. Among those, Juno has been developed as an "e-mail-only online service." This free service is financed through ads that are targeted to each user based on a profile that the subscriber completed when signing up for the service. Juno provides free software to access its service and encourages users to share that software with others. The only things needed to access Juno are a PC with a 386 or higher processor, Windows 3.1 or higher and a minimum 9600 bps modem. See the Resources section for the toll free sign-up number. Juno provides local connections in over 200 cities. In other cases, you will need to pay the long distance telephone charge to the city nearest you.

To whom can you send e-mail? With the right network connections, you can write to the President of the United States. His address is president@white house.gov. (There's no period at the end of his address.) Schools can join projects like "Computer Pals Across the World." This program links schools in different parts of the world to provide a learning experience for both sets of students. Students in Alaska and Australia became e-mail pen pals to share cultural information and discuss current events. With regular mail systems, the current events would almost have become history before a letter could be sent and a reply received. Teachers and SLMSs can use e-mail for professional growth by communicating with others in a school district, state, or throughout the nation.

E-mail and all online behavior have their own set of rules and conventions for use. There is "netiquette" (net etiquette) or rules governing your behavior online. In addition, most networks have a list of their own special rules and regulations that all users are expected to follow. In most cases, resist the impulse to e-mail everything to everyone. According to the Center for Business Innovation in Boston, unwanted e-mail is becoming a problem with trivial things mixed in with important items. My education network has a policy that prohibits the sending of any "chain" letters or similar documents through the network. Check your network and follow its rules. For some general hints on e-mail writing, such as keeping notes simple and short, or using the subject line as a headline, read the article by Ekhaml listed at the end of this chapter.

Frequent users of e-mail have developed a set of "emoticons" or symbols that allow a writer to express emotions on the computer screen. For example, send a smile with this symbol :-) Read sideways, that's a happy face symbol. Turn the last symbol upside down and you convey a less cheerful outlook :-(Check the Resources section for Intenet sites listing emoticons.

Some people see e-mail as fostering a rebirth of letter writing. However, a few words of caution are in order. Because of the immediacy of e-mail, it is tempting to reply as soon as you receive a message. While this is great in most cases, if a message upsets you, it may be best to delay your reply until it is controlled by reason rather than raw emotion. Also, remember that e-mail is not private. In the business world, courts have ruled that messages sent on a company-owned e-mail system can legally be read by administrators and used in the evaluation of employees. Even on a school network, you should assume that someone else can read your mail. "Packet sniffing" is a process to check the "packets" of data transmitted over networks and can be used to browse e-mail.

To keep e-mail private, people have developed encryption software which codes e-mail messages so that they can be read only by the specified recipient. PGP (Pretty Good Privacy) is a leading developer in this area. The U.S. Government, however, is concerned about the use of encryption software by terrorists and drug traffickers and has attempted to curtail the use of it.

If you are using a commercial service for e-mail, look for ways to cut down on your connect time. Try writing messages offline and going online to send it. (This works well with younger children, too.) Avoid retyping information by appending word processing files to your e-mail. Finally, purchase the fastest modem that your e-mail service will support.

What can students do with e-mail ?

When many librarians and teachers think about e-mail, they believe that you need an Internet connection to make it possible. However, many states provide e-mail accounts for teachers and students through state-wide networks. In addition, some services provide "free" e-mail accounts to anyone with a modem. There are a number of ways students can benefit from using e-mail:

- Practicing keyboarding skills
- Integrating writing, spelling, and grammar across the curriculum
- Developing questioning skills to obtain information
- Exchanging information about their community, state, country with other students
- Exchanging weather data and making comparisons
- Writing stories using information gathered through e-mail
- Investigating a profession or occupation
- Working collaboratively on solving a problem
- Interviewing an expert on a topic
- Becoming involved in supporting a community project

As with any curriculum project, advanced planning is important. Notices of students and classes interested in working with others on a project using e-mail are found in many places including newsgroups and listservs on the Internet, state and local network discussion groups, and print periodicals. If you don't see a "Call for Participation" that fits the curriculum project you are interested in, post a call of your own. Most of the planning is the same type that you would do in planning any assignment; identify the unit of instruction, establish objectives, identify how you will integrate information problem-solving skills and the use of e-mail into the unit, determine the information that the students will need to complete the project, and identify the possible learning outcomes and the assessment criteria (grading rubric, etc.) that will be used for student evaluation. There are, however, some special things you may want to check in advance when using e-mail.

- How long (days, weeks, months) will the students need to have access to e-mail ?
- How much time will the students have for daily computer access?
- Does the e-mail service limit the amount of time you can spend online? (Some state networks limit the amount of time that an individual teacher or librarian can spend online during a day.)
- What daily costs are there to connect to the mail service?
- How easily can the students use the software?
- Can e-mail be composed offline to save any connection fees?
- How will the students be accessing the e-mail each time?
  Whole class sending letters?
  Whole class, each individual sending a letter?
  Several groups, each group sending a letter?
  One small group from the class sending a letter?

- What types of projects will the students be doing?
    Informal electronic "keypals?"
    Simple information (cultural) exchange?
    Writing skills development?
    Collaborative writing projects?
    Mentoring?
    Information collection?
    Information collection and analysis of collected information?
    Collaborative problem solving and investigations?
    Contests?

School districts usually include an e-mail policy for students, faculty, and staff as part of a general "acceptable use policy" (AUP) for all information technology. (See Chapter 8 for more information on AUPs.) One caution to keep in mind when allowing students to do e-mail projects: remind them never to give their home address or phone number to any e-mail pal unless they have permission from home and from the school.

What have other schools done with e-mail? From Texas, Barbara Jansen reports that her students completed the following e-mail projects: fifth graders exchanged information with students in Finland for a history project while second graders worked with peers in Canada, New Hampshire and Finland to gather and compare weather data. Her fourth graders wrote folktales from information gathered through e-mail. In Pittsburgh, Pennsylvania, students use e-mail to send their work to other students for comments and evaluation. Students at Manhasset Junior High in New York sent e-mail to specialists to gather information for a debate on wetlands. Through CORE (California Online Resources for Education), high school students correspond with their peers in Germany and Austria.

What is a fax machine?

Telefacsimile or fax machines are showing up everywhere as prices begin to fall. In fact, they are now being sold for home use. Basically a fax machine is a scanner that translates the information on the printed page into a form that can be sent through the telephone lines to a fax machine on the other end. This machine reverses the process and prints out the document. Each fax document is accompanied by a cover page or note that lists the sender, destination, and number of pages being sent.

Fax machines are placed in two categories depending on their output. The top-of-the-line machines are plain paper faxes. They produce a high quality permanent image and tend to be expensive, although prices are falling. The cheaper thermal paper fax machines use a special thermal process to print and produce images that are not as crisp as the plain paper fax. In addition, thermal paper has a tendency to curl and the images on it fade over time. One solution is to photocopy all important thermal paper faxes when you receive them.

In selecting a fax machine, consider how it will be used. If most of your work will involve sending faxes, a thermal fax will work just fine. The quality will depend, in part, on the receiving machine. It will also depend on the quality of the original, so use the best copy you have when you send a fax. Other features to consider are the speed of transmission (between 6 and 20 seconds per page) and the number of pages that you usually send. Lots of pages sent over long distances mean you need a fast machine with an automatic document feed. Running out of paper when receiving a fax transmission can be a problem. Internal memory in some fax machines will store several pages until the paper supply is replenished. Other features to look for are broadcast faxing which automatically sends the same document to several numbers, and delayed transmission which delays sending documents until the night or evening rates go into effect.

FAX Machine Purchasing Checklist

Paper: plain _____ thermal _____

Printing speed: _____ pages per minute

Transmission speed: _____ pages per minute

Document feeder: manual _____ automatic _____

Internal memory: _____no _____ yes _____size

Special features

    Broadcast faxing _____

    Delayed transmission _____

Some people worry that if they purchase a fax machine they will begin to get the electronic equivalent of junk mail — junk faxes. The Federal Communications Commission has regulations about junk faxes. In the business world, faxes cannot be sent on an unsolicited basis unless there is an ongoing business relationship. The same would seem to hold true for the nonprofit community as well.

How are fax machines used in libraries?

Informal networks to deliver documents by fax have been in existence for some time. Now school libraries are beginning to formulate networks expressly for the purpose of providing periodicals by fax. Two excellent examples of such networks are the Houston Area Independent School Library Network (HAISLN) and Pennsylvania's Access Pennsylvania. These networks have established formal protocols that provide extensive guidelines for requesting and sending documents and cover such things as response times, hours when requests can be made, article length, and copyright compliance. HAISLN even gives members the right to suspend their participation in the network during periods called "end-of-term madness."

Extensive descriptions of these programs appeared in M. Wilson's article in the May 1988 issue of *Online* and in D. Hand's article in the February 1993 issue of *School Library Journal*. Copyright compliance, often a concern in establishing fax networks, is covered in Hand's article.

What is a fax modem and how is it used?

The newest advances in facsimile transmission are fax modems, which combine the advantages of a fax machine and a computer modem. They allow you to type information on your computer either by using a fax program or by typing the document in a word processing program and then selecting the fax modem instead of the printer for the output. With this arrangement, you can send a document to another person's fax machine or fax modem without ever printing it out. Many fax modems come with a "phonebook" program so that you can store the names and fax numbers of individuals as well as distribution lists. Other features include stock or user-designed cover pages for the faxes, delayed faxing to take advantage of cheaper nighttime rates, optical character recognition software so that you can edit the fax documents that you receive, and an automatic receive mode. Be sure that your fax modem meets either Class 1 or Class 2 transmission standards, preferably both. Only Class 1 modems allow you to transmit file attachments in fax modem to fax modem transfers

Like regular fax machines, fax modems have several advantages over the U.S. Mail and other delivery services. They are fast and usually cheaper than mail or delivery services, especially when express or overnight service is required. Even when long distance calls must be placed, software with a delayed faxing feature allows you to send the faxes when the phone rates are down instead of during peak business hours. A fax modem can send a document to and receive a document from a regular fax machine. In addition, a fax modem can act as a scanner so that you can then use OCR software for editing instead of retyping a document. There's more about this feature later in this chapter.

Depending on the computer's printer, when a document received by a fax modem is printed, the quality is higher than a thermal fax and as good or better than plain paper ones. In some cases, you will not even want to print a document received on a fax modem; it can be read on the computer screen without ever needing to generate a hard copy.

Many businesses are using a technology known as "fax-on-demand" so that consumers can obtain written information and technical support quickly and inexpensively. When calling a business with fax-on-demand capabilities, you are usually given a voice menu system. Using the telephone keypad, you select the numbers of the documents that you would like to receive. Finally, you enter your fax number and the documents that you selected are sent to your fax machine. This is an excellent way to receive answers to FAQ (frequently asked questions). See the Resources section of this book for some fax-on-demand phone numbers for technology suppliers.

What are the special concerns with fax modems?

When a fax modem receives a document from a fax machine, the incoming document is stored as a graphics file, not a text file. What does that mean? The page is stored as a complete picture with dark and light areas, not as individual letters that can be changed in a word processing program.

For the computer to change the graphic of the page into letters, you need to have optical character recognition (OCR) software that will translate the visual patterns on the fax into a text that the computer can recognize. This is an emerging field of technology and a lot of progress has been made since the first OCR programs appeared on the market. If you tried some of the early OCR programs that were distributed with computer fax machines or scanners, try some of the new programs. When I began writing the second edition of this book, one of my students helped me by using a scanner with current OCR software to "read" the text for two sections. It did the job perfectly.

One drawback of the fax modem is that the information to be sent must be in the computer. That means that it has to be typed or scanned into the computer. While many documents are typed on a computer, then printed and fed into a fax machine, others such as letterheads, signatures, graphics, and magazine articles are not on a computer and need to be scanned into the computer before they can be sent through a fax modem. A scanner is a computer peripheral (add-on electronic device) that converts a printed page into a digital form that can be stored on a computer disk. Scanners are available in both black and white (grayscale) and color models.

There are several types of scanners: hand-held, flatbed or desktop, sheetfed, and slide scanners. All of them, however, operate on the same principal of recording the areas of light and dark or the areas of various colors from the image being scanned into the computer where they can be stored on a disk, edited, printed, or faxed.

With a hand-held scanner, you hold the scanner in your hand and slide it across the text or graphic. The scanner transfers the information to the computer where it can be used or stored. Even if you use plastic scanning guides with a hand-held scanner, you need a steady hand to drag the scanner with a slow, easy motion. Often, hand-held scanners are limited in the size of the image that can be scanned unless accompanied by special software that allows several passes of the scanner to be placed side-by-side to create single image. Hand-held scanner software should be checked to see how complete this merger of strips actually is and how well the OCR software works. Hand-held scanners are not the best choice for printed material that you plan to edit.

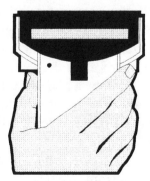

Figure 7.6 Hand-held scanner

Other scanners are designed for larger originals than the hand-held. With a sheetfed scanner, the original is fed into a unit similar to a fax machine. As the original moves under a scanning device, the image is read and transferred to the computer. Many sheetfed scanners have large trays and can feed a document through the scanner a page at a time, making them ideal for scanning large amount of single sheet materials such as photocopies.

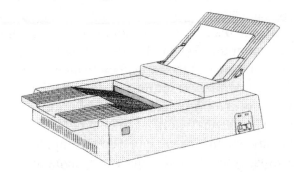

Figure 7.7 Sheetfed scanner

If you need to scan three-dimensional items or books, a flatbed scanner is the answer. This scanner is similar to a small photocopier. Place the text or graphic on the scanner, close the lid, push a button, and the transfer takes place.

Figure 7.8 Flatbed scanner

Did you ever wish you could copy the images from slides into the computer? With a slide scanner, you can. Not only will these scanners copy the slide image, they operate at a much higher resolution than other scanners, thus allowing you to enlarge the scanned image without a significant loss of quality.

Pressure from businesses and the growth of home office has encouraged the development of "multifunction" computer peripherals. What this means is that, instead of having a separate photocopier, scanner, printer, and fax machine taking up space near a computer, manufacturers have developed devices that combine the functions of several or all of these machines into one piece of hardware. A multifunction unit can be a real asset in a library. In addition to saving space, another advantage of the multifunction peripherals is that it usually costs less to purchase one of these devices than to purchase several single function ones. A disadvantage, however, is that when one part of the device is broken, the entire multifunction unit will need to be sent for repairs.

The computer treats data from any type of scanner the same way a fax modem handles information from a fax machine; it stores it as a graphics file. That means you need OCR software to use the text as anything other than a graphic. If you use OCR software, a flatbed scanner will help you achieve the highest accuracy. If you plan to use a scanner with your fax modem, look for one that is TWAIN (driver that sits between or "twain") compliant.

What hardware and software do you need?

Hardware is important. A fax modem needs to be connected to a computer with at least 640K to 1MB of RAM with 4 to 10MB of storage space on the hard disk. Part of that hard disk space is needed for the fax modem software and part is needed to store incoming faxes. (A fax document stored as a graphic takes up more space than a comparable text file.) A typical fax modem operates at speeds from 2400 to 9600 bps and comes in both internal and external varieties. That means you need a free internal expansion slot or COM port in the computer to connect it.

In addition to serving as a fax machine, a fax modem can be used as a plain modem to access other telecommunication services. A fax modem can be put on a LAN either directly at individual workstations, attached to the file server, or on a special fax server. No matter where it is placed, it does need access to a telephone line.

Although many fax modems come bundled with software, you might want to upgrade to a program with additional features. The software programs used with a fax modem should allow your computer to send and receive faxes in "background mode" while you are using your computer to do other things. Remember, however, that when the computer is turned off, the fax modem is turned off as well and cannot receive incoming documents. If you leave your computer on just to receive faxes, be sure to turn the monitor off or to use a screen saver program if you have an older monitor.

Most software has the ability to distinguish between regular phone calls and faxes and reacts differently to each. Other software features include those found in regular modem software programs as well as an automatic cover sheet for outgoing messages, a delay send feature to take advantage of evening phone rates, and a phone book feature to send the same fax to several people.

Fax modems are ideal replacements for fax machines when computer generated documents need to be sent. If the sender and the receiver were both on the same e-mail system or on interconnected networks, the document could be transferred that way. However, in many instances, it is easier and more private to send information via a fax modem.

What is computer telephony?

Basically, computer telephony or CTI (Computer Telephone Integration) is the combining of functions of telephones with computers. To put it into perspective, it is a $3.5 billion dollar industry that, according to *Computer Telephony* magazine, is growing at a rate of 30% a year. Projections are that e-mail will give way to "messaging" systems in which e-mail, voice mail, pagers, and faxes are managed by the computer in a single integrated system in which one electronic mailbox will hold all types of messages. Special programs will send voice mail messages to the "typed" e-mail inbox and will also allow e-mail to be "read" by the computer over the telephone. In addition, the voice mail component will provide custom messages for individuals who call into the system. All this can be combined with a database linked to phone numbers and an autodialer. With such a system, it would be possible for you to tell the computer to call the home of all students who have overdue materials at the end of the semester and leave a message to please return the items, leave a reminder in their e-mail boxes, and send a copy of the list to classroom teachers.

To take advantage of telephony, you will need to start with a modem, phone line, and a computer with sound, preferably one that switches to a power conserve mode when it is inactive since the computer will need to be left on for the system to function. Add to that a high-quality surge suppressor for both electric and telephone lines and voice modem software. A telephony board which you place inside the computer combines telephone, answering machine, phone dialer, fax, and sound interface on a single card. You can even add features for music on hold, speakerphone, and video conferencing. When purchasing additional hardware and software for a PC, be sure items meet the TAPI (Telephony Application, Programming Interface) standard established by Microsoft and Intel for the interface between a telephone system and a single computer. There is also the TSAPI (Telephony Services Application Programming Interface) developed by AT&T as a protocol for connecting telephones to networked computers.

There is a downside to telephony. In addition to the cost of leaving your computer on all the time, there is a possibility that a computer hacker can use the telephone connection to get into your computer to plant a virus. If you use telephony, protect your system with virus software.

What is videoconferencing?

When you think about the things that we currently do with plain vanilla telephone lines, it is amazing. In addition to carrying our voice conversations, these overworked lines are expected to carry computer data in analog format and even video. It's no wonder that the telephone lines cannot live up to all of our expectations, especially when we expect them to transfer moving video images. For smooth video, images need to be shown at the rate of 30 frames per second. At a lower rate, the video looks like a second-rate pre-1920 black and white film. Unfortunately, most telephone lines can only carry video at the rate of 5 to 10 frames per second. While ISDN lines are a solution, their higher costs often prohibit their use unless special arrangements have been made for educational institutions and libraries.

In spite of these problems, videoconferencing is a growing technology. The basic idea is to use a DSVD modem, video camera, microphones, speakers, and a computer with a video capture board or other method of getting video into the computer, sound card, and video conferencing software to send voice and moving images through the telephone lines to another computer. While picture can be transmitted over POTS lines, an ISDN-based system will provide the best quality. Videoconferencing done over a LAN can slow down other functions on the LAN.

Several packages have been developed for home and school videoconferencing, others for business and industry. A new standard from the International Telecommunications Union, known as H.324, is projected to eliminate many of the proprietary software problems and allow more cross-platform compatibility. Compare vendors and, for a quality conference, look for a system that will project the video at 15 or more frames per second with a full-duplex speaker phone and an interactive whiteboard. Other features to look for include application sharing, file transfer, audio and video quality, ease of use, and the ability to connect several people. Also check the minimum system requirements to be sure the program will work on your computers.

The following are some of the products listed in the resources section: *VideoPhone Kit* for the Mac, *CU-SeeMe* from White Pine, Shark Multimedia's *See Quest*, and Connectix *Quick Camera*. *CU-SeeMe* was originally developed at Cornell University (that's where the CU in the name originated). A free version is available at http://cu-seeme.cornell.edu. None of these are ideal but they will put you on the road to desktop videoconferencing with some options costing less that $100.

If you don't have your own camera, you can still become a lurker on conversations. Check the *Cu-SeeMe* event guide on the Internet or use one of the search engines to look for *CU-SeeMe*.

What is an electronic bulletin board?

An electronic/computer bulletin board system (BBS) is actually a messaging system. Originally designed as a place to post messages and to respond to them in an open manner (everyone reads everything) rather than a private manner (e-mail), many BBSs were started by special interest groups (SIGs) whose members needed a way to stay in touch and find answers to problems. When computers were still being built from kits and computer stores were few and far between, BBSs provided a place where people could get help with their computer problems. Post a problem today and receive some suggestions by tomorrow.

As they grew, many electronic BBSs provided more than public bulletins. E-mail, conferencing, online chats, software for downloading, information on a variety of topics and a gateway to other networks were some of the services that they began to provide. With the growth on the Internet/ World Wide Web, most BBSs have changed and have moved, in whole or in part, to the Internet. There are, however, still a few local BBSs, including some run by schools. In some instances these BBSs are similar to an intranet, providing Internet-like services to a local community.

Many of the features now accessed through the Internet began on BBSs including conferences and chats which have now become listservs and newsgroups. With a chat, a topic may be posted for discussion. Then, people could dial into the BBS and use their computer and modem to type comments about the topic. Several people may become active in the chat at the same time, and a lively "discussion" may occur. Lurkers are people who read but do not send messages. Flamers are those who are obnoxious or insulting. Unlike an informal chat, a conference is a little more structured, held at an announced time, and may even be restricted to individuals who have previously been given special passwords. The actual conference format, however, is similar to a chat.

Many BBSs are easily accessed and free except for the price of the telephone call. Others may charge a fee or may only be accessed through another service that has a fee. If fees are involved, direct BBS fees are usually minimal. Fee online services are discussed later. However beware; although BBSs are often a source of shareware or even free programs that you can download to your own computer for future use, programs downloaded from bulletin boards are often a source of a virus.

Open BBSs have limited controls; anything except illegal or obscene activities are permitted and anyone can access it. A closed BBS can be accessed by passwords only. People entering the system as a guest (a first-time user or someone without passwords) are not allowed to write or post messages on the system.

Some schools have set up their own BBSs for faculty, staff, students, and even the community. Depending on the number and variety of services that are offered and the number of telephone lines into the BBS, different computers are necessary to manage the data. Usually allowing e-mail, messages, chats, and conferences, an education BBS is often managed by a microcomputer. For a large scale BBS, a mainframe or minicomputer may be necessary.

To set up a small system, you'll need a computer, modem, and dedicated phone line. If the BBS will only operate during evening hours, you can get away with using a telephone that carries voice messages during the day but is unused after school. Special BBS management software governs the operations and should monitor the activities of the users. Some software will even keep a record of who uses the BBS and what they do. This record keeping is not much good, however, unless there is someone to serve as the systems operator or SysOP to administer the bulletin board. This person oversees all the operations, troubleshoots problems, and makes sure everything on the BBS is legal. The resources section of this book contains a list of some BBS software programs.

How do WANs fit in?

For this discussion, we will define WANs as the regional and state networks that are developing for education and library services.

In the library field, several states began to develop union catalogs of library materials on WANs to publicize the holdings of libraries and to share cataloging responsibilities. Using a modem, a participating library could search the WANs file server for information. At first, only academic and large public libraries put their holdings on the centralized computer's database. Later they were joined by school libraries, special libraries, and small public libraries. With the development of CD-ROM, the central database was often distributed to all member libraries in that format and the network began to add other telecommunications functions.

At the same time, regional and state education agencies began to develop their own telecommunications networks. By 1997, 38 states either had or were planning networks that include schools. Complete information on a state by state basis is available on the Texas Education network (TENET). See the Resources section for the compete online address. States including California, Florida, North Dakota, Texas, and Virginia started to provide state-wide access by K-12 educators to a variety of resources free or for a minimum charge. With a computer, modem, telephone line, and appropriate passwords, it has become possible for any teacher, SLMS, administrator, or, in some cases, student to access the network.

To see exactly what activities might occur on a WAN, look over the shoulder of one middle school librarian as she uses Virginia's educational network called VA.PEN. After she calls a local telephone number (or an 800 number) she enters her passwords and begins a busy telecommunications session in which she:

Reads and answers her e-mail. One of her messages tells her that a draft copy of the state's new recertification proposal is in her mailbox. Pressing a series of keys on her computer, she directs VA.PEN to download the information to her computer's floppy disk. She can print that out once she ends her telecommunications session.

Sends an e-mail message to a SLMS across the state about coordinating an author's visit to both schools.

Sends a message to all seven members of the Virginia Educational Media Association (VEMA) committee she chairs.

Selects an item labeled "electronic news, conferencing, and bulletin boards" and sees the following list:

1. local newsgroups for norfolk.vak12ed.edu
2. Virginia's PEN newsgroups
3. k12net newsgroups
4. USENET national/international newsgroups
5. Student Discussion Groups
6. Daily Report Cards
7. CNN Newsgroup Guides
8. USA Today news summaries
9. Access *all* newsgroups at the Same Time

Enters option 2 and selects the VEMA group. She reads the latest messages on the network's special VEMA bulletin board and notes an announcement of a special workshop at one of the state universities that she would like to attend. Seeing that the date of an event that she listed on the bulletin board has passed, she removes the outdated listing.

Uses the foreign language bulletin board to post a request for suggestions about some foreign language computer programs she is thinking about purchasing.

Enters option 1 and reads the notices on her local school district's special librarian's bulletin board and sees that one of the elementary schools that just "lost" their sixth grade to a new middle school has some books to give away. She sends a request for a copy of the list directly to that librarian's e-mail address.

Scans the librarian's bulletin board from a neighboring school district and notes that they are having a lively debate over which of two CD-ROM encyclopedias to buy for the middle schools. Remembering her own experiences, she posts a quick suggestion about the quality of the illustrations in one of the sources they are considering.

Downloads the curriculum guide for today's CNN program so that she can print it out later for the teachers.

Remembers that there was a lot of discussion at yesterday's faculty meeting about an education article in *USA Today* and checks the news summaries for more information or a follow-up.

Returns to the main menu and checks Only the Best, a selection aide for media, to see if it has a review of those foreign language programs.

Looks at the listings in Academy One, a special student-oriented gateway section of VA.PEN that is sponsored by the National Public Telecomputing Network. She sees a project is just starting and makes a note to mention it to the seventh-grade teams for possible use.

Accesses the online catalog of the University of Virginia to check on a book that a teacher doing graduate work has requested.

Running out of time, she logs off and begins a busy day in the library.

If this SLMS had more time, she could have used her state network as a gateway to other networks and services that we will talk about later in the section on the Internet. The total cost to her local school for all of the time that she spent online was zero; her state pays for funding the VA.PEN network.

WANs are useful, but beware. Think about the use of photocopy machines in schools. Somehow, paper has proliferated. The thinking seems to be: it's so easy to make one copy, why not make 10 copies and send one to everybody? WANs can be addicting in almost the same way. It's tempting to read every message on every bulletin board on the system, post replies to every query, and explore all of the services. The result is busy signals and long waits to get connected. Some state networks limit the time that an individual can spend on the network each day. In most cases, they do provide the option for individual teachers and librarians to negotiate for longer access times when completing special projects.

Unfortunately, there is not enough time in the day and enough people staffing every library to allow the amount of time to be spent on the WAN as the librarian in our example spent. But, while WANS can be addicting, with a little self-control, they can expand the resources of your library significantly.

What are online services or online networks?

Online services or networks have been developed that combine bulletin boards and e-mail with the features of WANs; add other special features such as home shopping, travel reservations, or research in a variety of specialized reference sources; and make the services available to people on a national or international level. According to a 1996 national survey, 35% of the people connect to the Internet through online services. Some of these online services are recreational, others are educational. Some are free, others charge a fee for access and use.

Commercial Services

Telecommunications networks such as America Online (AOL), Prodigy, CompuServe, and the Microsoft Network (MSN) are commercial services whose business is making money. The fees charged by these and other networks generally fit into one of the following categories:

- Basic monthly fee: the user pays a monthly fee for unlimited use of the network's services.

- Basic fee plus: the user pays a basic monthly fee that entitles him to a core of services. There is an additional charge per hour for the use of additional services.

- Pay for use: there is no monthly fee. The user is billed only for the actual time spent online. Again, telephone charges may be added to the bill. In some cases, a pay-for-use service may have a small fee to obtain passwords or a small annual membership fee. This is especially true if the service sends print newsletters or other publications to users.

In addition to the basic fees, there may be telephone charges to connect to the network. If the network has an 800 number or a local number, the telephone charges are minimal or are even eliminated. Some services are accessed through special telephone networks which, while they may have a local number, still charge a telecommunications fee.

When working with students and nontypists, it is important to note that keyboarding skills are very important when using a network, especially when using a commercial one. The "hunt and peck" method becomes expensive when you are being charged for each minute that you are using the service.

Commercial services can be further subdivided into three types: those with very specialized interests for a particular profession, those with a wide research emphasis (KnightRidder, WilsonLine), and those that have a wide variety of services (Prodigy, America Online, and CompuServe).

Research Networks

Of special interest to school librarians are the online database services or online reference services that provide access to research information. They can be used in a manner similar to print reference sources but with the help of a computer to do the searching. In general, these services have a variety of research databases in several categories:

Bibliographic. These index-style databases provide the bibliographic citation to indicate where the complete information can be found. Some bibliographic databases also contain abstracts.

Full Text. The complete document can be found in this type of database. An encyclopedia is a full-text reference source.

Numerical. Statistics and other strictly numerical information are contained in numerical databases.

Directory. Electronic versions of reference directories can be found online.

These computer-accessed reference tools have many advantages over their print counterparts. They are:

- updated more frequently.
- ideal for locating rapidly changing information.
- an excellent source for infrequently used but important reference materials.

- often less expensive, per use, than print sources.
- a means to locate information that is not usually found in a school library
- ideal for information on very current subjects that are not found in traditional reference sources.

Although the fee structures of the research services vary, some provide special rates for school libraries. In addition, most of the online services used in school libraries provide training and free access time to help librarians become familiar with the sources that the services offer.

Most of these services rely on a search strategy called Boolean logic, which is the same strategy that is used to locate information in some online library catalogs. Boolean logic is simply the use of the terms "and" and "or" in a special way. "Or" is used to identify synonyms; "and" is used to link different terms. Appendix A has more complete information on Boolean searching using ERIC as an example.

Sometimes users are intimidated by Boolean search strategies used to locate information on these online services. It seems difficult at first glance, but the services have developed worksheets that simplify the process. In addition, some services have menu systems that you can use instead of relying on your knowledge of Boolean searching. There are also programs such as SmartSearch from SearchWare that allow you to structure your search in advance (offline) before you even connect to that expensive online service.

The use of online database services is so widespread in school libraries that several states have incorporated online searching as a skill in the library skills curriculum. One excellent curriculum guide that contains online skills is Pennsylvania Online, issued by the Pennsylvania Department of Education. It was reprinted, in part, in the May 1987, issue of *School Library Journal* in the library computing section.

ERIC

Sponsored by the U.S. Government, ERIC (Educational Resources Information Center) is a free database that, because it is in the public domain, is available in a variety of places including CD-ROM in many libraries, through state WANs, on commercial services such as AOL and CompuServe, in research databases such as KnightRidder, and through the Internet. Because many people use telecommunications to access ERIC, we'll look at it in this section.

ERIC is the world's largest database of educational resources and is used by teachers, librarians, students, and administrators, among others, to find references to current information about all areas of education. Individual ERIC Clearinghouses collect, abstract and index the material related to their area of interest. Obtaining information is as simple as searching the ERIC database in one of its many forms. The information that you find will consists of references to current journal articles, books, research reports, conference papers, curriculum guides, and special reports. While the complete text of some of the reports are available online, in most cases you will need to visit a library that has the journals or the microfiche of the documents or you may purchase a copy from the ERIC Document Reproduction Service. If you have problems finding information, each ERIC Clearinghouse has a toll-free number where an information specialist can help you with your questions. There's even a general toll-free number (1-800-LET-ERIC) if you don't know where to start.

ERIC is one of the greatest educational resources available via telecommunications. Thankfully, most of the materials produced by ERIC (materials that explain how to use the database, not the articles and reports that are indexed) are in the public domain and may be freely reproduced, in whole or in part, for your use. That makes them excellent, inexpensive teaching tools. Appendix A of this book contains ERIC's own overview of its database and suggestions for accessing its various resources.

One way to search many computer databases is through the system known as Boolean logic. This tells the computer system how to search for the information that you need. Yes, you can search by typing in a single term. Boolean logic, however, makes your searching more powerful by allowing you to combine terms. Recently I performed a search for a teacher who was looking for information on horror books for children. He had been typing the word "horror" as his search term. What he found were hundreds of references to all the horror stories that teachers tell and references to the horror of the Holocaust along with references to books by Steven King and R. L. Stine. By combining terms through the system of Boolean logic, I helped him narrow his search. The expression that we used was "horror AND children's literature." Information on constructing a search with Boolean Logic and ERIC's search worksheet are also in Appendix A.

Free Networks

Educators have developed networks to provide for an exchange of information and to move their free WANs beyond the regional and state boundaries. Bitnet became the international network for colleges and universities to exchange research and professional communications but has since given way to the Internet. Other free networks developed to serve a variety of needs. As noted above, many states have developed educational networks. In addition, public libraries and other community agencies have also developed free networks that, in many cases, now serve as gateways to the Internet. In the next chapter of this book, we will take a closer look at the Internet and the information that it provides.

What lies in the future for telecommunications?

The Telecommunications Act of 1996 mandated discounted rates for libraries and schools for networking/wiring projects and for Internet access, especially in low income areas. In addition, the Technology Literacy Challenge Fund was funded for its first year. A lot depends on how these programs are managed. However, they should make telecommunications more available in all schools. The job of the SLMS is to help make sure that the technology is used in the curriculum.

Bibliography

Abilock, D. (1996). Integrating e-mail into the curriculum. TECHNOLOGY CONNECTION, 3 (5), 23-25. Abilock presents examples of ways to integrate e-mail into both the elementary and secondary school curriculum.

Belliston, W. (1996). E-mail—the teacher's pet. *Tech Directions,* 56 (Aug.), 27-8. Contains advice for teachers on using e-mail.

Cohen, S. E-mail basics. (1996). *Training and Development*, 50 (8), 48-50. Along with information on the World Wide Web, this articles contains mail etiquette and tips.

Coogan, D. (1995). E-mail tutoring, a new way to do new work. *Computers and Composition,* 12 (2), 171-181.

Dyrli, O. (1995). Telecommunications: Gaining access to the world. *Technology & Learning*, 16 (3), 79-84. Although this is part one of a series of articles about the Internet, there are some lists of e-mail activities for students.

Dyrli, O. (1995). E-mail bridges to school collaboration. *Technology and Learning*, 16 (2), 26. Discusses the teaching of several science units in grades 3-8 through e-mail.

Ekhaml, L. (1996). Making the most of e-mail. TECHNOLOGY CONNECTION, 2 (10), 18-19. A guide to being "concise, courteous, and correct online."

Ekhaml, L. (1997). Scanningmania! *School Library Media Activities Monthly,* 13 (7), 34-37. Along with an overview of scanning, Ekhaml provides some "words from the wise" and tips to make better use of your scanner.

Hand, D. and Weathers, B. (1993). Periodicals by fax: a Houston experience. *School Library Journal*, 39 (2): 29-32. Describes the "periodicals by fax" network set up by area private school librarians.

Hinton, W.D. (1997). Elementary e-mail. *PC Novice,* 9 (2), 38-41. Hinton explains "how to get started with electronic messaging" and reviews the e-mail services of CompuServe, Prodigy, and America Online.

Holzberg, C. (1995). Scanners make the grade. *Technology and Learning*, 16 (3), 53-61. Holzberg reports on the ways the special education teachers in the Norfolk (Virginia) Public Schools use scanners to help them provide instruction for visually impaired and physically handicapped students.

Huber, J. (1996). Modems 101. TECHNOLOGY CONNECTION, 3 (1), 35-36. Basic information about modems and phone lines.

IFLA fax guidelines. (1996). *Journal of Interlibrary Loan, Document Delivery & Information Supply*, 6 (4), 5-10. Contains the policy statements of the International Federation of Library Associations for the use of fax machines for interlibrary loan.

ISDN, Again. (1995). *Software and Networks for Learning,* 21 (3), 7. Discusses ISDN and the connections needed to use it for both PCs and Macs.

Jansen, Barbara A. (1996). Connected to the Internet; Now what? *School Library Media Activities Monthly*, 13 (1), 29-31. The subtitle of this article is "Using E-mail in Collaborative Curriculum Projects." While the examples in the article were done on the Internet, they could be done through any e-mail provider.

Lent, A. F. & S. Miastkowski (1996). Modems. *Multimedia World*, 3 (4), 85-90. The authors test 28.8 kbps modems from 14 manufacturers.

Mather, M. A. (1996). Cutting-edge connectivity: ISDN and beyond. *Technology & Learning,* 16 (8), 28-30. Information on ISDN, videoconferencing, and distance learning is contained in this article.

Phelps, A. (1997). E-mail grows up. *PC Novice,* 9 (2), 28-31. An overview of "paging, fax, voice, & text" as parts of e-mail.

Robinson, M. (1995). Improving science teaching with e-mail. *Computers in the Schools,* 11 (1), 95-107. Presents an overview of the use of e-mail in science education in Nevada.

Salvador, R. (1997). State education networks spread. *Electronic Learning,* 16 (6), 8. This brief article summarizes the *State Networking Report: Progress, Policies, and Partnerships Bring Internet Connectvitity to K-12 Schools*. Copies of the complete report are available from the Southwest Educational Development Laboratory at (512) 476-6861.

Salvador, R. (1995). What's new in kids' e-mail? *Electronic Learning*, 15 (2), 14. Discusses commercial systems that promote "E-mail and Internet readiness without actually sending messages through cyberspace."

Silva, P. U. (1996). E-mail: Real-life classroom experiences with foreign languages. *Learning and Leading with Technology*, 23 (5), 10-12.

Sunden, J. (1996). Desktop videoconferencing. *PC Today,* 10 (11), 54-56. Sunden reports on four color videoconferencing systems.

<u>Notes</u>

Chapter 8

The Internet and the World Wide Web

Today, mention the word "network" and everyone automatically responds with the words Internet and World Wide Web. Sometimes these words are accompanied by a horror story about the pornographic information that is out there just waiting to be found by unsuspecting children. At other times, there is a description about the wonderful information to be found on the Internet and the great educational opportunities that the 'Net and the Web provide for all students, teachers, and SLMSs. Whether educational tool or educational management problem, the Internet is a fixture in many public schools today. According to *Classroom Connect* magazine, the "Internet guru" for most schools is...(drum roll, please)...the school library media specialist.

Unfortunately, most SLMSs have not been trained to be the guru. In this chapter, we will provide some Internet basic training by looking at what the Internet is, how to connect to it, how to search for information, and what to do with the information that we find. As part of that process, we will also explore the problems associated with Internet usage and look at acceptable use policies as well as monitoring and filtering software. Then, we will consider the process of building a Web site and installing an Internet/Web server. In conclusion, we will examine Web/Net appliances and the future of Internet access.

What is the Internet?

The Internet is not a network in the usual sense. Actually it is a network of networks consisting of more than two million computers in more than 200 countries. These networks pass information to each other using a set of rules called the Internet Protocol; that's how the Internet got its name. Growing out of a Department of Defense project begun in 1969 and the National Science Foundation Network (NSFNET) to serve the academic and educational communities, the NSFNET today provides the backbone or high speed central superhighway for the Internet.

When access to the resources of the Internet first became available to the general public, it was not easy to locate information, and use of the Internet's resources was limited. That changed with the development of the World Wide Web, the graphical interface to the Internet, and the corresponding development of user-friendly Web browser software. No longer is it necessary to type in long, complex commands to move from location to location in cyberspace. With the Web came hyperlinks that provide point-and-click connections between sites. Use the mouse to click on a highlighted word, phrase, or picture, and you are transported to the next location on the Internet. Whether you use a PC, Mac, or even a Unix-based computer, Web access is the same because of the HTML (hypertext markup language) standard for Web pages that allows all Web browsers to display HTML the same way.

The introduction of the Web interface has been followed by a tremendous growth in the use of the Internet. According to statistics published in the October, 1996, issue of *PC Novice*, the Internet is really being used! Just counting adults, there are approximately 35 million users in the United States and 89 million users worldwide. Add to that the 21 million nonusers who said they planned to go online by the end of 1997. Then factor in the 20% of the Internet users who are students and not counted in the previous statistics. Now consider that the average weekly Internet usage in the United States and Canada is 5 hours and 28 minutes. That's a lot of use for the current Internet system.

The success of the Internet has been responsible for many of its problems. Basically, the Internet is now underpowered and overused. If you live in the eastern time zone, you can experience the problem firsthand. Just log on to the Internet at 8:00 a.m. and begin working on a project. After you've worked for awhile, you will feel that it is taking longer for the computer to respond to your requests. Check the clock; it should be five or ten minutes after 9:00 a.m. Keep working, but be prepared for the next slowdown. Around 10:00 a.m. you will find things grinding to a halt. Response time is so long, you pick up a book to read while you are waiting for the next site to download information. The problem is not in your computer. It's just the rest of the country waking up and signing on the Internet.

Unfortunately, the slowdown has been accompanied by more serious problems. First, some of the commercial vendors who provide access to the Internet were not prepared for the number of people using their services. In late 1996, America Online, a commercial Internet access provider, offered unlimited monthly access for a set fee. People subscribing to that service reported trying for days to get online and receiving nothing but busy signals. Even though that problem may have been solved, there are still other problems. In the February 3, 1997 issue of *InfoWorld*, Bob Metcalfe reported that there is a 30% packet loss of information during peak usage periods for major Internet Service Providers. While this does not mean that all the information is lost, it does mean that information has to be resent (usually this is done automatically by computers) and that there is between a 2% and 4% delay/loss rate daily on the Internet. (Report at: http://nic.merit.edu/~ipma/netnow.)

But, in spite of the problems, the Internet is here to stay as a major factor in education. Colleges and universities have come to rely on the Internet to share information. Currently, there is a proposal under consideration to build Internet II and to restrict its use for research only.

In contrast, K-12 schools will be using the current Internet for the foreseeable future. The declining costs and the access to information that the Internet affords everyone make Internet access a top priority for many schools today. To help that occur, the Telecommunications Act of 1996 established a discount rate for schools and libraries. The idea was to provide affordable Internet access by linking the cost of access to a school's poverty rate (subsidized school lunches) and local telephone costs. Discounts between 20% and 90% are anticipated not only for Internet access but also for the wiring needed to make the Internet connection.

It is really not surprising that the SLMS is expected to be an expert on the Internet since the Internet provides many resources for librarians. In fact, some people find using it is addicting. Through the Internet, a SLMS can use e-mail, participate in chats and conferences, retrieve information from online databases, access bulletin boards, play games, browse the online catalog of a major reference library, read a college or university's campus-wide information system (CWIS), check out a technical report, help a teacher locate information for a class, guide students who are trying to complete reports, reach a vendor's technical service help page, find out about the programming on Cable in the Classroom channels, and the list goes on.

In many respects, the Internet is not very different from print information that SLMSs have been working with for years. In a speech at a 1996 Computers in Libraries conference, Hope Tillman made the following comparison between traditional print materials and the Internet. First, she noted that individual home pages are a form of vanity or self-publishing. That does not make them inherently bad; they just lack, for the most part, the peer review of published print materials. Then there is the "grey literature" (pamphlets and technical reports) that exist on Internet sites. Tillman equated these with those brochures and clippings that librarians kept in the vertical file. In another category are the advertising and public relations materials that used to arrive in schools as promotions and "free and inexpensive" materials from publishers and other commercial sources. Now they appear on commercial sites on the Internet. Tillman's point is that, just as librarians have, for years, had to evaluate and use materials from a wide variety of sources, now they have to evaluate and use similar materials that are housed on the Internet.

How does a school connect to the Internet?

There are a number of ways that an individual school can connect to the Internet. These include through an online service, a national or local Internet Service Provider (ISP), a non-profit institution, or through a dedicated direct link to the Internet. In addition, you will need the communications software to make either a SLIP (Serial Line Internet Protocol) or PPP (Point-to-Point Protocol) connection to the Internet. But, before we look at each of these options and at a few less well-known alternatives, let's review some transmission basics.

One of the major concerns in selecting an Internet service is the bandwidth, carrying capacity, or speed of the connection. (There's additional information in Chapter 7 on telecommunications.) Slowest are the modem connections through POTS (plain old telephone service) lines with 33.6 Kbps being the fastest speed with a set of standards making it universally accepted. While there are 56 K modems, there is no set of standards for a 56 K connection, resulting in two different methods of connection and a need to have the same type of 56 K modem on each end of the connection. (It is similar to the old feud between VHS and Beta videotapes.) For faster connections, special ISDN telephone lines or dedicated lines are needed. With ISDN telephone service, you also need an NT-1 network terminator or an ISDN modem with a built-in NT-1 terminator. In addition to the extra costs, a problem with ISDN lines is that they do not work when the power goes off, so they supplement but do not replace POTS lines.

Unfortunately, a fast modem or an ISDN line does not guarantee fast processing on the Internet. Things like the time of day and usage on the Internet all play a part.

Online Service

Dial-up access through POTS lines can link a school to the Internet through an online service such as America Online, Compuserve, or Prodigy. In addition to providing access to the Internet, these vendors provide other special services for their subscribers including chat groups, forums, special electronic magazines or "zines," and online reference sources. While online services were, initially, the only way some people had to connect to the Internet, their market share has fallen with the development of national and local Internet Service Providers (ISPs).

Figure 8.1 shows the number of accounts on each service based on their published figures. This is different from the number of users since an individual on America Online can have up to five accounts.

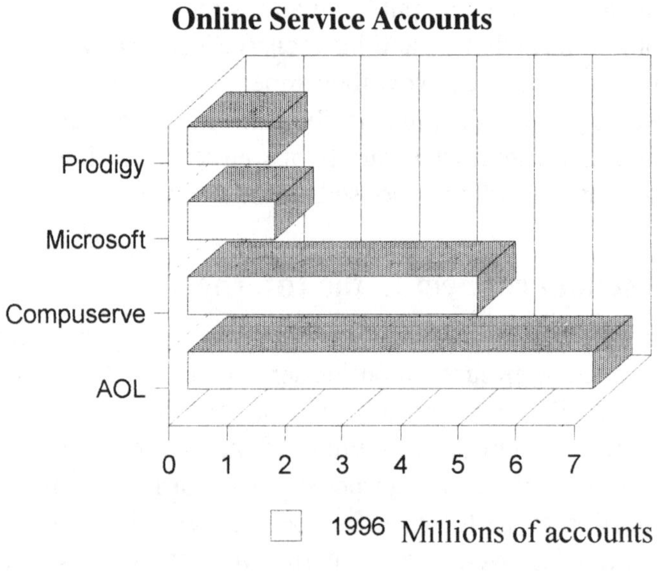

Online Service Accounts

Figure 8.1 Online service accounts in 1996 in millions

Internet Service Provider (ISP)

Another type of dial-up service is an Internet Service Provider whose sole function is to connect you to the Internet. Not included are all of the special features of the online service. Of course, most people would agree that, with Internet access, those special features are really not necessary. Most ISPs provide an e-mail box, access to a number of newsgroups (my ISP currently lets me select from 46,000+ groups), and space for a home page on the Web. Generally, for a setup fee and a monthly charge, the ISP provides a software package including an e-mail program and Web browser, and a local or 800 number for you to call to access the Internet.

There are some national ISPs with a mixture of local and 800 numbers. Recently they were rated for tech support, speed of connection, installation, navigation, and user extras. According to the test results reported in the May 1997 issue of *SmartMoney* magazine, the top five national ISPs were, in order from top down, AT&T, Earthlink, Mindspring, MCI Internet, and NetCom. When online service providers were added to the test, Compuserve placed third behind Earthlink.

Gaining in popularity are local ISPs. Selecting one of these can have benefits in better service and faster connection speeds. However, this is a tremendous growth area and some of the providers have been in business only a short time. They may not have the money to upgrade their system as technology changes, or to pay recurring costs and stay in business. There have been reports of some local ISPs taking money for one, two or three year contracts and then going out of business within six months.

Most ISPs provide you with software to connect to their service as well as other applications. Fortunately, installation is usually easy, at least if you have an account with a good ISP. Although other people report horror stories and configuration problems, my ISP (Exisnet) provided me with a set of 3.5" floppy disks which I loaded into the computer that I use for Internet access. It's a 486 PC with 8MB RAM running Windows 3.x and a 28.8 Kbps modem. After following the easy instructions and completing the installation, I rebooted the computer and was ready to surf the 'Net.

Freenet Connection
In many states, schools are able to access the Internet for free through a state or regional network. In Virginia, VA_Pen is a k-12 network with local or 800 numbers to provide free access throughout the state. Any school personnel can obtain passwords and telecommunications software to access this network which, in turn, provides access to the Internet. One problem of this system is that telephone lines into the network are often limited and the result is delays and busy signals. This can be especially frustrating during the school day when students are trying to go online to work on a project. An option has been to limit the number of hours per day that an individual can go online by setting a usage limit per password. That presents a special problem for librarians who need full-day access for students accessing the Internet in the library. However, in many cases, this free connection is the only option for budget conscious schools.

Dedicated Direct Access
Most SLMSs agree that, given a choice, they would have direct access to the Internet, not a dial-up service. Usually a direct connection is made through a dedicated high speed, high capacity T-1 or T-3 line that connects a school's own internal network to the Internet. In those cases, the school will have its own Internet server, network adapter cards, and server software with TCP/IP (Transmission Control Protocol/Internet Protocol) standards. Added to the installation costs, there will be monthly connection fees.

Other Options
In addition to the dedicated line and dial-up services there are other ways to access the Internet. Cable modems attached to television cable lines and wire-

less modems with speeds equal to T-1 lines are available. DirectPC provides Internet service via a satellite dish at a transmission rate of 400 Kbps. Costs include the installation and purchase cost of the dish as well as monthly fees.

There are also new categories of telephone lines on the way. xDSL (digital subscriber lines) come in several versions: SDSL (symmetrical digital subscriber lines) and RADSL (rate adaptive digital subscriber lines). Developed by telephone companies as a response to possible challenges by cable companies for your business, the xDSL lines can work as fast as 1.5 Mbps. For even faster speeds, ADSL (asymmetric digital subscriber lines) allow data to be compressed and downloaded at speeds between 1.5 Mbps and 6 Mbps with a special modem. There is, unfortunately, a slower upload speed.

Figure 8.2, based on figures supplied by the Odyssey Homefront study in September, 1996, provides an overview of Internet access.

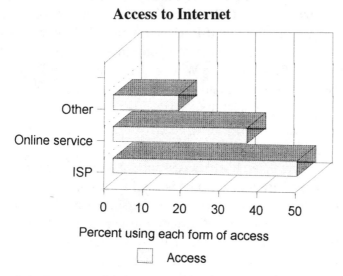

Access to Internet

Figure 8.2 Percent of Internet users who use each form of access

Access Fees
Use of the Internet itself is free. However, a charge may occur depending on how an individual accesses or gets on the Internet. Schools using a freenet access, such as a state education network or library network, pay nothing. Using a commercial online service brings a monthly fee for unlimited usage or a monthly fee for a set number of hours plus a per hour charge for each hour over the maximum. In addition, if you use a high speed ISDN connection, your ISP may charge a higher rate.

What should you look for in selecting an ISP?

In selecting your Internet access, the first thing to do is check with others in your locality. Ask them, or the ISP that they recommend, the following questions:

What services does the ISP provide?

Does the service provide single or multiple e-mail accounts ? With a multiple account, the SLMS can have his/her own account plus a separate one for general student use through the library.

Can you access other e-mail accounts through this service? Through my home ISP, I can access my school account, making it easy to check my mail on holidays and vacations.

What newsgroups can be accessed through this service? Some ISPs filter or regulate the number of newsgroups that a user can access through their service. While this may be beneficial, it may also be a form of censorship that is not needed.

Does the service provide space for personal WWW pages? If so, could the school or school library develop its own Web page and make it available through the service?

Does the service have a local or 800 phone number? If an 800 number, is there any additional charge for it?

If you are purchasing/renting a direct Internet connection, determine who will install and maintain the lines.

If the service provider upgrades his end of the system, what responsibilities will you have? Will you need to purchase additional equipment?

What technical services are provided?

When is technical help available? What hours? What days?

Is the technical support line a free call?

What additional costs, if any, are there for technical help?

What is the response time? With one ISP that I used, you had to call and leave a message on the voice mail. The only time that I called, I had to wait two days for a response.

What is the quality of the service?

How many subscribers does the ISP have per modem? Too few modems to support a large subscriber base will result in busy signals.

What is the speed of those modems? If there are several different speeds, how many are there at each speed? Remember, your connection speed cannot exceed the speed of the slowest modem, yours or the service modem.

If the service has 56K modems, what type are they?

Does the service have ISDN modems? Is there any additional charge to connect to them?

How often do subscribers get a busy signal when they attempt to log on to the service?

What are the peak hours? How often do subscribers get busy signals then?

Are subscribers frequently disconnected from the service when they are online?

What software is provided?

Is communications software provided? What are its features? My home ISP's software package has a great graphical interface. I click on one button to connect and then on different buttons to go on the Web, check my mail, check my school mail account, Telnet to another computer, download files via FTP (file-transfer proto-col), and various other services.

Is a commercial Internet browser provided? Is it a major brand such as Netscape Navigator or Microsoft Explorer? Is it free? Is it the latest version?

Is there e-mail software? What is it and how easy is it to use?

What other software is provided: News Reader? Telnet? FTP? Internet Relay Chat?

Will upgrades to these programs be provided? Will there be a fee? How can they be obtained?

Does the software require a certain operating system on the user's computer? Windows? Windows 95? Windows NT? Mac?

What hardware do you need to access the service?

Are there any suggested systems requirements for using the service?

What platform(s) will the software (if any) provided by the service run on?

What is the cost of the service?

Is there a set charge for unlimited service? While it may seem that unlimited service is best, there may be cases, especially for personal use, when unlimited is not best. Generally, with unlim-ited access, people tend to access the system and just leave their computer connected to it all the time whether they are using it or not. This could be tying up a connection for another user. Of course, in a school, unlimited access is probably the most cost-effective choice. If there are different fee schedules, can you switch from one to the other to take advantage of the decreased usage during the summer months?

How can you pay the charges? Will the service accept a purchase order?

What is the length of time for a contract? Monthly, semi-annual, and yearly are the usual options. Beware, however, of taking a year contract with a brand new service.

Are there any additional charges for services?

Is there an initial set-up or connection fee?

In some cases, you can also find a rating of the ISPs that you are consid-ering. CNET, the Computer Network, includes a consumer satisfaction guide to ISPs on its Web page which is searchable by location. The URL is http://www.cnet.com/Content/Reviews/Compare/ISP/. (That final period is the end of the sentence.)

What is a Web browser?

When the Internet first became accessible, it was difficult to use. However, the development of the World Wide Web and the graphical interfaces for using it made it easier for everyone to explore the Internet.

Basically, a Web browser is a software package that is stored in your computer or LAN and allows your computer to find and read HTML (hypertext markup language) Web pages. This graphical, point and click interface allows you to move from one URL (Universal Resource Locator) or address on the

Web to another by just moving your mouse and clicking on a highlighted word or graphic. These highlighted words are hyperlinks, or special "buttons" that automatically send your browser to another location on the Internet where it downloads information from that site to your computer. In addition, the browser allows you to access newsgroups, and keeps a history of your travels over the Internet.

The first Web browser was Mosaic, which was created in 1993 by the National Center of Supercomputing Applications (NCSA) at the University of Illinois. Commercial companies quickly copied the idea. While NCSA Mosaic or a commercial clone is still used by some people today, Mosaic does not have a large share of the current browser market.

Currently there are two major Web browsers. *Netscape Navigator* has the lead with 70% of the market. But *Microsoft Internet Explorer* is trying hard to catch up. Both perform similar functions and are enhanced by browser plug-ins. These are add-ons, often from third-party developers, which allow the browser to perform certain tasks such as digitizing signatures so that you can "sign" a document over the Web or use special features such as Internet telephony and videoconferencing, Internet filters for objectionable material, and multimedia support.

Web Browsers

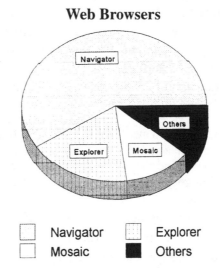

Figure 8.3 Market share of major Web browsers

Browsers do their basic work of moving you around the graphical portion of the Internet by reading the URL of the location that you would like to visit. Usually, a site consists of a home or main "page" and related pages. Each page has its own address. This address usually begins with "http://" followed by the domain and subdomain names of the location. The "http" at the beginning of the address means that the site was created with the hypertext transfer protocol. The "html" often found at the end of the URL means that hypertext markup language was used to create the page. You should begin to see "vrml" at the end of URLs. These letters signify that virtual reality markup language, a 3D standard, was used in the creation of that page.

Additional information on some of the subdomain abbreviations can be found in Chapter 7.

One feature that you really need to be aware of on a Web browser is the one that keeps the browser from downloading graphics. With the limited bandwidth of POTS lines, graphics often take a long time to load into your computer and slow down your navigation through the Internet. As a result, browsers contain a feature which allows you to view text-only. This really speeds things up. Many sites now allow you to click on an icon for a text-only version. If you get to a site were the graphics are important, you can turn on the command to load the graphics and instruct your browser to reload the site.

How can you find things on the Internet?

Even with a good Web browser, looking for information on the Internet can be as much of a challenge as finding a needle in a haystack unless you know the URL where the information can be found. If you don't, you can just "surf the net," using hyperlinks to move from site to site. However, that technique has been compared to going into a library and finding all the books on the floor in a pile. The process of locating information becomes one of dig until you find. While you can locate lots of interesting things with this method, it is very time consuming and not very efficient.

Because of that, users have developed special Internet tools to help anyone search worldwide for information. Some were developed when the Internet was basically text-based. These include Veronica, Archie, Jughead, and Gopher. We won't spend much time with these since most of their functions have been replaced by the Web browser. In fact, when using them to search you will frequently encounter the following message: "This gopher is closed, please visit http://" followed by a Web URL.

Gopher: This menu-driven system was developed to organize text. By moving through a series of increasingly more specific menus, users were able to find the information that they needed. One great remaining gopher is at the following URL: gopher://peg.cwis.uci.edu.

Veronica: A text search engine used to search gophers.

Jughead: A site- or topic-specific form of Veronica.

FTP site: A method used to transfer files, hence the name file transfer protocol (FTP).

Archie: A text search engine for FTP sites.

The World Wide Web has its own search tools which include search engines and Web directories. Although these two tools are different, they are often lumped together and called search engines or search utilities. There are now even search utilities called metasites that allow you to search several directories or search engines at the same time. However, the lines between these utilities are flexible with search engines sometimes incorporating directory features.

In reality, a true search engine is a computer-created database. First a "spider" or robot program makes its way through the Web, locating information and relaying new data and changes back to the main search engine computer. At the main computer, this data is added to the search engine's database. When you try to locate information using that search engine, a program at the search engine's main computer looks through the database to find information related to your request. Major search engines include *AltaVista, Excite, HotBot, Lycos,* and *OpenText*.

In contrast, a Web directory is a people-created database. First people search the Web to find information, analyze it, and arrange it by subjects or in categories. When you use a Web directory to locate information, a program searches its database to find the information. *Yahoo, Magellan, Point, InfoSeek Select Sites*, and *Excite NetDirectory* are all search directories.

Searching with either of these types of utilities is fairly easy. With a Directory, you access the Web site by typing in the URL or using the bookmark feature on your Web browser if you have been to the site before. (There are lists in the resources section.) Then you work your way through a series of increasingly more specific menus until you reach the topic that you are interested in. Clicking on that topic will produce a list of Web sites where the information can possibly be found. In doing a directory search, your success depends not only on your skill as a searcher but also on the skills of the people producing the directory.

Using a search engine is a little different. After you access the site, you find a blank space where you can enter your search query. At this point, it is very important to know how the search engine works because the success of your search with a search engine depends a great deal on your skills. Most search utilities have rules and guidelines available at their site to help you become a better searcher. Read them when you first begin searching and re-member to check them at least monthly in case the rules change.

There are several online sources that rate search utilities. One of these sites is The Spider's Apprentice at http://www.monash.com/spidap.html. (That final period is the end of the sentence.) In addition to providing tips on searching the Web, there are FAQ (frequently asked questions) about search engines, an explanation of how they work, and a guide for planning the best search. Check out the rankings and the in-depth ratings and analysis page.

For a look at search engines from a different perspective, visit the search engine watch page of Calafia Consulting at http://searchenginewatch.com/major.htm. (There's no period at the end of a URL.) The goal of this site is to help Web page developers get their sites indexed. Learn which search utilities base their information on the full-text of a page and which depend on an abstract. Some utilities sell keywords. Pay the designated fee and your site will be in the top 10 sites on a given topic. Other search engines look at page popularity and use that to place a site higher in the list than a less popular site. Finally, some search engines penalize sites for "spamming" or using a word too often. In an attempt to have your Web page come out higher in a search for school sites, you might be tempted to put the words "school, school, school" at the top of your page. Some search engines will actually penalize a site for doing this. The Calafia site has a wealth of information from the Web page developer's point of view.

Reviews of search engines appear in periodicals. In the May 12, 1997 issue, *InfoWorld* published a test of some of the search engines and metasites. They rated the sites on a scale of 1 to 10 for ease of searching, quality and accuracy of results, usefulness of the online documentation, cost, and the level of the support provided. Ratings of 10 were outstanding, 8 very good ("meets all essential criteria and offers significant advantages"), 6 good ("meets essential criteria and includes some additional capabilities"), 4 satisfactory (meets essential criteria), and 2 poor. The results of this test are shown in figure 8.4.

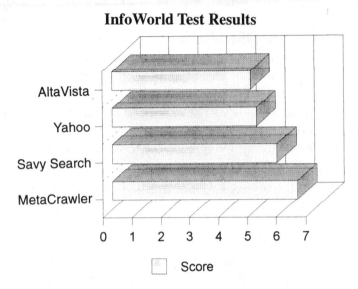

InfoWorld Test Results

Figure 8.4 InfoWorld ratings of search engines on a 1-10 scale

Another test of major search utilities was published in volume 5, issue 3 (1997) of *PCNovice Guide to Going Online*. In this test, search engines and directories were rated on the basis of how up-to-date the listings are, the quality of the results of the search, how much control the user had over the search, and other factors such as the ease of use, helpfulness of instructions, and warnings, if any, about objectionable material. These test results are shown in figure 8.5.

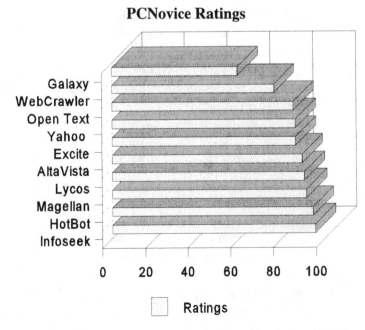

PCNovice Ratings

Figure 8.5 PCNovice ratings of search engines out of 100 points

As you can see from the ratings, not even the experts agree. What you can do is perform your own test of the search utilities that you frequently use. In fact, you might be able to ask a few students to do the test and then compare the results. Select three or four topics that have been or might be searched in your library. Be sure at least one of them is a current topic. Now use each of the utilities in your test and compare the results. How many hits are there? Look at the first 10-20 and determine how many of those seemed likely to contain the information that you are seeking. What levels of searches can you do? What is the difference between the basic and advanced searches? Would students be successful? Follow a few of the links to the actual sites. Are they active sites or does your browser indicate that it cannot locate that server? How long does it take to run the search on each utility? (In all fairness, you need to do the searches at the same time of day for each utility.)

No matter which search utilities you decide to use, there are some ways you can improve your success. Here are a few hints:

- Limit your searches to three or four search utilities and learn how to use them.

- Know what is included in the database for each utility. Some include newsgroups in their database while others do not. Newsgroups often contain information that might not be appropriate in a school setting.

- For the sites that you search, find and read the searching tips. Usually the site will have a list of guidelines to help you with basic and advanced searches. Print these off and keep a copy where you and other searchers can consult it before you go online.

- Structure your search in advance. Unless you have lots of time or a lot of experience searching, plan your search before you access the search engine. Think of synonyms, narrower terms, and related terms. Identify alternate spellings.

- If you are using a directory, learn the vocabulary of the utility. Keep notes so that you can refer back to them later.

- Learn the Boolean searching techniques for your sites. Most search engines allow you to do Boolean searches (for more information see the ERIC appendix in this book). However, they do not use the same abbreviations for the Boolean operators. One site may let you use the Boolean operators AND, OR, and NOT as long as you capitalize them, while another utility requires graphic symbols such as + and -. Keeping a phrase such as school library media specialist together may mean using parenthesis on one search utility and quotation marks in another.

- Don't forget to use your Web browser to bookmark your search utilities.

What are newsgroups and listservs?

Sometimes the best way to find an answer to a question or to locate information is to ask an expert. Fortunately, the Internet provides access to experts world-wide on any topic imaginable through two of its features: newsgroups and listservs.

There are over 46,000 newsgroups, or online discussions, on the Internet. You can locate a newsgroup on almost any topic by using some of the general search engines. (Check the specifics of the utility; not all index newsgroups.) In addition, you can search Deja News (http://www.dejanews.com) for your subject or visit the Web's site of Publicly Accessible Mailing Lists. A newsgroup is like an open bulletin board on which e-mail messages are posted for everyone to read. The software to read the postings is usually built-in to your Web browser or the software furnished by your Internet access service. Each group has its own "personality" and rules of conduct, so most people only "lurk" at first by just reading the messages. After they become familiar with the rules of the group, they become active participants and post their own messages. To help people learn the rules quickly, most newsgroups have sets of FAQs that can be read. In addition, some newsgroups maintain "archives" of previous postings that you can read.

Listservs or mailing lists are also discussion areas of the Internet. However, unlike newsgroups, listservs are for members only through a subscription. Subscriptions are free, but this process limits access to those who are really interested in the topic, not just surfing by. In a few cases, subscriptions are only available to members of a particular organization or profession. Liszt (http://www.liszt.com) is the search engine for listservs. Once you have identified a listserv that you would like to join, you follow the instructions, generally, to send an e-mail to a specific address and request membership. After becoming a member, you will receive the mailing list postings as e-mail directly to you. Members on really busy listservs may receive several hundred e-mails a day. That's why many listservs offer the feature known as a digest where they bundle the e-mail and deliver a bundle several times a day or week. This results in less space being taken up in your electronic mailbox.

One listserv that is especially interesting to school librarians is LM_NET which is operated by Mike Eisenberg of Syracuse University and Peter Milbury of Pleasant Valley High School in Chico, California. Here you can post a question about anything dealing with school libraries and know that SLMSs throughout the world will give you advice. See the resources list for subscription information.

There is one word of caution about using a listserv. Once you subscribe to that list, you will automatically receive all the messages posted by members of that interest group. If the group members are very active (like SLMSs), that can amount to hundreds of messages each week.

Douglas Wells, of the Virginia Department of Education, was called in to work on a problem at one of the local nodes (area server computers) for VA_PEN. It seems one of the school librarians had subscribed to LM_NET in June and then left school for the summer. In a few weeks, there were more than 1,400 unread messages in the librarian's e-mail box. They occupied more than four megabytes of space on the network's local server computer and were creating problems for the entire system.

If you subscribe to a listserv, remember to read your mail regularly and discard messages after you read them. Otherwise, your old mail will be taking up space on some computer. If you go on vacation, ask your listserv to suspend or cancel your mail for a period of time.

Also, when using a listserv, remember that anything sent to the listserv's posting e-mail list address will be sent to everyone in the group. To respond privately to one person, use that person's personal e-mail address. More than one embarrassed group member has accidentally sent a "confidential" reply to every member of the listserv rather than just to the intended person.

One other thing needs to be mentioned at this point. It is the process known as "spamming." In spamming, an individual sends an inappropriate or unrelated message to several newsgroups and/or to everyone in a number of listservs. (Some people make a distinction and call it "spam" if the unrelated message is sent to one newsgroup or one listserv and "velveeta" if the message goes to several groups and/or listservs.) The message might be a commercial, a chain letter, or a request to send business cards or some other document to someone whom you do not know. Spamming is a violation of netiquette (net etiquette). Unfortunately, there are even programs known as "spambots" that are designed to assist in spamming. In his last "Howgoesit" general message to all subscribers, my own ISP announced that anyone caught spamming through his service will be automatically disconnected with no warning and no refund of connection fees.

Related to spam are the great urban legends that have been born on and currently reside on the Internet. The best example is the true story that got out of hand. A boy in Britain was trying to break into the Guinness Book of World Records for the number of "get-well" cards received. Unfortunately, the story continued and grew after the boy was well and released from the hospital. It was "spammed" across the Internet. The hospital and the local post office are still flooded with cards whenever the story reappears on the Internet. Other stories may not have any basis in fact. Know your source and do not believe everything that you read. Refer to the urban legends site on the Web (listed in the Resources section) for more tall tales.

What can you do about objectionable material on the Internet?

With so much information available on the Internet, some schools are allowing students to access Internet resources from classrooms and libraries. In other places, schools are providing e-mail accounts for students as well as Internet access. Educators, however, have raised several concerns about this access. Some center around the problem of students becoming hackers and violating laws while using school computers. Other concerns are related to the problem of students accessing inappropriate or objectional materials via the Internet. Everyone has heard at least one story about the pornography and sexually explicit materials on the Web.

Acceptable Use Policies

While schools have developed several ways to cope with the problems created by student access to the Internet, the most common solution is the development and implementation of an acceptable use policy (AUP) for the school district. While guidelines on Web publishing are sometimes included in a district's AUP, they are often in a separate document. (See later in this chapter for additional information.) Generally the AUP is developed by a committee representing all concerned individuals including library media specialists, teachers, individual school administrators, central office administrators, staff members, parents, and representatives from the community. In some districts, students are also included on the committee since they may have a great deal of experience using the Internet. Although the policies that these committees develop vary in exact format and content, they generally contain the following items:

Statement about the Internet; what it is, and what resources are on it. Discussion of the benefits of providing Internet access to students and teachers.

In this section of the UP, the school district will usually indicate the benefits of using the Internet in the curriculum and for staff training and development.

General overview of the types of sites found on the Internet; from private citizen's homepage and community bulletin boards to commercial corporations and adult bookstores. This should be a frank discussion, in which the school district points out the variety of materials that are available.

Explanation of the ways in which students and staff will access the Internet and use the computers at school. Some indication is given if the access will occur only in the classroom with a teacher present, in a computer lab, in the library, or in other locations within the school. Also, it should be pointed out whether the access will be with a whole class, groups, or with an individual. Obviously, in a school district, there may be many combinations of access.

Warning about the content of some of the sites and newsgroups.

Statement of the responsibility of any user of school computer resources. It should be made clear that access to the Internet is a privilege granted only to responsible users who follow the guidelines of the AUP.

Clear indication of the uses and behaviors that are and are not permitted. There may be a statement that the computers cannot be used for any commercial, political, or illegal purpose; to vandalize another computer; to invade another individual's privacy; to harass another individual or group; to engage in the practices known as "spamming," or 'hacking;" or to violate any copyright laws. The problems of hate mail and discriminatory actions may be addressed. The use of inappropriate, vulgar, or obscene language and/or visuals is usually forbidden.

Consequences of any violation of the policy. The results for any unauthorized uses should be clearly spelled out. There should be a clearly stated procedure for lodging complaints against any individual, whether student, faculty, or staff.

Statement limiting a school district's liability.

Discussion of the privacy or lack thereof for individual users. The school may reserve the right to: read any e-mail received or sent through school computers; read or view any materials residing in student or teacher areas of the school network server computer(s); review or monitor the Internet site history (listings of the Internet sites visited) of any users; use filters or monitoring software to limit access to portions of the Internet; limit access to certain newsgroups or listservs.

A place for signatures. Usually, a student form is signed by the student, a parent or guardian, and a representative of the school, generally a teacher or SLMS. When school employees sign the AUP, their signature is accompanied by the signature of a school administrator.

Offline browsers

Another solution to the problem of students to access inappropriate materials on the Internet is the use of a type of program known as an offline Web browser. *WebWacker* is one of the best known of these programs. Most of these programs work with the Web browser on your computer to find information on the Web. The difference is that the offline Web browser then allows you to download the information from the Web onto the hard drive of your computer. Then you can disconnect from the Internet in order to view the downloaded material. To use an offline browser you will need at least 20MB free on your hard disk.

By using an offline Web browser, a teacher or SLMS can locate sites for students in advance and then allow the students to access only the materials that have been downloaded. Since many of the offline Web browsers allow you to schedule the time for the downloading to take place, you can arrange to have sites downloaded at night when Internet traffic is light. With the scheduling part of the offline Web browser, you can also arrange to have news and frequently updated information downloaded every day. You can also save time when working with a class of students by downloading the information in advance. By doing this you will be avoiding the delays and slowdowns that often occur on the Internet during the day.

There are special benefits to using an offline browser with elementary students. In a study reported in the Winter 1997 issue of *School Library Media Quarterly*, researchers found that younger elementary students have difficulty evaluating Web sites and tend to think that if something is on the Internet, it is true. This brings out the need for teachers and library media specialists to identify sites in advance. Only when children are older do they begin to develop critical skills to evaluate the sites that they find.

There are, however, some down sides to the offline Web browser. When a teacher or SLMS preselects and downloads the sites, students are not given the opportunity to learn search strategies or how to evaluate a wide variety of sources of information. In essence, an adult has done the evaluation for them. Students are also not being allowed to accept responsibility for their actions and to learn the proper use of school computers. While this can be an advantage with elementary students, it can lead to a problem with middle school and high school students.

Rating systems

PICS (the Platform for Internet Content Selection) is a voluntary rating system that is sanctioned by the World Wide Web Consortium. Under the PICS guidelines, individual organizations can set up their own rating scale. RSACi (Recreational Software Advisory Council - Internet) rates sites based on language, sex, nudity, and violence. Internet Explorer 3.0 has a PICS filter option that can be set to alert you to any site that exceeds the ratings that you designate. You can override the alert with a password.

Monitoring and filtering programs

Today there are many Internet filtering or monitoring programs on the market. The purpose of these is either to block access to specific sites or to provide a record of the sites accessed through the school computers.

Most filter programs block access to specific sites and to searching by specific keywords. Usually the list of these sites and keywords is developed by the software producers. Unfortunately, both public and school librarians, have found that this can create problems. A local school district found that their filtering software blocked the word "breast," thus making it difficult for high school students to find information on breast cancer. Other filters may eliminate any site that has a tilde (~) in its URL. Although the tilde often is the sign of a personal Web page, many excellent sites have a tilde in their URL.

As a result, librarians are establishing guidelines for evaluating filtering software. In the May 1997 issue of *American Libraries*, ALA's journal, Karen Schneider reported on these efforts. A rebutal to her article by David Burt appeared in the August issue. Some of the other debates appeared in messages on the Public Library Listserv and are maintained on the PubLib Internet Filters resource (http://sunsite.berkeley.edu/PubLib/pubref.htm). From those discussions, Schneider developed the following list of features that librarians should examine when considering purchasing filtering software.

- Enabling or disabling blocking based on individual keywords and sites.
- Access to the filter product's list of blocked Internet sites and keywords.
- Ability to add and remove sites and keywords from the site list.
- Ability to block based on developing rating schemes, such as PICS.
- Ability to block according to 'time, place, manner.'
- Variable access control.

She adds that, from the patron's end, she would expect:

- Methods for alerting patrons these products are in use.
- Feedback mechanisms for requesting that sites be added or dropped.
- Ability to request or view site and keyword lists.

Schneider's recommendation for filtering software was to install Squid, a free program for Unix-based servers, or Net Nanny.

There are other sites on the Internet that discuss filtering software. One of the best is Carolyn Caywood's site called Guiding Children Through Cyberspace - URLs. She has wonderful links to other sites. (http://www6.pilot.infi.net/~carolyn/guide.html)

Unlike filtering software, monitoring software keeps a record of the sites that an individual visits while using the Internet. This site history can then be checked randomly or whenever inappropriate use of the Internet is suspected. When monitoring software is used, it is important that everyone knows, in advance, that a record will be kept of the sites visited by anyone logging on with their passwords.

Other actions

In addition to filters, monitoring software, and offline browsers, there are a number of other ways that SLMSs have developed to cope with the potential problem of improper use of the Internet. Some SLMSs require students to schedule an appointment for using the Internet and to provide a written plan or search statement in advance. Others use a large screen television monitor situated at the circulation desk and hooked to the Internet computer to see what students are doing. If there are several computers with Internet access, many librarians make sure they are in a visible area of the library, not hidden in a corner. For classroom use, some schools issue passwords only to teachers and hold the teacher accountable for any searching done on that password. Unfortunately, where there is multiple access, whether in a classroom, lab, or library, techniques other than direct monitoring need to be used.

How should you evaluate a Web site?

Basically, you should evaluate a Web site the same way you evaluate any material. In fact, as SLMS, we really have an advantage in that we have always been trained to evaluate materials whether they are books, periodicals, or audio visual materials. Web sites are no different. But, just to help you out, here are a few things to consider:

Evaluating a Web Site

What is the scope of the site? What does it say it covers? How well does it actually do that? How complete is it in comparison to similar sites?

How applicable is the information on this site to the student's assignment or your purpose?

Who or what is the authority or source behind the Web site? If it is a person, look at his or her credentials. If it is an organization, how reputable is it? Look at the URL. What clues does it provide? (~ usually denotes a personal user)

Check the accuracy of the materials on the site. How well do they fit into the facts that you already know about a topic?

What is the purpose of this site? Why was it developed? To inform? To persuade? Is it an advertorial (combination ad and editorial)?

Is the design and layout of the site one which suggests a reputable source or are there grammatical, mathematical, or spelling errors?

How appropriate are the materials on the site for your intended use?

Is there any bias? What is the point of view of the writer? Is the site balanced in its presentation of controversial material? Remember, even a biased site can be very useful if balanced with other information.

How is the site organized? How easy or difficult is it to locate information? Is there an overview or map of the information contained on the site?

Are there navigation aids to help you move through the site? Does the site have its own search engine to locate information?

How up-to-date is the site? When was it last revised? Has it been put on the Web and then abandoned?

Are there links to other sites? Does someone keep the links current or do many of them lead to dead ends? Are the links pertinent to the main purpose of the site or are they unnecessary distractions?

For what audience is the site intended? Is it designed for experts or does it assume visitors are novices? What is the reading level of the site?

Does the site have a text-only feature to save the time of downloading graphics? Does it depend so much on graphics that it takes forever to download?

Is this a stable site or will it likely have moved or disappeared the next time you look for it?

Is there a way to contact the author or authority behind the site such as an e-mail address?

How can students and teachers use the Internet?

We've spent a lot of time talking about the technical aspects of Internet access and about the problems associated with it. In fact, sometimes this discussion seems to overpower what should be the real focus — how to use the vast resources of the Internet in a school. The following are just a few examples of the ways teachers and librarians have used the Internet:

Use a search engine to locate specific information. In a weather unit, use the resources found at WeatherNet. (http://www.cirrus.spri. umich.edu/wxnet)

Post a question for an expert on a mailing list or listserv. KidsConnect, a part of AASL's ICONnect, is a question-and-answer-service for kids. Students can post an e-mail question to AskKC@iconnect.syr.edu and have a SLMS respond within 48 hours with Internet sources to help provide the answer.

Read the archives of a mailing list to locate information on a topic.

Develop a Web site for your school or library. See the Resources section for some URLs of school sites.

Become part of a discussion group. Join LM_NET.

Work with other schools on online projects. Listings of ongoing and upcoming projects appear in many Internet resources including those listed in the Resources section of this book. One ongoing project is to gather information about the environment and report it on GLOBE's (Global Learning and Observations to Benefit the environment) Web page. (http://www.globe.gov)

Develop a cooperative project of your own with another school. Team with a school in another state or country to exchange information. Turn your students into researchers as they try to answer questions about their own locality.

Use e-mail and have "keypals" instead of pen pals.

Take an Internet field trip and visit another city, state, or country. Visit the reconstructed Colonial Williamsburg (http://www.history.org/twentieth-century/visit.html) or tour Albania. (http://www.netlink.co.uk/users/albpub/index.html). If you prefer something a little farther away, look at the information on Mars. (http://cmex-www.arc.nasa.gov/)

Use Internet resources for your own or teacher staff development. AASL's ICONnect offers online courses in basic and advanced Internet subjects. Also, individual school districts such as Bellingham, Washington, have posted staff development courses on the Internet. (http://www.bham.wednet.edu/resource.htm)

Download lesson plan ideas. Available plans range from a unit plan on worms in the food chain (http:www.greatlakes.12.mi.us/ members/newberry/) to guidelines for teaching about the Holocaust. (http://www.ushmm.org/education/guidelines.html)

Read a periodical online. You can find Internet versions of many periodicals from the *Atlantic Monthly* (http://www.theatlantic. com/atlantic/) to *Byte* magazine. (http://www.byte.com)

Keep up to date in a specific subject. EurekAlert (http://www. eurekalert.org) has great science information.

Teach students how to evaluate Internet resources. An electronic slide show at Widener University's site is great for high school students and adults. (http://www.science.widener.edu/~withers/webeval. htm)

The list could go on and on, but there are several ways you can develop ideas of your own. First, checkout the listings of Internet sites in current educational journals, not just the technology ones. Almost all of the practical journals from THE BOOK REPORT and LIBRARY TALK to *Emergency Librarian*, *Classroom Connect*, and *Teaching PreK-8* consistently run lists of appropriate Internet sites. In addition, there are new journals and publications to consider. *Online-Offline* is a new journal that is designed to "help K-8 teachers and librarians with the growing demands of planning lessons that incorporate both new technology and traditional media." Each issue has a theme with extensive listings of Web sites and other media to support it.

You can also find Internet ideas in ready-made lesson plans. Many commercial lesson plans contain Internet sites. In addition, you can use the links from Web pages such as *School Librarian Links* (one of my favorites) to find free lesson plans on the Internet itself.

Some SLMSs develop a computer database of frequently used Web sites. Included in the database are the URL of each site, the name of the site, relevant curriculum area(s), appropriate grade levels, and a section for comments. Because knowledge of the curriculum is important, it would be ideal for a group of librarians in a district to work together on this project and to share the results. In a networked school, the database can easily be made available on the network for all teachers and SLMSs to use.

An extension of the database idea is to develop a master list of bookmarks to curriculum sites. Bookmarks are a feature of Web browser software. They allow users to place a "bookmark" in one of the browser's files to record the URL of each site they might someday wish to return to. If all the schools use the same Web browser software, the relevant curriculum sites from the database can be bookmarked, the file saved to floppy disk, and the disk of ready-made bookmarks distributed to each school. In addition to a master bookmark file, the bookmarks can be sorted and rearranged so that all bookmarks for a particular class or subject appear on a single disk. This helps students and teachers visit pertinent sites.

Writing in *School Library Media Activities Monthly*, Barbara Ripp Safford reported on an assignment that she gave to her students in the School Library Media Studies program at the University of Northern Iowa. They were to "teach a lesson about the World Wide Web, but its objectives must be something beyond how to access information." The students outdid themselves. They:

- developed a lesson on how to "use key words to identify and refine an appropriate subject for a report" using search engines.
- used information on authors to compare the data found on the Web to that found using traditional reference sources.
- compared and contrasted several Web sites on the same subject.
- used Web sites to show the difference between fact and opinion.
- examined "bias in the presentation of information by looking at two Web sites about the Vietnam War."
- examined a site from a white supremacy group to show how Web sites can be made to look authentic, authoritative, and very professional.

One word of caution in using the Internet: some of the evaluation exercises are not appropriate for use with younger students. Most of the higher level evaluation activities designed by Safford's students were developed to be used with secondary students. As with any lesson plan, you need to match the age and skills of your students to the tools that they will use. Realize, also, that you need to match the resource to the appropriate unit goals or lesson objectives. The Internet is a resource: a means to teach something, not an end in itself.

Are there any specific things to remember when using the Internet in lessons?

While SLMSs and teachers have developed some wonderful lesson ideas using Internet resources, they have also reported some problems. These include time problems such as expecting to cover too much in a single lesson and not allowing enough time to complete a search. There are also problems with slow response times during certain portions of the day and slow downloads because of too many graphics on a Web site. Also, SLMSs report some frustration in not being able to help students evaluate the results of a search, and a fear that the students will accept anything found on the Internet as a fact.

Another problem is how to cite Internet resources. Many teachers require that students doing research must submit a bibliography of their sources and must follow a specific style manual. Unfortunately, many of these manuals provide no hints as to the correct citation format for a Web site, e-mail, or usenet message. Here is one place where the Web can help solve a problem that it creates. There are several sources on the Web that provide examples for citing Internet resources. Some of these are listed in the Resources section. Check them out while you still can. At least one of these sources has been threatened with a copyright lawsuit by a major publisher of a print style manual. While the developer of the site claims the right to apply the rules by using his own examples, he has still removed the citation information from his Web site.

SLMSs and teachers have developed more tips for using Internet resources in the library and in the classroom. The following tips were developed by Mary Alice Anderson, Media Specialist at Winona Middle School in Winona, Minnesota and Cathleen Wharton, US WEST, and published in the Internet Supplement to TECHNOLOGY CONNECTION and LIBRARY TALK, September 1996.

Tips for Using the Internet

Teachers, have you...

selected more than one relevant WWW site?

set bookmarks or Web pages on the computers or saved a bookmark file to disk?

checked the sites to be certain everything works with the browsers the students will be using?

made sure the links are not out of date or moved to another location?

designed thinking questions for the students?

instructed the students in the mechanics using the Internet (explained menus, taught them how to save and download text and graphics)?

provided instruction about good search strategies?

explained that all search engines do not provide the same results?

instructed the students in how to save/export bookmarks, download files, and print only what is necessary?

scheduled the use of the computer labs or computers?

made sure the necessary helper apps (such as graphic converters and other tools to help) are installed on the computers?

arranged for team-teaching with the media or technology specialist or others who can assist you, if necessary?

talked with your students about netiquette including guidelines for downloading, saving, and printing?

developed "Plan B," for students who cannot use the Internet or in case there are technical problems?

included Internet-specific directions to your students such as...

Did you pay careful attention to the instruction?
Did you look at all of the resources your teacher has pointed you to?
Did you record or bookmark URLs and any information you might want to use later?
Have you recorded information you will cite in your bibliography?
Did you answer all of the questions using your own words?
Did you investigate only project-related sites?

Do I have to worry about copyright on the Internet?

Yes. The information on the Internet is protected by copyright. All original information placed on the Internet or WWW after March, 1989, is legally considered to be the property of the person or organization that owns the original information. A copyright notice does not need to be present, but having one never hurts. Usually, e-mail is considered the property of the sender or the sender's employer. For text and graphics, the copyright law is the same as for print materials. Some of the software available on the Internet is freeware, and some is shareware. With shareware, if you decide to use the program after trying it out, you should send in the registration fee.

When a Web page is created, it automatically is protected by copyright. Web page copyright is owned by the creator, the creator's employer, or the individual or company paying for the development of the site. A school district should have a policy that addresses the ownership of Web sites created on its computers or with its resources.

What should I do if I want to build a Web site for my school or library?

Many schools are building their own Web sites, either on their own Internet Web server or on a commercial site. Before you begin, you need to decide where your Web site will reside. There is no use developing a site if you do not have a home for it. Because your site will need to be accessible 24 hours a day, you either need direct dedicated Internet access in your school or school district, or you need to find another home for it.

If you have direct dedicated Internet access, you will need your own Web server hardware and software to hook to that connection. In selecting the hardware for your server, you need to decide where the processing for animation, audio, 3D and other video will be done. Currently most servers download that information to the user's machine. A new trend is to have dynamic Web pages created for the individual user by the use of databases on the Web server. Software known as middleware creates what are called "dynamic" pages and "server-side" scripts. You can visit Web66 (http://web66.coled.umn.edu) and read the Classroom Internet Server Cookbook for Mac, Windows 95, and Windows NT for technical advice.

Each computer platform has its own entries in the server market and many are sold as complete packages. The usual configuration for a Web site is an internal network that is connected to a UNIX, Windows NT, or Mac server which acts as a bridge between the internal network and the Internet. Apple sells its own Apple Internet Server Solution 8550/200 which has a 200 MHZ PowerPC 603 chip with 32 MB RAM, expandable to 512 MB and SCSI interfaces. On the PC platform look for Sun Netra 1/170E, Silicon Graphics WebFORCE O^2, or the NeTpower Calisto Web 3. These have Pentium or Pentium Pro chips running between 167 MHZ and 200 MHZ with 64MB RAM expandable up to 1GB on the WebFORCE. Most have fast SCSI interfaces.

In addition to the hardware, you will need the software. First, there will be the usual computer operating system, such as UNIX, Windows (95 or NT) or Mac. In addition, you will need Web server software. Currently this is a growing, changing market. However, a few more commonly used server software programs include: *Netscape FastTrack Server*, *Microsoft Internet Information Server*, Luckman *Web Commander*, O'Reilly *WebSite*, and Quarterdeck*WebSTAR*.

If you do not wish to have your own Web server, you need to find another place to house your Web site. Possible locations are on the server of a local ISP, college or university, or town or community server. Another place might be on the server of a local commercial business with an Internet connection. In making a decision about where to place your site, consider such things as the ease of uploading the information to it, and how accessible it will be for updates. Ask yourself if just one person will need access to the site or if several classes, a middle school team, or individual students will also need access. If you are approaching an outside business or agency to host your site, be realistic in determining the space it will occupy. While the homepage for an individual might be 2MB or 3MB, a fairly plain school site will need a minimum of 15MB to 20MB with additional space needed for a lot of graphics.

Once you have identified a possible home for your Web site, you need to think about what you want to put on it. Before you make any decisions, use the Internet to visit sites developed by other schools to determine what you like and do not like. As you look at the other sites, examine their organization, content, and use of text versus graphics.

Some things you might see in your Internet visits are:

- An overview of the school and/or library
- Profiles of the school and/or library faculty, staff, and administration
- A community profile
- Information about the school and community that has been gathered by students
- Links to other sites
- Displays of student work and projects
- History of the school and/or community (some call this a "virtual museum")
- Online experiments in which you can participate
- Issues of an electronic magazine (a "zine")
- Individual classroom pages with information on class members, projects, and upcoming assignments.
- Descriptions of successful lessons with links to the specific plans and activities

In the past, designing a Web site meant using html (hypertext markup language) itself. Now, however, the simplest way is to use a graphic editor software program that lets you see the site as you build it. Examples of this software are Claris *HomePage*, Microsoft *FrontPage*, *Web Weaver* (a shareware program simple enough for even upper elementary students to use), and Adobe *PageMill*. These and other graphic editors are listed in the Resources section. There are even Internet sites listed there to help you develop your Web site.

Once you have your development software, plan your Web site using the same planning guidelines that you would use for any multimedia project. You can refer to the guidelines in Chapter 11 of this book for some advice and some checklists.

Basically, you'll need to think about who your audience will be and what you want to say or convey to that audience. Since a Web site often consists of several linked Web pages, you will need to organize your information. A good idea is to storyboard your site and plan the links that you will provide. Strive for a consistent look to your site and limit the things that look pretty or impressive but that increase the time that it will take for your site to download. Unless people know your site is really great, there is a limit to the amount of time they will spend waiting for it to download.

Don't forget to lead people to your Web site. Once your site is up and running, you will want to contact some of the search utilities to have your site added to the database. Check the Calafia Web site in the Resources section for some helpful hints.

In response to the growing number of school Web sites, some districts are developing Web publication guidelines. While this is sometimes included in the district's AUP, often it is a separate document. The Web site guidelines include such things as who is responsible for maintaining the Web site, who has final authority over what goes in the site, who must approve any links to other sites that are included, and how the site will be updated. In addition, some determination must be made concerning how much personal information about any individual will be placed on the Web site. Check the Stafford County (Virginia) guidelines on the Internet. (http://pen1.pen.k12.va.us/Anthology/Div/Stafford/tech/tech.html) (Note that's the number one after the first "pen" in the URL)

How can I use the Internet as a telephone or for videoconferencing?

Chapter 7 of this book discusses the growing field of computer telephony. Most of the information discussed there applies to the Internet as well.

To take your telephone on the Internet, you need a computer with an Internet connection, sound card, speakers, microphone, and telephony software. To send your message, the Internet takes it, breaks it into pieces, sends the pieces to their destination and then reassembles it. One problem with the Internet is that not all of the packets take the same route. In addition, with the previous lack of standards for telephony hardware, there were often problems making the connection. Even now, slow connect speeds on the Internet can mean poor audio quality even with speech compression technologies. Of course, the person you call must be logged on to the Internet in order for you to talk to him or her.

Desktop videoconferencing (DVC) via the Internet has been plagued by the lack of standards. Only recently has H.323 DVD been adopted as a TCP/IP standard. It is scalable to work with modems between 14.4 Kbps and 1.5 Mbps. Among software developers, the first to meet those specifications were Microsoft's *Net Meeting 2.0* and Intel's *Internet Video Phone*. The later also meets the t.120 data-sharing standard for file-transfer, whiteboarding, and applications sharing.

What are some of the other issues surrounding the Internet?

A major concern of Internet users is privacy. One issue centers around e-mail and grew out of a situation where an Internet service read the e-mail of some of its subscribers. Courts have ruled that e-mail housed on a business computer can be read by the employer. A school's UP should clearly define the confidentiality, if any, of school e-mail.

Another problem is "cookies." Cookies are placed on your hard drive by a Web site and contain information including the name of the site and information about what you did there. Some people, however, have raised objections as to the information that is in these cookies and how much personal information the Web site can extract about a visitor. The May 1997 issue of *Consumer Reports* discusses the DoubleClick Network which is "an ad agency collecting dossiers on the millions of people who visit dozens of popular Web sites daily—and who may not be aware that someone's gathering private information."

Both Netscape and Microsoft have announced that the next upgrades to their browsers will place limits on cookies. In the meantime, you can search your hard drive for any file with the word "cookie" in it and consider deleting it. One word of caution; some cookies contain Web site passwords so be sure you do not delete these. Other options for refusing cookies are listed in the Resources section.

A relatively new tool on the Web is "push" technology, sometimes called Web-casting or channel-casting. With push technology, information is sent automatically to a "subscriber." Push works in the background and, when your computer keyboard is idle for a set period, displays its data. The best example is *PointCast* (http://www.pointcast.com) which delivers news, weather, sports, and financial information to your computer. Your regular screen saver is replaced with *PointCast*'s information. (Of course, for this to work, your Internet connection must be active.)

Cookies and push technology are related to the problem of "online safecrackers." These hackers can, technically, gain entrance to your hard drive while you are on the Internet. While this does not seem to be a serious problem, there are "firewall" programs to limit their access. *SecureCast*, a software program from McAfee (http://www.mcafee.com) can be downloaded free from their Web site. It will run in the background whenever your Internet connection is idle to be sure nothing is sneaking into your computer. In addition, there are programs that allow you to partition your hard drive and limit access to each part with a password. Other than having a separate computer for Web access, the best thing you can do is to turn off your modem when you are not using it.

What's in the future for the Internet?

The Internet is constantly growing and changing. New programs for Web site developers such as Java (an add-on for HTML to include animation and video), and VRML (Virtual Reality Modeling Language) continue to add to the once text-based Internet. However, they share the problem of limited bandwidth, resulting in slow transmission rates. On the horizon are a variety of Internet "appliances" or non-traditional ways to access the Internet, some of them with much faster speeds than POTS lines.

Some companies are backing NCs (Network computers) or Web PCs (Web personal computers). NCs are proposed as a cheap alternative to the microcomputer to provide Internet access. Rather than requiring a powerful microprocessor, the processing for the NC is done on a central server. Without any disk storage, the NC comes with a keyboard and a mouse and uses a TV monitor for display.

Accessing the Internet via the fast television cable connection is possible with @Home (http://www.home.net). This service allows computers to access the Internet or cable lines owned by Cox, TCI, and Comcast. Current projections are for transmission rates of 128 Kpbs "upstream" and 10 Mbps "downstream" or back to you. Time Warner is also planning to offer a similar television/cable modem system.

There are still other Internet appliances. WebTV (brand name) provides the subscriber with a box to place on top of the television and a connection to the WebTV network, a paid online service. This service then provides an Internet connection. Some cellular telephones have built-in e-mail and Internet access on a four-line screen that allows the user to access Web sites with HDMT (Handheld Device Markup Language). Intel is taking television to the computer with Intercast technology. This allows people to view television on their personal computer as they download related Web pages.

Who knows what the Internet will look like by the year 2000? Just don't expect it to slow down so you can catch up.

Bibliography

Anderson, M.A. & Wharton, C. Guidelines for Using the Internet. TECHNOLOGY CONNECTION, 3 (5). A checklist and reminders of things to consider before implementing a class project.

Barkhouse, N. (1997). Grasping the thread: Web page development in the elementary classroom. *Emergency Librarian,* 24 (3), 24-25. The author, a grade 2/3 teacher, discusses how her class set up their own Web page.

Blenz. Clucas, B. (1995). Hooking up to the Internet; Are freenets an option? TECHNOLOGY CONNECTION, 2 (3), 33-34. The author looks at community networks as a free access road to the information superhighway.

Burt, D. (1997). In Defense of filtering. *American Libraries,* 28 (7), 46-48. Burt responds to the 10 major arguments that have been presented to protest the use of Internet filters in libraries.

Cahlin, M. & Schuman, K. (1996). Downloading and viewing images. *PC Novice,* 7 (4), 81-83. Contains specific directions for downloading images using any of the major commercial online service providers.

Clyde, L.A. (1996). Kids going online. *Emergency Librarian*, 24(2), 54-55. Reviews some of the Internet books that have been published just for children.

Descy, D. (1996). Create your own home page; a step-by-step guide. Technology Connection, 3 (2), 19-21. Directions for using HTML and your word processor to create a Web page.

Doyle, B. & Doyle, D. (1997). Dynamic and interactive Web servers. *NewMedia*, 7 (3), 48-59. The authors "test drive" Web server hardware and software.

Dyrli, O. (1997). Online privacy and the cookies controversy. *Technology & Learning*, 17 (6), 20. Should you refuse all cookies through the Internet? The author claims they serve a very useful purpose.

Eckhouse, J. (1997). The Web on TV. *HomePC*, 4 (2), 73-82. A look at Internet appliances that connect your television to the Internet.

Ekhaml, L. (1996). Make your presence known on the Web. *School Library Media Activities Monthly*, 12 (10), 33-35. Provides some basic information about Web publishing and design techniques.

Fitzgerald, M. A. (1997). Misinformation on the Internet: Applying evaluation skills to online information. *Emergency Librarian*, 24 (3), 9-14. Discusses the problems of unregulated information on the Internet and some signs that may indicate misinformation.

Garlock, K. & Pionetk, S. (1996). *Building the service-based library Web site*. Chicago: ALA. Includes design principles as well as addresses of other library sites.

Gentili, K. (1997). School library media specialists new to the Internet ask: Where do I begin? *School Library Media Activities Monthly*, 13 (5), 25-27. The creator of the *School Librarian Links* page on the Web talks about why she constructed it and what it does for SLMSs.

Harrison, E. Andrews, M. & Kalis, L. (1997). The right connections. *SmartMoney*, 6 (5), 116-125. Compares and rates the major national Internet providers on factors such as reliability, speed, installation, tech support, and navigation.

ICONnect: How to connect to the Internet. (1996). Chicago: ALA. A handbook on searching the Internet.

Internet roadmap for educators. (1996). Arlington, VA: Educational Research Service. This guidebook for Internet use covers uses in the classroom, educational projects and sites, copyrights, and acceptable use policies.

Is your computer spying on you? (1997, May). *Consumer Reports*, 62, 6. Take a look at cookies and what they can tell advertisers about you.

Johnson, D. (1995). Emerging technologies, emerging concerns. Technology Connection, 2 (8), 50. Read the letter that the author wrote to a school board member who was concerned about pornography on the Internet.

Johnson, D. (1995). Selection skills are critical to evaluating resources. Technology Connection, 3 (2), 50. Johnson provides some guidelines for evaluating World Wide Web sites.

Jones, T. (1997). Using search engines on the World Wide Web and where to find search engine help. *School Library Media Activities Monthly*, 14 (1), 35-36. Explains how to find the help screens at many of the major search engines.

Junion-Metz, G. (1996). Bounce onto the net. *School Library Journal,* 42 (2), 34-38. "An easy-to-understand guide to the terms techies use...for choosing the right Internet connection."

Kafai, Y. & Bates, M. (1997). Internet Web-searching instruction in the elementary classroom: Building a foundation for information literacy. *School Library Media Quarterly*, 25 (2), 103-111. In the SNAPdragon Project, elementary school children evaluated Web sites and constructed their own online directory.

McKenzie, J. (1995). Planning a voyage into cyberspace. TECHNOLOGY CONNECTION, 2 (2), 9-11. In this first of a series of six articles, McKenzie explains how to plan before students actually go on the Internet.

Metz, R. & Junion-Metz, G. (1996). *Using the World Wide Web and creating home pages. A how-to-do-it manual for librarians.* New York: Neal-Schuman. From browsing the Web, to building a Web site and using Web resources in the library, this 269-page book covers it all.

Miller-Widrick, M. & Thomas, C. (1995). Listservs teachers will Love. TECHNOLOGY CONNECTION, 2 (8), 32-33. In addition to telling you how to locate listservs, the authors provide information on listservs in a number of curriculum areas.

Minkel, W. (1997). Lost (& found) in cyberspace: How to make search engines work for you. *School Library Journal*, 43 (3), 102-105. Reviews search utilities and includes "8 ways to outsmart an engine."

Novelli, J. (1997). Speed surfing for educators. *Electronic Learning*, 16 (5), 52. Suggestions to save time and money when searching for information on the Internet.

Palgi, R. (1996). Rules of the road. *School Library Journal*, 42 (8), 32-33. Explains why you need an AUP and what to put in it.

Philman, M. (1997). See you on the Internet. *NewMedia,* 7 (4), 37-40. Provides information on and comparisons of desktop videoconferencing software.

Rosenberg, S. (1997). Changing channels. *NewMedia,* 7 (4), 45-50. Looks at alternatives to the current telephone access to the Internet including WebTV, satellite, and cable.

Silliamson, C. (1996). Another look at acceptable use policies. TECHNOLOGY CONNECTION, 3 (2), 23-24. Provides an overview of the content of AUPs along with some disclaimers.

Schneider, K. (1997). Selecting Internet filtering software: Buyer beware. *American Libraries,* 28 (5), 84. Discusses nine features of filtering software and makes some software suggestions.

Seiter, C. (1997). *Internet for Macs for dummies starter kit.* Foster City: IDG Books. Another title in the popular "Dummies" series.

Simpson, C. & McElmeel, S. (1997). *Internet for schools.* Worthington, OH: Linworth. Includes the basics of Internet use and methods for introducing students and teachers to the Internet.

Stafford, B. R. Axdahl, P., Dohrmann, J., Ehlers, B., Freidhof, J., McCabe, A., Stickfort, S., & Throckmorton, A. (1996). What do we teach about the World Wide Web? *School Library Media Activities Monthly,* 13 (4), 44-46. What can you teach about the Web beyond how to find neat sites? These University of Northern Iowa library science students have the answers.

Stoll, C. (1995). *Silicon snake oil.* New York: Doubleday. According to the *National Review,* September 11, 1995, this book is "incisive, fascinating and indispensable." Stoll explains the hype surrounding the Internet and tells us what's wrong with it.

Tillman, H. (1997). Evaluating quality on the Net. [http:www/tiac.net/users/hope/findqual.html]. This is a February 1997 update of a paper that Tillman, Director of Libraries at Babson College, presented at the Computers in Libraries conference in Arlington, Virginia, in February 1996.

Tips and tools for building a school Website. (1997). *Technology & Learning,* 17 (4), 25-38. Discusses how educators are building Web sites and the tools that they are using to do it.

Valauskas, E. & Ertel, M. (1997). *The Internet for teachers and school library media specialists.* New York, Neal-Schuman. From funding Internet access to using the Internet in the curriculum and publishing on the Web, this book uses case histories to show how others have succeeded.

Van Hoff, A., Shaio, S., & Starbuck, O. (1996). *Hooked on Java.* New York: Addison-Wesley. *Byte* magazine says "if you want an overview and some sample code, this book is the place to start." (April 1996).

Varhol, P. (1997). Web fetchers. *Mobile Computing & Communications,* 8 (4), 80-90. Evaluates eight offline Web browsers.

Notes

Chapter 9

Distance Learning: Television and Beyond

Technology has done much to change the way a SLMS manages a school library, provides library resources, and teaches library or information skills. Many teachers and administrators have embraced the new technologies, changing the way instruction takes place in entire school districts. But while some schools have made use of new technologies, others, for various reasons, have not. Some schools may simply not be able to afford to purchase equipment or resources. Others may find that there are too many demands for funds on a budget that has already been cut to the bare bones. Small school districts may not have the resources to hire teachers for special or advanced placement classes when only a few students would enroll in those classes. Collections suffer as videotapes of "current events" become history videos and science resources become outdated.

One solution to this problem of inequity of resources has been to depend more on technology itself. In previous chapters we have looked at using fax networks to obtain periodical articles, computers and modems to search distant databases for information, and computer telecommunications networks for forming instructional partnerships with schools around the world. In addition, educators have begun to rethink the old concept of distance learning or distance education and to use the changes in technology to change the way in which instruction and information is delivered to students, faculty, staff, and administrators.

What is distance learning?

Distance learning or distance education can be described as the delivery of instruction or information through the use of radio, broadcast television, cable television, satellites, telephone lines, fax machines, or a combination of these technologies. In the past, distance learning often had a teacher in a television studio teaching a lesson that was videotaped or sent out as a live broadcast television signal. The teacher never met the students in the class and there was little, if any, interaction between students and instructor. This "distance learning" was almost like using a videotape for instruction. In many cases, it was nothing more than a "talking head" on a television screen.

Technology is beginning to change all of that. Entering the picture are two-way video and audio delivery systems, satellite uplinks and downlinks, multisite delivery systems, interactive cable television, and distance learning via the Internet and World Wide Web. Even broadcast and cable television companies are offering distance education opportunities to schools in the form of free or inexpensive resources.

To understand how this all fits together, let's look first at the ways that distance education has, historically, been delivered to schools and the content of that education. Then we'll look at television, a major provider of distance education, by exploring the types of television that are available today, some specific examples of distance learning networks, and the ways television networks are assisting in providing information to schools everywhere. We'll end by looking at the impact the Internet is beginning to have on distance learning and by examining how you, as a school librarian, need to work with distance education.

There is, however, one major point to keep in mind as we look at the various forms of technology used in distance education. Technology should be used only as a means to accomplish an educational goal. Problems exist when that technology, rather than the curriculum and instructional content, becomes the goal of distance learning. As Donald Ely stated in his address entitled "Distance Education: by Design or Default," presented at the June, 1996, conference of the Association for Educational Communications and Technology, "The most successful distance education programs in the world are those that respond to real needs and offer an alternative to learning which would otherwise be denied or prohibitive in terms of cost and time."

What are the main forms of distance learning?

There is always a problem with trying to put things in distinct categories since many times there are exceptions and overlaps. That's true when trying to describe the types of technology used with distance learning. Thus, you have to realize that the following is only a general description.

Text only

The first form of distance learning was the correspondence course in which students were expected to read and respond, usually by taking a test or answering a set of questions that were then mailed to the instructor. Originally this text was delivered through the mail. Technology, however, has made it possible to deliver text materials in other formats. Instructors can use e-mail to send materials to students who e-mail their tests or papers to the instructor for grading. If e-mail is not convenient, printed materials can be faxed. Sometimes videotapes are added to the instructional packages. In other instances, text materials can be posted on homepages on the Internet for students to download or to read. It seems interesting that one of our latest technologies, the Internet, is fostering the regrowth of an early form of distance learning: the correspondence course. Unfortunately, with text-only distance learning, students often feel isolated from the instructor and other students, although the modern telecommunications have made the instructor more accessible to the students.

Audio Only

With the advent of radio and audio recording came the use of these technologies for distance learning. Recordings of lectures could be used for distance learning. In a way, today's booming "books-on-tape" market is a form of audio-only distance learning. In "live" format, lectures and discussions could be sent by radio to provide one-way audio communication from a central transmission point to one (point-to-point) or many (multipoint) sites. This expanded to two-way audio, or audioconferencing, with the use of special telephone equipment (microphones and speakers) and with the regular telephone lines for transmission.

The problem with the audio-only format is the lack of visual contact between the students and the teacher or, in the case of multiple sites, among all of the students. Since most people are not primarily auditory learners and since people seem to remember most of what they hear and see, audio-only distance learning is not successful for the majority of students. In addition, because the instructor cannot see the students, he/she cannot react during the program to the students' questions and concerns unless those concerns are actually voiced by the students over a two-way audio connection.

Several ways have been tried to make audio distance learning more successful. One is to transmit still visuals to the remote site before the audio program begins. In some cases, mail delivery is used; however, in recent times, it is more common to use fax machines or computers to download text information. In other instances, a trained "facilitator" is placed at the reception sites to assist the learners. However, the use of a facilitator is not always practical or possible. Now, with the use of computers, modems, and appropriate software, still graphics can be sent to distant computers to supplement the lecture or discussion in what is called audiographic conferencing. Still missing, however, is the visual contact between student and instructor.

One-way Video

With the advent of television, many educators saw the technology as a way to deliver instruction. An instructor at a central site taught a class. That class was viewed, either live or on videotape, by students in one or more remote sites. This form of instruction has grown into our use of television programs to provide distance education. Missing here, however, was any direct communication between the instructor and the students. Research on this model of distance learning has shown that it works best when there is an adult facilitator or teacher in each receiving classroom.

One-way Video, Two-way Audio

The next step was to provide one-way video with two-way audio connections. This "simulated lecture" is usually done through the use of telephone lines to carry some of the audio. The video can be sent as regular broadcast television, ITFS (Instructional Television Fixed Service), or satellite link. Sometimes the video courses are locally produced, while other times the courses are received via satellite and then transmitted to other sites. Again, facilitators at each site are important and are often used as troubleshooters for technical problems. Many states use staff development teleconferences to transmit information about new programs to all teachers in the state. AASL has used the teleconference distance learning format to publicize its programs. Unfortunately, the emphasis in this method is on the sending location with limited interaction of the students or other viewers.

Two-way Video and Audio

Perhaps the ideal set-up for distance learning is to have both the audio and video as two-way communications. (See Figure 9.1) In this videoconferencing, fully interactive format, all of the sites (whether only the teacher and one group of students in a point-to-point system or teacher and many sites in a multipoint system) are set up with cameras, monitors, microphones, and speakers. Signals can be sent in a variety of ways: by satellite, fiber optic telephone cables, or microwave. Using a control panel, the instructor can select the images to display on all of the monitors. These images can range from video of the instructor, pictures of documents or manipulatives used by the instructor, or live video of students at any of the sites. Ideally, each receiving class has the potential to see each of the other classes. Students in one remote site can see students in another remote site during a discussion. One problem of this method of distance learning has been the expense for the live satellite television transmission.

In the past, it was impossible to send full-motion video through telephone lines. However, these problems have been solved, to some degree, through the use of video compression technologies and fiber optic cables, T-1 or ISDN lines, and the development of what are known as CCITT (Consultative Committee International Telegraph and Telephone) standards for the transmission of audio and video. As a result, several networks have been established that use telephone lines for two-way video and audio distance learning. Sometimes called group-videoteleconferencing, these networks may have multiple cameras and sophisticated audio setups in all sites, and permit the instructor to use a variety of media (slides, transparencies, computers, videotapes) in instruction. See the videoconferencing information in Chapter 7 of this book for more information.

While informal distance learning often takes place during conferences and chats on computer networks, desktop video conferencing systems have been developed for the Macintosh and for PCs. Using the new digital telephone lines (some of these systems will also work on analog telephone lines), two users can share data on their computers. In addition, there is a "live video window" on a portion of each computer monitor. A video camera, mounted on top of each computer monitor, can send a motion video to the other computer for display in the small (3" x 3") "live video window."

Another new technology on the horizon is interactive cable television, sometimes called Interactive Video and Data Services (IVDS). Linked with HDTV (High Definition Television), IVDS will not work with the television sets and video cameras that are currently in use. It uses an entirely different set of broadcasting standards and is not compatible with the existing NTSC format. The idea is to combine computers and television into a single interactive format. While some forms have been tried in Europe, no one seems to know exactly what will be used in the United States.

Combinations of the above

Schools have tried various combinations of the above to make distance learning more meaningful for students. One current delivery method is what is called the "online mentored seminar" or computer mediated communication (CMC) that relies on the Internet for portions of the instruction. Used primarily with

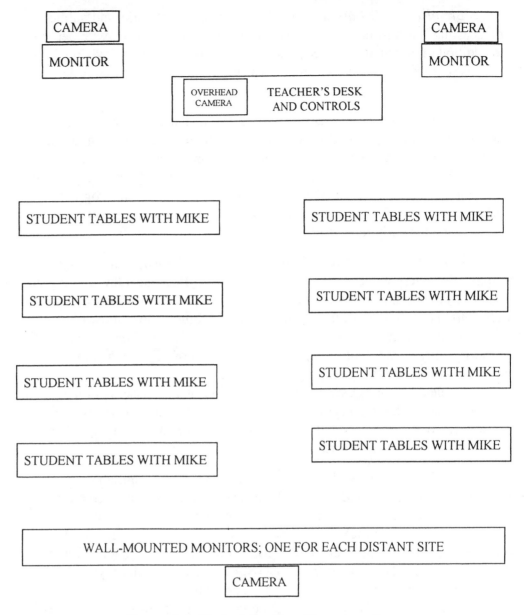

Figure 9.1 Typical Sending Classroom Setup

advanced placement high school students and college students, this seminar method requires student to gather information using text and television and then to exchange that information with the instructor and other students through e-mail, BBSs or newsgroups, chat rooms on the Internet, and listservs which route the e-mail to all members of the group. There may even be interactive tutorials on the World Wide Web. Factored in are also live videoteleconferences at various times throughout the semester.

What types of television networks are involved in distance learning?

Traditionally, television has been a major factor in distance learning. However, to understand the role of television networks, you first need to look at the basic types of television services available.

Broadcast or Off-air. Usually the commercial networks and public broadcasting stations that are received free on any television set, with perhaps the addition of an antenna, are considered broadcast or off-air television. The signal is sent from a transmitter over the airwaves to the television. A device known as a relay can be used to boost the signal so that it reaches farther.

Public Television Networks. A form of broadcast television found in many communities is the noncommercial or public television station. Some of these are established to provide local community information and televise local government. Others have an instructional role and carry instructional programming during the daytime hours and Public Broadcasting System programs during the evening. These stations may even broadcast college courses for credit during the early morning hours.

Cable Television. Living in the mountains of Pennsylvania, I grew up thinking that everyone had to have cable television. Because television signals do not bend over mountains and down into valleys, cable television companies were started to bring television programming to "remote" locations. With cable television, a main antenna and/or a satellite dish receives television signals. These signals are then sent through wires to cable subscribers who pay a monthly cable fee to view the programming.

Cable companies usually offer a "basic service" consisting of a number of channels and additional specialized channels, each with its own fee. Subscribers can opt for only the basic service or can add as many additional channels as they want or can afford.

Satellite Television. Satellite television uses a retransmitter on a satellite in space. When a signal from earth hits the satellite, it is beamed back to earth where it is picked up by a satellite receiver or satellite dish. Satellites are used to beam a network television broadcast from its point of origin to the satellite and back to your local network affiliate or cable television company. The affiliate then sends the program out over the airwaves where your television set or antenna picks it up and plays the program.

In addition, you might have your own satellite receiver in your school or at your home that would allow you to receive some free broadcasts directly from the satellite. Pay programs are usually scrambled (the signal is mixed up) and can only be received by someone with the appropriate unscrambling device.

Satellite receivers can be classified as either agile or fixed. A fixed satellite receiver is permanently set to receive the signal of only one network. More versatile is the agile satellite receiver that can be moved to pick up a variety of signals.

Closed Circuit Television. Closed circuit television or CCTV is often found in a single school building, school campus, or a school district. A television signal is sent from a distribution point to receivers that are connected to it by wires. Many schools use CCTV to show student-produced news programs or to rebroadcast cable, off-air, or satellite programs throughout a school.

Instructional Television Fixed Service. Often called ITFS, Instructional Television Fixed Service is educational programming broadcast in the high frequency microwave spectrum that is not received by regular television sets. Its range is limited and only sites with a special high frequency converter can receive an ITFS signal.

How are these television networks involved in distance learning?

Public Broadcasting Stations

Traditionally, many local public television broadcasting stations have aired educational programs during the daytime hours. While only one-way audio and video, these programs are valuable resources for classroom teachers and school librarians who incorporate them into their own lessons.

Selecting the programming for these daytime instructional shows is usually a joint responsibility of the local public broadcasting station and area school districts who pay a membership fee to the station each year. If your school district is a member of such a group or consortium, you can help select the programs that are aired by contacting your district's representative to the consortium.

While some programs on the network might be produced locally, most are purchased for broadcast and include generous copyright privileges. For example, you might have permission to tape each show in a series and to keep the tapes on file in the library for a year. Teachers and students could use the tapes at any time. Should the network purchase the rights to the program the next year, you could continue to use your tapes.

In addition to the programs, the network may provide other services as well. PBS Video News and other resources can be obtained from the national PBS Elementary/Secondary Service center. For many of the special educational programs and the after-school and evening programming, PBS or the local affiliate purchases, prepares, or lists a source of instructional guides for the classroom teacher. Copies of these can be obtained for each teacher using the series, with additional copies placed in the professional collection of the library. Then, when you circulate a videotape of a program, you can also circulate the teacher's guide. Staff members from the local affiliate might also be available to provide face-to face staff development activities on using specific programs, teaching with television, or complying with copyright.

PBS is a partner, along with Texaco, Thirteen/WNET, and other local public television stations, in the National Teacher Training Institute. Begun in 1990, this program targets math and science teachers with a goal of providing training, materials, and advice in creating lesson plans for individual class-rooms. By 1996-97, over 115,000 teachers were trained in the Institute's methods.

General Cable Television Services

Many local cable television networks provide some services to school districts. In many cases, they provide a local channel that schools and municipalities can use to air programs of local interest. In addition to the local services, cable networks have developed a national educational project called Cable in the Classroom.

Cable in the Classroom

The idea behind Cable in the Classroom is to provide free cable service and educational programs (without commercials) to schools. Currently more than 8,500 local cable companies and 33 cable networks (sometimes called programmers) participate in this project, which reaches over 75,000 schools throughout the United States. Member cable companies provide free installation and basic service to all public and state-approved private schools that are passed by cable. In addition to the regular programming with commercials, Cable in the Classroom networks offer special commercial-free programs (540 hours per month in 1997) and services to schools. These services include such things as information on copyright and curriculum-based support materials..

Some of the Cable in the Classroom commercial-free programs are aired during the early morning hours. Use the instructions that came with your VCR to set the timer and record the programs you want.

The following are brief overviews of a few of the networks that belong to Cable in the Classroom and offer special programming for schools. Remember, however, not all of these networks may be aired by your local cable service. Check with your local cable company for details. Check the Resources list for addresses and URLs of the networks.

Arts & Entertainment Network. Commercial-free programs on history, drama, performing arts, biography, archeology, and anthropology air each weekday on ABE Classroom. The copyright on these shows allows unrestricted educational use for one year.

Black Entertainment Television (BET). Each month, BET provides a copyright-free "teen summit" feature that focuses on current teen problems. On request, BET will send schools commercial-free copies of some of their regular programs.

C-SPAN. These public service networks (C-SPAN I and C-SPAN II) for the cable television industry offer commercial-free and copyright-free coverage of the U.S. House of Representatives, U.S. Senate, selected congressional hearings, international legislatures, and other public events. Two audio-only channels (C-SPAN Audio 1 and C-SPAN Audio 2) provide international news in English and the BBC World Service from London. Free teaching guides, lesson plans, and monthly newsletters are also available. A 24-hour schedule hotline gives a two-day schedule as well as some long-range information. Purdue University's School of Liberal Arts maintains C-SPAN's Public Affairs Video Archives which records and stores C-SPAN programs for educational use.

CNN. CNN Newsroom is telecast each weekday at 4:30 a.m. with CNN WorldView at 4:45 a.m. Both may be recorded for later unrestricted use. Daily classroom guides for the two programs are available over many telecommunications networks and include summaries, background information, discussion questions, activities and bibliographies.

The Discovery Channel. In a one-hour block called Assignment Discovery, this network presents shows that can be used in a school for one year. Featuring curriculum-related topics, these shows cover science and technology, social studies, natural science, arts and humanities, and world events and contemporary issues. Vocabulary words and study questions are presented before the program, and a bibliography appears at the end.

The Learning Channel. Aired during one hour each week are several 5- to 15-minute programs in the TLC Elementary School series. These programs, which may be taped and kept for two years, cover curriculum-related topics for grades K-6.

Knowledge TV (KNOW). KNOW, formerly Mind Extension University, provides instruction for students from elementary school through graduate school as well as professional development and enrichment classes ("useful programming for everyday life") from more than 25 distance education providers.

The Weather Channel. Learn about the weather by viewing The Weather Classroom, which is broadcast Sunday at 4:00 p.m. with a repeat Monday at 4:00 a.m. for 30 minutes with unrestricted educational use. In addition to the nation's weather for the day, the show features a meteorology topic. A textbook/workbook for the series is available.

In addition to the programs, the members of Cable in the Classroom provide a variety of services to educators including a variety of staff development items, teacher training workshops, an online electronic bulletin board for educators, and competitive grants for video equipment.

Cable in the Classroom Magazine. Published monthly except for a combined July/August issue, this magazine is generally made available free to schools by the local cable television network or for a nominal fee. Containing feature articles about teachers and SLMSs who use the programming, program listings, a taping calendar, and information about contests and support materials, each issue is also available online with search features.

The Family & Community Critical Viewing Project is a partnership uniting Cable in the Classroom with the National Partner Teacher Association and the National Cable Television Association. In addition to providing training on critical viewing and media literacy, the partnership presents "Taking Charge of Your TV" workshops and a free video of the same title.

Ingenious X*Change

Information such as news, weather, sports, and stock quotes is transmitted by the local cable company to a computer in the school. Also provided are lesson plans and "Video Connections," a daily educational programming guide.

Channel One

Channel One (sometimes called the classroom channel) is a commercial venture developed for schools by Whittle Communication. It has since been sold to ABC and then to Disney. Upon joining the Channel One network, each school receives, at no cost, a television monitor for each classroom, a fixed satellite dish, and a VCR. In return, the school must arrange for students to view a

12-minute television news program each day. This program is sent each night via satellite to the school where it is recorded for viewing later that day. When not being used for Channel One, the monitors and VCR can be used to show other educational programs. Quick repairs (no waiting for days before you see the repair person) for any Channel One equipment is just a phone call away.

This news show is not the only resource available on Channel One. During the day, Channel One airs several hours of educational programs. Its Classroom Channel has a variety of noncommercial curriculum-related programs, and its Educators Channel airs staff development features.

Since shows on both are copyright-free, one SLMS reports adding over 180 videotapes on current topics to her collection as a result of recording shows from these channels. Channel One provides a copy of a monthly magazine with program listings and program notes for each faculty member so there is plenty of time for the SLMS and the teachers to decide in advance what they want to have sent out over the network in the school or to have recorded for future use.

What's the catch, you ask? The 12-minute news program contains two minutes of commercials that are aimed at students. These two minutes have caused some heated debates. While some people see Channel One as an opportunity to receive badly needed technology at no cost, others see it as the selling of America's school students. A 1993 study did find that students viewing Channel One scored 5% to 8% higher on current events than nonviewing peers, with retention hinging on the ways teachers used the newscasts in discussions and whether the programs were shown in homeroom or in academic subjects. View the program, review your state and school district policies, and look at the alternatives before you make up your own mind.

What other television distance learning resources are available?

In addition to the materials provided by many of the networks, other resources are available to help you locate and select television programs for use in your school. While designed for home rather than school use, periodicals such as Satellite Orbit list programs available to anyone with a satellite receiver.

In a computerized database, KIDSNET, a clearinghouse for information about audio and video materials for children and young adults, identifies appropriate radio and television programs by curriculum area. It also provides some print materials and information about copyright. Check the resources list for addresses of distance learning networks and other distance learning resources.

How are states involved in distance education?

Many networks use new technologies to deliver distance education to various parts of the United States. While some are regional, extending across many states, others have developed within the boundaries of a single state or a region within a state.

Wisconsin is one state that has been active in developing distance learning. With many small and remote schools, the state of Wisconsin wanted to provide all of its students with an equal opportunity for a quality education including the chance to take highly specialized courses. To do this, it has encouraged the development of regional networks that work with local telephone companies to provide and transmit instruction and staff development programs.

Using the fiber optic telephone lines of the telephone companies, the networks provide high quality, reliable two-way audio and full-motion video instruction. Fax machines are used to deliver documents (handouts, tests) needed to supplement instruction. Some networks are planning to add CD-ROM, laserdisc, e-mail and other computer communication capabilities to the network.

Now, imagine that you are the SLMS in a K-12 school with a total enrollment of 120 students. You are located in the middle of the metropolis that extends from Atlanta to Boston on the eastern seaboard of the United States and are less than 125 miles from Washington, D.C. However, your town cannot be reached by car, train, or bus; in fact, there is only one car in your whole town, and it is used to teach driver education. Living on Tangier Island in the middle of the Chesapeake Bay, your only way to get to the rest of the country is by plane or boat.

Nina Pruitt, SLMS at Tangier Combined School, sees distance learning as one way of providing educational opportunities for her students. Using a satellite link, Tangier students take classes such as marketing and trigonometry. The interactive video satellite connections with two-way audio and video give the Tangier students an opportunity to interact with other students over the statewide network and over the direct link to a county high school on the mainland. Handouts, assignments, and tests are sent both ways using a fax machine.

Tangier received its equipment as part of a turnkey package given to every Virginia high school by the Virginia Department of Education as part of VSEN (Virginia Satellite Educational Network). Consisting of an agile satellite receiver, fax machine, television monitor, VCR, conference telephone, and storage cart, the system allows a school to receive programs from sites throughout the state and the world. VSEN itself has three broadcast sites in the state and transmits courses in Latin, Japanese, AP English, calculus, statistics, and U.S. history.

Other states are also involved in distance learning. The following are a few additional examples.

Iowa. Using a fiber optic network, the ICN (Iowa Communications Network) began with fiber optic links to a classroom in each county. Plans are to develop 300 school sites and 100 library sites. In the spring of 1995, over 47,000 hours of instruction were held on the network.

Texas. Texas Educational Telecommunications Network (TETN) is a 24-hour telecommunications link to educators throughout the state and provides two-way videoconferencing as well as data transmission.

Kentucky. KET or Kentucky Educational Television offers a variety of courses such as German, Latin 2, pre-calculus, and physics to sites within the state and to members of a consortium.

ESN (Education Satellite Network) was created by the Missouri School Boards Association.

Multi-state:

The Satellite Education Resources Consortium or SERC is active in 23 states ranging from New York and Florida to Mississippi and Nebraska.

IDEANET is a joint venture of the Missouri School Boards Association, Northern Arizona University, Oklahoma State University, and Satellite Telecommunication Educational Programming.

Distance Learning Associates was created by the Massachusetts Corporation for Educational Telecommunications, Central Educational Telecom Network, Fairfax (Virginia) County School System Satellite Network, and the Prince William County (Virginia) Satellite Network.

Why use distance learning?

Traditionally, distance learning has been seen as a way to:

- Provide equity of access for all students, no matter how remote or poor the school district.
- Make available a wide range of subjects (including advance placement and foreign language classes) even to small school districts.
- Allow students to be exposed to "expert" teachers.
- Take a "field-trip" without leaving the school.
- Foster collaboration and develop shared problem-solving skills.
- Develop partnerships with other schools and with businesses.
- Provide up-to-date instruction.
- Deliver instruction for special-needs students.
- Provide enrichment opportunities.
- Present current events programs.
- Provide training and staff development opportunities.

In addition, many educators advocate the use of the Internet as a distance learning component because of its flexibility, use across computer platforms (PC and Mac), availability, currency and realistic costs.

Teachers on all levels promote the use of distance learning. Joan Horvath, a middle school social studies teacher in California, reports the success she has had using CNN Newsroom with 7th and 8th grade classes while Joan Bennet, a teacher in Hawaii, uses the same program with her high school social studies classes. Mary Widen and Mary Jukubiak, elementary teachers in Wisconsin, used World Flight 1997 on A&E , the re-creation of Amelia Earhart's attempted flight, to learn geography by using a video, teaching package, and Web site to follow the path of the flight. Exploring life in colonial America becomes more interesting with "electronic field trips" made possible by Colonial Williamsburg and PBS. Registered classes receive live telecasts and faxes and participate in online forums. In Chicago, Lilla Green uses the PBS series *The New Explorers* with kids from the toughest inner-city neighborhoods to explore science in elementary school. Art activities can grow out of distance learning. Middle schoolers in Pennsylvania watched "The Face of King Tut" and created a life-size paper sarcophagus.

What are the disadvantages of distance learning?

Although distance learning has many advantages, there are some disadvantages. Most of these involve situations in which regularly scheduled classes are offered with two-way audio and one- or two-way video connections. A few also involve the use of educational television programming.

Instruction. Some programs become nothing more than "talking heads." Not all television programs are educationally sound. Good distance learning classes require good instructors who are trained in effectively teaching on television and are willing to spend the time to develop the lessons. One distance learning instructor states that the preparation time for television instruction is three or four hours of preparation for each hour of instruction. Remember to evaluate distance learning resources in the same way you evaluate all instructional materials. Consider also, the inservices that will be provided for both the sending and receiving teachers or facilitators.

Location. For distance learning with two-way audio and video, there must be a facility in the sending and receiving locations that can be set-up for and dedicated to distance education. Having the set-up in a regularly scheduled classroom and "bumping" the regular class out of the room when the distance learning program comes on is not a good situation. Nor is locating the special classroom or receiving equipment away from the library if the SLMS is responsible for the hardware.

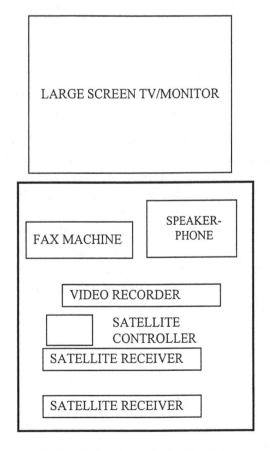

Figure 9.2 Locking Video Console Unit for Each Electronic Classroom

In Virginia, as part of the Electronic Classroom program, high schools and middle schools each received equipment to be used to receive satellite broadcasts. In the receiving classroom, all equipment was designed to be stored in a locking cabinet to provide security when the classroom was used for other purposes.

Class materials. Whether distributed by mail or by fax, class materials need to be received in time so that they are available for all students. With off-air or cable television programs, teachers guides and other materials need to be obtained and distributed before the programs are broadcast.

Library resources. Whenever new classes on new subjects are offered, resources to support those classes must be available. If the resources are not available in the individual school, some provision must be made for obtaining them whether on loan or as part of the permanent collection.

Schedules. Class schedules of the sending and receiving schools need to match to take best advantage of the programming. This requires coordination between the sending site and all receiving sites.

Facilitators. Most receiving sites need a monitor or facilitator to be in the receiving classroom during the class session.

Internet. While the Internet can be a useful tool in distance learning, there are problems with its use, including the social isolation problem and the need to provide adequate access for all students. In addition, heavy Internet traffic during the day often results in slow transmission and increased waiting times.

Technology for technology's sake. In a few cases, school are using distance learning because of the status the new technologies bring rather than for the educational benefits that the students derive from it.

Copyright. Be sure you and your teachers comply with the copyright guidelines when taping distance learning programs or any off-air or cable television shows. In addition, problems arise when teachers transmit commercial materials by any means as part of distance learning. Permission is usually required for any rebroadcast or duplication of materials, including videotapes. Showing a video to the on-site class and allowing the remote sites to see it is rebroadcasting and is probably a copyright violation.

The following is an adaptation of a form used by Old Dominion University in Norfolk, Virginia, when requesting permission to use materials in satellite television classes.

Request for Permission to Broadcast Materials

Date: _____

To: _____
Company: _____
Telephone: _____
Fax: _____

From: _____
Department of Instructional
Television Services
Name of your school
Anytown, USA 00000-0000

Phone: _____ Fax: _____

I am requesting permission for _____, an instructor
teaching _____(Course title)_____, to use the following material in
a televised course being broadcast closed-circuit (with limited access)
to _____(location_____ at no profit. Unless otherwise specified,
each item will be used only once in the course of regular instruction
during the time period specified. Copies _____will _____ will not
be retained on the videotape of the class which is used only for
student review and instructional planning.

Titles of material to be used   Date of use

A self-addressed, stamped envelope is enclosed for your reply.
Thank you.

Request Approved: _____ Disapproved: _____
Fee required, if any: _____

Comments:

Name: _____Title: _____
Company: _____Date: _____

How should you plan for distance learning?

Planning for distance learning is similar to planning any educational activity.
Begin by explaining why you are even considering distance learning. Look at
the curriculum, the purpose of the instruction, the audience for it, and the
alternative methods for delivering that instruction. Examine the costs for each
method including any new equipment, instructional materials, and structural
renovations. Evaluate the quality of teaching involved, and the benefits for the
learners. If the Internet is to be used, investigate current and needed student
access. Only after a careful comparison should you consider distance learning.

Perhaps distance learning will be only one component in the delivery of instruction. As Donald Ely noted in his speech to the Association for Educational Communications and Technology, the most successful distance education programs are those that are based on real needs with strong instructional practices that involve learners.

If you do decide to begin a distance learning program, be sure you plan for its implementation in order to ensure its success. For an article in *T.H.E. Journal*, William Boone surveyed over 50 teachers to develop a list of tips for those considering implementing distance education. Included are the following suggestions:

- Look for teaching styles that limit the amount of "lecturing".
- Develop a "human bond" among all participants.
- Encourage interaction among all sites by limiting enrollment and encouraging questioning.
- Consider having an adult proctor at each site to keep students "on task".
- Develop back-up plans in case of transmission failures.
- Provide training for all participating teachers and SLMSs.

Boone's tips are echoed by Gloria G. Musial and Wanita Kampmueller in their article on the misconceptions about distance learning via television. Their list of 10 misconceptions about teaching and learning through two-way television points out that:

- Not all students will succeed in the classes.
- Not all teachers can teach well via television.
- Television classes will not always save money.
- Distance learning classes do not replace the need for qualified teachers.

In addition to curricular and instructional decisions, you will need to establish rules and regulations for distance learning classes. The regulations that you establish should be based on your individual situation, the needs of your students, the types of classes being delivered, and the demands of your curriculum. The following are some of the guidelines that the Virginia Satellite Educational Network recommends for student participation in middle school and high school classes that are sent across its distance learning network throughout Virginia and other participating states. While the courses on this network are primarily small advanced-placement classes, the following criteria can be modified to fit individual situations.

Criteria for students:

Students should:

Be motivated and able to work independently.

Have a minimum grade point average of 3.0.

Score at or above the 75th percentile on an ability test.

Express a strong desire to succeed academically.

Have demonstrated success in other academic courses.

Attendance records should not reflect chronic absenteeism.

Recommendations by principals, guidance counselors or teachers for students who cannot meet the minimum criteria will be considered on a case-by-case basis.

Student Conduct and performance:

Students should:

Arrive on time, be seated, and begin class work immediately.

Behave as in the usual classroom setting.

Participate in the classroom broadcast by calling periodically.

Arrange for make-up tests with the instructor.

Assume responsibility for their progress in the Electronic Classroom program.

All assignments must be turned in on time.

Late or incomplete work will not receive full credit.

At the instructor's discretion, missed quizzes may or may not be made up.

There are many different ways to set up both the sending and receiving classes for distance learning. Things to take into consideration include the room arrangement, lighting, microphone and camera placement, the size and location of the television monitors, and the quality and location of the cameras.

What is the school librarian's role in distance learning?

Technology is only valuable if it is used. To ensure the use of television and distance learning opportunities, many SLMSs work with and promote these technologies in a number of ways.

Working with Equipment

The school librarian's role in distance education varies from school to school. In some cases, if you are the SLMS in the receiving school, you may have to set up the satellite or other equipment to receive the program, being sure that all the hookups are correct. In other cases, you may not actually be involved in sending or receiving the programs but may find that the site selected to function as the receiving classroom is in the library (perhaps the library conference room).

If you are responsible for setting up and troubleshooting the equipment, be sure this equipment is located near the library. It is frustrating to run between the receiving classroom at the other end of the building and the library whenever minor adjustments are needed.

Providing Instructional Resources

If you are the SLMS in a school where a program originates, you should be involved in providing instructional resources and support for the teacher of the distance learning class. Whether you are in a sending or receiving school, you will also need to provide information sources to support the students. Online computer networks, telecommunications, and fax may help you obtain that information and make it available to others.

In addition, you can maintain a collection of teacher's guides and free materials from many of the Cable in the Classroom networks. This is an excellent place to use volunteers. If you don't have volunteers who can come to school during the day, think about using evening volunteers. Many of the Cable in the Classroom resources can be obtained through the Internet. Often, parents who work during the day would like to volunteer to help the school if there was a way. You might have one or more volunteers who would be willing to download the program guides at home each week or each month and send them in to school.

Selecting Resources

You may also be called upon to give your professional advice when distance learning resources are being selected. Even though some of these resources are free, the American Library Association has cautioned about the need to apply the same selection criteria to distance learning resources and television programs as are applied to selecting other materials for the schools's collection and for use in instruction. The ALA Council adopted a resolution, sponsored by the American Association of School Librarians and ALA's Intellectual Freedom Committee, stating that "the selection of...services must be made within the established guidelines of written materials selection policies, without regard to gifts or premiums."

Managing the Collection

Videotapes will frequently be made, following the copyright guidelines, of cable and off-air television programs and of distance learning classes. Sometimes they will be tapes that are made for students who are absent or for review purposes. Other times they will be tapes of curriculum-related programs that have liberal copyright conditions. Often these tapes will become part of the school library's collection. As SLMS, you need to think about several things:

- Where will the tapes be stored?
- Will you obtain related teaching guides on the programs? If so, what will you do with them?
- Will tapes and guides be added to the library's catalog? If so, will you do full cataloging on each of them?
- If they are not in the catalog, how will you let your patrons know about them? A list? An index? A computer database?
- Will they circulate? To whom? Students? Teachers? For what time period?
- Will you provide a video workstation so they can be used in the library?
- How will you keep track of the copyright regulations for each tape? Will you put a sticker on each with the copyright expiration date or will you use some other method?
- What procedure will you use to remove tapes as the copyright dates expire? (Remember the expiration date will often depend on the date the individual tape was made and will not necessarily correspond to the school year.)

Coping with Copyright

Recently a SLMS said that school librarians have become the "copyright police" in the school. Whether or not you, as a SLMS, like that role it is true that the burden for copyright compliance for use of many instructional resources will fall on your shoulders. In Chapter 1 of this book, we reviewed some basic copyright guidelines and stressed the need to follow and inform others of these regulations. Since people are often guilty of violating the copyright law when videotaping television programs and using those videotapes, let's look at a few copyright basics.

Off-air taping guidelines. According to the report of U.S. Congressman Robert Kastenmeier's Negotiating Committee on the recording, retention, and use of television broadcast programs for education purposes:

> A broadcast program may be recorded off-air simultaneously with broadcast transmission (including simultaneous cable retransmission) and retained by a nonprofit education institution for a period not to exceed the first 45 consecutive calendar days after date of recording. Upon conclusion of such retention period, all off-air records must be erased or destroyed immediately. "Broadcast programs" are television programs transmitted by television stations for reception by the general public without charge.

> Off-air recordings may be used once by individual teachers in the course of relevant teaching activities and repeated once only when instructional reinforcement is necessary, in classrooms and similar places devoted to instruction within a single building, cluster or campus, as well as in the home of students receiving formalized home instruction, during the first 10 consecutive school days in the 45 calendar day retention period. "School days" are school session days—not counting weekends, holidays, vacations, examination periods, or other scheduled interruptions—within the 45 calendar day retention period.

> Off-air recordings may be made only at the request of and used by individual teachers, and may not be regularly recorded in anticipation of requests. No broadcast program may be recorded off-air more than once at the request of the same teacher, regardless of the number of times the program may be broadcast.

Kastenmeier's report contains additional fair use guidelines to be followed in using off-air recordings. Note that they apply to off-air and not to cable programs.

The following is an adaptation of a form used by the Norfolk, Virginia, public schools for off-air recording.

Off-Air Recording Statement

This tape (_____)
was recorded (select one of the following) _____ by me _____ by
_____(name) at my request on _____(date)
from _____(television channel). The 10th
consecutive school day from the recording date is _____(date).

Following the copyright laws, I will not use this recording more than
once in relevant teaching activities in each of my classes and will not
repeat it more than once in each class for reinforcement during the ten
day time period.

The 45th day after the recording date will be _____(date).
I understand that the only use that can be made of this tape from the
11th day until the 45th day is teacher evaluation unless permission has
been obtained from the copyright holder.

_____(number) of copies of this video have been made. Each
bears a copy of this statement.

This recording and all copies will be erased or destroyed no later than
the 45th day as indicated above.

In signing this form, I agree to abide by all off-air copyright laws and
guidelines:

Teacher signature _____

Library Media
Specialist signature _____

In many school districts, additional policies have been implemented
regarding the use, in the classroom or school library, of videotapes that are not
owned by the school. These policies apply not only to "off-air" recordings but
also to rented videos and videos purchased by individual teachers. These
policies are a response, in part, to problems arising out of the inappropriate use,
by some teachers, of videos. Thus it is not unusual for a teacher or SLMS to
need to obtain written permission in order to use non-school owned materials.
The following is a modification of a form used by the Norfolk, Virginia, and
Chesapeake, Virginia, public schools for using non-school owned materials,
including off-air video tapes. This form is used in addition to the standard off-
air taping form.

Video Usage Form

Teacher: _____ Class: _____

Video title: _____

Date to be shown: _____ Length of time required: _____

Source of video: _____ Television "off-air"
(Select one)   Off-air recording form must be attached
          _____ Educational institution
                  Name of institution _____
          _____ Ordered directly from company or business
                  Name of company _____
          _____ Local video rental center
          _____ Personal copy
          _____ Other (specify) _____

Summary of content:

Objectives to be taught:

Description of any possible objectionable sequences:

____Approved ____Disapproved   Requested by:

_____   _____
Administrator's signature   Teacher's signature

_____   _____
Date   Date

Cable television guidelines. There are different interpretations of the copyright law as applied to cable television. One of the safest things you can do is use the Cable in the Classroom magazine to help you determine the copyright restrictions for many of the programs that are commonly used for educational purposes.

Most of the cable networks have purchased very liberal copyright clearance for these shows. Beware, just because one program on a network is listed as "free: unrestricted use for educational purposes," does not mean that all programming on that network is unrestricted. While all programming on SPAN is unrestricted, only programs produced in-house on BET have liberal copyright provisions. Although the Arts and Entertainment network gives one year rights for its A&E Classroom, its prime-time programming is governed by Kastenmeier's fair use guidelines. Cable networks also air some "restricted" shows that may only be shown when they air or be taped for home use (not for use in a school). In some cases, a video of these restricted shows is available for purchase.

In addition, some of the cable channels which participate in Cable in the Classroom post a list of frequently asked questions (FAQ) on their Web sites. (See the Resources section.) Particularly useful is the FAQ list for media specialists on the Discovery Channel site. This list is in addition to their general list of questions and provides answers to a lot of copyright questions.

Copyright policies. Even with the fair-use guidelines and the program listings by cable networks, there are still gray areas and situations that the guidelines do not cover. In addition, schools have made rulings about where the taping can take place, whether tapes brought from home or rented from a video store can be shown in school, and who is responsible for monitoring copyright compliance. Be sure you read your school's copyright policy.

If a policy has not been approved, send to associations and other districts for sample policies and encourage your school to adopt a formal policy. Charles Vlcek's Adoptable Copyright Policy contains a computer disc of policies that you can adopt or adapt. Make a copyright policy part of the library's policy manual. The May/June 1992 issue of *Technology & Learning* magazine has some excellent information. Other sources of information are in chapter one (CH1) of the Resources section.

Inform your teachers about the copyright regulations. The Association for Information Media and Equipment (AIME) has information on television copyrights that you can distribute to faculty and students. While this organization is dedicated to fighting copyright crime with its copyright hotline, it also provides assistance in copyright matters. As AIME states in one of its brochures: "If you're one of those who are walking by, ignoring the thieves who are stealing what companies manufacture, you're going to have a hard time convincing anyone that you are one of the 'good guys.'"

It's up to you to know the law, how to find information about specific programs, and whom to contact for additional information. It's also your responsibility to tell others about copyright.

Promoting the Use of Distance Learning Programs

While many of the general activities we discussed in Chapter 1 for promoting the use of technology in general can be used with television and distance learning, there are some specific things you can do.

- Schedule and publicize staff development programs. Use distance learning programs such as Teacher TV on The Learning Channel or programs from the Educator's Channel on Channel One as well as videotapes and activities provided by various cable networks and public television.

- Obtain lesson plans, study guides, activity packets, and other materials from distance learning providers and television networks and make them accessible to teachers. Let them know about additional resources that they can order for their classrooms.

- Demonstrate the proper use of distance learning and television resources in your own teaching. Show how to prepare yourself and your class for a program. Help students use critical viewing skills and have a post-viewing discussion.

- Contact your local PBS affiliate and the local cable company to see if they have any promotional information on upcoming programs. Often they can provide posters, photos, and other materials that you can use on bulletin boards, in newsletters, and on school-wide television news shows.

- Use bibliographies, research guides, sample instructional units, and other guides to show how existing library resources and technology (reference books, CD-ROMs, online databases) can be used to supplement distance learning.

What is in the future for distance learning?

As school districts, localities, and states tackle the question of how to provide equity in education to all students while keeping within a tight budget, distance learning seems to provide an answer. Even with its limitations, distance learning, in its various forms, has filled a significant void in the education of students and will probably continue to do so with increasing frequency. As new technologies come on the market and as Internet access becomes more prevalent in classrooms and for all students, the avenues available for the delivery of distance learning will increase and with these will come the increased use of distance learning technologies.

Bibliography

Barker, B. (1996). Factors in determining rural school readiness to use distance learning. *Rural Educator*, 17 (3), 14-18. Here are a series of questions to consider in assessing your readiness to use distance learning.

Boone, W. J. (1996). Developing distance education classrooms. *T.H.E. Journal*, 24 (3), 61-63. Drawing his discussions with k-12 teachers, Boone lists some of the issues that should be considered when planning for distance education.

Bruwelheide, J. H. (1994). "Copyright concerns for distance educators." In Willis, B. *Distance education: Strategies and tools*. Englewood Cliffs, N.J.: Educational Technology Publications. Addresses some specific copyright concerns.

Developing a distance learning program. (1996). Columbia, MO: Missouri School Boards Association. Prepared for school districts, this handbook contains basic information on planning and implementing distance learning. Also included is an explanation of satellite downlinks and satellite system components.

Distance learning for all learners. United States education and instruction through telecommunications. (1995). Washington, D.C.: Council of Chief State School Officers. This report on distance education is available from the Council of Chief State School Officers, One Massachusetts Ave., N.W., Suite 700, Washington, DC 20001-1431.

Elliot, I. (1995). Taking the fast lane on the information superhighway. *Teaching PreK-8*, (2), 34-39. Visit Mary Paasch and her sixth graders in Atlantic, Iowa for a first hand view of the benefits of distance learning.

Ely, D. P. (1996). *Distance education: By design or default.* Paper presented at the Conference of the Association for Educational Communications and Technology (Tallahassee, FL, June 21, 1996). Ely looks at the questions that should be addressed before distance education is selected as a solution.

Fyock, J. J & Sutphin, D. (1995). Adult supervision in the distance learning classroom: Is it necessary? *T.H.E. Journal*, 23 (4), 89-91. The authors report on a study of high school students taking distance learning classes.

Itzel, W. J. (1996). Distance learning through wide area networking. *Media & Methods,* 32 (Mar./April), 6. In Baltimore, courses in Japanese, math, creative writing, and African-American literature are offered through distance learning.

Johnston, J. (1995). Channel One, the dilemma of teaching and selling. *Phi Delta Kappan*, 76 (5), 437-442. A 1990-1993 study examines what students learn from Channel One news and what teachers and principals think about the program.

Jordahl, G. (1995). Bringing schools closer with "distance" learning. *Technology & Learning*, 15 (4), 16-19. Jordahl presents five examples of the benefits of using satellite technology in distance education.

Kerka, S. (1996). *Distance learning, the Internet, and the World Wide Web.* Columbus, OH: ERIC Clearinghouse on Adult, Career, and Vocational Education. Provides an overview of distance learning on the Internet and Web including e-mail, bulletin boards/newsgroups, interactive tutorials, interactive teleconferencing and downloading of materials.

Laney, J. D. (1996). Going the distance: Effective instruction using distance learning technology. *Educational Technology,* 36 (2), 51-54. Distance learning brings an economics course to second graders.

McKay, G. (1995). " Copyright in the pipeline." In *The Internet—Flames, Firewalls and the future.* Proceedings for the 1995 Conference of the Council for Higher Education Computing Services, Roswell, New Mexico. Examines the problems that distance educators have in transmitting materials over television or through the Internet. Recommends the adoption of Multimedia Fair Use Guidelines.

Mood, T. A. (1995). *Distance education: An annotated bibliography.* Englewood, CO: Libraries Unlimited. Beginning with a history of distance education and television in the classroom, this book lists 297 books as well as periodicals and electronic journals.

Musial, G. G. & Kampmueller, W. (1996). Two-way video distance education. *Action in Teacher Education,* 17 (4), 28-36. As the subtitles states, this article discusses "ten misconceptions about teaching and learning via interactive television."

Nasstrom, R. & Gierok, A. (1996). *Channel One and CNN Newsroom: A comparative study of seven districts*. Paper presented at the National Council of Professors of Educational Administration (Indian Wells, California; August 10, 1994) and at the National Conference on Creating the Quality School (Oklahoma City, Oklahoma, March 30, 1996).

Repman, J. (1996). Will distance learning go the D\distance? Technology Connection, 2 (10), 11-12. Provides an overview of distance learning delivery systems from correspondence courses to video teleconferencing.

Sanchez, R. (1996). Star Schools. *Principal*, 76 (1), 46-47. A report on TEAMS Distance Learning, one of the U.S. Dept. Of Education's Star Schools, which delivers learning through satellite, cable, public television, and the Internet.

Simonson, M. R. (1993). *Encyclopedia of distance education research in Iowa*. Ames, IA: Iowa Distance Education Alliance. In addition to a review of the literature on distance education, this reference source contains information on individual research projects conducted in Iowa including teacher training, student assessment, science instruction, and student perceptions of effective instructional methods.

Notes

Chapter 10

Video and Computers

Most school libraries have computers and video cameras. In fact, videos have become an important part of the school library collection, and video production by students and faculty has become a major component of many library media programs. Likewise, the computer is recognized as a valuable instructional and management tool as well as a great learning aid for students. Being able to combine the two, video and computers, to establish a complete editing studio on a desk brings us into the world of desktop video.

While video projectors take items from a computer monitor and show them on a screen, and scanners import printed visuals into a computer, taking motion video images and using them in a computer presents more of a challenge. We'll begin this chapter by looking at how to take video from a computer by projecting or displaying a computer image on a screen or television and by videotaping a computer image. Then we'll explore how to put images into a computer through a scanner or a still or video digital camera. Finally we'll turn our attention to the field of desktop video by looking at the ways to use a computer to edit video and to create video. Because some programs and computer add-ons have almost become standards, we will refer to certain products by brand names.

One word of caution. This is a rapidly changing field in which new products are constantly breaking down some of the barriers. To keep up with the technology, you will have to read general and specialized periodicals. Try to buy hardware that will allow you to add additional boards or replace some existing components as the field changes.

How can a computer image be projected for a group to see?

Having a whole class gather around a 14" monitor while you explain how to search the online catalog or a CD-ROM database can be a problem. Thankfully, there are ways to project a computer image onto a screen.

One alternative is to use a computer video projection system to show the computer image on a large screen. Currently two main types of systems are on the market: video projectors and liquid crystal display (LCD) panels. Although the cost of video projectors continues to fall, these projectors are most frequently found in advanced computer labs and in auditoriums. There are several types on the market including the high end CRT(Cathode Ray Tube) or RGB (Red, Green, Blue) projectors (see Figure 10.1), and the less expensive LCD projectors.

A few years ago, LCD projectors were almost ignored; they were not as good as the CRT projectors and were too expensive to compete with the LCD panels. Today, they have found their niche in the business world for mobile presenters, salespeople, and corporate trainers. If you do have the good fortune to become involved in purchasing one, be sure that it will accept a Mac, VGA and/or SVGA signal from a computer as well as a broadcast television NTSC (National Television Systems Commission) signal and other video formats that you might need. A few other things to keep in mind include:

- Brightness of the projected image.
- Evenness of the image when viewed from all angles.
- Contrast and color saturation of the image.
- Special features such as a remote control.
- Sound system (Built-in speakers? Stereo?).
- Type of mounting (Ceiling? Rear-projection?).
- Image size required for the room it will be used in.
- Lighting conditions of the room it will be used in.
- Replacement cost of lamp.
- Ease of set-up and ease of use.
- Compatibility with the computers in your school.
- Repair record.
- Noise generated by projector's fan.
- Extras such as presentation software.

A side-by-side comparison of the projectors that you are considering should be the final test.

Figure 10.1 Video Projector

While video projectors are the ideal, the system found most frequently in schools is the LCD panel. Like the projector, the panel allows whatever is shown on a computer's monitor to be projected on a large screen for a class to view. The difference is that the LCD panel is usually used with an overhead projector providing the light source, and the set-up is quite similar to using a transparency on an overhead projector. In this case, however, the visual to be projected is coming from a computer.

The quality of projection with an LCD panel depends, in part, on the brightness of the light source, with 3000+ lumens being a minimum. Some older overhead projectors do not emit enough light to project an image that can be seen clearly on a projection screen. To overcome the lighting problems and to produce more compact hardware, some manufacturers are building the panel and light source into a single unit. Some models of overhead projectors can use two types of lamps: a regular one for transparencies and a special one which produces increased light for an LCD panel.

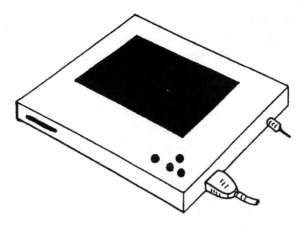

Figure 10.2 LCD panel with power and computer hook-ups.

The LCD panel is simple to use. With an overhead projector at the front of a room, the panel is placed on the stage of the overhead and the panel and computer are connected following the directions that come with the panel. These directions and the necessary cables vary from manufacturer to manufacturer, so read the instructions for the panel you are using. When purchasing an LCD panel, be sure it is compatible with the computers with which you intend to use it and that it provides ports for all of the connections (computer, videodisc, VCR) that you want. If you plan to project full motion video from a computer, you need to have a special converter. While some panels have the converter built in, most require separate hardware. To use video computer images, be sure the panel you select has full motion video capabilities.

While LCD panels are great for projecting some types of computer images, they are not without their problems. Inexpensive panels on the market today are capable of projecting good black and white still images in a regular sized classroom, but not in a very large room or in a bright location. To use many panels, you need to be able to dim or turn out the lights in order for everyone to see the image, even when using a strong overhead projector for the light source. This may present some problems when using the panels with students. If you plan to use the panel in one particular room, have your electrician install a dimming switch for the room lights or use accent lights to keep the room from being totally dark.

You may hear people refer to active matrix or thin film transistor (TFT) panels and passive matrix LCD panels. These terms refer to the way in which the panel is constructed. Active matrix panels are more expensive, but they have a higher quality display with better color than the passive matrix panels. If you intend to project full-motion video, you will need an active matrix panel.

How can you take a picture of the image on your computer's monitor?

Have you ever wanted to prepare a pathfinder or guide to demonstrate the use of a new database? To make it effective you might have wanted to have an exact copy of what is shown on the monitor. In order to do that, you have to go through the process known as screen-capture. This takes the on-screen image (complete with any pull-down menus) and saves it as a text or graphics file on your computer where you can print it or edit it.

Screen-capture can be done in one of several ways. First, you can use the software that is built into the operating system of most PCs and Macs. Another way is to use special screen grabber or screen capture software such *Capture, Desktop Imager, Flash It!, FreezeFrame, Hot Shot Graphics, Hypersnap, QuickShot, SnagIt, Snapz,* or *Wincopy.* Finally, you may find screen capture software as part of an integrated utility program or productivity package.

While the features vary from program to program, most allow you to:

- Take a full screen snapshot.
- Identify a portion of the screen to copy.
- Exclude pull-down menus from the picture.
- Save the image as a graphic file in a common graphic format such as .BMP, .PCF or .TIFF.

In addition, individual programs have other features including special effects, cropping, resizing, color changes, and photoediting.

The simplest, although not the most creative form of screen capture can be done through the operating system on either Macs or PCs. In a Mac, the capture takes the form of [Command & Shift & 3] held down at the same time. This saves the screen on the hard drive. You can call it into a graphics, wordprocessor, or integrated program such as *ClarisWorks* to manipulate it.

For more sophisticated captures, Leticia Ekhaml recommends *FlashIt,* a shareware utility.

Screen capture on a PC using Windows is a little tricky. In her article in the April 1997 issue of *School Library Media Activities Monthly,* Ekhaml writes the following;

> Screen images can be captured by Windows users by pressing the
> PRINT SCREEN key... This will send the captured image to the
> Clipboard... To edit the captured images, one can go to Paintbrush,
> located in the Accessories group in Windows' Program Manager,
> press the PASTE command. When you are finished editing the image,
> choose Save As under the File Menu to save your screen capture.

For more advanced features with Windows, she recommends *Hijack.*

How can you videotape a computer image or show it on a television?

Sometimes you have an image or a video in a computer that you want to show to a class but you don't have access to a video projection system. In that case, you may want to take the image from the computer and show it on a television set.

To record a computer's video signal on videotape or to show it on a television, you can use a computer such as the Apple IIGS that outputs an analog video signal and hook it up as described in *Making It With Media* (Linworth, 1992) by Augie Beasley.

If you use an Apple IIGS, plug one end of an RCA cable into the composite "video out" and the other end into the "video in" on the videotape recorder. When you turn on the equipment, the computer image should be on the monitor and on the television screen. To do this with an Apple IIe, plug an RCA "Y" jack (the bottom of the "Y") into the "monitor out" on the computer, attach an RCA cable to one branch of the "Y" and plug the other branch into the "video in" on the video cassette recorder. Plug another cable into the "Y" and run it to the computer monitor.

Any Mac with an AV card such as the Macintosh Centris AV or the Quadra AV, or any in the 680x0 series (68020, 68040, etc.) offers video hook-ups as standard features or optional accessories. The Amiga computer has a built-in NTSC encoder that also allows a direct connection.

With most other computers, a problem arises because of the differences between computer images and television images. These differences are in the scanning methods used to display an image, and in the size and sharpness of the images. For all PCs and many Macs, you will need to add a video output card or a converter. This is an internal expansion card or an external device that changes a computer signal to one that can be shown on a regular television by eliminating screen flicker and making the fuzzy images look crisper. Some scan converters include all the necessary software for operation while others do not. Included can be features such as zoom, freeze frame, and remote control. While cheaper scan converters hook to the television antenna input jack, the better ones plug into the AV input jacks. On the computer, the convertor usually hooks to the computer's VGA output. The same convertors will allow you to send the computer's video output to a VCR instead of a television. The set-up of the video output cards varies. For exact instructions on how to set up the card and cables, you need to check the directions on the video output card and the software that is supplied with it. In selecting a scan converter, check for the following:

- Color accuracy
- Resolution
- Image size shown on the screen
- Ability to scroll up and down if needed to see complete image
- Screen flicker

Recording a computer presentation on videotape is ideal when you know that a computer will not be available for playback when you make a presentation. This often happens at conferences or inservice workshops where the computer hardware is not the same as you have at your own school. Most places do, however, have a VCR that will allow you to show your videotaped computer presentation.

What about putting still pictures into a computer?

We've discussed taking visuals from a computer and projecting them or videotaping them. But what if you want to reverse the process? Instead of taking visuals out, you might want to put video into your computer. There are several ways to do this depending on the type of visual. Since motion video presents the most challenges, let's start with still pictures that you or your students might want to add to a presentation or use in your media center's newsletter.

One method is to take your visual and use a scanner to convert the image to a digital picture. (See Chapter 7 for a discussion of scanners.) That's fine if you already have the picture. But what if you need to take the photographs before you can scan them? In that case, using the scanner presents some problems. Chief among them is that you lose the immediacy. Once you take a picture, do you wait until the whole roll is exposed before you have it developed? Or do you hurry down to the one-hour photo shop knowing that you have only taken four exposures on a roll of 24? What do you do when you find the pictures did not turn out the way you wanted? Do you use a Polaroid camera, knowing that the image might not be the best for scanning into a computer?

There is an alternative that allows you to take a picture and transfer it directly into the computer or display it on a television set. It's the still digital or filmless camera. Over the past four years, this technology has developed from the original XapShot to quite sophisticated cameras with features that rival those of a 35mm SLR (Single Lens Reflex) camera with interchangeable lens. However, instead of taking pictures on a roll of film, the still digital camera stores images on a photo-sensitive ship or CCD (charged-coupled device). Once stored as a digital image, there is no risk of the pictures fading or being scratched.

There are several things that you can do with the images. First, there is direct input from the camera into a computer with no film processing required. High-end cameras may also allow you to instantly review your photos on a built-in LCD screen. Some cameras have a cable that allows you to hook the camera to the video-in port on a television set. Buttons on the camera allow you to show the images, go forward and reverse, and to erase the images. With other cameras, you can transfer the images to videotape by running the cable to the video-in jack of a VCR. It is fun, easy, and immediate. For example, the Apple QuickTake Digital Camera takes 32 standard resolution shots or eight high resolution shots in color and allows you to transfer them via a serial cable. Once the photos are in your computer, you can use one of a number of photo finishing or image editing programs such as *Adobe Photoshop, Corel Photo-Paint6, Picture Publisher,* and *PhotoEnhancer* to edit them.

There are, however, some drawbacks. In addition to the expense of the camera, you need a large storage space on your computer's hard drive or disk for the pictures. Depending on the detail of the picture, whether you shoot in color or black and white, and the file compression technology that the camera uses, each digital photo can require up to 1MB of storage space. Check your computer to see that it meets the camera's minimum requirements for storage and for processing power. Another cost factor with the digital cameras is the need to replace or recharge the batteries frequently because of the large amount of power that the cameras use. Then, too, there's the quality of the image produced by some of the cameras. Tests done with several brands of color digital cameras show wide variations of color and quality of image when shooting the same scene. Whites may become blue or light pink. If you are planning a purchase, test a few models before you make a decision. If that's not an option, read a few of the test results in articles in the Bibliography for this chapter.

The price that you will pay for a still digital camera is based very much on the amount of control that you have over the settings on the camera. Simple point-and-shoot cameras are the cheapest. However, this is a high growth field, and prices should continue to fall while quality and features of the cameras increase.

What can you do with a still digital camera? The images can be loaded into a computer where they can be used in desktop publishing or edited for use with a number of different multimedia computer programs. You will be able to produce computer slide shows featuring photos from your library as part of library orientation, library instruction, or public relations programs. Or, you can turn students loose with the camera.

Connie Scott, SLMS at Hampton High School in Hampton, Virginia, reported great success when a group of business education students used a digital camera to take pictures of local businesses. The full-color pictures became part of a computer slide show on economic development in the city, which the class developed using a computer program known as *HyperCard*.

There are some less expensive alternatives to a digital still camera. One is to use your regular camera and have a Kodak photo finisher put your pictures directly on a 3.5" floppy disk with a technique known as Picture Disk. This disk can then be used in your computer. Another way to bring your photos into your computer is through the process known as PhotoCD. With this method, you take photographs with your own camera and then have them processed onto a special CD that can be played in any multisession CD-ROM drive. On its Web site, Kodak maintains a list of places that will develop Picture Disks and PhotoCDs. While Kodak sells special software that allows you to view and edit these images on the computer, many photo programs such as *Photoshop* allow you to do the same thing.

Occasionally you may want to put one frame or still visual from a video or television show onto a computer. In that case, you need a video frame grabber to produce a still picture. The most popular one today is Snappy, Video Snapshot by Play. This small box-like device attaches to the printer port of your computer and to a video source such as a television set, camcorder, or VCR. When you press a button, Snappy captures 1 frame of video and stores it as a .PCX, .TIFF, or .BMP file, ready for editing.

Finally, you can download visuals from a photo-archive service or the Internet. Beware, most things on the Internet are not in the public domain and are protected by copyright in the same way that printed images are. Included in the resources section are some places to check for possible images.

What are some difficulties of putting motion video into a computer?

Until this point we have been discussing putting still pictures into a computer. But many times you will want to use motion video in your productions. The ideal full-motion video on a computer should have the visual image fill the entire screen with full color and with the same crisp resolution as on a television. In addition, to eliminate jerky movement (think of the old silent pictures), the video should run at 30 frames per second. This is the standard that we are used to seeing in movies and is considered real-time or full-motion video. Unfortunately, older computers did not have the power to transmit a full screen image at that rate. The result was a compromise that either slowed down the speed of the video to an almost unacceptable speed or reduced the size of the image shown on the monitor. However, while more powerful computers and video compression technologies have eliminated some of the problems, getting real-time on a computer is neither easy nor inexpensive.

Analog versus Digital

To understand some of the problems involved in using a motion video image on a computer, you need to realize that there are differences between analog and digital signals. Analog deals with continuous waves of a signal while digital deals with on-off discrete signals. There are books that explain these technical differences if you want more specifics, but from a nontechnical standpoint all you really need to know is that the video world is based on analog signals, while the computer world is based on digital signals. Video components (VCRs, camcorders, television receivers, and videodiscs) speak a different "language" than computers. For a computer to understand an analog signal, it needs an internal video digitizing card (sometimes called a video capture card or motion video digitizer board) or an external video/computer interface. While some computers now come with built-in video digitizers, and some camcorders have digital formats, in most cases there must be some kind of "translation" device for a video component and a computer to communicate.

The video digitizing card takes the analog information from the video, translates it into digital information, and stores the visual image in digital form. This same card or interface can usually work in reverse to show a computer image on a television or to record it on videotape. A frame grabber is a video card that is designed especially to take one frame (or a very short segment) of analog video and convert it to a digital computer graphic.

Hard Disk Storage

If the difference between analog and digital did not create enough problems for the development of true desktop video, the problem of storage would. Let's say you want to take several short video clips and store them on the computer's hard drive before you edit them. Storing one frame of video in digital format on a computer's hard drive takes about 1MB of memory. Since video usually runs at 30 frames per second (30 fps), it would take 30MB of storage for each second of video. At that rate, a 2GB hard drive would be full in a minute. You would also find that the information about each frame could not be written to the hard disk fast enough to keep up with the incoming video information.

Video Compression

To overcome the storage problem, video compression was developed. This is a bit of an oversimplification, but video digitizers with compression features save only the important information on each frame of video. By eliminating the things your eye cannot see or using other shortcuts, the cards decrease the amount of information that needs to be stored with each frame.

Thus, a video capture or compression card may allow your computer to store one second of video in only 10MB of hard disk space, a third of the amount that it would take to store only one second of noncompressed video. This sounds great, but there is a tradeoff. The more digital data about each frame that is eliminated, the less you will have to work with to edit and produce your final video. Fuzzy and blurred images can result from compression.

The recording and playback of video from a computer is managed by a software codec (video Compressor/DECompressor). It probably will not surprise you to learn that there are several different codex for video. Unfortunately, these different codecs are incompatible (like Beta and VHS tapes). Chief among these are technologies such as Indeo (originally called DVI), Cinepak, JPEG (Joint Photographic Experts Group), and MPEG (Motion Picture Experts Group). In an effort to ease playback, Windows 95 does include the Indeo and Cinepak codecs. Otherwise, a device known as a filter is required when digital video from one system is to be used on a system with another standard. The ideal is to capture television-quality (or better) video, full-screen, full-motion at 30 frames per second. The ideal is seldom achieved without expensive equipment.

Is there a simple solution?

If you do not want to worry about digitizing video, there are still some ways you can use your computer to help with video production. If you happen to have an Apple II, Apple IIGS, or Commodore Amiga, you can use some graphics programs such as VCR Companion or Slide Shop to add text and produce some simple special effects without adding any special video interface. The Amiga computer has a built-in video interface. Macs have, traditionally, been built with video playback capabilities. The PC manufacturers responded by developing the MPC (Multimedia Personal Computer) specifications (see Chapter 2 and by using the MPC label to identify video playback ready computers. The MMX enhanced Pentium processor by Intel was developed specifically to allow better video editing and faster playback. Apple, in turn, has developed FireDrill, a multimedia coprocessor that it will include on its PowerExpress systems to accelerate video, audio, graphics, communications, and 3D animation.

Can motion video be shown but not stored on a computer?

A way to get around the storage and compression problems of using video on a computer is to use the computer just to display the video. Usually this is done through the use of a special board called a real-time video display card. Although these cards do not digitize the analog video signal, they do allow the video to be shown at a full 30 fps on either the complete monitor screen or only a small portion of it. Some of these boards even allow you to overlay or put computer-generated information on top of the video image.

How can a computer show CD-ROM video?

With all the problems of incompatibility between traditional video sources and computers, you might wonder how computers can play back the video from CD-ROMs. Most computers today come with a video playback system that has the minimum amount of hardware and software needed for video playback. Traditionally, this has been a standard feature of Macintosh computers. The MPC standards have helped the PC world catch up by setting minimum hardware requirements for playback. In addition, the Plug-and-Play standard for PCs signals the end of problems on installation and compatibility with existing hardware.

There are times, however, when you might need to increase the power of your computer by adding a graphics board or video accelerator card. While the PCI-bus of the Power Macs may not need a card, most Macs and PCs can benefit from an upgrade when lots of video is used on the computer. Contained on the video accelerator card is memory in the form of VRAM (Video Random-Access Memory) or DRAM (Dynamic Random Access Memory). While DRAM is cheaper, VRAM is faster. By doing the work of preparing and processing graphics, a video accelerator card frees the main computer processor. A card controls the screen resolution, scan rate, interlacing, and refresh rate of the monitor. While the card can only make the computer go as fast as the monitor will allow, many cards do not meet the display potential of the monitor.

Purchasing a video accelerator card for a Mac is simple. With a PC you need to know what type of expansion slots you have so that you can buy the appropriate video accelerator card. Common types include the ISA (Industry Standard Architecture), VLB (Video Electronics Standards Association local bus), and the PCI (Peripheral Components Interconnect) bus slots.

How can you digitize your own video?

One way to digitize video is to use a digital video (DV) camera to take the original footage. The ideal is to have a DV camera that allows a camera to computer transfer with no analog-digital conversion. On the market are cameras that outperform the Betacam, and are smaller in size and lighter in weight at half the cost and with twice the storage capacity. Faster than using a traditional camcorder, the DV camera means that there is no "generation" loss when copies are made. The process is similar to that for digital video still cameras but the price tag is higher, depending on the quality. On one end there is the QuickCam by Connectix. At the other is the DV camera, announced by Hitachi, that records full-motion (30 fps) MPEG-1 video and stores up to 20 minutes of video or 3,000 photographic images on its internal hard drive. The results can be played back on the camera's own slide-sized LDC monitor or on a computer.

If you are not fortunate enough to own or have access to a DV camera, you need to look to your camcorder or VCR as your video source. Then you will need to hook the video source to a video capture card or board in your computer. The card converts (digitizes or captures) the analog signal to digital and compresses the information. This reduces the amount of space it takes to store the video on the hard drive. Remember, without compression it would take 30MB of space on the hard drive to store one second of video.

Video compression cards come in all varieties. Some follow one of the industry accepted standards such as Indeo, JPEG, Cinepak, and MPEG. On the other hand, cheap cards may accomplish compression by skipping video frames, resulting in poor image quality. When selecting a card, look for one of the standard formats, the compression rate, and the picture quality of the video.

How can a computer be used to edit video?

Once you have a video capture card, editing video with a computer is easy, in theory. You take a camera, record video clips, digitize the clips, store them on the hard drive, use a software program to edit them, and then send the final result out to videotape or play them on your monitor.

The problem is that many different products are available. These products perform in very different ways, and there is a wide range of prices. Before we discuss some of these products, let's review a few editing basics. For a more thorough review of video production, check *Looking Great with Video* by Augie Beasley (Linworth, 1993). This book also gives excellent examples of ways to use video with students and teachers.

Linear Editing

With linear editing, you begin by shooting the videotape. Then, using a VCR, you play the tape (a lot of winding and rewinding) and mark the clips that you want to use. Then you copy those clips in proper sequence onto the master. Once done, it is hard to change unless you re-edit and prepare a new master. Of course, with every generation of tape, you loose quality.

Nonlinear Editing

In nonlinear editing, the videotape is digitized and stored as a video file on the hard drive. You use the computer to access and mark the precise clips that you want. However, unlike the VCR, the computer does not have to search from front to back of a tape with all the accompanying winding and rewinding, The computer can quickly find any frame in the video file.

The ease or difficulty of this process is determined by the software that vou use. Some programs allow you to use a mouse to mark the beginning and the end of each clip that you are considering for your video. Then, they display the first frame of each clip on the computer's screen. The mouse is used to arrange and rearrange these pictures until you have a final product.

What you are doing is creating an edit decision list (EDL). The computer uses this list of starting and stopping points to access the precise segments in the order that you want to use them. You can actually view your product on the computer screen as you go along, making changes as necessary. Because you are not actually generating a new analog tape, each version will be as clear as the original video that was stored in the computer.

When you have your final list, you can do one of two things to produce a videotape. If this is an offline edit, you can take your video and your computer-generated EDL to a professional video studio to have the final tape produced. This is usually done when you need to produce a video with broadcast quality.

With an online edit, you use your computer to record the final sequence on videotape. Broadcast-quality video is possible from a microcomputer, but it is currently very expensive. Many online editing programs allow you to manipulate the images, create special effects, and provide special "transitions" (dissolves, wipes) between clips. Titles and text overlays can also be added. The goal of true desktop video is to use a PC, Macintosh, or Amiga computer for online editing to produce a broadcast-quality product.

What hardware is needed for desktop video?

Before we look at hardware or software for desktop video, keep one thing in mind. This field is changing rapidly. Prices for hardware and software are declining. The same high-quality results as those obtained from a hardware and software package that cost hundreds of thousands of dollars several years ago can now be obtained from a package in the $5,000-$15,000 range. Low-end setups are now within the budgets of many schools, and many of the low-cost programs give quite satisfactory results if you are not after broadcast quality.

To determine the hardware that you want and that you actually need (the two often are not the same), begin by deciding what you want to do with your desktop video setup. What output will you have: videotape, computer presentation, your own CD-ROM? What quality will you want? Will you need full broadcast quality? Will you be using it for professional-style productions; will your teachers use it to prepare instructional tapes; or will your students be using it for video production and to make video reports for classes? Will you be content with seeing your video in a small window on the computer screen or do you want full-screen video? How fast will your video need to be shown? Five fps is very jerky, while 20 fps is much smoother. Broadcast quality will require 30 fps. Do you need color and, if so, how much? Hardware that can display color at 8 bits per pixel can show 256 colors, while 24 bits per pixel shows 16 million colors. Start by dreaming a little; the budget figures will bring you down to reality.

Camcorder

Some desktop video systems allow you to create everything on the computer. In other cases, you will be editing and adding to a videotape. Since your final product can only be as good as the video that is supplied to it, you need to use the best camcorder you have. If you are purchasing one to use with desktop video, look for a model with high resolution and a variety of special features. Be sure that the video digitizer card on your computer will accept your camera. Some digitizers will not work with S-VHS or Hi-8 video.

Computer

Do not scrimp in getting a computer to use with video if you are looking for a quality video product. Here are some options:

- Macintosh: While you can use a Macintosh with a 68020 chip and 4MB of RAM for low-end video, you really need a more powerful computer to take advantage of today's video software. For a middle-of-the-road choice, try a low-end PowerMac such as the 7600 with 32MB RAM and a 17" monitor. An excellent choice for quality desktop video use would be a Power Mac 9600 or a PowerTower Pro 250.

- PC: In selecting a PC to use with a good nonlinear video system, look for at least a Pentium 133 (plus) with 32MB RAM and a 2.1GB hard drive. For more intensive video usage, purchase a Windows NT computer or a Pentium with MMX technology. Some experts recommend a computer with dual Pentium processors.

- Amiga: If you will be using an Amiga for true desktop video, you will probably be using the NewTek *VideoToaster* software. A full configured setup will cost between $10,000 and $15,000, but, with this purchase, you will have a broadcast quality system. You can also use the *VideoToaster* on any Amiga that has a video slot (Amiga A2000 and up).

Hard Disk Drive

No matter what computer you select, your hard disk should provide from 300MB to 2 Gigabytes (2GB) of storage. (Remember 2GB will store less than 25 minutes of video.) For heavy video use, look for a single AV-rated SCSI drive or, for a top-of-the-line system, a RAID (Redundant Array of Independent Drives) which comes with its own RAID software. RAID units are hard drive arrays that provide improved performance by having a group of hard drives work together. Whichever you purchase, use it only for video. When purchasing a hard disk, look for one that has a fast access time (one that will find and read data quickly) and a fast throughput (sustained data transfer rate) or a high Sustained Read and Sustained Write speed.

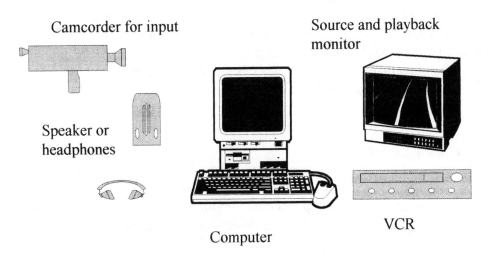

Figure 10.3 Desktop Video Set-up

Removable Storage

If you want to be able to move your digital video files from one machine to another, you need a local network or some type of removable storage. This is the term given to one of a number of devices that, unlike a computer's hard disk drive, can actually be moved from place to place without moving the entire computer. The most frequently used removable storage systems are removable cartridge systems such as a those by SyQuest or Iomega (Zip drive). (See Chapter 2 for more information.) Another device to consider is a magneto optical (MO) disk. While tape drives are another removable storage device, their slow, linear access is not recommended for use with desktop video production.

Video Digitizer (Capture)

Whether an internal card or an external device, your digitizer is the link between your video and your computer. A poor digitizer can destroy a good video during the transfer process. The digitizer should:

- have 24 bit color and 16 bit audio
- sync the audio and the video
- contain motion and still video frame grabbers
- show video in full screen with a resolution of 640 x 480
- run at 30fps
- come with or be compatible with popular video capture software

In reality, you need to match your digitizer to your needs and budget. Video that runs at 15 fps or that shows in only a small window on your computer monitor may be all you really need for your desktop video projects.

But remember, do not rely on someone telling you that a digitizer meets "the current video standards." Ask what those standards are in terms of the items mentioned above and make your own decision. If you are planning to output your video to tape or television and have different video input and output boards for your system, or use different computers for digitizing and outputting the final tape, be sure that the formats of the two boards match. Some digitizers that are used in schools are the *VideoSpigot* and *VideoSpigot for Windows* from SuperMac Technology and *ComputerEyes* from Digital Vision Company.

Time Base Corrector

Machines do not always run at a steady pace. The playing speed of a VCR may vary slightly, just enough to create editing problems. There are also different timing standards for desktop video and regular television video. Because of these timing and speed problems, a device known as a time base corrector is used to synchronize the video production and to eliminate phasing errors. All you really need to know is that if you want to produce high-quality desktop video, you need a time base corrector. Do not be surprised to find a good one costs almost half as much as a computer.

Turnkey Systems

Because of the complexity of coming up with all the proper components that will work together to produce desktop video, many manufactures are offering turnkey systems. You buy the complete system and only need to turn it on. This may be the best answer for someone just beginning desktop video production.

What desktop video software is available?

Mention the words desktop video and a few names come to most people's minds. *QuickTime* and *Video for Windows* represent one end of the scale. At the other end is the *VideoToaster*, which boasts broadcast-quality video and even has its own magazine. Let's look first at what video software programs can do and then look briefly at these programs as an indication of what is currently available.

Desktop video software programs handle the job of decompressing video files stored on the hard disk and displaying them on the computer monitor. In addition to allowing you to edit the video by marking and rearranging clips, they, or programs that work with them, may also let you add things to the video. Because compression works only on the video, not audio, part of information from the video source, the software must also keep the compressed video and the uncompressed audio together.

Some programs may allow image manipulation and may create digital video effects (DVE) such as stretching, rotating, flipping, and flattening images. They may also create transitions between scenes such as wipes, dissolves, and fades. Images from digital clip art libraries can be imported from CD-ROM and used in the production. Some very sophisticated programs allow morphing, or changing one shape or object into another in a series of realistic steps. Character generator features include simple overlays as well as scrolls (text moves from bottom to top) and crawls (text moves from right to left). These programs may have a graphic user interface (GUI) with lots of icons on the screen, or they may look like a professional editing studio. What makes it difficult to keep up with the desktop video software is that these features may be contained in one desktop video program or may be found in other programs that can be used with the main program.

Popular programs include *Digital Video Producer* by Asymetrix, *Adobe Premier* (regular and light versions) by Adobe Systems, *MCXPress Mac* by Avid Technologies, *Video Shop* by Strata, *Video Action Pro* by Star Media, *Luminere* by Corel, *VideoFusion,* and *After Effects* by Adobe Systems.

QuickTime

QuickTime is difficult to describe since the term is often applied to almost anything that deals with digital video on a Macintosh computer. In essence, *QuickTime* began as Apple's standard for storing motion video, decompressing it, and playing it back. It has grown to become the dominant digital video standard on Macs and for many uses on PCs. Its competitor is Microsoft *ActiveMovie.*

QuickTime is actually a file format, not a codec such as Cinepak or AppleVideo. That means you can select your own compression technology to use with it. Apple even teamed with Intel to use Indeo's compression technologies in *QuickTime*. The software uses time-based rather than frame-based recording. If you want the same picture on the screen for three seconds, *QuickTime* will leave the same frame on the screen for three seconds, not project 90 frames (3 seconds x 30 fps) of the same picture.

With its movie toolbox, component manager, and image compression manager, *QuickTime* is trying to become the Internet video standard. Its Fast Start feature lets a movie begin playing on your computer before the entire movie or video clip has been downloaded.

Getting video in a digital format on a Macintosh is just the beginning of the fun you can have. Once you have the video in *QuickTime* format, you can:

- edit it with a program such as *Adobe Premiere* or *VideoShop*.
- do post-production special effects work with *VideoFusion*.
- use a software package such as Passport's *Producer* to import graphics and animation from any of a number of compatible software programs.
- combine everything into your final product.

If you want to show your production on the computer screen, you are ready to go. Saving it to video tape requires the use of a video output card.

You, your faculty, and your students can use *QuickTime* to add video clips to presentations and projects. For example, a student may be preparing a visual report on a subject using a computer program that generates "slides" on the computer screen. As part of the presentation, the student may insert a short segment (remember the storage limitations) from a video clip art library or from a videotape into the presentation. The production work will need to be done on a computer with a digitizing card such as the VideoSpigot. Because the computer needs the digitizing board only to record the video, the presentation can be made on any computer with the appropriate software if you have removable storage to transport the data.

Video for Windows

Video for Windows AVI (Audio-Video Interleaved) is similar to *QuickTime* and was designed by Microsoft for the PC world. Used with a video digitizer, it can store and then playback and edit digital video. With an accelerated 486 CPU, the playback speed is 30 fps, and the video is shown on the whole screen. Its components consist of VidCap to work with the digitizer to capture video; VidEdit for cut and paste editing; PalEdit for color correction; BitEdit for changing images while editing; WaveEdit for working with sound data, and Media player to control it all. A video created with *Video for Windows AVI* can be played back on any PC with a VGA card.

Video Toaster

Produced as an add-on board for Commodore's Amiga computer, NewTek's *VideoToaster* (sometimes just called the *Toaster*) was the first desktop video product to produce true broadcast-quality video on a microcomputer. In honor of that feat and the effect that it had on television production technology, the designers of the *Toaster* and the president of the company were given Emmys at the 45th Annual Primetime Emmy Awards. You can see and be awed by *Toaster*-produced commercials and some television shows. Features of the *Toaster* 4000 include:

- a video switcher for handling multiple inputs (at least five) and editing them into one composite video with transitions such as wipes and dissolves
- a character generator that can add titles and text to video.
- ToasterPaint, a video effects generator that can capture a single frame and "paint" on it or use a variety of "tools" to change it.
- 3-D animation software known as LightWave 3D.
- a color effect generator called ChromFX.

A new add-on to the *Toaster* is the Flyer tapeless editing system.

While some schools have *VideoToasters*, these systems are usually found in technical high schools or in a school system's central television production facility. While an entry-level system with computer and *Toaster* board can be purchased for approximately $5,000, the many add-ons drive the price up and up and up.

There is also a problem of the compatibility of existing video equipment with the *Toaster*. Some SLMSs have found that, in order to use the full capabilities of the *Toaster*, they need to upgrade and purchase other new equipment to use with it.

When Frances Clark, SLMS at Booker T. Washington High School, Norfolk, Virginia, investigated the possibility of putting a *Toaster* in her video production studio, she found that adding the cost of upgrading her existing equipment to the cost of the *VideoToaster* and Amiga computer brought the price to more than $15,000.

But, while the *Toaster* platform is expensive, prices are declining as new systems come on the market. If you need broadcast-quality desktop video, you really do need to consider the *VideoToaster* or one of its competitors such as *Trinity* by Play, Inc.

What lies ahead for desktop video?

Writing in the December, 1996, issue of *VideoToaster User*, Burt Wilson made his predictions for the future.

> I am convinced that before the year 2000 we will be making commercials that will be broadcast from our home TV set into the middle of the room where 3-D holograms will preform on our living room rug right before our eyes, much the same way that R2D2 "broadcast" the message from Princess Leia in *Star Wars*.. ..digital is the future, but digital holograms are the ultimate end result to this technology. (p. 10)

While we probably won't find holograms dancing in our classrooms and libraries, there are several new products and ideas already on the way into the desktop video world, and many more are sure to come. This is a field where staying up-to-date means reading a variety of specialized publications, attending meetings, and chatting on the Internet.

Without a crystal ball, we can probably be safe in predicting two things. Some technologies that are currently in use will fall out of favor and be passed by entirely different technologies. In addition, prices will fall and more sophisticated hardware and software will become truly affordable. While you are waiting for those things to happen, you might want to keep an eye on the following.

Video on the Internet

Currently Internet video is limited by the bandwidth or carrying capacity of the communicationlines and maxes out at about 10 fps with compression technology. Better modems and faster connections should increase the transfer speed and improve the quality of video. DVOLive uses "streaming" technology to send video over the WWW and was used for the 1996 conventions.

Videoconferencing

An early videoconferencing technology developed by Cornell University, *CU-SeeMe* uses TCP/IP protocols and a 28.8 Kbps modem to provide videoconferencing. (See Chapter 7 for additional information.) Although you need your own camera in order for other people to see you, you can become a lurker on other video conversations by checking the *CU-SeeMe* event guide on the Web.

While early videoconferencing technologies required the use of the same software to participate in the conference, the introduction of H.320 standards and its accompanying substandards for audio and video compression and transmission should bring about a growth in videoconferencing.

3D and Animation

Fire and Light seem to be the key words in the rapidly growing 3D and video animation fields.

- NewTek's *LightWave 3D* software is now available for all platforms: Windows, Amiga, and Power Mac. It's an advanced, full feature 3D package for the video professional.
- *FireWalker* from Silicon Studio/Silicon Graphics is a 3D multimedia authoring, editing and rendering system.
- *FireDrill* is the multimedia coprocessor for the Apple Power Express systems.

On the Web, VRML (Virtual Reality Modeling Language) is doing for 3D what HTML (Hypertext Markup Language) did for two-dimensional graphics. As Web browsers are developed that can read the VRML pages, this technology will grow. Currently there are two standards: Netscape's Moving Worlds VRML and Microsoft's Active VRML. The Resources section lists Web addresses for VRML plug-ins.

Bibliography

(See also the listing for Chapter 11)

Abrams, Arnie. (1996). *Multimedia Magic*. Boston: Allyn and Bacon. An introduction to multimedia, this book comes with tutorials (and CD-ROM samples) for *Photoshop, Premiere*, and *Digital Chisel* on the Mac.

Agnew, P. W. (1996). *Multimedia in the classroom*. Boston: Allyn and Bacon. After introducing the fundamentals of multimedia hardware and software, the author provides examples of multimedia projects in a variety of classroom settings.

ABCs of LCD (1995). *Technology and Learning,* 15 (March): 39. Discusses LCD panels and projectors.

Beasley, A. E. (1993). *Looking great with video*. Worthington, OH: Linworth. An in-depth look at video production in a school library. While not about digital video, this book has good information about video production that would be useful with digital video.

Beasley, A.E. (1995). Becoming video literate. *School Library Media Activities Monthly,* 12 (2), 34-36. The basic camera movements, angles and projects discussed in this article can also be used in digital video production.

Beasley, A. E., & Palmer, C. G. (1990). Desktop videotapes: The computer connection. THE BOOK REPORT, 9 (1), 20-23. Overview of several programs to use with an Apple IIe or Apple IIGS. While the article is old, many people still use these computers for very simple video.

Communication in the age of virtual reality. (1995). Erlbaum. In reviewing this book, *Choice* stated that it was "a particularly thorough and well-organized collection of essays...not a surface, glitzy treatment of the hot topic of VR, but a solid, comprehensive overview of the domain and its possibilities in the context of communication. Highly recommended. (*Choice* (1995) 33 (Nov.): 498.)

Conger, S. (1996). Digital camera image enhancement "how to" for elementary teachers. *Technology Teacher,* 55 (May/June), 51-52. A feature article on digital cameras and image processing.

Connolly, B. (1995). Presentation hardware. *Online,* 19 (May/June), 12-14+, Color LCD panels, LCD projectors, and computer-to-TV options are explored in this review roundup.

Ekhaml, L. (1997). Taking electronic snapshots of your computer screen. *School Library Media Activities Monthly*, 13 (8), 40-42. In addition to looking at the various types of screen capture software, the author discusses techniques for screen capture on a Mac and PC.

Ekhaml, L. (1996). Those nifty digital cameras. *School Library Media Activities Monthly*, 12 (6), 33-35. Discusses the types and uses of "filmless cameras" and some of their educational applications.

Frankel. D. (1996). LCD projectors grow brighter and shrink lighter. *Presentations,* 10 (1), 38-52. A buyer's guide to more than 50 LCD projectors.

Frater, H. & Paulissen, D. *Multimedia mania*. Grand Rapids, MI: Abacus, 1993. An overview of multimedia for PCs with suggestions for using specific programs. Comes with a CD-ROM disc that holds demo programs and multimedia tools.

Graf, N. (1996). MPEG: Videos on CD-ROM. Technology Connection, 3 (2), 26. Graf looks at the basics of MPEG technology, system requirements, and the future.

Grotta, S.W. & Grotta, D. (1996). Are you ready to go filmless? *Presentations,* 10 (5), 76-84. Reviews some of the major digital cameras from a number of price ranges.

Guide to digital photography. (1996). Agfa. Produced by Agfa, this guide gives an overview of digital cameras, compares digital and film-based photography, and includes information on computer-based imaging. For information, contact Agfa at (800) 395-7007 or http://www.agfahome.com.

Holtz, M. (1997). *Multimedia workshop; QuickTime for Windows*. Belmont; Wadsworth Publishing. This title in the Multimedia Workshop Series provides information on using QuickTime with Windows.

Krushenisky, C. (1996). Putting pictures in your PC. *PC Novice,* 7 (1), 50-51. Provides an overview of the types of Kodak Photo CDs on the market.

McClelland, D. (1997). Digital cameras: Picture it now. *MacWorld*, 14 (3), 113-118. As prices fall for reliable digital cameras, McClelland looks at 10 inexpensive cameras.

Meyer, D. (1997). DV & FireWire; Direct-inject for desktop video gets closer to reality. *Interactivity,* 3 (2), 66-67. Meyer reviews the FireWire technology from Apple for a digital video standard known as DV.

Milano, D. (1996). Quicktime VR. *Interactivity,* 2 (3), 34-43. An in-depth review of Apple's *QuickTime* virtual reality software for Mac or Windows computers.

Popki, R. (1996). Turn your PC into a desktop video studio. *Multimedia World,* 3 (5), 76-86. Popki looks at some video capture cards and shares his own "installation nightmare." (And we thought the experts never had those kinds of problems.)

Rahmat, O. (1997). Uncle Apple wants you! *Interactivity,* 3 (1), 25-31. A technical discussion of QTML, Apple's QuickTime Media Layer for application development and the IMG (Interacture Media Group) at Apple.

Sauer, J. (1996). Harnessing the power of digital video. *Presentations,* 10 (10), 57-66. An overview of digital video with tips for editing and reviews of several popular programs.

Sauer, J. (1997). New tools give *QuickTime* muscle. *NewMedia,* 7 (1), 71-74. Sauer reviews five production tools for *QuickTime* video including some for Web publishing.

Sauer, J. (1997). Price-busting digital video. *NewMedia,* 7(4), 54-63. A review of under $2,000 full-screen video capture cards.

Sauer, J. (1997). Working with DV requires storage muscle. *Presentations,* 11 (3), 53-59. Sauer examines some of the AV-rated hard drives and disk arrays for storing video.

Schoor, J. (1994). Mac-to-TV converters. *Macworld,* 11 (8), 67. Schoor looks at external cross-platform video adaptors.

Stern, J. (1997). *QuickTime: The official guide for Macintosh users.* Indianapolis: Hayden Books. A handbook on the *QuickTime* video format.

Weiser, C. (1996). Spotlight on cameras in the curriculum. *Media & Methods,* 32 (Jan./Feb), 20.

Weiser, C. (1997). Using cameras in the classroom. *Media & Methods,* 33 (Jan./Feb), 16. Discusses the use of camcorders and digital cameras in the classroom.

White, C. (1997). Squeeze play—Video compression formats explained. *DV,* 5 (2), 41-44. A look at JPEG, Indeo, Cinepak, and some of the new compression formats for video.

Williams, G. (1995). Everything you want to know about desktop video. TECHNOLOGY CONNECTION, 2 (8), 20+23.

Wright, G. (1997). Comparing apples to oranges. *Interactivity* 3(5), 51-58. Wright looks at professional 3D graphics boards.

Notes

Chapter 11

Multimedia Presentation Systems and Hypermedia

In a speech given in October, 1993, U.S. Representative Edward Markey of Massachusetts, chairman of the House Telecommunications and Finance Subcommittee, compared keeping up with technology to riding in the front car of a roller coaster. "It may look like you're steering the cars, but in fact you're just holding on." While there are many areas of technology where you might feel that you're just holding on, with the new multimedia presentations systems and hypermedia, you are often lucky to be doing even that.

Just as it is difficult to describe the feeling you get when you are riding in that front roller coaster car, it is difficult to explain, in print, exactly how the new multimedia presentations work. But this chapter will try to explain the basics of multimedia, explore presentation software, look at hypermedia, provide some ideas for selecting presentation software and using it in a school library, and give some advice for student productions.

What is interactive multimedia?

Have you seen National Geographic's CD-ROM program *Mammals*? With this program, you can find out a great deal of information about almost any animal. For this example, let's say you are interested in finding out about animals that live in cold northern climates. You think of a polar bear and a moose, and decide to start by finding information about the moose. Beginning with the *Mammals* A-Z menu on your computer screen, you select the proper guide letters for the word "moose" and are presented with a list of animals. Using the mouse, you click on "moose" and are then shown a screen with a picture of a moose, some text, and several icons (small symbols) at the bottom of the page. The word "solitary" is highlighted in the text, so you use the mouse to click on it. The program shows you a definition of the word. Returning to the main moose screen, you click on the map icon to see an outline map with the moose's range highlighted, and then the camera icon to see a series of photos of a moose. A click on the page icon gives you a detailed description of the moose, and a click on the ear icon lets you hear the sounds a moose makes. Finally, you click on the film icon and watch a short action film about the moose. Finishing your study of the moose, you return to the main A-Z screen to learn about another animal. You have just used an interactive multimedia presentation system that was distributed on a CD-ROM disc.

True multimedia is a combination of many of the technologies that have been discussed in earlier chapters of this book. It is sometimes defined as bringing together data from a variety of sources (still visuals, animation, full-motion video, sound including speech and music, text, and graphics) and manipulating it with a computer. The resulting product can either be viewed sequentially or in a non-linear form called hypermedia. If the user of the product can, by his or her actions, vary the way in which it is displayed, it is called interactive multimedia. This allows the user to create his or her own approach to the information.

Beware! Do not assume that, whenever you see the word "multimedia" on a software package, the package will be truly interactive multimedia. As one teacher said, "if it has text and beeps occasionally, the producers call it multimedia." Multimedia is a hot topic, so know what you're buying before you write the purchase order.

In our multimedia example using *Mammals*, you were able to use graphics (the maps), still visuals (photos), full-motion video (the film clip), sound, and text to find out about the moose. In addition, because you could select how you approached your topic (animals of the cold north) as well as the icons (map, ear, page) that you used and the order in which you used them, the program is considered to be interactive and nonlinear. If you were only able to access a series of frames (think of a set of slides shown one by one on your screen) with information about the moose and used the mouse to click on an icon to view them in a set order, the program would be considered sequential.

The next step beyond using multimedia is for you or your students to create your own multimedia programs. Thankfully, there are many software packages on the market that simplify the job of producing a multimedia presentation. In fact, many of these authoring systems even make the work seem like fun.

What multimedia presentation systems are available?

Computer authoring systems have been in use in schools for a number of years. Designed to help someone who is not a programmer or who does not know a programming language, authoring systems provide prompts to take a user step-by-step through the process of creating a computer program. The first authoring systems were designed to create computer-based lessons and tests and included routines to monitor student progress through the lessons and to record grades.

Recently, the idea behind the instructional authoring systems has been expanded to the development of presentation systems. Like the traditional authoring systems, a presentation system can help you create a computer program. However, unlike the lesson created by an authoring system, the program that most of these systems create is like a "slide show" on a computer monitor. Information is seen in a series of frames or individual slides shown on the monitor. There can be a variety of transition effects (dissolves, wipes, fades) between each of the "slides" in the program.

In addition, the user can interact with the program by moving a pointer with a mouse and clicking on an icon on the screen called a button. Clicking on a button can control external hardware such as a CD-ROM player, show a full-motion digital video clip, play a music selection, or move to another slide in the presentation. A hypermedia presentation system allows you to create a web of "slides" that are interconnected with a projection sequence determined by the user.

The appeal of these multimedia presentation programs lies in the fact that the "slide shows" that they create are dynamic with color, sound, animation, and even some full-motion video clips. This means that they can be used with people who have a variety of learning styles. These same programs can create printed handouts or even transparencies to accompany or replace the computer presentation.

What is hypermedia?

Hypermedia presentations provide an interactive, nonlinear approach to information in which the user selects his or her own path through the data. What does that mean? Think about a "choose your own adventure" story. As you read the story, you select different paths depending on the way you react to different situations. Different readers may select different story lines and experience different situations, or everyone may make the same choices and read the same story. The decision is up to the user.

Now, let's say that, in that same adventure story, some words are highlighted and have a page number beside them. By turning to that page, you can find out more about the word such as a definition, historical information, or a picture. If that word is the name of a famous person, when you turn to the appropriate page, you might find biographical information, a picture, and a quote from a famous speech. You might become so interested in that person that you put down the adventure story and pick up a history book to read more about the person and the times in which he or she lived.

If all of that page turning and picking up another book were done for you by a computer whenever you clicked the mouse on an icon, you would have an interactive, nonlinear approach to information. And, if you could hear the famous speech or see a photo of the person, you would have a multimedia approach as well. Put them together and you have hypermedia, an interactive, nonlinear multimedia presentation system.

A few special terms are used to describe some of the actions in hypermedia. By using a mouse to click on a button or hot point (visible as icons or hidden behind an object or a highlighted word), you can link or branch (move) to other parts of the presentation. Bookmarks allow you to return easily to your original place in the program if you find yourself lost in hyperspace. (Hyperspace is that never-never land you started into when you branched off the adventure story and picked up the history book.) Concept maps provide an overview of the presentation and show where you are in relation to the whole.

With hypermedia you can explore a topic for just the basic facts, or you can go into more detail on all or just a few items. By providing lots of opportunities for branching, the originator of the presentation can let the user browse the information. To provide more structure, the originator can limit the choices the user can make or provide a suggested path through the information. Hypermedia is a true multimedia system.

Hypermedia software is used by many companies to develop CD-ROM programs. *Mammals*, which we used as an example at the beginning of this section, is a hypermedia program. Refer to the chapter on CD-ROM for a discussion of electronic books that are also hypermedia presentation systems.

What is *HyperCard?*

Hypermedia presentation systems really became popular when, in 1987, Apple Corporation distributed a program known as *HyperCard* free with all new Macintosh computers. It allowed people to author a presentation by creating cards (the slides in a slide show), arranging them in a stack (a group of cards that create a program) and linking them with buttons. Now there are many presentation programs on the market that use hypermedia links. Some people, however, still refer to any hypermedia program as *HyperCard.*

What are the benefits for teachers and librarians?

Multimedia presentation software can be used to produce attention getting, dramatic, audio and visual lessons and reports. Using sound instructional design principles (objective, content outline, materials list, storyboard, and so forth), a teacher or SLMS can produce a variety of multimedia instructional materials that should keep the interest of most students. Librarians can produce library orientation, reference guides, and skills instruction programs that students and teachers can use at any time. If you are tired of delivering the same demonstration on selecting a research topic, try using a multimedia presentation system to develop a product that students and teachers can access on their own.

In using presentation software, remember these words of caution. First, do not always try to produce a glitzy program. A well-produced presentation with relatively few special effects is better than a flashy one that will not run. Mary Alice Anderson reports that she has success using a program such as *ClarisWorks* or *Microsoft Works* to produce simple, but effective presentations by creating computer "slides" with page breaks between them. Then she plays the program back by using the software's built-in slide show option.

Second, don't use a multimedia system to produce a lesson that could be done more easily in another format. If transparencies would work better in a given lesson, use them. In fact, you might even use the presentation system to design the transparencies and then print them out on transparency film using a color printer.

Why should students use this software?

Let's go back in time several centuries to the year 1560. Gutenberg's invention of moveable type has been in existence for over 100 years. Yet, in a small room in a monastery, an apprentice scribe bends low and laboriously copies a book by hand. Hearing the master scribe enter the room, the weary apprentice asks why the monastery does not use the technique discovered by Gutenberg. That way many more books could be produced and learning would spread. The master replies that Gutenberg's idea is just a passing fancy and will never really catch on. Its product just cannot compare to a handwritten text, and, besides, copying by hand is a good exercise for the mind.

Now move back to the end of the twentieth century. Think about some of the reasons you may have heard against allowing students to produce multimedia presentations instead of written reports. Do you see any of the master scribe's logic in them? After all, how many "term papers" does the average person write once he or she completes school? Compare that to the number of presentations to clubs, church groups, civic organizations, and government agencies (city council, school board) that same person will probably give. Don't the presentations outweigh the research reports?

Contrary to some opinions, allowing students on all levels to create multimedia presentations to replace or supplement written reports does not mean the death of books and learning. In researching the information needed to prepare a multimedia presentation, students use the same print and electronic sources that they use to create a written report. In addition, students are able to combine traditional library/information skills (i.e., selecting and narrowing a topic, preparing an outline) with the higher level thinking skills (i.e., critical thinking, problem solving, and decision making) when they are actively engaged in authoring their own multimedia presentations. If they work in groups, they are developing cooperative learning skills.

The question always arises: Do students learn when they are producing multimedia presentations? Educators at Battle Ground Middle School in Indiana decided to find out. Technology and Media Director Joanne Troutner reported on the development of assessment rubrics and their applications in a pilot testing program at the school. (While all of the assessment rubrics can be found in her 1996 article in TECHNOLOGY CONNECTION, her computer skills rubric appears later in this chapter.) Students were evaluated on their computer skills, presentation, knowledge, and cooperative learning skills. Praise came from students and parents as well as the teachers involved in the project. In addition, the teachers found that the experience of developing the grading rubrics was "one of the most powerful forms of staff development we had ever experienced."

Giving students this opportunity also takes advantage of the students' various learning styles. Often, we forget that many high school students are tactile-kinesthetic and learn best by actually doing things.

To see how school librarians have worked with their teachers to help students make multimedia presentations part of their assignments, watch school librarians Connie Scott and Star Wolven at Hampton High School in Hampton, Virginia, as they work with an English class that is studying American poets. These dynamic librarians are fortunate that a Macintosh computer lab is located off the library and that Connie has become quite proficient in using *HyperCard*.

- In the classroom, the teacher has assigned groups of students to report on specific poets.
- Using the library's reference collection (print and CD-ROM), Star guides the students as they gather information.
- Since most of the members of this class had used *HyperCard* in their social studies class in the fall, Connie meets the groups in the Mac lab, reviews the basics of presentation planning, and helps the groups organize the information that they found through their research into a computer multimedia presentation.
- Students work on their presentations in the lab with their teacher (and sometimes Connie or Star) during their class periods and during other times when the lab is available.

- The scanner is used as one group decides to use a portrait of the poet in its presentation while another wants to incorporate some artwork that the students think illustrates the mood their poet tried to convey in some major works.
- Another group wants to incorporate a brief audio selection into its presentation.
- Finally the presentations are ready and are used as the groups present their reports to the class.

While both librarians agree that a project like this takes time, they also say that it is worth it. It's exciting to watch students become involved in their work and teach each other how to use the computers, software, and references. Everyone seems to be learning. Students who often are the first out the library door now return after school to polish their presentation or to try to find one more piece of information that they need. In fact, students who have been allowed to use the computers to create a multimedia presentation in one class help convince other teachers to try it.

What can students do?

With a little help from teachers and the SLMS, students in elementary, middle, and high school can use multimedia presentation programs. Although some teachers may be reluctant to allow students to create multimedia presentations because they are not familiar with the software or are not sure how to evaluate the product, with a few suggestions, most are willing to give multimedia a try.

Writing in TECHNOLOGY CONNECTION, Lesley S. J. Farmer explains how she helped a student create a presentation.

> A student at my school was researching influential artists of the 1930s. He looked up Dali in the Grolier's CD-ROM and discovered related articles. Going from one article to another, he generated a group of relevant entries, each with pictures that could be enlarged to fill the computer screen. Hooking the computer to a large-screen monitor, the student showed a sequence of pictures from the CD-ROM that demonstrated the influence artists had on each other and the society. Both he and the class were impressed! (p. 31)

Teachers and students have also found the benefits of using multimedia presentation software to develop portfolios. At Van Cortlandt Middle School in Croton-on-Hudson, New York, students are required to demonstrate competence in problem solving, communications, research, and "out-of-class" activities. The solution was to allow students to develop multimedia portfolios which included documents, video clips, audio, and still images. The teachers found that this assignment appealed to all students regardless of their academic achievement. They also were pleased at the high standards that the students set for themselves. Although some students developed their own format for preparing the portfolio and presenting it at the end of the year, others used a variety of authoring presentation packages.

In Florida, two schools used the templates from *Multimedia Assessment Tool* to develop what they called a "digital shoebox." The shoebox consisted of a home page for each student with links to administrative and academic information as well as a demonstration video of each student engaged in "performance assessment tasks." Each shoebox was used as part of a student-teacher conference and was shared with the parents.

While presentations can be created on almost any subject, here are some suggestions for various curricular areas.

Social studies:

Research local history. Supplement the text with illustrations that are scanned in from postcards.

Present a person in history, including a picture, the reading of a famous quotation, a brief part of an important speech or, for recent figures, a film clip.

Select a time period and present an overview of it. Include music (audio) and art (visual) as well as information about important historical events.

Prepare a brief economic report on a major U.S. corporation that is listed on the New York Stock Exchange. Include graphs and charts as well as illustrations of its products.

English:

Select a favorite poet. Provide biographical information and a visual interpretation of one of his or her poems.

Select one novel and have different characters tell their side of the story.

Develop a multimedia book report that will encourage others to read the book.

Write a short story that includes options for the reader. (Think of this as a computerized "choose your own adventure.")

Science and math:

Prepare a short tutorial that other students can use. Include an information section, an activity, and a short quiz.

Create a tutorial to help others learn basic science terminology.

Illustrate a mathematical concept or formula.

Using *Mammals* as a guide, prepare a report on an insect, bird, or fish. Use the results as the beginning of a class science encyclopedia.

Foreign language:

Instead of a written report on a foreign city, create a visual one. Any narration should be in the foreign language.

Prepare a tutorial stack that shows items or actions and then describes them in the foreign language. Then try the reverse by making a statement in the foreign language and letting the user click on a button to see what it represents and hear the English translation.

Art:

Prepare a biography of an artist and include samples of his or her major works.

Select one of the basic artistic elements (form, line, shape) define it, and show how several artists used it.

How should you select presentation software?

A variety of software programs are available to help you create your own multimedia presentation. In selecting one, you need to keep in mind some basic questions:

- How will the presentation be used? Class presentations by students, instruction created by teachers, staff development, or shows to groups outside the school?

- Who will be the audiences? Students, teachers, community?

- What types of things will you want to include? Text, photos, scanned images, created graphics, animation, sound, motion video?

- How interactive should it be? Should it run on its own without any need for user input or should it require some actions on the user's part? If so, how much?

- Should it be sequential or nonlinear? Will the product run as a straight slide show or will it allow branching to various parts?

Once you have some idea of the things you want in your presentation software, look at a few other questions to keep in mind when you actually select one.

What hardware is required? Look at the specific hardware requirements for each program you consider. Most require a large RAM (at least 8MB) and hard drive of at least 250MB. To use some, you will need a mouse, a barwand, audio board, or even a video adapter. Does the software support some brands and not others? Will you be able to store student presentations on floppy disks or will you need larger removable storage devices such as a Zip drive?

With what operating systems can it be used? Are there versions for both the PC and Macintosh/Apple? On a PC, will it work with Windows? Does it need System 7 to run on a Macintosh?

Is it WYSIWYG (What you see is what you get)? Is what you see on the screen as you create the program the same thing that is shown during the presentation? Can you see the combined text and graphics as you create the presentation?

Does it give you an overview of all the slides? A master view of the presentation shows all of the slides (or a portion of a long presentation) on the screen, in miniature, at one time. In some cases, you can rearrange, copy, or delete any of the slides by moving the miniature pictures on the computer screen.

Does it have a word processor and spell checker? Some programs include a basic word processor and spell checker to assist you in entering text information. Others allow you to bring information into the program from another word processor. Some do both.

Does it have an outline feature? With some programs, you can create an on-screen outline of your entire presentation and use that outline in various ways to design your presentation.

What type fonts are provided? Will the type fonts provided by the program suit your needs? Can you purchase additional fonts? Can you bring text and accompanying type-style information into the program from another source?

What are the graphics tools? Most programs have "tools" to help you create your own computer graphics. These include chart tools to prepare pie, graph, and bar charts; drawing tools to make lines, circles and curves; "paint brushes" to create, shade, and color objects; and manipulation tools to flip, rotate, skew, and move objects. Some programs allow you to import graphics from computer or CD-ROM clip art files and from scanners.

Does it have transitional effects? One advantage computerized "slide-show" presentations have over traditional transparencies and slides is that they provide transitional effects from one slide to the next. Wipes, dissolves, barn doors (opening from the middle of the screen) and fades are only a few of the effects that can add pizazz to a presentation.

Are there templates or can you customize the design? Some programs have built-in templates or designs for the layout of the slides. You select a design and fill in your information. Other programs offer templates plus an option to let you create your own designs. If a program has templates, look at them to determine how useful they will actually be in your situation.

Can you import information from other programs? Spreadsheets and word processors sometimes contain information that you would like to use in a presentation. How easy is it to import that data? Can data from spreadsheets be used to create charts and graphs?

What are the output possibilities? In addition to showing a presentation on a computer monitor, some software programs can provide print copies for handouts (in miniature or full-page size) and transparencies. A complete "slide-show" can be printed on paper as 12 small (1 1/2" by 2") frames per page and used as notes for the presenter or handouts for the audience. Some high-end programs produce data that can be turned into color 35mm slides or color prints.

How helpful is the documentation? Look at the documentation provided with the program. Is it clear with step-by-step instructions? Can you understand it? Are there illustrations? Are there tutorials or on-screen help?

Are the commands easy to remember? Are there icons on the screen to help you? Do you need to remember commands or are there lots of prompts?

Does it have sound capabilities? Can you include sound with your presentation? If so, what hardware is required to record and playback the sound? Can you create or import your own digital sounds?

Are there video and animation features? If you plan to use full-motion video or animation as part of the presentation, be sure the software will support it. If you plan to use the software on a Macintosh, does it support/require *QuickTime* or require System 7 as the operating system? What type of animation does it produce? With path-based animation, the user identifies the path for an object to follow and the computer makes the object move along that path. (For example, the image of the dinosaur "walks" from right to left on the screen, however the legs do not actually move back and forth as it walks.) In cel-based animation, there are a series of successive images that provide the illusion of full-motion. Television cartoons are cel-based animation. True cel-based animation requires a great deal of time and artistic ability.

What sources of video can you use? Can you bring digital video from CD-ROM, CD-I and other technologies into the presentation? Can it work with a video digitizer or DVI technology to convert images from analog sources such as videotape and videodiscs? (See Chapter 8 for more information about digital and analog video.)

How long will it take to learn to use it? If it takes too long to learn to use the program, you may never use it no matter how many great features it has. On the other hand, do expect to put some time and effort into learning to use most of the major presentation systems. Depending on the program and your computer skills, you should be able to use the basics of many programs in less than six hours.

Checklist for Presentation Software

General ease of use

Word processing features

Slide show features (templates, sorter, outliner)

Layout and design capabilities

Graphics tools (draw, graph)

Format for imported graphics (BMP, GIF, JPED, PICT, TIFF)

Format for imported video (*QuickTime*, MPEG)

Video special effects

Audio (recording and playback)

Format for imported audio (MIDI, WAV)

Included clip art images

Included video clips

Included sound clips

Multimedia features (hyperlinks, transition effects, animation)

Minimum hardware requirements

Documentation provided

Price

Figure 11.1   Features of Presentation Software

Can you try out the program before you buy it? Some schools, colleges, universities, and computer stores offer classes in using presentation software. Take a class to see how easy the program is to use before you buy it. If no one in your area offers a class, check with neighboring school districts.

Does the program have a special playback feature? Some programs have a special replay option. With this, you can create a presentation and give it to someone else to use. That person can play the completed presentation on a computer even though that computer does not have a copy of the software that you used to create the presentation.

What presentation software is available?

The purpose of this book is not to evaluate or recommend specific software programs. However, with something as new and special as multimedia presentation programs it might be helpful for you to know a few brand names to consider. These programs range from the very simple to the true hypermedia programs and professional multimedia production packages. If you are thinking of developing presentations to show to the school board, parents, or the community, take a tip from the business world. There, the most widely used presentation software packages are, in descending order: *Powerpoint, Harvard Graphics, Word Perfect Presentations, Persuasion,* and *Astound.*

Some companies such as Microsoft, Corel, and Lotus include HTML (hypertext markup language) in their presentation packages. You can then use a program feature to "publish to the Internet." This creates an HTML file which can be uploaded using FTP/IP to move the file to your own Web site. Add a link from a page on your site and you have put your presentation on the Web.

Here are two words of caution to keep in mind when selecting presentation software. First, while some of these programs can be used on any level, others are better for elementary, middle, or high school. You are the only one who knows your students and their abilities. Second, like most technologies, this field is changing and new products are coming on the market. Included in the Resources section is a list of presentation tools. In some cases, the Internet address is provided. Some companies provide samples of their programs on their Web sites.

What hardware is necessary?

Remember, whenever possible, select the software first and then purchase the hardware. The software package and the types of presentations that you want to create will help determine the hardware that you need. If this does not happen and the hardware arrives first, accept reality and be prepared to work with what you are given. However, realize that your hardware may limit how well your software will work.

For example, if you want to use full-motion video in your presentations (check Chapter 10 for additional information and hardware requirements), you will need more equipment than if you only plan to use text and computer graphics. For some applications with either the Macintosh or PC, you might want to have a CD-ROM drive, a scanner, and a videodisc player.

While some presentation software programs will run on older model PCs with less than 640K of RAM, others may require a computer that meets the standards set by the Multimedia PC Marketing Council (MPC) or the Interactive Multimedia Association (IMA). (See Chapter 4 for more information on MPC standards.) Currently, the highest level, MPC3, requires a 75Mhz Pentium with 8MB RAM, a 4x CD-ROM drive, 16-bit digital sound, and a 540MB hard drive. However, most of the presentation software packages will run with a 486 processor. If you plan to use a lot of video and audio, more power is better.

The Apple and Macintosh platforms offer a wide variety of computers that will run multimedia presentation software. Depending on the software, you can use anything from an Apple IIe to a PowerMac. A lot of people suggest the Performa 575 with extra memory.

Remember, you do not need high-powered equipment to begin creating multimedia or hypermedia presentations on your computer.

What are the problems of using multimedia presentation systems?

Multimedia presentation systems are useful tools for students and teachers. However, they do have some drawbacks.

Hardware costs and accessibility. Depending on the software that you select, you may need a powerful computer with a variety of peripherals. If you plan to allow students to produce multimedia reports, you will need either a network with the software running on it, access to a computer lab, or several computers to handle the demand.

Skills required. While some programs are easy to use and most have tutorials and on-screen help, a certain amount of skill is necessary to use most presentation software. Anyone who uses it will need some initial training. Usually you will find that students catch on to using it faster than teachers.

Time involved. It takes time and planning to develop a good multimedia presentation. As a person becomes familiar with the software, that time does decrease.

Addiction. Once you begin working with multimedia and hypermedia presentation systems, you can become addicted. Hours fly by as you animate that dinosaur, launch that rocket, or make that reference book talk. (Yes, I am speaking from experience.)

What are some things to remember in planning a multimedia presentation?

Planning a multimedia presentation is similar to planning a slide-tape show or a video with the addition of branches and jumps. In fact, it could be called storyboarding with branches instead of its usual linear approach. With a group, you will probably use a linear approach. If individuals or small groups will use your presentation themselves, you will want to include more hypermedia features.

To begin planning, ask yourself a few basic questions. What is the goal of the presentation? What do you hope to accomplish? Do you want to inform? Convince? Persuade? Educate? Who is your audience? Students? Teachers? Parents? Administrators? Community? A combination of these? What resources do you have available?

Once you have a plan in mind, remember the following general suggestions.

- Remember the basic design principles of unity, contrast, repetition, consistency, balance, proportion, and restraint.
- Avoid white backgrouds.
- For text, try black, dark blue or dark green ink on a light background, or yellow on a black or dark blue background.
- Keep graphics simple; do not overuse them.
- Use "white space." Do not clutter the screen.
- Do not mix the formats of the slides (vertical and horizontal).
- Check and recheck your spelling.
- Use graphics that you scan or capture with video capture or a still digital camera.
- Use video and or animation as an integral part of your presentation, not merely for entertainment.
- Use "bullets" rather than numbers to make your points.
- Do not use all caps. This slows down reading by 25% or more.
- Keep the text simple. Follow the old transparency 6x6 rule. No more than six words per line, no more than six lines per screen.
- Do not use solid blocks of text.
- If you have several lines of text, justify the left margin but do not justify the right.
- Be consistent, not creative, with your type fonts. Readability is the key.
- Use large, legible fonts with a minimum of 20-22 points.
- Make your headlines 2 to 4 points larger than the text

If students will be developing presentations, help them be successful by providing them with a presentation checklist or a grading rubric in advance. The following is an adaptation of a simple checklist that I developed to use with middle school students. It originally appeared with a multimedia social studies lesson on Native Americans in the October, 1996, issue of *School Library Media Activities Monthly.*

In his article on rubrics, Harry Grover Tuttle of the Ithaca City (New York) School District reported on the use of analytical, holistic, and primary rubrics to evaluate multimedia productions. The holistic rubric illustrated in his article evaluates the entire project on the basis of preparation, documentation, content, response to class questions, and use of multimedia. These are similar to the topics cited by Cornelia Brunner in her 1996 article in *Electronic Learning.*

Presentation Checklist

For text use:
No more than two styles (fonts) of type.
A type size between 24 and 36 points.
No more than six words in a line.
No more than six lines on a slide.
Upper and lower case letters.

For colors on text slides use:
One color for the background.
No more than two colors for the text.

For visuals, use:
Images to add, not detract.
A minimum of special effects.

Be sure to check:
Your spelling.
Your facts.

She grouped the "fifteen criteria teachers need to effectively assess kids' projects" under the broad headings of preparation, sources, organization, navigation, and media integration.

The rubric on the next page was developed by teachers for evaluating student-developed hypermedia projects and was published by Joanne Troutner of the Tippecanoe School Corporation in Lafayette, Indiana, in Technology Connection, March 1996.

What do you need to keep in mind about copyright?

On September 27, 1996, the nonlegislative report on Fair Use Guidelines for Educational Multimedia was adopted by the Subcommittee on Courts and Intellectual Property of the U.S. House of Representatives. (See Appendix B.) This report provides "permitted uses of educational multimedia projects" created by students and teachers. The report is endorsed by a number of educational organizations including the Software Publishers Association and the Association for Educational Communications and Technology and supported by the U.S. Copyright Office. In addition, many major companies and organizations participated in the development of these educational multimedia fair use guidelines.

Basically, the guidelines allow students and teachers to use portions of "lawfully acquired copyrighted works when producing their own educational multimedia projects" to maintain them in their own portfolios. For students, the project must be part of a specific course and may be kept as part of the student's portfolio for "personal uses such as job and graduate school interviews." Educators are provided rights related to production of teaching tools "in support of curriculum-based instruction activities at educational institutions" and may keep the materials for up to two years before they need to seek permission from the copyright holder(s).

Section	Description	Rating Key
Research	• Uses varied sources — books, magazines, vertical file, databases • Has notes with source documented • Has bibliography • Cites sources • Avoids plagiarism	1 Has less than required number of resources 2 Has required number of resources 3 Has more than required number of resources
Subject Knowledge	• Mentions factors leading up to or resulting from topic • Related topic to time period • Historically accurate	1 Little or no understanding of where topic fits in history 2 Some understanding 3 Clear understanding
Organization of Information	• Logical progression of information • Thesis is clear • Conclusion clear • Graphic further explains or clarifies text • Supported facts	1 Strange connections between information 2 Limited connections between information 3 Logical connections between information
Content and Accuracy	• Facts are up-to-date • Pictures accurately tie to text • Sound ties to text • Demonstrates depth of knowledge	1 Inaccurate/lack of ties 2 Accurate but partial requirements 3 Accurate and fits

Copyright 1993 Tippecanoe School Corporation, Lafayette, Indiana
Published in TECHNOLOGY CONNECTION, March 1996.

The guidelines provide "portion limitations" for each type of work. For example, up to 10% or three minutes of motion media, whichever is less, may be used. With "music, lyrics, and music video," up to 10% but no more than 30 seconds can be used. Entire illustrations or photographs may be used but no more than five images by an artist or photographer may be used, with some exceptions, in a single project. If the images come from a collective work, the limit is the lesser of 10% or 15 images.

In addition to the specific limits and permitted uses, the guidelines contain a set of reminders. These include cautions about downloading digital material from the Internet. As the report notes, "access to works on the Internet does not automatically mean that these can be reproduced and reused without permission or royalty payment." The report also reminds educators to include the copyright notice for all materials including those governed by the fair use criteria.

Bibliography

(See also the listing for Chapter 8.)

Anderson, M.A. (1995). The easy way to create computer slide shows. TECHNOLOGY CONNECTION, 2 (3), 16-17. Anderson explains how to use *ClarisWorks* to develop a presentation slide show.

Bett, S. (1995). New and improved slide shows with presentation software. TECHNOLOGY CONNECTION, 2 (3), 22-24. Compares five of the leading presentations software packages.

Brunner, C. (1996). Judging student multimedia; Fifteen criteria teachers need to effectively assess kids' projects. *Electronic Learning*, 15 (6), 14-15. Explains a set of guidelines to evaluate student-made productions.

D'Ignazio, F. (1995). A multimedia publishing center from scratch (and scavenge). TECHNOLOGY CONNECTION, 2 (5), 21-25. D'Ignazio provides a sample student contract for a multimedia club and a multimedia workstation starter kit.

Downs, E. & Clark, K. (1997). Guidelines for effective multimedia design. TECHNOLOGY CONNECTION, 4 (1), 8-9. An overview of design principles.

Ekhaml, L. (1994). Add sizzle to your presentation with electronic slide shows! *School Library Media Activities Monthly*, 11 (3), 38-40. After an introduction to the uses of electronic slide shows in schools, the author provides a tutorial for *Aldus Persuasion* 2.1 presentation software package.

Farmer, L.S.J. (1995). Multimedia: Multi-learning tool. TECHNOLOGY CONNECTION, 2 (3), 30-31. Farmer discusses ways she has helped students integrate text, graphics, sound and motion into their presentations.

Farmer, L.S.J. & Hewlett, J. (1992). *I speak HyperCard*. Englewood, CO: Libraries Unlimited. (See the review in the May/June 1993 issue of THE BOOK REPORT, p. 50.)

Hinkin, S. (1996). How to dodge a speeding bullet; and other tips to help avoid death by terminal presentation predictability. *Presentations,* 10 (3), 27-30. Hinkin uses color slides from presentations to show how the good slides could be made better. When you've mastered the basics, there are great ideas in this article to make your presentations truly professional.

Holzberg, C. S. (1994). Teacher-tested ideas: Hypermedia projects that really work. *Technology & Learning*, 14 (4), 31-36. Examples of projects from schools throughout the United States in the areas of language arts, science, social studies, and other subjects.

Hubbard, G. (1993). Multimedia. *School Library Media Quarterly*, 22 (Fall), 45-47. Discusses multimedia and provides some suggestions for overcoming reluctance to using it in a school.

Krushenisky, D. (1997). Multimedia to the max. *PC Novice,* 9 (2), 24-27. Contains reviews of the leading interactive encyclopedias and reviews CD-ROM vs. Internet vs. hardcopy encyclopedias.

LeCrone, N. L. (1997). Integrating multimedia into the curriculum. TECHNOLOGY CONNECTION, 4 (1), 14-15. Using *ClarisWorks* and *KidPix*, students created slideshows as sixth graders developed travel brochures on Egypt, and fourth graders completed a Native American unit.

Legal land mines, how to avoid licensing litigation. (1996). *InterActivity,* 2 (2), 63-73. If you use music in presentations for non-instructional purposes, check the extensive listings of stock audio sources in this article.

Milone, M. N. (1995). Electronic portfolios: Who's doing them and how? *Technology & Learning,* 16 (2), 28-36. Gives examples of schools in which students and teachers are using digital portfolios.

Multimedia, the complete guide. (1996). London: Dorling Kindersley. This book has the same illustrated approach to multimedia that makes the DK books perennial favorites in school libraries.

Simpson, C. (1997). *Copyright for Schools: A Practical Guide, 2nd edition.* Worthington, OH: Linworth. This edition includes many more practical "real life" examples.

Simpson, C. (1997). How much, how many and when? Copyright & multimedia. TECHNOLOGY CONNECTION, 4 (1), 10-12. A look at the new fair use guidelines for multimedia.

Stafford, D. (1997). PowerPointing the way. TECHNOLOGY CONNECTION, 4 (1), 16-17. LM_NET subscribers provide examples of the ways they use *PowerPoint* software in the curriculum.

Teaching information literacy using electronic resources for grades 6-12. (1996). Worthington, OH: Linworth. Contains lesson plans for multimedia.

Tolhurst, Denise. (1990). A checklist for evaluating content-based hypertext computer software. *Educational Technology,* 32 (3), 17-21.

Troutner, J. (1996). Yes, they put on quite a show, but what did they learn? TECHNOLOGY CONNECTION, 3 (1), 15-17. In addition to a discussion of hypermedia projects with middle school students, Troutner provides four grading rubrics for multimedia presentations.

Tuttle, H.G. (1995). Do's & don'ts of multimedia presentations. *MuliMedia Schools,* 2 (5), 28-31. Discusses a structured approach to planning multimedia presentations and illustrates a multimedia planning sheet.

Tuttle, H.G. (1996). Rubrics; keys to improving multimedia presentations. *MultiMedia Schools,* 3 (Jan./Feb.), 30-33. Tuttle shares a rubric for evaluating a multimedia report and explains its use in the classroom

Yoder, S., Bull, G. & Harris, J. (1992). *LinkWay for educators: an introduction.* Eugene, OR: International Society for Technology in Education. Basic instructions for using LinkWay and LinkWay Live!

Notes

Chapter 12

Technology Staff Development for Teachers

Throughout this book, we've looked at computers and related technologies that are becoming part of every school. But technology is a means, not an end in itself. The sole reason to have technology in the schools is to provide better education for the students. The technology may free the SLMS from filing cards in the card catalog, but the end result should be that the students and teachers have better access to the materials in the collection and that the SLMS has more time to become involved in the curriculum of the school. With proper use, the Internet can extend that access to materials located throughout the world.

But even if the SLMS is technology literate, he or she cannot be the sole participant in the technology revolution in the school. For computers and related technologies to be successful and not relegated to the back of the closet like film loop projectors, teachers have to participate in the revolution. That's why the final, and most important, technology-related task that SLMSs need to perform is staff development.

Why do schools need technology staff development?

Few people seem to doubt the benefits technology can bring to education. Many, however, do seem concerned about the lack of use of technology, believing that if you put enough computers in a school, teachers will learn to use them, perhaps through osmosis. After all, if you put children in front of computers with a new piece of software, most will dig in and explore. However, many teachers in the same situation will sit and wait for someone to show them or lead them step by step. Sure, there will be a few who want to jump right it. But most will wait apprehensively.

Some people see the lack of the use of technology as part of a conspiracy. Writing in the May 15, 1996 issue of *USA Today*, James Snider contends that teachers resist technology because they fear they will lose money, status, and power. According to Snider, distance education can put an expert in each classroom and eliminate the need for the individual classroom teachers. Thus, to keep their jobs, teachers refuse to use technology.

I don't think there's any conspiracy on the part of teachers to keep technology out of the school. There is, however, a lot of fear and anxiety; and that fear is shared by some SLMSs as well as classroom teachers and administrators.

In a recent article, one SLMS advocated splitting the library in two parts. One would contain technology and one would contain print materials. The more I read, the angrier I became. I wanted to tell that librarian that she was missing the point. Information was the important thing; just the carrier was different. I could read a novel via a computer. However, I like to read it in paper format so I can lean back in my recliner and be comfortable or take it with me on vacation. I could search for information using the paper copies of the *Readers' Guide*. Thankfully, I have the option to search using a CD-ROM or online database. But whether I locate the information in a paper or electronic format, I still need to apply the same evaluation strategies in order to use it. The carrier is not the important thing. What is important is the information (and I'm including fiction as a type of information).

Fortunately, most SLMSs have embraced the new technologies. But it hasn't been easy. Often it has meant taking the computer home weekends or during the summer and working through the programs and tutorials. It has meant buying a home computer and experimenting with it. For most librarians, there has been no other alternative. As one library supervisor told a group of prospective SLMSs, "when you become a librarian, don't think I can come or send someone to your school to teach you every software package. You have to jump in and learn it yourself." And, for the most part, we librarians have done just that. We've jumped in and taught ourselves how to use the technology in our libraries.

In a 1996 article, Alice Yucht, a SLMS, draws parallels between "Aunt Lily" who is starting to drive again after the death of her husband, and a librarian like herself who is trying to get on the Information Superhighway. Although Yucht, like Aunt Lily, already knows how to "drive" (or operate) computers and related equipment, she knows that she needs "intermediate Navigator's Ed" that includes new highways "with names that sound like secret codes: CD-ROM, ftp, URL, HTML." But if she, as an experienced SLMS, knows that she needs more training and practice, what about the teachers? As Yucht states:

> Classroom teachers are already over loaded with curriculum mandates, and find themselves having to teach more, in less time, to kids who are often less willing/able to learn than ever. Many teachers still need basic computer Driver's Ed., and certainly can't teach Navigation Skills when they don't know how or where they are going themselves. Yet the powers-that-be seem to think that electronic access to Info-Chaos will be the next universal panacea. It won't be, unless both students and teachers learn how to use all the data they find out there. (p. 15)

The technology that SLMSs and teachers are facing is continuing to grow. Unfortunately, the expenditures for technology have not been accompanied by expenditures for staff training. In the report of the Quality Education Data, figures show that U.S. schools spent over $4 billion on technology in 1995-96, or approximately $95.00 per pupil. At the same time, these schools spent only 4% of the technology funds, or less than $4.00 per pupil, on technology training. While experts recommend allocating at least 30% of the technology budget for training, a 1995 report from the Congressional Office of Technology Assessment shows the breakdown is approximately 55% for hardware, 30% for software, and 15% on training and repairs.

Why does this happen so often? One reason is that hardware is easy to see and talk about. You can show a parent group $25,000 in a computer lab. But it is difficult to show the $25,000 spent on staff training. At other times, states follow the seagull method for distributing technology. Buy the hardware, then fly in and dump it in individual schools, and, just as quickly, fly out again. When attending a meeting with his/her colleagues, an administrator can brag that "my district has an XYZ digital video camera and an ABC computer editing studio." That seems to sound a lot more impressive than "we trained teachers to use the computers that we bought."

In the Spring, 1997, issue of the *Journal of Staff Development*, Rosie and Robert Vojtek write that:

> Access to technology and staff development must occur simultaneously for the integration of technology to become institutionalized in the classroom. Simply providing computers in the classroom and/or connecting classroom computers to the Internet does not mean teachers will use the computers in day-to-day instruction. (p. 61)

Educators are beginning to see the results of the lack of training. Hardware and software are sitting unused in schools. Little is being done to teach educators how to integrate technology into the curriculum. Therefore, many states and local districts have developed a technology training initiative. Unfortunately, what's being offered for training is usually how to run a piece of equipment or how to use a specific program such as a word processor or database rather than how to integrate those programs or that equipment into the curriculum of the school.

What do teachers want for staff development programs?

Mention the words staff development to a group of teachers, and you will probably be met with a collective groan. Unfortunately, most educators have been the victim of at least one poorly planned in-service or similar program.

Planning staff development is like planning a lesson or a curriculum. You need to find out where your learners are in terms of knowledge and compare that to where you would like them to be. Then you look at the means to get them there.

One additional consideration in staff development is to involve the learners, in this case teachers, to identify the things that they need help with. In a 1995 study, Philip Turner did just that. He asked teachers to identify the top five things they would like help with in their teaching. These items were further rated by the amount of assistance needed: in-depth, moderate, initial level. Among the items listed by the teachers at the "In-Depth Level" were:

- Provide in-service training on use of newest multimedia resources.
- Conduct workshops on latest instructional techniques, especially model teaching critical-thinking skills.

Although Turner only surveyed a small group of teachers, these same topics seem to come up over and over again for staff development.

In a 1996 article in the *NASSP Bulletin,* Maria Shelton and Mary Jones reported on a survey conducted by the Fort Worth, Texas Independent School

District. In trying to determine the factors that affect the use of technology in the classroom, the district asked teachers for their input. As a result, the teachers identified four things as "critical to support technology integration into the curriculum: time, training, technology, and teacher-type tasks." What that meant is that teachers wanted:

- specific time for training.
- training that is relevant to the classroom.
- technology in their classrooms for follow-up use.
- active participation in the training with expectations for use of the new skills after the training is over.

What model of staff development is best?

There is no one magic model of staff development that works for all situations. In fact, there are many models for staff development training with each having its own strengths and weaknesses. Some of the following types overlap, but here are just a few ways staff development can be delivered:

Top-down. This approach is often used by central school administrators. Although this model is easy to plan and implement, topics may be selected with little input from the building level personnel. The result is that this training is rarely effective and is frequently met with resistance.

One Shot. An expert is hired to conduct a workshop. While the workshop may be excellent, there frequently is no one at the local school to provide any follow-up.

In-house. This model may rely on experts from within the school district or a mixture of internal and external experts with personnel from the district doing the follow-up sessions for an outside expert. A problem is that an internal expert may not be given the same respect as an external one.

Topic of the Month/Year. With this method, there is a set of constantly changing topics for staff development. Although this is an effective way to provide information on new ideas, it has its problems. Just as soon as school personnel begin to understand one topic and begin to incorporate it into their teaching, another topic is introduced. People tend to give up in frustration.

Modeling Workshops. It is one thing to talk about technology, and another thing to use it. Seeing someone model the appropriate use of technology in a classroom setting can be very practical and very convincing. To be meaningful, however, the uses of technology modeled in the workshops need to be appropriate for the specific group of teachers attending. Modeling the use of CD-ROMs for primary children to a group of high school teachers will not work.

Comprehensive and Consistent. This model calls for a team of experts and school personnel to develop a single staff development program to train all professional personnel of a school district. Teachers, SLMSs, and administrators attend workshops over one or two years in an effort to make a long-term commitment and change in the school district. Under this model, a program may take as long as five years to implement.

Curriculum-Related. Tying technology to changes within the curriculum can be successful when technology is used to model lessons in the new curriculum. Just as successful are staff-development programs where all the technologies introduced relate to the existing curriculum or to the state's standards of learning. Both Virginia and California report great results in helping social studies teachers use the Internet when staff development workshops modeled the use of Web sites to support the newly adopted standards of learning in each state.

Conferences. While sending individuals to conferences can be an excellent form of staff development, a lot hinges on the ability of those individuals to implement what they saw at the conferences and to pass their knowledge on to others.

Distance Learning. Television and the Internet offer many opportunities for staff development, but they are not very effective unless participants are able to work with the demonstrated technology themselves.

See it Through Students' Eyes. Gail Lovely reports that she includes students in some of the staff development programs that she designs. As she writes in the October, 1996, issue of *Electronic Learning*, "Teachers who bring one or two students with them are able to watch how they react to products and projects without having to take the trainer's word for it and without discounting new ideas with thoughts like, 'My students could never.....'"

15 Minute Quickie. Faster than a speeding bullet, this model suggests designing short training modules that can be tacked on to the end of other meetings. They're great as teasers to interest people in longer, more in-depth training.

How can you be sure your staff development is successful?

While you can never be entirely sure that the staff development program that you are planning will be successful, there are some things that you can do to help it succeed. But keep things in perspective; not even the best advertising campaign or the best teacher can reach 100% of the audience 100% of the time.

With that in mind, here are a few tips for having a successful technology staff development program:

- Find out what your teachers need and want. It may not be what you assume. You may want to introduce the Internet while the social studies teachers want resources for the new standards of learning the state has developed. Combine the two and show the teachers some new resources using the Internet.

- Garner administrative support. Be sure your building level and district administrators know what you have planned and that you have their support. Invite them to attend.

- Insure success. Start with teachers who have shown an interest in the topic you are presenting. Hook them and let them help you spread the word to the other teachers. Don't start with the teacher who has vowed never to put his hands on a computer.

- Schedule a convenient time. Ask your teachers for input. Talk to your administrator for his or her advice and consider some of the alternatives listed later in this section.

- Select a catchy title, but be sure to deliver what you promise. The following are modified from titles suggested by Augie E. Beasley and Carolyn Palmer in Linworth's *PR Notebook for School Librarians*:

  > If all Else Fails - Kick (Maintenance and repair)
  > Without a Glitch (Editing video with a computer)
  > To Byte or Not to Byte (Selecting software)
  > Searching' Every Way I Can (Using search engines)
  > What You See is What You Get (Using presentation software)
  > The Best is Yet to Come (Introducing some new equipment)
  > Reach Out and Touch Someone (Using videoconferencing software)
  > Multiple Copies, Multiple Problems (Copyright laws)
  > It's a Snap! (Using a digital camera)

- Identify the objectives that you want to cover and stick to them. Few things are more upsetting than to attend a workshop and hear the presenter say, " I know the title says this is a workshop for advanced Internet users, but we're going to begin with some basics anyway."

- Be sure you have enough hardware for the participants and be sure that the equipment is working. Nothing can be more frustrating for a beginner than to try all morning to get a piece of equipment to work only to find out that the problem was with the equipment, not the operator.

- Begin with the basics (on either an introductory or advanced level) and build on them. Don't start out to impress your teachers with your knowledge of technology.

- Allow multiple entry points to a workshop or program. If you have several teachers at different levels who need training, don't make the experienced teachers sit through the basics. Allow them to come into the program at a later point. This works especially well for multi-session staff development programs.

- Try to appeal to all learning styles: verbal, visual, tactile.

- Make things relevant to classroom practice. Use examples from the topics covered in the classes that the teachers in each group teach.

- Provide breaks if the program extends over 1 1/2 hours.

- Use small groups. If you have a big interest in a particular program, repeat it rather than let it grow too large. With technology training, a ratio of 8 to 1 is good. If you have to have larger groups, be sure to have someone to assist you. You'll usually find a least one person who can't keep up with the group and needs individual attention.

- Allow collaboration. One teacher may be afraid to try something. Two or three working together can help each other.

- Model what you teach. If you are showing teachers how presentation software can be used in the classroom, use presentation software, not transparencies, for the demonstration.

- Focus on integrating the technology into the curriculum not on the use of technology for its own sake.

- Give teachers something to take away from the program with them. If you are introducing specific hardware or software, try producing tip sheets that the teachers can keep in a notebook and refer to. You might also challenge teachers by providing some suggestions of ways to implement a specific technology into their classrooms and inviting them try one. If they do, be sure to publicize the results. A sample challenge is shown later in this section.

- Try to keep the program relaxed. Keep the format flexible. Learn to laugh.

- Provide time for plenty of hands-on guided practice during the program. Let the participants work with the technology on their own while you are there to provide help if necessary. Remember, people learn best by doing.

- Use food as a drawing card. Bribery is a harsh word, but a few munchies never hurt. No, you don't want teachers eating chips and dip at the computers, but plan a time for a short break or for refreshments before or after the program. While everyone loves those sinfully rich pastries and cookies, be sure to include something lighter such as a veggie plate with a fat-free dip for the health-conscious members.

- Provide incentives for attendance. In Virginia, staff development classes that are approved by the district superintendent can carry recertification points for teachers. Your state may have a similar option. If that's not possible, try one of the other types of rewards listed later in this section.

- Evaluate the program. Give the participants an opportunity to tell you what they liked, what they didn't like, and how they would modify the training. Don't rely on word-of-mouth. Get the evaluation in writing. There are sample forms later in this section.

- Be available after the program for questions. Some people will not ask questions when in a group, but may approach you individually afterward.

- Publicize the results. Let everyone know, not what *you* did, but what the *teachers* in your staff development did. Make them the center of attraction.

- Schedule follow-ups to the initial staff development program. The National Center for Restructuring Education, Schools and Teaching says that it might take as many as 20 follow-up sessions before teachers feel comfortable using what they have learned in a staff development program.

- Use teachers in follow-up programs. Allow teachers to show their peers what they have done.

What are some possible staff development topics?

There's always a danger in listing possible topics. To be successful, staff development should depend on the needs of individual teachers. However, there are some general topics on which SLMSs frequently provide workshops. These include the following areas with a few examples of each.

Specific Computer Programs:

Using computer programs such as an electronic gradebook.

Using a wordprocessing or database program to support a particular curriculum area.

Using a Web browser to locate information.

Taking a scavenger hunt on the Internet using search utilities.

Teaching (name of subject) using (name of program).

Specific Computer Hardware:

Using a videodisc player to teach geology.

Preserving history with a digital camera.

Using the Internet and World Wide Web Sites:

Applying the criteria in Chapter 8 of this book and letting teachers evaluate Web sites related to the units that they teach.

Locating Internet sites for curriculum area.

Citing Internet references, some tools and Web sites.

Learning to use the Internet via e-mail. AASL offers staff development seminars through ICONnect. Check the resources section for this and other URLs of training materials on the Internet.

Copyright and Ethics:

Reviewing the new guidelines for the use of multimedia technology as well as the guidelines for off-air taping.

Designing assignments that discourage plagiarism. Rather than writing a report, have students gather information that they can use to produce something other than a written report. In a Native American unit, have students compare the life styles of various tribes, build a model of a dwelling used by a specific tribe, or write a journal entry describing an imaginary visit to a tribe.

Integrating Technology in the Curriculum:

Across the Curriculum

Creating a multimedia portfolio for students and teachers.

Creating a school/classroom Web page.

Language Arts

Publishing a classroom newsletter with desktop publishing.

Setting up and monitoring e-mail pals for your students.

Adding illustrations to your stories for primary teachers.

Science

Using experts on the Internet in your classroom. The how and whys of newsgroups and listservs.

Conducting weather experiments over the Internet.

Participating in world-side science experiments.

Math

Solving geometry problems on the Internet.

Social Studies

Planning an online field trip using the World Wide Web.

Making history come alive with Internet resources.

Using interactive CD-ROMs in the classroom.

Art

Preparing a multimedia presentation about an artist.

Comparing the works of several artists through a multimedia presentation.

Visiting a museum via the Internet.

Music

Composing music with a computer.

Using Information and Problem Solving Skills:

Exploring one of the models of problem solving discussed next in this chapter.

Using an information skills model in your classroom.

Why should information and problem solving skills be part of staff development?

You may have wondered about the last topic in the previous chapter. While SLMSs teach information skills to students, they often forget a critical link: teachers. If SLMSs want students to use these skills, their teachers need to be familiar with these models of locating information. In the study done by Philip Turner, teachers ranked the need to have workshops modeling teaching critical thinking skills as a top priority.

There are several models of information and problem solving skills that you might use. A few are outlined here. Complete information on each of them can be found by consulting titles in the bibliography at the end of this chapter.

ALA's Information Problem-Solving Skills:

I.   Defining the Need for Information

II. Initiating the Search Strategy

III. Locating the Resources

IV. Assessing and Comprehending the Information

V.   Interpreting the Information

VI. Communicating the Information

VII. Evaluating the Product and the Process

From: *Information Literacy: a Position Paper on Information Problem Solving*. American Association of School Librarians.

The Big Six

1. Task Definition
    Define the information problem
    Identify the information needed

2. Information Seeking Strategies
    Brainstorm all possible sources
    Select the best sources

3. Location and Access
    Locate sources
    Find information within the source

4. Use of Information
    Engage the source (read, hear, view, touch)
    Extract relevant information

5. Synthesis
    Organize information from multiple sources
    Present the information

6. Evaluation
    Judge the process (efficiency)
    Judge the product (effectiveness)

From: Eisenberg, M. And Johnson, D. (1996) *Computer Skills for Information Problem-Solving: Learning and Teaching Technology in Context.*

Information Seeking

1. Initiation (contemplating the task and possible topics; uncertainty)

2. Selection (selecting a topic; optimism)

3. Exploration (encountering inconsistency and improbability: confusion)

4. Formulation (forming a focused perspective; clarity)

5. Collection (gathering and extending; satisfaction or disappointment)

6. Presentation (connecting and extending; satisfaction or disappointment)

7. Evaluation

From: Kuhlthau, C. C. (1993) *Implementing a Process Approach to Information Skills.*

Research Process

1. Choose a broad topic
2. Get an overview of the topic
3. Narrow the topic
   Reflection: Is my topic a good one?
4. Develop a thesis or statement of purpose.
   Reflection: Does my thesis or statement of purpose represent an effective, overall concept for my research?
5. Formulate questions to guide research
   Reflection: Do the questions provide a foundation for my research?
6. Plan for research and production
   Reflection: Is the research/production plan workable?
7. Find/Analyze/Evaluate sources
   Reflection: Are my sources usable and adequate?
8. Evaluate evidence/Take notes/Compile bibliography
   Reflection: Is my research complete?
9. Establish conclusions/ Organize information into an outline.
   Reflection: Are my conclusions based on researched evidence? Does my outline logically organize conclusions and evidence?
10. Create and present final product.
    Reflection: Is my paper/project satisfactory?

From: Stripling, B. K. And Pits, J. M. (1988) *Brainstorms and Blueprints: Teaching Library Research as a Thinking Process.*

Information Skills Model for Teaching Electronic Information Skills

I. Presearch activities

II. Searching for Information - Develop a strategy for each function:
   Browse (Most simplistic)
   Hierarchial (More complex)
   Analytical (Boolean logic)
   Filtering (Choosing criteria which will limit topic)

III. Interpreting Information - Summarizing and paraphrasing

From: Pappas, M. L. (1995) *Information Skills for Electronic Resources.*

Where can you find resources to help you?

There are many print resources about conducting in-service programs. Some books, such as *Workshops for Teachers: Becoming Partners for Information Literacy* by Lesley S.J. Farmer, even contain workshop outlines. Periodicals such as TECHNOLOGY CONNECTION and *Classroom Connect* often feature ideas for technology inservice programs. In addition, *The Journal of Staff Development* has a column that runs under the heading: Technology in Staff Development.

The Internet is also an excellent resource for staff development ideas. At the Web site of the Bellingham (Washington) Schools, there are several plans you can look at. One, an eight-hour class on "Information Literacy and the Net," emphasizes "student investigations as vehicles to explore the information available over the Internet," and provides answers to the following questions:

- What is Information Literacy?
- What is Visual Literacy?
- What is Textual Literacy?
- What is Numerical Literacy?
- How might we use the Research Cycle to achieve literacy and build insight?
- In what ways do we gather information?
- How might we Sort, Analyze, and Synthesize Information most effectively?
- How do we provide the social foundations and group skills needed to make this kind of research work? How will we measure student progress with literacy?
- In what ways could this type of learning support multiple intelligences and different learning styles?
- Where are the good curriculum resources on the Web and how might I use them?
- Where are the good teacher resources on the Web and how might I use them?
- Where are the good information sites for virtual field trips, weather, and daily news? How might I use them?
- Now that I've visited a variety of good sites, how will I use this information to design an effective learning experience for students?
- How do we use indexes and search engines to find information efficiently on the Web?
- How do I connect globally using Telecommunications and Mail?
- How does your lesson plan support the district policy?

The complete lesson plans are available at the school site (http://www.bham.wednet.edu/literacy.htm). Permission is given to copy them for use by "non-profit public learning institutions only for use with their own staff." Other classes at the schools' general site include "Creating Online Student Investigation Units" and a workshop on databases.

Associations may also provide staff development assistance or ideas. ASCD (Association for Supervision and Curriculum Development) in Alexandria, Virginia, has a kit entitled Teaching and Learning With Technology. AASL offers training through its ICONnect site on the Internet.

ISTE (International Society for Technology in Education) maintains a list of "Recommended Foundations in Technology for All Teachers." While this list of competencies was designed as a checklist for teacher preparation programs, it is an excellent description of the basic technology competencies. Check yourself and let the teachers in your school see where they stand. Areas needing work can become topics for staff development programs. (http://www.iste.org/standards/found.htm)

Douglas P Crispen of the University of Alabama started a listserv that became so popular that it is now closed to new members. His "Roadmap96" listserv covers basic topics about the Internet in short, easy to follow lessons. While you can't get lessons e-mailed to you, you can consult the archives of all previous lessons and you can share them with others. (http://www.gnofn.org/whs1/education/teacher/rdmap96/remap96.html)

For help with science and math, the Eisenhower National Clearinghouse (http://www.enc.org) has a professional development exchange. This searchable site has information on workshops, classes, institutes, summer interships, and other professional development opportunities that you can share with your staff.

The "Electronic Library Classroom 101" is the other name for BCK2SKOL, an initiative of librarians in South Carolina. (http://web.scd.sc.edu/bck2skol/bck2skol.html) The lessons at this Web site even provide hot links to sources as part of the lessons.

Another set of training tools is Tools for the Internet Trainer, which can be accessed through the home page of LITA, the Library and Information Technology Association. (http://www.lita.org/) The link will lead you to a series of 15-minute training modules on Internet-related topics.

In addition to the free materials, there are several commercial vendors selling technology training packages. Some include Classroom Connect's *Educators' Essential Internet Training System* and Decision Development Corporation's *Creating the Technology Classroom,* which uses a videodisc for training.

When should you schedule staff development?

There is no one best time to schedule a staff development program, yet scheduling can have a direct effect on the success of a program. Two things you need to do are listen to your teachers and keep your options open. Here are a few of the times available.

Before and after school. No one likes to come to work early or stay late on a regular basis, but some teachers may be willing to extend their day for technology training, especially if the training is linked to a reward such as recertification, or continuing education credit. Some schools report success with evening classes just for teachers.

On special staff development days. Many states provide staff development or training days as part of the regular school calender. Some of these days can be used in the individual schools for hands-on training. Also consider teaming with subject specialists so that technology training is combined with a language arts or science staff development program.

During the school day. Depending upon the staffing patterns of your school and the size of the library staff, it might be possible for staff development to occur during the regular school day during teacher planning time. In some cases, principals have hired substitute teachers to free classroom teachers to attend staff development sessions. Tom Kranz, principal of Roberto Clemente Middle School in Germantown, Maryland, used the district's four half days of staff development time for initial technology training. For reinforcement, he hired substitutes to release the teachers by academic department with each teacher being released for one-half day. With one substitute, he could provide two teachers with follow-up training and, by releasing teachers by discipline rather than grade level, there was minimal disruption of the work on an individual middle school team.

In Iowa City, Iowa, students go home one hour early every Thursday while the teachers stay for staff development. While the second and fourth Thursdays are reserved for district-wide staff development programs, the agendas on the first and third Thursdays are determined by the individual schools. This is an ideal arrangement for technology training.

A similar plan is followed in Holt, Michigan, where middle and senior high school students don't arrive at school until after 11:30 on Wednesdays. Teachers start their days four hours earlier and spend the time collaborating. In return, the teachers voted to give up their daily planning periods and to have a "slightly longer" school day on the other weekdays.

In the teacher's lounge. Some SLMSs report success when they put new equipment in the teacher's lounge and allow teachers to use it during the school day. This works well for follow-ups to staff development programs.

With individualized learning packets linked to take the technology home. In some instances, the only way to learn technology is to do as the author Gary Paulsen claims he did: take the technology into a room and don't leave until one of you wins. It may be possible to develop learning packets for teachers to check out with the appropriate technology for a weekend or a summer. This is an excellent incentive for follow-up education. In some school districts, teachers who attend a scheduled technology workshop or participate in a series of programs are given priority to check a computer out to use at home over the summer.

At each person's convenience. No, I'm not suggesting that you offer one-on-one personal training to an entire school staff. However, there are ways to allow people to pick the time of their training. You can do this by letting technology help you teach technology. There are several sources such as ICONnect or BK2SKOL, mentioned above in this chapter, that allow you to deliver instruction via e-mail. Another alternative is to develop learning packets and tutorials that teachers can work through on their own.

During summer camp. Our local PBS TV station holds a summer camp each year. Schools provide part of the funding and participants go to a nearby camp or resort for a week of immersion in technology as well as a few hours in the pool. This is so popular that the selection process has become highly competitive.

The Fort Worth, Texas, Schools hold a "Technology Bootcamp" during which participants receive five intensive days of training. The reward is a multimedia computer, software, and printer for their classroom use. For follow-up, each "bootcamper" develops two technology-based lessons for the school district's database.

What rewards or incentives can you offer teachers for their participation?

Do you tease with a carrot (cake) or motivate with a stick? That is the perennial problem when planning staff development programs.

Here are some things to consider:

- Will a local college provide continuing education units for the training?
- Will your state department of education accept the training for recertification credits or points?
- Will your school district use attendance at the programs as a factor in granting a salary increment or a master teacher designation?
- Can the school district offer a bonus or incentive pay for attendance?
- Will teachers who complete the workshops be the first to have access to the technology in their schools or be eligible to check equipment out over the summer vacation?
- Teachers in one Canadian school district gave up a week of summer vacation and every Tuesday evening for an entire school year for the opportunity to attend technology training and have a Macintosh Powerbook to use as their own for a year. (Oh yes, food was included with the workshops.)
- Will the school district or school publicize the names of individuals completing the programs?
- Will first consideration for student teachers or interns be given to teachers who have completed a certain number of technology training sessions?
- Can you or a community sponsor or business partner provide certificates, t-shirts, keychains, or other prizes for completion of technology programs?
- Will completion of a certain amount of technology training qualify a teacher for additional paid professional leave days to attend off-site conferences and/or workshops?

How should you evaluate a staff development program?

There are several types of evaluation you need to consider after conducting a staff development program. Perhaps the most difficult evaluation is measuring the long term changes that you hope will occur as a result of any technology training. These changes are often linked to goals in the affective domain of behavior; objectives such as having two more teachers use the videodisc in their curriculum as a result of a workshop or having one more teacher bring his/ her class to the library media center for instruction in information/research skills in preparation for going online to locate information.

Other long term goals are also intangible or difficult to relate directly to a technology staff development program. These include things such as higher scores on student achievement tests, better attitudes of students, and the use of a wider variety of instructional materials in the classrooms of the school.

There are, however, more immediate evaluations that should be done as the program is ending. One is your self-evaluation. After the program, you will need to reflect on the session. Use a form similar to the following one and file it away with an outline of the inservice for future reference. Don't rely on your memory.

Then, too, there is the immediate evaluation that you give to the participants at the end of your program. While a few words of "that was the best staff development I've ever attended" from the participants are great for the ego, provide them with an opportunity to give you more formal comments. Then use these comments in planning future sessions. Don't be discouraged if some of the comments relate to items beyond your control. You probably can't do much about the temperature of a room, but you can learn to request an air-conditioned one or a fan to help with the heat generated by most equipment.

There's no one right format for a participant's evaluation. The following are several formats of evaluations that might help you construct one of your own. As you will see, all of them are simple and easy to complete with space provided for those individuals who want to comment on specific items.

Model Self-Evaluation

Program Title:_____Date:_____

Audience:_____

Location:_____ Length of program_____

Summary of content (attach outline or handouts)

Rate the program on the following:

Content in relation to this audience:
Too easy	Just right	Too difficult
Not useful	Useful	Very useful

Comment:

Format of program:
Too loose	Just right	Too structured

Comment:

Order of program:
Rearrange topics	Just right

Comment:

Pacing:
Too fast	Just right	Too slow
Too many breaks	Just right	Not enough breaks

Comment:

Room:
Too small	Just right	Too large
Too hot	Just right	Too cold
Inflexible		Flexible

Comment:

Equipment:
Not enough	Just right	Too much
Not working		All working

Comment:

Workshop Evaluation Form

Use the scale below to respond to each statement:

The inservice was well planned		1	2	3	4	5
The material presented was useful to me		1	2	3	4	5
The inservice allowed for hands on participation	1 2 3 4 5					
The presenters were knowledgeable about the subject matter		1	2	3	4	5

Comments: _____

_____

_____

Scale:
1 = poor
2 = below average
3 = average
4 = above average
5 = excellent

Based on an inservice evaluation prepared by Dorothy Goff, Virginia Beach, Virginia and Patricia Rideout, Surry County, Virginia.

Technology Inservice Evaluation

Please answer the following questions:

	NO				YES
1. This inservice presented ideas on incorporating technology that are relevant to my classroom	1	2	3	4	5
2. This inservice gave me ideas for how I can continue learning on my own.	1	2	3	4	5
3. Time was allowed for practicing with technology tools and collaboration with my colleagues.	1	2	3	4	5
4. The presenters seemed knowledgeable and well prepared.	1	2	3	4	5

5. The best thing about this inservice was:

6. Ways this inservice could be improved:

Adapted from a form developed by Kaye Alsbrooks, Newport News, Virginia and Patty Waller, Norfolk, Virginia.

How can you provide effective follow-up to your technology training?

Providing follow-up to technology training is very important. Too often SLMSs do a great job delivering the initial staff development program and then drop the ball. Here are some ways that you can help teachers keep learning after the formal staff development training has ended.

- Use existing PR tools. Use your library newsletter or Web page to provide short information on technology topics related to your programs. Publicize teachers who are using technology in their classrooms and include samples of their students' work in library displays.
- Develop a school e-mail news bulletin. Use e-mail to deliver technology updates to the staff.
- Make information on technology available to teachers. Keep technology magazines in the teacher lounge or workroom. Put up a technology bulletin board where teachers can find Internet links to help them in the classroom.
- Encourage a teacher's technology support group. Volunteer to host the first technology support group meeting one day after school. Provide refreshments and encourage teachers to share their problems and their successes.
- Help teachers identify peer-coaches or mentors to help them use technology.
- Schedule brief follow-up sessions to technology training workshops.
- Lobby to have technology training included in your school or school district's instructional plan.
- Enlist other teachers to provide one-on-one tutoring sessions.
- Provide teachers with a technology challenge to keep them involved after the workshop ends. See the example of a challenge issued after an Internet workshop.

The Teacher Technology Challenge

Challenge #1. Brighten up an old lesson plan. Select one of your favorite lessons. Then identify at least three Web sites to use with it.

Challenge #2. Check out the listing of e-mail projects for students by using the links on the school library's home page. Find at least one that your students could participate in next year.

Challenge #3. Use the offline Web browser to cut (actually download) at least five Web sites that your students could use.

When you've completed one of these challenges, come into the library media center for a special reward.

Technology is wonderful, exciting, fantastic, and scary. For adults, learning to use technology can be traumatic. Anne Russell has identified six stages that most of us go through when learning to use technology:

- Awareness
- Learning the process
- Understanding and application of the process
- Familiarity and confidence
- Adaptation to other contexts
- Creative application to new contexts.

A good staff development program takes these stages into consideration. The creative application may not develop as the result of the first workshop that a teacher attends. But, as Alice Yucht says:

> As the Information-Navigation specialists, we must position ourselves (and our profession) as the crossing guards, the engineers, supervisors, mass transit providers, even the highway patrol at times... I think we owe it to the kids—and our fellow teachers—to be at their sides, helping them learn how to safely and successfully navigate the highways and byways of this vibrant new Info-Nation.

Hang on for a fascinating trip!

Bibliography

AASL. *(1994). Information Literacy: A position paper on information problem solving*. Chicago: AASL. AASL statement on information literacy and an outline of problem-solving skills.

Anderson, M.A. (1996). *Teaching information literacy using electronic resources for grades 6-12*. Worthington, OH: Linworth. Loads of lesson plans for using electronic reference tools, online services, and the Internet.

Armstrong, D. (1996). Technology integration at the middle and high school levels: A model for staff development. *NASSP Bulletin,* 80 (582), 81-88. Computer Assisted Teacher Talk is a summer-institute program just for teachers.

Eisenberg, M. & Johnson, D. (1996). *Computer skills for Information Problem-Solving: Learning and teaching technology in Context*. Syracuse, NY: ERIC Clearinghouse on Information & Technology. The authors take the Big Six information skills and use examples from technology to discuss each point.

Farmer, L. (1997). *Training Student Library Staff.* Worthington, OH: Linworth. How librarians can effectively train student staff without neglecting their own responsibilities.

Farmer, L. (1995). *Workshops for teachers: Becoming partners for information literacy*. Worthington, OH: Linworth. Includes sample workshops which, while not all on technology topics, provide complete information for holding the workshop.

Harrington-Lueker, D. (1996). Coming to grips with staff development. *Electronic Learning,* 16 (1), 32-43. Contains lots of ideas for staff development programs with technology.

Hoffman, B. (1996). Managing the information revolution: Planning the integration of school technology. *NASSP Bulletin*, 80 (582), 89-98. Identifies the things that principals can do to remove the barriers to technology integration in the classroom.

Holzberg, C. (1997). Teach your teachers well: Successful strategies for staff development. *Technology & Learning*, 17 (6), 34-40. Provides an overview of several staff development programs.

Inquiring minds: Creating a nation of teachers as learners. An 'Education Week' special report. (1996). Washington, D.C.: Education Week. This special report first appeared as a supplement to *Education Week* on April 17, 1996, and contains seven essays on professional development.

Kranz, T. (1996). Squeezing out training time. *Electronic Learning,* 16 (1), 74. By using substitutes, a middle school freed teachers to participate in follow-up training for staff development.

Kuhlthau, C.C. (1993). Implementing a process approach to information skills. *School Library Media Quarterly,* 22 (1), 11-18. This model addresses the feelings that a student has as he or she works through the research process.

Lovely, G. (1997). After the workshop is over. *Electronic Learning,* 16 (5), 53-54. Lovely discusses "six effective ways to follow up any staff development session."

Lovely, G. (1996). Make every minute count. *Electronic Learning,* 16 (3), 51. Here are some "innovative ways school can find more time for technology staff training."

Lovely, G. (1996). One size does not fit all. *Electronic Learning,* 16 (2), 51. A consultant looks at a few training models.

Lovely, G. (1996). Secrets of motivation. *Electronic Learning*, 16 (1), 72. Tips for providing rewards for teachers attending technology training.

McElmeel, S. (1997). *Research strategies for moving beyond reporting*. Worthington, OH: Linworth. Using a six-step process, the author uses primary sources including WWW sites to teach the research process.

McKenzie, J. (1993). *Administrators at risk*. Bloomington, IN: National Educational Service. Contains an overview of a process to "develop a delivery system capable of establishing technological literacy and skill across the district's instructional and administrative staff."

Moody, R. (1997). On the process of inquiry: A synergy of teacher, school library media specialist, and student. *School Library Media Activities Monthly*, 14 (1), 13-34+. After looking at the goals of the SLMS and the teacher as well as the goals held in common, Moody explores how the two can work together to help students.

Pappas, M. L. (1995). Information skills for electronic resources. *School Library Media Activities Monthly*, 12 (8), 39-40. Discusses a search model that discourages plagiarism and that guides a student through the vast amount of information available on the Internet.

Pope, S. (1996). Singing the praises of on-site training. Technology Connection, 3 (3), 16-17. As a district "media specialist/technology/trainer/unofficial trouble-shooter/tech coordinator," Pope shares her experiences with on-site training.

Richardson, J. (1997). Smart use of time and money enhances staff development. *Journal of Staff Development,* 18 (1), 46-50. Richardson looks at some innovative ways of making time for staff development.

Russell, A. (1996). *Six stages for learning to use technology.* Paper presented at the meeting of the 1996 National Convention of the Association for Educational Communications and Technology, Indianapolis, Indiana, 1996. Identifies the six stages which adult learners go through as they learn to use technology.

Sharp, P. (1993). *Sharing your good ideas: A workshop facilitator's handbook.* New York: Heineman. Lots of practical advice for improving your staff development presentations.

Shelton, M. & Jones, M. (1996). Staff development that works! A tale of Four T's. *NASSP Bulletin,* 80 (582), 99-105. The authors identify four factors of a successful technology integration staff development program: time, training, technology availability, and teacher-type tasks.

Skeele, L. (1994). Hands-on technology inservice that works. TECHNOLOGY CONNECTION, 1 (4), 1-2. With new technology throughout the school, the faculty embarked on an ambitious program of training with excellent results.

Skeele, L. (1996). *Teaching information literacy using electronic resources for grades K-6.* Worthington, OH: Linworth. From the electronic card catalog to desktop publishing and the Internet, this book has lesson plans that librarians and teachers can really use.

Stripling, B.K. & Pitts, J.M. (1988). *Brainstorms and blueprints; teaching library research as a thinking process.* Englewood, CO: Libraries Unlimited. This book teaches a research method that can be used by all students.

Turner, P. (1996). What help do teachers want, and what will they do to get it? *School Library Media Quarterly,* 24 (4), 208-212. Turner asked a group of teachers to identify the ways they could become better teachers and how their SLMSs could help them do this.

Yucht, A. (1996). Ignition anxiety. LIBRARY TALK, 9 (3), 15+. Alice Yucht compares her keeping up with technology to Aunt Lily's learning how to drive again after twenty years. There's lots of truth behind the humor.

Glossary

The following definitions are not meant to replace a good computer/technology dictionary. They are meant to provide simple definitions and to provide a cross reference to the chapter(s) in this book where a term is discussed.

Acceptable use policy: A written agreement which is developed by a school district, outlines rights and responsibilities for Internet use, states penalties for violations, and is signed by teachers, students, and parent(s)/guardian(s). (Chapter 8)

Access time: The amount of time that it takes a computer drive to locate information on a disk. Can also be applied to a CD-ROM drive. (Chapters 4 and 5)

Acoustic coupler: see **Modem**

Active matrix LCD panel: An LCD panel that has a higher quality display, with better color, than a passive matrix panel. Required for projecting full-motion video. (Chapter 10)

ADC: Analog digital convertor; used in telephone lines. (Chapter 7)

Agile satellite receiver: A satellite receiver that can be moved or adjusted to pick up a variety of television signals. (Chapter 9)

Analog: Signals used in the video world by television receivers and VCRs. (Chapter 10)

Appliance: A single-purpose computer, for example, one that can be used only for Internet access. (Chapter 2)

Applications program: Computer program that allows users to perform tasks such as word processing, graphics design, database development, or specialized tasks such as library circulation. (Chapter 2)

Archie: An Internet retrieval program used to locate information on anonymous ftp sites. (Chapter 8)

Archive copy: A copy of a computer program that is made and kept in a secure place while the original program is being used. (Chapter 2)

ARCnet: A network transfer architecture that determines how information is shared on a LAN. (Chapter 6)

Artificial intelligence: A computer program that "thinks" or works like the human brain. (Chapter 11)

Assistive technology: Hardware and software designed for special-needs users. (Chapter 2)

ASVD: Analog simultaneous voice and data; a protocol for personal conferencing. (Chapter 7)

Asynchronous transfer mode (ATM): A protocol used on many fiber optics networks. (Chapter 6)

AUP: See **Acceptable use plan**

Authoring software: See **Authoring system**.

Authoring system: A computer program designed to help someone, who is not a programmer or who does not know a programming language, create a computer program or a computer presentation. (Chapter 11)

Autochanger videodisc player: A videodisc player that can play both sides of up to 72 discs. (Chapter 5)

Automatic log-on: A feature of some communications software programs that will automatically provide passwords to a remote computer each time they are connected. (Chapter 7)

Backup: An exact duplicate or copy of software (program or data). (Chapter 2)

Baseband co-ax: See **Coaxial cable**

Baseplate: A security device in which one part of the plate is attached to the hardware device and the other to the equipment's normal home or storage place such as a large cart or a piece of furniture. (Chapter 1)

Baud: A transmission rate of a modem that includes the bits per second and additional information. (Chapter 7)

BBS: see **Bulletin board system**

Bits per second: Rate of transmission, usually applied to the speed at which a modem sends and receives information. Abbreviated bps. (Chapter 7)

Boolean logic: A search strategy used to locate information in an electronic database. (Chapter 7)

Bookmark: A marker used with Internet browser software to allow a user to easily return to a site. (Chapter 8)

bps: see **Bits per second**

Bridge: A network device used to connect similar systems. (Chapter 6)

Broadcast television: Television stations that are received free on any television set with, perhaps, the addition of an antenna. (Chapter 9)

Browser: Software used to navigate the World Wide Web. (Chapter 8)

Buffer: A temporary storage space for electronic information. Printer buffers take information from the computer, store it, and gradually send it to be printed. (Chapter 2)

Bulletin board system: An electronic messaging system on a computer that can be reached via a modem. See also **Open BBS** and **Closed BBS**. (Chapter 7)

Bus: A network topology in which one cable connects everything. (Chapter 6)

Button: A point in a hypermedia program that, when clicked on with the mouse, leads to another part of the program or provides additional information. (Chapter 11)

Byte: A unit of measurement used with computers. (Chapter 2)

Cable television: Television signals that are received locally with a main antenna and/or satellite dish and then sent through wires to cable subscribers who pay a monthly cable fee to view the programming. (Chapter 9)

CAD: Computer assisted design. (Chapter 2)

Caddy: The hinged plastic carrier into which a CD-ROM disc is placed. (Chapter 4)

Carrier Sense Multiple Access: See **Ethernet**

CAV: A videodisc format that stores information in concentric rings with about 30 minutes of motion video and audio tracks on each side of the videodisc. CAV format allows a user to access each individual image by its frame number. (Chapter 5)

CAVI: A computer controls a videodisc and combines audio, still video, and motion. (Chapter 5)

CCITT: see **Consultative committee international telegraph and telephone**

CCTV: see **Closed circuit television**

CD-I: Compact disc interactive. A technology that is being developed to allow the CD-I hardware to work directly with a television set without an additional microcomputer. (Chapter 4)

CD-R: A recordable compact disc. (Chapter 4)

CD-ROM: Compact Disk-Read Only Memory. This optical media uses light to store and retrieve information. In addition to containing animation, video, and audio information, a single CD-ROM disc can store between 250,000 and 2.5 million pages of information that can be accessed quickly by a computer. (Chapter 4)

CD-ROM database: A collection of information that is stored on a CD-ROM disc. (Chapter 4)

CD-ROM Server: A central computer on a network with multiple CD-ROM drives that can be accessed through the network. (Chapter 6)

CD-ROM XA: An emerging technology that allows multimedia with compressed audio. (Chapter 4)

CD-WORM: Compact disc, write once, read many. (Chapter 4)

Central processing unit (CPU): The "brain" of a computer; it is also called a microprocessor, microchip, or chip. (Chapter 2)

CGA monitor: A computer monitor that can display up to 16 colors. (Chapter 2)

Chat: A "live" informal discussion on a computer telecommunications network. (Chapter 7)

Checkdisc: A type of videodisc that can be produced from a 3/4" videotape. Less expensive (less than $500) to produce than a regular videodisc, it does not have the quality of a regular videodisc. (Chapter 5)

Chip: An abbreviation for microchip. See also **Central processing unit**. (Chapter 2)

Client server LAN: see **Server LAN**

Clock speed: see **Operating speed**

Clone: A computer that "acts like" or is compatible with a major brand. (Chapter 1)

Closed BBS: An electronic bulletin board system that can only be accessed with passwords. (Chapter 7)

Closed circuit television: Television in which signals are sent from a distribution point to receivers that are connected to it by wires. Often found in a single school building, school campus, or school district. (Chapter 9)

CLV: A videodisc format that stores information in a continuous spiral like the grooves on a record. Only expensive videodisc players can display still images from CLV videodiscs or access a single image by its frame number. (Chapter 5)

Co-ax: see **Coaxial cable**

Coaxial cable: Network wiring that consists of a single conductor with shielding and insulation. Thick co-ax is 1/2" to 5/8" in diameter, while thin or baseband co-ax is about the diameter of a pencil. (Chapter 6)

Communication ports: Connectors on a computer that allow external devices such as the monitor, external drive, mouse, and modem to be attached to it. (Chapter 2)

Communications parameters: see **Communications protocols**

Communications protocols: The protocols that are used in telecommunications with a modem. These include the transmission rate, parity, stop bits, and number of bits in a word. (Chapter 7)

Compact Disk, Read Only Memory: See **CD-ROM**

Compatible: A computer that can run the same software programs as another computer because it "acts like" that computer. (Chapter 1) See also **Clone**.

CompuServe: A commercial telecommunications network. (Chapter 7)

Computer assisted videodisc instruction: see **CAVI**

Concept map: An overview of a hypermedia presentation system. (Chapter 11)

Conference: A structured exchange of information on a telecommunications network. (Chapter 7)

Constant angular velocity: See **CAV**

Constant linear velocity: See **CLV**

Consultative committee international telegraph and telephone: Standards for the transmission of audio and video over fiber optic cables. (Chapter 9)

Consumables: Items such as ribbons, paper, disks, and telephone charges that are used or consumed. (Chapter 1)

Continuous power source: See **Uninterruptible power supply**

Continuous read drive: A CD-ROM drive with a buffer. (Chapter 4)

Controller card: A card that, when inserted into a computer, allows it to work with another hardware device. (Chapter 2)

Cookies: An information file placed on your computer when you visit some Web sites. (Chapter 8)

Crawl: Text or image moves from right to left on a monitor. (Chapter 10)

Cross platform compatibility: Ability of software on one platform to read files created on another platform. (Chapter 2)

CTD: Cumulative trauma disorder (Chapter 1)

CTI: Computer telephone integration. (Chapter 7)

Daisy-chained network: An unconnected ring network topology. (Chapter 6)

Daisy chain: Connecting several peripheral devices to a computer by linking one peripheral to the computer and then another peripheral to the first, etc. (Chapter 4)

Data: Information. (Introduction)

Data bus: An electronic carrier which takes information from the microprocessor to the other parts of the computer. (Chapter 2)

Database: A collection of data or information that is organized to allow retrieval of the information. A shelf list is a print database with one card (one record) for each unique item in the library. (Chapter 3)

DD disk: A double-density floppy disk. Density refers to the spacing of information on a disk. (Chapter 2)

Dedicated: Term used to describe a piece of hardware (computer, telephone line, etc.) that is used for only one purpose. For example, some people have a dedicated phone line to use only with their modem. (Chapters 1 and 7)

Desktop video: The use of a computer and special video software and accessories such as the *VideoToaster* to generate video, to add graphics, titles and special effects to video tapes, and to function as a video editing system. (Chapter 10)

Desktop videoconferencing systems: Use of digital telephone lines to share computer data and video information. (Chapter 9)

Digital: Electronic signals used in the computer world that consist of on and off pulses. (Chapters 7 and 8)

Digital video effects: Effects produced by desktop video software programs such as stretching, rotating, flipping, and flattening video images. (Chapter 10)

Digital video interactive: A video compression technology that allows up to 72 minutes of full motion video to be compressed, stored on a single CD-ROM disc, and then played back at full screen size. (Chapter 10)

DIMM: Dual in-line memory module, a form of DRAM. (Chapter 2)

Direct PC: Internet service via a satellite dish. (Chapter 8)

Disk operating system: See **DOS**

Diskette: See **Floppy disk**

Distance education: see **Distance learning**

Distance learning: Delivery of instruction or information to students, faculty, staff and/or administrators through the use of radio, broadcast television, cable television, satellites, telephone lines, fax machines, or a combination of these technologies. (Chapter 9)

Documentation: Instructions that accompany (in print or on disk) hardware and software. (Chapter 2)

DOS: An operating system for PCs. (Chapter 2)

Dot matrix printer: A high speed, low cost impact printer. (Chapter 2)

Download: Using a computer and modem to receive information from another computer. (Chapter 7)

DRAM: Dynamic random access memory, a type of main computer RAM. (Chapter 2)

DSVD: Digital simultaneous voice and data; a protocol for personal conferencing on telephone lines. (Chapter 7)

Dumb terminal: A workstation on a network that cannot be used as a standalone computer. (Chapter 6)

Duplex: The directions in which data travels over telephone lines, part of communications protocols. (Chapter 7)

DVD: Digital video disc or digital versatile disc. (Chapter 2)

DVE: see **Digital video effects**

DVI: see **Digital video interactive**

E-mail: Using a computer to send a message to another person over the telephone lines via a telecommunications network. (Chapter 7)

Edit decision list: A list of the starting and stopping points to access precise segments of a video in the order that they are to be used. (Chapter 10)

EDL: see **Edit decision list**

EISA: Extended industry standard architecture. (Chapter 6)

Electronic bulletin board: see **Bulletin board system**

Electronic mail: see **E-mail**

Emerging technologies: Newer technologies including such things as virtual reality, digital video interactive (DVI), video information systems (VIS), artificial intelligence, and expert systems. (Chapter 4, 5, 8, 10)

Emoticons: Symbols that allow a writer to express emotions on a computer screen. Often used in E-mail. (Chapter 7)

Encrypt: To hide and/or not display information on a computer screen. Passwords are often encrypted. (Chapter 6)

ERIC: Educational Resources Information Center. (Chapter 7)

Ethernet: A network transfer architecture. (Chapter 6)

Expansion card: An electronic device that is installed internally in a computer to expand its capabilities. For example, an internal modem. (Chapter 2)

Expansion slot: The space inside a computer that allows the installation of an expansion card. (Chapter 2)

Expert system: A program that directs a computer to use a pattern of logical "thought" similar to that used by an expert in the field to solve a problem. (Chapter 11)

External modem: see **Modem**

FAQ: see **Frequently asked questions**

Fax: see **Telefacsimile**

Fax modem: A computer peripheral that combines a fax machine and a computer modem to send and receive faxes with a computer. (Chapter 7)

FDDI: Fiber distributed interface, an alternative to Fast Ethernet. (Chapter 6)

Fiber optic cable: A network/telephone cable that uses glass fibers to transfer data rapidly over long distances. (Chapter 6)

File: A collection of related data (records) that is stored together. (Chapter 2)

File server: The central computer in a server network. (Chapter 6)

File server LAN: see **Server LAN**

File transfer protocols: Standards for transferring data files from one computer to another with a modem. (Chapter 7)

Filter: A device required when digital video from one system is to be used on a system with another digital video standard. (Chapter 10)

Filtering software: See **Internet filtering software**

FireWire: A high speed bus designed for PC video. (Chapter 10)

Fixed satellite receiver: A satellite receiver that is permanently set to receive the signal of only one network or source. (Chapter 9)

Flamer: An obnoxious or insulting person on a telecommunications network. (Chapter 7)

Floppy disk: A removable device for storing computer information. There are two basic types: a 5.25 inch disk with a flexible plastic cover and a 3.5 inch disk with a hard plastic cover. (Chapter 2)

Format: The process of preparing a floppy disk or hard disk to receive and store information. (Chapter 2)

FPS: Frames per second. In video, the number of frames shown per second. (Chapter 10)

Frame grabber: A video digitizing card which is designed to take one frame or very short segment of an analog video and convert it to a digital computer graphic. (Chapter 10)

Frequently asked question: Many Internet sites have FAQ lists of questions that are frequently asked by users of that site. (Chapter 8)

FTP: see **File transfer protocol**

Full motion video: Video that fills the entire computer screen and runs at 30 frames per second. (Chapter 10)

Gateway: A network device used to translate between dissimilar systems. (Chapter 6)

GIGO: Garbage in; garbage out. If a user puts bad (incorrect/incomplete) information into the computer, bad information comes out. (Chapter 3)

Gopher: A protocol for accessing information on the Internet through a system of menus and submenus.

Graphics: A visual/picture generated by a computer. May be shown on a monitor or printed out. (Chapter 11)

Graphics adapter board: see **video adapter card**

Ground fault circuit interrupter (GFCI): A device in an electrical circuit that will cut the current if any electricity leakage is detected and will prevent shock if the equipment comes in contact with water. (Chapter 1)

Group-video-teleconferencing: The use of fiber optic telephone lines for two-way video and audio distance learning. (Chapter 9)

Groupware: Programs designed for use by several people working together on a project on a network. (Chapter 6)

Guest: A first time user or someone without passwords on a closed bulletin board system or network. (Chapter 7)

GUI: Graphic user interface. This term is often used to describe the operating system on a Macintosh computer or the PC world's Windows program. (Chapter 2)

Half-height unit: An internal CD-ROM drive that takes up about the same space as a 5.25" floppy disk drive. (Chapter 4)

Hard disk: A large capacity non-removable device for storing computer information. (Chapter 2)

Hardware: Equipment consisting of its physical components and electronic parts. (Introduction)

Hayes-compatible: A universal standard for modems. (Chapter 7)

HD disk: A high density floppy disk. Density refers to the spacing of information on the disk. (Chapter 2)

HDTV: High definition television. (Chapter 9)

HHPC: Hand held personal computer. (Chapter 2)

High Sierra: A standard for CD-ROM set by the International Standards organization. (Chapter 4)

Home page: The first computer screen that appears at any Internet address. (Chapter 8)

Hotlist: See **bookmark**

HTML: See **Hypertext Mark-Up Language**

Hub: A junction on a network where cables meet. (Chapter 6)

HyperCard: A hypermedia program for the Macintosh computer. (Chapter 11)

Hypermedia: An interactive, nonlinear approach to information in which the user selects his or her own path through the data. (Chapter 11)

Hypertext Mark-Up Language: Programming language used to create a hyperlinked Web site.

Icon: picture. (Chapters 2 and 10)

IDE: Integrated drive electronics. An Interface for computers and peripherals. (Chapter 4)

IEEE: Institute of Electrical and Electronic Engineers. (Chapter 6)

IEEE1394 bus: See **FireWire**

ILS: see **Integrated learning system**

Inkjet printer: A non-impact printer that squirts ink on paper to print the characters. (Chapter 2)

Instructional technology: The hardware and software used in an educational setting. Often referred to simply as technology. (Introduction)

Instructional television fixed service: Educational television programming that is broadcast in the high frequency microwave spectrum and is not received by regular television sets. (Chapter 9)

Integrated learning system: The name given to a package that combines the hardware, NOS, applications programs, and management software for a network. (Chapter 6)

Interactive: see **Interactive multimedia**

Interactive cable television: New technology to combine computers and television into a single interactive format. (Chapter 9)

Interactive multimedia: A multimedia product in which the user, by his or her actions, can vary the way in which the information is displayed. The user can create his or her own approach to the information. (Chapter 11)

Interactive multimedia videodisc system: see **Videodisc Level III**

Interactive video: see **Videodisc**

Interactive video and data services: see **Interactive cable television**.

Interactive videodisc: see **Videodisc Level III**

Interface: An electronic device that allows two different pieces of hardware (i.e., computer and printer) to communicate. (Chapter 2)

Internal modem: see **Modem**

Internet: Our global computer network of interconnected networks and computers. (Chapter 8)

Internet Account: An account with a commercial online service or Internet Service Provider that gives you access to the Internet. (Chapter 8)

Internet appliance: Hardware other than a personal computer which is designed to allow access to the Internet. (Chapter 8)

Internet filter software: Used to block access to specific Internet sites. (Chapter 8)

Internet service provider (ISP): Any service through which you gain access to the Internet. Usually a commercial vendor. (Chapter 8)

Internetworking: A process that allows different LANs to interact. (Chapter 6)

Intranet: An organization's internal network that uses Internet protocols. (Chapter 5)

ISDN: Integrated services digital network for high speed communications. (Chapter 7)

ISO 9660: See **High Sierra**.

ISP: See **Internet service provider**.

ITFS: see **Instruction television fixed service**

Jaz: A high-capacity (1 GB) removable storage disk/drive made by Iomega. (Chapter 2)

JPEG: A digital video compression standard used in the popular Macintosh program called *QuickTime*. (Chapter 10)

Jukebox: A configuration in which several pieces of software are housed in a single unit. Used for CD-ROM and videodiscs. (Chapters 4 and 5)

Kilobyte: A measure of computer storage/processing capacity. Roughly corresponds to 1000 bytes. (Chapter 2)

LAN: Local area network. A LAN connects computers, printers, CD-ROM drives and other electronic equipment within a room, building, or several buildings and allows sharing of information. (Chapter 6)

LAN card: see **Network interface card**

Laser printer: A professional quality non-impact printer. (Chapter 2)

Laser videodisc: see **Videodisc**

LCD panel: Used with an overhead projector to provide the light source; a LCD panel projects whatever is shown on a computer's monitor on a regular projection screen for viewing by a group. See also **Active matrix LCD panel.** (Chapter 10)

Level I videodisc: see **Videodisc level I**

Level II videodisc: see **Videodisc level II**

Level III videodisc: see **Videodisc level III**

License: A legal agreement concerning the use of certain software programs. There are site licenses and network licenses. (Chapters 2 and 6)

Liquid crystal display panel: see **LCD panel**

Listserv: A process that allows a user to "subscribe" to all of the communications sent on a network by members of a special interest group. (Chapter 7)

LocalTalk: A network transfer architecture developed for Apple and Macintosh computers. (Chapter 6)

LQ: Letter quality printer. (Chapter 2)

Lurker: A person who reads but does not send messages on a telecommunications network. (Chapter 7)

Mac: An abbreviation used to refer to the Macintosh series of microcomputers made by the Apple Corporation. (Introduction)

MARC: Machine Readable Cataloging. A format for cataloging information entered into a computer database. (Chapter 3)

Media retrieval system: A combination of hardware and software that allows access to the audio/visual resources of the library from classroom by remote control. (Chapter 3)

Megabyte: A unit of measurement to describe an amount of information. Often used to describe the amount of storage space on a computer hard drive. Abbreviated MB and sometimes referred to as simply "meg." Roughly equivalent to one million bytes. (Chapter 2)

Megahertz: Abbreviated MHZ. A measure of the operating speed or clock speed of a computer's central processing unit. (Chapter 2)

Memory: The part of the microcomputer where the microchip processes information. It consists of RAM and ROM. (Chapter 2)

Menu driven: A program design that allows users to select choices from an on-screen menu rather than enter commands. (Chapter 2)

Microchip: see **Central processing unit**

MicroLIF: Microcomputer Library Interchange Format. A version of MARC developed for microcomputers. (Chapter 3)

Microprocessor: see **Central processing unit**

Microsoft Internet Explorer: A Web browser. (Chapter 8)

MMX: See **Multimedia extensions**

Modem: A modulator/demodulator that translates the computer's digital information into analog information that can be sent over telephone lines. Modems can come as cards plugged into the expansion slot inside a computer (internal) or as an external device. (Chapter 7)

Monitor: The screen or display device used with a computer. (Chapter 2)

Monitoring software: Used to provide a record of the Internet sites accessed through a given computer. (Chapter 8)

Monochrome monitor: A monitor that displays images in black and another color such as white, orange, or green. (Chapter 2)

Morphing: A digital video effect that allows one shape or object to change into another in a series of realistic steps. (Chapter 10)

Motherboard: The electronic component in the computer that holds the microprocessor, RAM chips, ROM chips and contains the electronic pathways between these components. (Chapter 2)

Motion video digitizer board: see **Video digitizing card**

Mouse: A pointing device used with microcomputers. (Chapter 2)

MPC Standards: Standards for multimedia hardware and software that were established by the Multimedia PC Marketing Council. (Chapter 4)

MPEG: A standard for digital video compression and decompression. (Chapter 10)

MRS: See **Media retrieval system**.

Multidisc videodisc player: A videodisc player with the ability to play 12" and 8" videodiscs as well as audio CDS. (Chapter 5)

Multimedia: The use of a computer to integrate and control graphics, video, audio, and text information. (Introduction and Chapter 4)

Multimedia extensions: Built into Intel's P55c chip to increase speeds for video, graphics, and games. (Chapter 2)

Multiple machine loading: A process by which one copy of a computer program is loaded into several computers by loading each machine separately. (Chapter 2)

Multitasking: The ability of some computers to run several programs at the same time. (Chapter 2)

NC: Network computer. Although it looks like a regular PC, all of its power comes from a central server. (Chapter 8)

Netiquette: Etiquette and rules of conduct for using the Internet.

Netscape Navigator: A Web browser, (Chapter 8)

Network: An arrangement in which two or more computers are connected electronically so that they can exchange data. (Chapter 6)

Network adaptor: see **Network transfer architecture**

Network adaptor card: see **Network interface card**

Network administrator: The individual who has the responsibility of the day-to-day operation of a network. (Chapter 6)

Network architecture: see **Network transfer architecture**

Network interface: see **Network transfer architecture**

Network interface card: Governs how data is sent through a LAN. (Chapter 6)

Network interface unit: see **Network interface card**

Network license: A copyright agreement that allows software to run legally on a specific network. (Chapter 6)

Network management utilities: Programs such as anti-virus software, menu programs, and metering utilities designed to be used on a network. (Chapter 6)

Network operating system: The operating system that manages an entire network. (Chapter 6)

Network transfer architecture: An interface that governs the flow of data over a network. (Chapter 6)

Network transport: see **Network transfer architecture**

Networking: Getting access to and sharing information and resources. (Chapter 6)

Newsgroup: An open bulletin board on the Internet. (Chapter 8)

NIC: see **Network interface card**

NLQ: Near letter quality printer. (Chapter 2)

Node: A connection of a hardware device to a LAN. (Chapter 6)

Nonlinear editing: A process in which a videotape is digitized and stored as a video file on a hard drive and edited by the computer through the use of editing software programs. (Chapter 10)

NOS: see **Network operating system**

NREN: National Research and Education Network proposed by the U.S. government as a high-speed link between businesses, government agencies, educational institutions, research facilities, and libraries. (Chapter 7)

NSFNET: National Science Foundation Network. (Chapter 8)

OCR: See **Optical character recognition**

Offline browser: Software that allows you to download Web sites onto the hard drive of your computer for viewing offline. (Chapter 8)

Offline edit: Videotape and computer generated EDL are taken to a studio where the final tape is produced. (Chapter 10)

OLE: Object linking and embedding protocol developed by Microsoft. (Chapter 2)

Online edit: Computer is used to record the final edited video sequence on videotape. (Chapter 10)

Online database service: An online reference service, accessed with a computer and a modem, which can be searched electronically for information. (Chapter 7)

OPAC: Online public access catalog; a card catalog on a computer. (Chapter 3)

Open BBS: A bulletin board system that has limited controls. Anything except illegal or obscene activities are permitted, and anyone can access it. (Chapter 7)

Operating speed: The speed at which the central processing unit is able to process information. Also called clock speed. (Chapter 2)

Operating system: The program that manages the operations of the computer. Common operating systems include DOS and System 7. (Chapter 2)

Optical character recognition: Software used with a scanner to translate the visual patterns on paper into characters that a computer can recognize and use. (Chapter 7)

Optical videodisc: see **Videodisc**

Packet: A piece of information on a network. It contains information about the source of the data and its destination as well as the data itself. (Chapter 6)

Parallel port: A connector that allows peripheral devices to be attached to a computer (i.e., printers usually attach to parallel ports). (Chapter 2)

Parity: Error checking; part of communications protocols. (Chapter 7)

Passive matrix LCD panel: Lower price and lower quality than an active matrix LCD panel. (Chapter 10)

PC: An abbreviation used to refer to IBM personal computers and to microcomputers that act like those made by IBM. (Introduction)

PC Card: Credit card sized peripherals developed by the Personal Computer Memory Card International Association (PCMCIA). (Chapter 2)

PCI bus: Peripheral component Internet bus, a 32 bit bus. (Chapters 2, 6)

Peer-to-peer LAN: Every computer on the network is equal. These LANs are less expensive, require less maintenance, and are simpler to change than server LANs. (Chapter 6)

Phosphor burn-in: A ghost-like image that becomes permanently etched into a computer monitor when an image is left unchanged on the screen for a long time. (Chapter 2)

Photo CD: A Kodak product that takes film shot with a regular 35mm camera and "develops" it on a Photo CD disc that can be used in many CD-ROM players. (Chapter 4)

Pixels: The sharpness of the image on a computer monitor is measured in dots called pixels. The more pixels or dots per inch, the higher the resolution. (Chapter 2)

Platforms: A term used to refer to a group or family of computers. Two of the major platforms are Macintosh and IBM PC-compatible computers. (Introduction and Chapter 2)

Port: The electronic connection that allows peripheral devices to be attached to a computer. (Chapter 2)

POTS: Plain old telephone service. (Chapter 7)

Presentation system: A computer authoring system that allows an individual to create "a slide show" on a computer. (Chapter 11)

Printer: The hardware device that is used to produce a hard copy (printed copy) of information from a computer. (Chapter 2)

Prodigy: A commercial telecommunications network. (Chapter 7)

Program: The set of instructions that controls the actions of a computer. (Chapter 2)

Proprietary interface: An interface that is hardware dependent and is designed to be used only with a certain brand of hardware. (Chapter 4)

Public domain software: Programs that are available free of any charge. (Chapter 2)

Public television: A form of broadcast television that is public and noncommercial. (Chapter 9)

Pullwires: Wires placed in conduit during the building or renovation of a facility. Later, if additional wiring is required, the pullwires can be used to pull the appropriate cables through the conduit. (Chapter 1)

QuickTime: Apple's standard for storing motion video, decompressing it, and playing it back. A name generically given to a motion video on a Macintosh computer. (Chapter 10)

RADSL: Rate adaptive digital subscriber line; a new category of telephone line. (Chapter 8)

RAM: Volatile or temporary "random access" computer memory. When the computer is turned off or disconnected from a power source, the information in RAM is lost. (Chapter 2)

Random access memory: See **RAM**

Read only memory: See **ROM**

Real-time video display card: A card that allows a video to be displayed on a computer monitor without digitizing an analog signal. (Chapter 10)

Remote log-in: The process of using a telecommunications network to connect to a computer located some distance away and actively look in that computer for information. (Chapter 7)

Removable storage: Computer storage that is capable of storing a large amount of information (100+ MB). Unlike a hard drive, it can be moved from place to place without moving the entire computer. (Chapter 10)

Repurposing: A term used to describe the process of creating the user's own script for using a videodisc. To repurpose, the computer operator can use the remote control, create barcodes, or author a computer program. (Chapter 5)

Resolution: The sharpness of a computer image on a screen as measured in dots called pixels. (Chapter 2)

RGB projector: see **Video projector**

Ring: A network topology in which each workstation is connected to the ones on either side of it. (Chapter 6)

ROM: The non-volatile or permanent "read only" computer memory. (Chapter 2)

RS-232 interface: A connection that allows hardware such as a videodisc player to be used with a computer. (Chapter 5)

RSI: Repetitive stress injury. (Chapter 1)

Satellite television: Television in which the signals are sent from earth to a retransmitter on a satellite in space and then back to earth where it is picked up by a satellite receiver or satellite dish. See also **Agile satellite receiver** or **Fixed satellite receiver**. (Chapter 9)

Scan converter: see **Video output card**

Scanner: An electronic device that is used to transfer an image from a printed page into a computer. Generally, information scanned into a computer is treated as a graphic rather than text. (Chapter 7)

Scanning frequency: A measure of how fast an image forms on a computer monitor. (Chapter 2)

Scroll: Text or image moves from the bottom to the top of the monitor. (Chapter 10)

SCSI: Small Computer System Interface. A non-proprietary common communication standard for computers and peripherals. (Chapter 4)

SDSL: Symmetrical digital subscriber lines; a new category of telephone line. (Chapter 8)

Search engine: An online searchable database for locating information on the World Wide Web. (Chapter 8)

Serial port: A connector that allows peripheral devices to be attached to a computer (i.e., a modem and a mouse connect via serial ports). (Chapter 2)

Server: The computer on a server network that can be accessed by anyone on the network. (Chapter 6)

Server LAN: Uses a main computer that is dedicated to monitoring and controlling the network. (Chapter 6)

Shareware: A computer program that allows users to "try before you buy." Those who like the program send a registration fee to the developer. (Chapters 2 and 7)
Shielded twisted pair: see **Twisted pair cable**

Shrink wrap license: A copyright statement that goes into effect when the purchaser opens the plastic shrink wrap to use a computer program. (Chapter 2)

SIG: A special interest group. (Chapter 7)

SIMD: Single instruction multiple data technology for MMS processors. (Chapter 2)

SIMM: Single in-line memory module: a form of DRAM. (Chapter 2)

Simultaneous machine loading: see **Multiple machine loading**

Site-license: A copyright agreement that allows a set number of copies to be used in one building or throughout a school district. (Chapter 1)

SLIP/PPP: An interface which allows computers to have graphical access to the Internet.

SLMS: School library media specialist or school librarian. All three are used interchangeably in this book. (Introduction)

Slots: Places on the motherboard to add more memory or internal devices to the computer. See also **Expansion slots**. (Chapter 2)

Sneaker network: Sharing information by physically walking from place to place. (Chapter 6)

Software: Programs or the information and instructions used by the equipment to perform a function. This includes traditional audiovisual software as well as computer programs, videodiscs, CD-ROM discs, and so forth. (Introduction)

Spamming: Sending inappropriate messages to individuals in newsgroups or listservs. (Chapter 8)

Star: A network topology in which a separate cable is used to connect each of several workstations to a central computer. (Chapter 6)

Step: A command that allows a videodisc player to advance or back up one frame at a time. (Chapter 5)

Still digital camera: A camera that takes pictures in a format that can be transferred directly into a computer or displayed on a television set. One brand is Canon's ZapShot. (Chapter 10)

Stop bit: Used to signal the end of a character, part of communications protocols. (Chapter 7)

Surge suppressor: An electrical device that compensates for power surges or spikes. (Chapter 1)

SVGA monitor: A computer monitor that can display up to 256 colors at a high resolution. (Chapter 2)

SysOP: The administrator of an electronic bulletin board system or a network. (Chapter 7)

System 7: An operating system for Macintosh computers. (Chapter 2)

TAPI: Telephony application, programming interface. (Chapter 7)

TCP/IP: Transport control protocol/Internetworking protocol. A communications standard used on intranets and the Internet. (Chapters 6, 8)

Telecommunications: A term applied to a method of communicating over a distance via a telephone line. (Chapter 7)

Telefacsimile: A scanner that translates the information on the printed page into a form that can be sent through the telephone lines to a fax machine on the other end. (Chapter 7)

Terminal emulation: Description of the way in which a computer is handling information, part of communications protocols. (Chapter 7)

Thin co-ax: See **Coaxial cable**

Time base corrector: A device used to synchronize a video production when several machines are used. (Chapter 10)

Time code-based: A VCR that records a time code on a videotape and uses this code to search for a specific part of the tape. (Chapter 9)

Token ring: A network transfer architecture often used with IBM PCSs. (Chapter 6)

Topology: The physical layout of the cables that connect the nodes on a network. (Chapter 6)

Touch pad: Another name for a remote control on a videodisc player. (Chapter 5)

Tower: A device that can hold up to 21 CD-ROM drives. (Chapter 4)

Trackball: A pointing device used with computers. Unlike the mouse, the trackball device remains still while the ball it contains is rolled to move a pointer on the computer screen. (Chapter 2)

Transfer speed: The amount of information per second that a drive can transfer to a computer. Used to describe transfer on floppy disk drive, hard drive, or CD-ROM drive. (Chapters 2 and 4)

Transitions: A term in video to describe dissolves, wipes, etc. (Chapter 10)

TSR program: "Memory resident software" that runs in the background behind other programs such as virus protection programs. (Chapter 2)

Turnkey system: A system of hardware and software that is purchased as a single unit. Purchasers only need to turn it on to use it. (Chapter 3)

Twisted pair cable: An inexpensive network cable consisting of two copper wires twisted for each pair. Shielded twisted pair wire has a layer of aluminum foil or copper mesh around the twisted pairs. (Chapter 6)

Uninterruptible power supply: A power source used to provide power for a computer or network for a brief period of time or to shut down the network during a major power outage. (Chapters 2 and 6)

Unshielded twisted pair: see **Twisted pair cable**

UPS: see **Uninterruptible power supply**

URL: Universal resource locator; an Internet/WWW address. (Chapter 8)

USB: Universal serial bus. (Chapter 2)

Utility program: A computer program that assists in the management of a computer. Examples include programs for hard drive backup, virus protection, data compression, hard disk maintenance, and data recovery. (Chapter 2)

Vaporware: Products that are planned but do not really exist. (Chapter 1)

Velveeta: See **Spamming**

Veronica: A search program used on the Internet to obtain access to gopher servers.

VGA monitor: A computer monitor that can display up to 256 colors. (Chapter 2)

Video adapter card: The card (also called a graphics adapter board) that controls the monitor in a PC. (Chapter 2)

Video capture card: see **Video digitizing card**

Video compression: A technique developed to save digitized video information on a computer's hard disk by saving only the important information on each frame of video. (Chapter 10)

Video digitizing card: An internal card that allows a computer to understand an analog video signal. (Chapter 10)

Video output card: An internal expansion card that changes a computer signal to one that can be shown on a regular television. (Chapter 10)

Video projector: A projector used to show a computer image on a large screen. (Chapter 10)

Videoconferencing: Method to transmit voice and video information over telephone lines or the Internet. (Chapters 7, 8)

Videodisc: A mass storage medium. A single videodisc the size of a 33rpm record can hold over 100,000 still pictures, each of which can be accessed by the player in one second. Videodiscs can also store text and video data. (Chapter 5)

Videodisc interactivity: Three levels of videodisc usage that are determined by the amount of control the user has over the disc and by the hardware and software that provides the control. See also **Videodisc Level I**, **Videodisc Level II**, and **Videodisc Level III**. (Chapter 5)

Videodisc Level I: The videodisc is controlled by the buttons on the videodisc player, by a remote control, or by a barcode reader. (Chapter 5)

Videodisc Level II: The videodisc is controlled by a special videodisc player with a microchip. (Chapter 5)

Videodisc Level III: The videodisc player is connected to a microcomputer. Software programs on the computer control the videodisc player. (Chapter 5)

VideoToaster: An add-on board for the Amiga computer. It is a top-of-the-line video system that can produce broadcast quality video with a computer. (Chapter 10)

Virtual reality: An attempt to use technology to create a simulated three-dimensional environment that appears real to the user. (Chapter 11)

Virus: An "infection" that is spread from computer to computer. A benign virus may only display a humorous message on the monitor while a destructive virus may silently destroy or change data. (Chapter 2)

Volatile: Term used to describe RAM. When a computer is disconnected from a power supply, the information in RAM is lost. (Chapter 2)

VR: see **Virtual reality**

VRAM: Video RAM, video memory. (Chapter 2)

WAN: Wide Area Network. Sharing resources over a long distance through dedicated cables, microwaves, or telephone lines. (Chapter 6)

Web browser: Software that allows a computer to find and read HTML Web pages. (Chapter 8)

WebPC: Web personal computer. (Chapter 8)

WebTV: Device to provide Internet access via a television set. (Chapter 8)

Windows: A GUI program that makes DOS appear to be icon-driven. (Chapter 2)

Windows 95: A true GUI, 32 bit operating system for PCs. (Chapter 2)

Wireless networks: Networks that use radio frequency transmitters to relay information. (Chapter 6)

Word processing: The use of a computer and program to write and edit text. (Chapter 2)

Workstation: An individual computer or input device on a network. (Chapter 6)

World Wide Web: The graphical access to the Internet. (Chapter 8)

WORM: Write one, read many. An emerging compact disc technology. (Chapter 4)

WWW: See **World Wide Web**

WYSIWYG: "What you see is what you get." A program with WYSIWYG displays information on the computer monitor in exactly the same way that it will be printed. (Chapter 2)

XapShot: A still digital or filmless camera. (Chapter 10)

Xmodem: A file transfer protocol used on telecommunications networks. (Chapter 7)

Zero-slot network: A network that uses an external rather than an internal network transfer architecture. (Chapter 6)

Zip drive: A 100 MB removable cartridge drive made by Iomega. (Chapter 2)

Resources for Further Information

Introduction

While books and articles are included in the bibliographies at the end of each chapter of this book, this chapter is a guide to some sources you can consult for additional information about the topics covered in this book. In general, the information is arranged under the title of the chapter in which a concept is discussed, but, because there is a lot of overlap of information, be sure to check Chapter 1 and related chapters for additional information. A table of contents to help you locate information in the Resources chapter follows this introduction.

The inclusion of a source in this chapter *does not* constitute an endorsement of a vendor or recommendation of a product. Rather, these sources are starting places for you to gather information.

> ***Remember, it is not always necessary or practical to deal with a national vendor. Your local, state, or regional dealers may be just as good or better in supplying products and after-the-sale service.

There are a few additional things to keep in mind as you use this information:

Company information. Many times a company will have several addresses and phone numbers. Use the information given here as a starting point.

Phone numbers. Please note that phone numbers listed are for voice communications (not fax or computer bulletin board) unless otherwise noted.

Periodical information. For additional information on periodicals (price, frequency, etc.) consult a standard periodicals directory such as *Ulrich's International Periodical Directory*. If you are unfamiliar with a periodical, request a sample issue before ordering. Beware that, just like technology, periodicals about technology often change, merge, and/or die.

Chapter numbers. To help you find the information related to a specific chapter, each subheading includes a reference to the chapter it supports. (ie. CH1 means the materials relate to Chapter 1 of this book.)

Contents of Resources Chapter

Chapter 1: Working with Instructional Technology

CH 1: Directory

Web site for toll-free telephone directory
http://www.tollfree.att.net/dir800/

Smith, D. L. *Web Site Source Book, 1996*. (1996). Omnigraphics. Lists "businesses, agencies, institutions, and other information resources on theWorld Wide Web."

CH 1: Professional Associations for Technology & SLMSs

American Library Association
American Association of School Librarians (Division)
50 East Huron Street
Chicago, IL 60611
(312) 944-6780
http://www.ala.org

Association for Educational Communications and Technology
1025 Vermont Av., NW
Suite 820
Washington, DC 20005-3547
(202) 347-7834
Fax (202) 347-7839

International Society for Technology in Education
1787 Agate Street
Eugene, OR 97403-1923
(800) 336-5191

International Visual Literacy Association
Educational Technologies Learning Resource Center
c/o Alice D. Walker
Old Security Bldg.
Blacksburg, VA 24061-0232
(540) 231-8992

National Telemedia Council
120 E. Wilson St.
Madison, WI 53703
(608) 257-7712
Fax (608) 257-7714

Strategies for Media Literacy
1095 Market St., #6176
San Francisco, CA 94103
(415) 621-2911
Fax (415) 255-2298

CH 1: Professional Journals for SLMSs

THE BOOK REPORT
480 East Wilson Bridge Road
Suite L
Worthington, OH 43085
(800) 786-5017
E-mail newslin@aol.com
http://linworth.com

Computers and the Media Center (CMC NEWS)
515 Oak Street North
Cannon Falls, MN 55009
(507) 263-3711

Computers in Libraries
Mecklermedia
20 Ketchum St.
Westport, CI 06880
(800) 632-5537
Note: Annual consultants directory and buyers guide.

The Electronic Library
143 Old Marlton Pike
Medford, NJ 08055-8750
(609) 654-4888

Emergency Librarian
Box C34069, Dept. 284
Seattle, WA 98124-1069
(604) 925-0566
Email: eml@rockland.com

LIBRARY TALK
480 East Wilson Bridge Road
Suite L
Worthington, OH 43085
(800) 786-5017
http://linworth.com

Media and Methods
Wagman Publishers
1429 Walnut Street
Philadelphia, PA 19102-3299
(215) 563-6005
(800) 555-5657

MultiMedia Schools
Online Inc.
462 Danbury Rd.
Wilton, CT 06897-2126
(800) 248-8466

School Library Journal
249 W. 17th St.
New York, NY 10011
(212) 645-0067
Fax (212) 463-6689

School Library Media Activities Monthly
LMS Associates
17 E. Henrietta St.
Baltimore, MD 21230
(410) 685-8621

School Library Media Quarterly
American Association of School Librarians
American Library Association
50 E. Huron St.
Chicago, IL 60611
(800) 545-2433
Fax (312) 440-9374

Tech Trends
Association for Educational Communications and Technology
1025 Vermont Ave., NW, Suite 820
Washington, DC 20005
(202) 347-7834

TECHNOLOGY CONNECTION
480 East Wilson Bridge Road
Suite L
Worthington, OH 43085
(800) 786-5017
http://linworth.com

CH 1: General Technology/ Computer Journals

Computerworld
375 Cochituate Rd.
Box 9171
Framingham, MA 01701-9172
(508) 879-0700

Computers in Education Journal
American Society for Engineering Education
Box 68, Port Royal Sq.
Port Royal, VA 22535
(804) 742-5611

Computers in the Schools
Haworth Press
10 Alice St.
Binghamton, NY 13904
(800) 342-9678

Educational Technology
Educational Technology Publications
700 Palisade Ave.
Englewood Cliffs, NJ 07632
(800) 952-BOOK

Electronic Learning
Scholastic Inc.
555 Broadway
New York, NY 10012-3999
(212) 343-6100
http://scholastic.com/EL

ERIC/IT Update
ERIC Clearinghouse on Information
& Technology
Syracuse University
4-194 Center for Science and
Technology
Syracuse , NY 13244-4100
(800) 464-9107

InfoWorld: *The voice of personal
computing in the enterprise.*
155 Bovet Rd., Ste 800
San Mateo, CA 94402
(415) 572-7341
Fax (415) 358-1269
Note: Free to qualified individuals

InterActivity
Miller Freeman, Inc.
600 Harrison St.
San Francisco, CA 94107
(415) 905-2200
http://www.eyemedia.com

Learning and Leading with Technology
Formerly: *The Computing Teacher*
Journal of the Society for Technology
in Education
1787 Agate Street
Eugene, OR 97403-1923
(800) 336-5191

New Media
Hyper Media Communications, Inc.
901 Mariner's Island Blvd, Ste. 365
San Mateo, CA 94404
(415) 573-5170
Fax (415) 573-5131
Note: Free to qualified individuals
http://www.hyperstand.com

Multimedia World
PC World Communications
501 Second St. #600
San Francisco, CA 94107
(415) 281-8650
Fax (415) 281-3915

Presentations
Lakewood Publications
50 S. Ninth St.
Minneapolis, MN 55402
(800) 328-4329
Note: Free to qualified individuals.
http://www.prese ntations.com

Technology & Learning
Peter Li, Inc.
PO Box 49727
Dayton, OH 45449-0727
(800) 543-4383

*T.H.E. Journal (Technological
Horizons in Education)*
150 El Camino Real, Suite 112
Tustin, CA 92680-3670
(714) 730-4011
Note: Free to qualified individuals

CH 1: *Specialized Computer Journals*

A+
A+ Publishing
80 Elm St.
Peterborough, NH 03458
(800) 441-4403
Note: also publishes *inCider*, a
newsletter

Amiga World
A+ Publishing
80 Elm Street
Peterborough, NH 03458
(603) 924-0100

Byte
McGraw-Hill
One Phoenix Mill Lane
Peterborough, NH 03458
(800) 232-2983

COMPUTE
Compute Pubs.
324 W. Wendover Ave., Ste. 200
Greensboro, NC 27408
(919) 275-9809
Fax (919) 275-9837

Home Office Computing
Scholastic Inc.
411 Lafayette St., 4th Fl.
New York, NY 10003

Home PC
600 Community Drive
Manhasset, NY 11030
(800) 829-0119
http:www.homepcmag.com

Mac Addict
Imagine Publishing Inc.
150 North Hill Drive, Suite 40
Brisbane, CA 94005
http:www.macaddict.com

MacWEEK
Ziff Davis Publishers
301 Howard St., 15th Fl.
San Francisco, CA 94105
Fax (415) 243-3651

Macworld
Macworld Communications
501 Second St.
San Francisco, CA 94107
(415) 243-0505

PC Computing
Ziff-Davis Publishing
One Park Avenue
New York, NY 10016
(800) 365-2770
Note: Picks 100 best products of the
year in December

*PC Home Journal and Mac Home
Journal*: *For work, play & education*
MacHome Journal Ind.
612 Howard St., 6th Fl.
San Francisco, CA 94105
(800) 800-6542

PC Magazine
Ziff Davis Publishing
1 Park Ave.
New York, NY 10016
(415) 243-3500
(800) 289-0429

PC Today
Peed Corporation
120 West Harvest Drive
P.O. Box 85670
Lincoln, NE 68501
(402) 479-2144
Fax (402) 479-2108
http://www/pctoday.com

PC World
PC World Communications, Inc.
501 Second Street, 5th Floor
San Francisco, CA 94107
(415) 243-0500
Fax (415) 442-1891
http://www.pcworld.com

Smart Computing in Plain English
formerly *PC Novice*
Peed Corporation
120 West Harvest Drive
P.O. Box 85380
Lincoln, NE 68501
(800) 848-1478
http://www.smartcomputing.com

Wired
544 Second St.
San Fransisco, CA 94107
(415) 276-5000

CH 1: Electronic Resources

See the listings for Chapter 8 of this book.

CH 1: Meetings to Attend

(Note: To determine exact dates and contact persons, check the calendar listings in professional publications.)

American Association of School Librarians
(Conference held every two years)

American Library Association

Association for Educational Communications and Technology

Computers in Libraries

Connected Classroom Conference

Databases in Schools

Microcomputers in Education Conference

National Educational Computing Conference (NECC)
(Sponsored by the International Society for Technology in Education)

CH 1: Selection Aids for Computers and Technology

In addition to periodicals listed above such as TECHNOLOGY CONNECTION, *Multimedia Schools,* etc., sources to check for reviews include the following:

Booklist
American Library Association
50 East Huron Street
Chicago, IL 60611
(800) 545-2433

California Instructional Technology Clearinghouse
(Note: searchable database of reviews under California Technology in the Curriculum Evaluations Database)
http://tic.stan-co.k12.ca.us/

Eisenhower National Clearinghouse
(Note: Source for math and science information)
http://www.enc.org/

International Society for Technology in Education
1787 Agate Street
Eugene, OR 97403-1923
(800) 336-5191

Media Review Digest
Pierian Press
5000 Washtenau
PO Box 1808
Ann Arbor, MI 48106
(800) 678-2435

New Mexico Educational Software Clearinghouse
http://www.enmu.edu/~siegelj/nmescx1.htm

Only the Best. The Annual guide to highest rated educational software.
Association for Supervision and Curriculum Development
Curriculum/Technology Resources Center.
1250 N. Pitt St.
Alexandria, VA 22307
(703) 549-9110 x514.

TESS: the Educational Software selector
Educational Products Information Exchange
103-3 W. Montauk Nwy
Hampton Bays, NY 11946
(516) 728-9100
Fax (516) 728-9228

Way Cool Software Reviews
http://www.ucc.uconn.edu/~wwwpcse/wcool.html

CH 1: Sample Job Descriptions for a Computer Technician, Network Manager, and Computer Coordinator

Send e-mail request to Doug Johnson, District Meida Supervisor for the Mankato (Minnesota) Public Schools at the following e-mail address: djohns1@west.isd77.k12.mn.us
(Note: That is the number one after "djohns.")

CH 1: Resources for Developing Technology Plans

Anderson, L. S. (1995). Making dreams come true; how to write a technology plan. *MultiMedia Schools,* 2 (5): 14-19. Outlines the process for developing a plan.

Baule, S. M. (1997). *Technology planning.* Worthington, OH: Linworth Publishing.
An overview of the process with sample documents.

Dyrli, O. E. & E. D. Kinnaman. (1994). District wide technology planning; the key to long-term success. *Technology & Learning* 14 (7): 50-56.

National Center for Technology Planning
Larry S. Anderson, Director
Mississsippi State University
Mississippi, State, MS 39762
URL: http://www.2msstate.edu/~lsa1
FTP: ftp.msstate.edu
Subdirectory: /pub/archives/nctp
Gopher: gopher.msstate.edu
Subdirectory: /Resources

CH 1: Resources for Developing Bid Specifications

Educational Products Information Exchange Institute
Writing Equipment Specifications: A How-To Handbook
Educational Product Report 28
103-3 W. Montauk Nwy
Hampton Bays, NY 11946
(516) 728-9100
Fax (516) 728-9228

International Communications Industries Association
Directory of Multimedia Equipment, Software and services
3150 Spring Street
Fairfax, VA 22031-2399
(800) 659-7469

CH 1: Sources of Grant Information

Aid for Education (newsletter)
CD Publications
8204 Fenton St.
Silver Spring, MD 20910
(800) 666-6380

Annual Register of Grant Support
RR Bowker/Reed Reference
Publishing
121 Chanlon Rd.
New Providence, NJ 07974
(800) 521-8110

The Chronicle of Philanthropy
1255 23rd. St. NW, Ste 775
Washington, DC 20037
(202) 466-1200
Fax (202) 466-2078

Directory of Corporate and Foundation Givers and
The Foundation Reporter
Taft Group
12300 Twinbrook Pkwy, Ste. 520
Rockville, MD 20852
(800) 877-TAFT

Education Grants Alert
Capitol Publications
1101 King St., Ste. 4444
Alexandria, VA 22314
(800) 327-7203

Education Technology News
Business Publishers
951 Pershing Dr.
Silver Spring, MD 20910
(800) 274-6737

Foundation Grants Index and
Foundation Directory
Foundation Center
79 Fifth Ave.
New York, NY 10003
(800) 424-9836

Funding Resource Bulletin
Government Information Services
4301 N. Fairfax Dr., Ste. 875
Arlington, VA 22203
(800) 876-0226

Grant Getter's Guide to the Internet
gopher://gopher.uidaho.edu:70/11/s/
e-pubs/grant

Grants for Libraries and Information Centers
Also *Grants for Elementary & secondary Schools* and *Corporate Foundation Profiles*
Foundation Center
79 Fifth Ave.
New York, NY 10003
(800) 424-9836

How to Write a Mini-Grant Proposal
Educational Activities
1937 Grand Avenue
Baldwin, NY 11510

Office of Educational Research and Improvement
Library Programs/OERI
U.S. Department of Education
555 New Jersey Ave. NW
Washington, DC 20208-5571

Winning Federal Grants (1994)
by Phale Hale
Capitol Publications
Alexandria, VA

CH 1: Help with Stolen Computers

Stolen Computer Registry
(914) 757-2626
http://www.nacomex.com/stolen/
stolen.html

CH 1: Some Manufacturers of Computers and Peripherals

To locate company information on the Internet, try searching the following site: http://www.Companies Online.com/

Apple Computer, Inc.
1 Infinite Loop
Cupertino, CA 95014
(800) 959-2775
(408) 996-1010
http://www.apple.com/

Canon U.S.A.
1 Canon Plaza
Lake Success, NY 11042
(800) 652-2666

Compaq PC
(800) 345-1518
http://www.compaq.com

Dell Computer Corporation
2112 Kramer Ln.
Austin, TX 7878758-4055
(512) 338-4400
http://www.del.com/

Digital Equipment Corporation
(800) 344-4825

Eastman Kodak Company
343 State Street
Rochester, NY 14650
(716) 724-4000
(800) 242-2424
http://www.kodak.com/

Epson America
P.O. Box 2842
Torrance CA 90509
(800) GO EPSON
http://www.epson.com/

Gateway 2000
610 Gateway Dr.
North Sioux City, SD 57049
(605) 232-2000
(800) 846-2042
http://www.gw2k.com/

Hayes Microcomputer Products
P.O. Box 105203
Atlanta, GA 30348
(770) 840-9200
Fax (770) 441-1213
http://www.hayes.com

Hewlett-Packard
(800) 333-1917
http://www.hp.com

Hitachi Home Electronics
3890 Steve Reynolds Blvd.
Norcross, GA 30093
(770) 279-5600
http://www.hitachi.com/

IBM Corporation
Old Orchard Rd.
Armonk, NY 10504
(800) IBM 3333
http://www.ibm.com

Logitech
6505 Kaise r Dr.
Fremont, CA 94555
(510) 795-8500

MicroNet Technology
80 Technology
Irvine, CA 92618
(714)453-6100

Mitsubishi Electronics America Inc.
1050 East Arques Ave.
Sunnyvale, CA 94086
(408) 730-5900
http://www.mitsubishi-drives.com/

Mitsubishi Electronics America
Information Systems Division
5665 Plaza Drive
Cypress, CA 90630
(714) 220-2500
http://www.mitsubishi-display.com/

Motorola
http://www.mot.com

NEC Technologies, Inc.
1250 Arlington Heights Road, Suite 5000
Itasca, IL 60143-1248
(800) NEC INFO
http://www.nec.com

Philips Professional Products
1 Philips Drive
Knoxville, TN 37914-1810
(423) 541-5803
http://www.philipsmcg.com/
http://www.philips.com

Pioneer Entertainment USA
2265 E. 220th St.
Long Beach, CA 90810
(800) 367-2467
http://www.pioneer-ent.com/

Power Computing
http:www.powercc.com/BYOB/

Sharp Electronics
Sharp Plaza
Mahwah, NJ 07430
(201) 529-8731
http://www.sharp-info.com/

Sony Educational System Division
3 Paragon Drive
Montvale, NJ 07645
(201) 358-4223
http://www.sel.sony.com/SEL/

Sony Computer Peripheral Products
3300 Zanker Rd.
San Jose, CA 95134
(800) 352-7669

Star Micronics
70 Ethel Road West
Piscataway, NJ 08854
(800) 506 STAR

Tandy Corporation
100 Throckmorton St.
Fort Worth, TX 76102
(817) 390-3700
http://www.tandy.com/

Toshiba America Information Systems
9740 Irvine Blvd.
P.O. Box 19724
Irvine, CA 92713
(800) 334-3445
http://www.tais.com/

Xerox Corp
(800) 34XEROX

CH 1: Information on RSIs Caused by Computers

The following WWW sites have information on RSIs

http://engr-www.unl.edu/ee/eeshop/rsi.html

http://ergo.human.cornel.edu

http://web.mit.edu:1962/tiserve.mit.edu/9000/34823.html

CH 1: Equity and Technology

Alliance for Technology Access
2173 E. Francisco Blvd., Suite L
San Rafael, VA 94901
(800) 455-7970

National Database of Assistive Technology
8455 Colesville Road
Suite 935
Silver Spring, MC 20910-3319
(800) 227-0216

Women in Technology Web Site
http://gse web.harvard.edu/TIEWeb/STUDENTS/STUDENTGROUPS/WIT/wit.html

Chapter 2: Computer Basics

CH 2: To Locate a Users Group:

Association of Personal Computer User Groups
(914) 876-6678

CH 2: Free Directory of Public Domain/Shareware

Austin ProSoft
P.O. Box 1811
Austin, TX 78767
(512) 323-2323
Edu-Ware Database on Disk
Free information on public domain and shareware programs.

CH 2: Information on Microprocessors

Intel
http://www.intel.com

Motorola
http://www.mot.com

CH 2: Diagnostic Software for Windows

First Aid for Windows
CyberMedia
(800) 721-78824

WINCheckIt
TouchStone Software Corp.
(800) 531-0450

WinSleuth
E Ware
(909) 279-0469

CH 2: For Tips On Using Windows

Microsoft's WinNews
To subscribe send an E-mail to the following:
Enews@nicrosof.nwnet.com
In the subject line type:
Subscribe winnews
In the text of the message type:
Subscribe Winnews

CH 2: Computer "Appliance" Producers
see also the general manufacturers listed in chapter 1

Network Computer Inc.
http://www.nc.com

U.S. Robotics: Pilot Palmtop
http://www.usrobotics.com/palm

CH 2: Removable Storage Manufacturers

Connor Peripherals
Tape Division
1650 Sunflower Avenue
Costa Mesa, CA 92626
(800) 626-6637

Iomega
1821 Iomega Way
Roy, UT 84067
(800) 697-8833
http://www.iomega.com

Kanguru Disks
Interactive Media Corp
(508) 429-9070

LaCie (SyQuest compatible)
Beaverton, OR
(800) 999-1179
http://www.lacie.com

Matsushita/Panasonic
2 Panasonic Way
Seacaucus, NJ 07094
(201) 348-70001
(800) 742-8086
http://www.panasonic.com/alive

MicroNet (SyQuest compatible)
Irvine CA
(800) 800-3475
http:www.micronet.com
Quantum
(800) 624-5545

Symbios Logic
2001 Danfield Dt.
Fort Collins, CO 90636-2905
(970) 226-9566
http://www.symbio.com

SyQuest
47071 Bayside Pkwy.
Fremont, CA 94538
(800) 245-2278
http://www.syquest.com

CH 2: Producers of Scanners

Apple Corporation
(408) 996-1010
www.apple.com

Hewlett-Packard
Roseville, CA
(800) 386-1117

Logitech
6505 Kaiser Drive
Fremont, CA 94555
(800)231-7717

Panasonic Communications
(800)742-8086

Pentax Technologies
(800)543-6144

Pixelcraft
(800) 933-0330

Polaroic Corporation
(800) 662-8337, x971

Umax Data Systems
3553 Gateway Blvd
Fremont CA 94538
(510) 651-4000

Visioneer
2860 West Bayshore Road
Palo Alto, CA 94303
(800) 787-7007
http://www.visioneer.com

CH 2: Resources for Assistive Technologies

American Council of the Blind
http://www.acb.org

Americans with Disabilities Act
http://www.usdoj.gov/crt/ada/adahoml.htm
(Note: That's the number one after adahom in the URL)

Assistive Technology Disabled Computer Users
http://www.iat.unc.edu/guides/irg-20.html

Center for Information Technology Accommodation
http://www.gsa.gov:80/coca/

Instant Access Treasure Chest
(Foreign Language Teacher's Guide to Learning Disabilities)
http://www.fln.vcu.edu/ld/ld.html

National Center for Accessible Media
http://www.boston.com/wgbh/pages/ncam/captionedmovies.html

New York State Commission for Blind and Visually Handicapped
http://www.state.ny.us/dss/cbvh/cbvh301.htm

Washington Assistive Technology Alliance
http://weber.u.washington.edu/~atrc/

CH 2: Mac/PC Translator Programs

DOS Mounter
Dayna Communications
505 Main St., 5th Floor
Salt Lake City, UT 84144
(800) 531-0600

Macintosh PC Exchange
Apple Computer
20525 Mariani Av.
Cupertino, CA 95014
(800) 776-2333

MacLink Plus/PC
DataViz
55 Corporate Dr.
Trumbull, CT 06611
(800) 733-0030

SoftPC
Insignia Solutions

CH 2: Windows NT Compatible Software

Microsoft web site at:
http://www.microsoft.com/ntworkstation/compat.htm

CH 2: Screen Saver Programs

After Dark/More After Dark
Berkeley Systems
2095 Rose
Berkeley, CA 94544
(510) 540-5535

Energizer Bunny
PC Dynamics
31332 Via Colinas, Suite 102
Westlake Village, CA 91362
(818) 889-1741

Pyro
Fifth Generation Systems
10049 N. Reiger Rd.
Baton Rouge, LA 70809
(800) 873-4384

CH 2: Virus Protection Software

Cheyenne AntiVirus
Cheyenne Software
(800) 424-3936
http://www.cheyenne.com

Dr. Solomon's Anti-Virus Toolkit
S&S
17 New England Executive Pk
Burlington, BA 01803
(888) 377-6566
http://www.drsolomon.com

FolderBolt Pro
Kent Marsh Ltd.
3260 Sul Ross Street
Houston, TX 77098
(713) 522-5625

Fortres 101
Fortres Grand Corporation
P.O. Box 888
Plymouth, IN 46563
(800) 331-0372

Full Armour for Windows
Micah Development
955 Massachusetts Avenue, Suite 365
Cambridge, MA 02139
(617) 641-1500
526 Clyde Ave.
Mountain View, CA 94043
(800) 848-7677

IBM AntiVirus
IBM
(800) 742-2493
http://www.av.ibm.com

Norton DiskLock and *Norton Anti-Virus*
Symantec Corporation
10201 Torre Ave
Cupertino, CA 95014
(800) 441-7234
http://www.symantec.com

Pc-cillin II
Touchstone Software
(800) 531-0450
http://www.checkit.com

SuperLock Pro
Joe Lyons Programming
10551 Regent Circle
Naples, FL 33942
(813) 598-4780

VirusScan and WebScan
McAfee Associates
(800) 332-9966
http://www.mcafee.com

CH 2: Other Information on Viruses and Virus Protection Software

Computer Security Institute
600 Harrison Street
San Francisco, CA 94107
(415) 905-2626

Datafellows
http://datafellows.cityhall.com:80/vir-info/virother.htm

CIAC (Department of Energy)
http://ciac.llnl.gov/ciac/ToolsDOSVirus.html

List of bogus viruses and virus alerts
http://www.kumite.com/myths
http://www.microsoft.com/msoffice/prank.html
http://www/sands.com/news/concept.html

CH 2: Sources of and Homes for Older Computers and Software

Boston Computer Exchange
210 South St.
Boston, MA 02111

Computers for Schools Program
(800) 939-6000

Computer Recycling Center
(415) 428-3700

Gifts in Kind America
(703) 836-2121

International Computer Users
Fellowship of Rotary International
(203) 248-8896

National Cristina Foundation
(800) 274-7846

National Materials Exchange Network
http://www.earthcycle.com/g/p/earthcycle

Non-Profit Computing Inc.
(212) 759-2368

P.E.P. (Parents, Educators, and publishers)
http://www.microweb.com/pepsite/Recycle/recycle_index.html

Surplus Software
(800) 753-7877

CH 2: Copyright Information

AIME, Association for Information Media and Equipment
P.O. Box 865
Elkader, Iowa 52043
(319) 245-1361
Copyright hotline: (800) 444-4203

ASCAP (for music)
One Lincoln Plaza
New York, NY 10023
(212) 595-3050

Association for Educational Communications and Technology
1025 Vermont Ave., NW
Suite 820
Washington, DC 20005
(202) 347-7834

Broadcast Music, Inc. (BMI)
40 W. 57th St.
New York, NY 10019
(212)586-2000

Copyright Clearance Center
222 Rosewood Dr., Suite 910
Danvers, MA 01923
(508) 750-8400
Fax (508) 750-4744
http://www.copyright.com/

Crash Course in Copyright
http://www.utsystem.edu/OGC/IntellectualProperty/cprtindx.htm

ILT Guide to Copyright
http://www.ilt.columbia.edu/projects/
copyright/index.html

Software Publishers Association
1730 M NW, Suite 700
Washington, DC 20036
(202) 452-1600
(800) 388-7478 (anti-piracy hotline)
WWWSPA.org (Web page)
(800) 637-6823 (fax on demand for
anti-piracy information)

U.S. Copyright Office
Library of Congress
Washington, DC 20559
(202) 707-3000
Note: Has a variety of free
publications
http://lcweb.loc.gov/copyright/

Additional copyright Web sites:
http://www.law.cornel.edu/topics/
copyright.html

http://www.benedict.com

Chapter 3: Library Management with a Computer

CH 3: Library Management Software

Ameritech Library Services
Resource Module
30 S. Wacker Dr.
Chicago, IL 60606-7413
(312) 750-5000

Brodart Automation
Precision One
500 Arch Street
Williamsport, PA 17701-7809
(800) 233-8467
http://www.brodart.com/

CASPR, Inc.
LibraryWorks
100 Park Center Plaza
Suite 550
San Jose , CA 95113
(800) 852-2777

Chancery Software
Mac School Library Pro
4170 Still Creek Dr., Suite 450
Burnaby. British Columbia, Canada
V5C6C6
(800) 999-9931

COMPanion Corporation
Alexandria
1831 Fort Union Blvd.
Salt Lake City, UT 84121
(800) 347-6439

Electronic Online Systems (EOS)
Formerly **Data Trek, Inc.**
GoPAC and *Manager Series*
5838 Edison Place
Carlsbad, CA 92008
(800) 876-5484

Dynix Scholar
Scholar and *Kids Catalog* (graphical
interface)
400 Dynix Drive
Provo, UT 84604
(800) 288-1145

Follett Software Company
*Circulation Plus, Catalog Plus,
Unison*
1391 Corporate Drive
McHenry, IL 60050-5589
(800) 323-3397

Gaylord Bros.
Community information module
Box 4901
Syracuse, NY 13221-4901
(800) 962-9580

Library of Congress
Cataloging Services
National Bibliographic Service
Cataloging Distribution Customer
Service
Washington DC, 20541
(800) 255-3666

The Library Corporation
1 Research Park,
Inwood, WV 25428-9733
(800) 325-7759
http://www.bibfile.com/

Marcive, Inc.
Record upgrade service
5616 Randolph Blvd.
San Antonio, TX 78233
(800) 531-7678

McGraw-Hill School Systems
Columbia
20 Ryan Ranch Rd.
Monterey, *CA 93940*
(800) 663-0544

Media Flex, Inc.
P.O. Box 1107
Champlain, NY 12919
(800) 361-1407

Nichols Advanced Technologies
Molli and *Athena*
3452 Losey Boulevard South
La Crosse , WI 54601
(800) 658-9453

Scarecrow Press
52 Liberty Street
P.O. Box 4167
Metuchen, NJ 04167

SIRS
Mandarin
(800) 232-SIRS

SIRSI Corporation
Unicorn
689 Discovery Drive
Huntsville, AL 35806
(205) 922-9825

SWLI Inc.
Laser Guide
(800) 933-5383

Winnebago Software Company
Winnebago CAT
P.O. Box 430
Caledonia, MN 55921-9900
(800) 533-5430

WLN
LaserCat
P.O. Box 3888
Lacey, WA 98503-0888
(800) DIALWLN

CH3: Media Retrieval Systems

AMX Corporation
11995 Forestgate Drive
Dallas, TX 75243
(214) 644-3048

Crestron Electronics
101 Broadway
Cresskill, NJ 07626
(201) 894-0660

Dukane Corporation
Instructional Technology
780 W. Belden Ave.
Addison, IL 60101
(800) 281-5991

Dynacom Corporation
63855 M40 Highway
Lawton, MI 49065
(616) 624-7123

Rauland-Borg Corporation
3450 West Oakton St.
Skokie, IL 60076-2951
(708) 679-0900

CH 3: Sources of Other Information

Computer Services
North Carolina Dept. of Public
Instruction
116 West Edenton St.
Raleigh, NC 27603-1712
Online catalog project and CD-ROM
encyclopedia project

Chapter 4: CD-ROM and Other Types of Compact Discs

CH 4: Journals

Note: CD-ROM information is often
included in general technology/
computer journals. Check Chapter 1
for titles.

CD-ROM End User
DDRI, Inc.
501 N. Washington St., Suite 401
Falls Church, VA 22046-3537
(703) 237-0682

*CD-ROM Librarian: The optical
media review for information profes-
sionals*
Note: title changed to *CD-ROM
World*

CD-ROM Professional
Note: title changed to *EMedia
Professional*

CD-ROM Today
GP Publications
23-00 Route 208
Fair Lawn, NJ 07410
(201) 703-9500

CD-ROM World
Meckler Corp.
11 Ferry Lane West
Westport, CT 06880
(203) 226-6967

Emedia Professional
formerly *CD-ROM Professional*
Pemberton Pr.
462 Danbury Rd.
Wilton, CT 06897
(203) 761-1466

Laserdisk Professional
Note: title changed to *Emedia
Professional*

Online and CD-ROM Notes
Learned Information Inc.
143 Old Marlton Pike
Medford, NY 08055-8750
(609) 654-6266
Fax (609) 654-4309

CH 4: Bibliographies and Selection Aids

(Note: Many of the periodical articles
appear on a yearly basis.)

Berger P. (1996). CD-ROM reviews
for schools. *Information searcher*, 8
(March), 24-6. Also in the May 1996
issue.

CD-ROMs in Print 1998 (1997).
Detroit: Gale Research. An annual
guide to CD-ROMs.

Couts, B.E. (1997). Best reference
sources 1996. *Library Journal*, 122
(April 15, 1997), 36-40. Includes CD-
ROMs and Web sites with the print
materials.

Dewey. P. R. (1995). *Three hundred
CD-ROMs to use in your library*.
Chicago: American Library Associa-
tion. Contains "descriptions, evalua-
tions & practical advice" on CD-
ROMs.

Jacso, P. (1996). State-of-the-art
multimedia in 1996: the 'big four'
general encyclopedia on CD-ROM.
Computers in Libraries 16 (4) 26-29.
An "exhaustive look at the good-and
the not-so-good" of Compton's,
Encarta, Grolier, and World Book
encyclopedias on CD-ROM.

Media: CD-ROMs. (1996). *Booklist*;
93 (Dec. 1, 1996), 674-6. A review of
CD-ROMs that continues in the
January and February 1997 issues of
Booklist.

*Multimedia & CD-ROM Directory
1997; Marketplace*. (1997). New
York: Groves Dictionaries.

Sorrow, B. H. & B. Lumpkin (1993).
*CD-ROM for librarians and educators:
a resource guide to over 300 instructional programs*. McFarland. This book
for teachers and librarians from K to
college received three checks (Read It)
in the January-February 1994 issues of
Emergency Librarian.

Reviews on the Internet from the
University of Texas Graduate School
of Library and Information Science:
http://volvo.gslis.utexas.edu/~reviews

CH 4: CD-ROM Shareware and Preview Suppliers

American Databankers
(918) 497-1201

BMUG
(800) 776-BMUG

CD-ROM LAN listserv
CDROMLAN@IDBSU.IDBSU.EDU

CD-ROM Source
(317) 726-0022

Digital Diversions Software
(800) 879-1150

Limelight Media
(812) 234-8800

Most Significant Bits
(216) 529-1888

Night Owl
(716) 484-3066

Pacific HiTech
(801) 278-2042

Quantum Leap Software
(800) 762-2877

Software Dispatch
P.O. Box 876
Brea, CA 92622-9903
(800) 937-2828, ex. 600

Walnut Creek
(800) 786-9907

Wayzata Technology
(800) 735-7321

CH 4: Sources of Products Mentioned in the Chapter

ADLib
50 Staniford St.
Boston, MA 02114
(800) 463-2686

Adobe Photoshop
Adobe Systems, Inc.
1585 Charleston Rd., Box 7900
Mountain View, CA 94039
(800) 492-3623
http://www.adobe.com

CD-I
Philips Professional Products
1 Philips Dr.
Knoxville, TN 37914
(800) 223-4432
http://www.phhilipspro.com

Photo CD
Eastman Kodak Co.
343 State Street
Rochester, NY 14650
(800) 242-2424

PhotoEdge
Eastman Kodak Co.
343 State Street
Rochester, NY 14650
(800) 242-2424

PhotoMagic
Micrografax
1303 Arapaho
Richardson, TX 75081
(214) 234-1769

PhotoPaint
Corel
1600 Carling Ave.
Ottawa, Ontario, CAN K1Z8R7
(800) 772-6735

Picture Publisher
Micrografax
1303 Arapaho
Richardson, TX 75081
(214) 234-1769

Renaissance
Eastman Kodak Co.
343 State Street
Rochester, NY 14650
(716) 724-4000

Sound Blaster
Creative Labs, Inc.
1901 McCarthy Blvd,
Milpitas, CA 94035
(408) 428-6600

CH 4: Manufacturers of CD-ROM Drives and Recorders

Electronic Vision, Inc.
5 Depot St.
Athens, OH 45701
(614) 592-2433
http://www.ev.net/fitne

Fidelity International Technology
215 Campus Plaza, Raritan Center
Edison, NJ 08837
(908) 417-2230
http://www.ourworld.compuse
rve.com/homepages/fiti

Hewlett-Packard Company
PO Box 58059,
Santa Clara, CA 95051-8059
(800) 752-0900

Micro Design International
6985 University Blvd.
Winter Park, FL 32792
(407) 677-8333
http://www.mdi.com

MicroNet Technology
80 Technology
Irvine, CA 92618-7019
(714) 453-6100
http://www.micronet.com

NEC Technogies
1414 Massachusetts Ave.
Boxboro, MA 01719-2298
(800) 632-8377
http://www.nec.com

Pioneer New Media Technologies
2265 E. 220th St.
Long Beach, CA 90810

Plextor
4255 Burton Dr.
Santa Clara, CA 95054
(408) 980-1838 (4 PLEXTOR)
http://www.plextor.com

Sony Electronics
3300 Zanker Road
San Jose , CA 95134
(800) 352-7669
http://www.sony.com

TEAC
7733 Telegraph Road
Montebello, CA 90640
(213) 726-0303

Toray Marketing & Sales
1875 S/ Grant St. Suite 720
San Mateo, CA 94403
(415) 341-7152
http://www.toray.com

Toshiba American Information Systems
9740 Irvine Blvd.
P.O. Box 19724
Irvine, CA 92713-9724
(800) 334-3445
http://www.toshiba.com

Yamaha Corp. of America
100 Century Center Court
San Jose , CA 95112
(800) 543-7457

CH 4: Producers of CD Recording Software

Corel Corp.
1600 Carling Ave.
Ottawa, Ontario Canada K1Y0J3
(800) 772-6735

Creative Digital Research
7291 Coronado Dr. #8
San Jose , CA 95129
(408) 255-0999

Dataware Technologies
Cambridge, MA 02141
(617) 621-0820

Incat/Adaptec, Inc.
Milpitas, CA 95035
(800) 774-6228

Multimedia Design Corp.
8730 Red Oak Blvd., Suite 404
Charlotte, NC 28217
(704) 523-9493

Promax Technology
16 Technology Dr. #106
Irvine, CA 92618
(714) 727-3977
http://www.scsidisk.com

Rimage Corp.
7725 Washington Ave. S.
Minneapolis, MN 55439
(800) 445-8288
http://www.rimage.com

StorNet
1109 Saunders Court
West Chester, PA 19380
(610) 692-8400
http://www.stornet.com

CH 4: Manufacturers of CD-i Players

Diamond Multimedia Systems
2880 Junction Ave.
San Jose , CA 95134-1922
(408) 325-7284
http://www.diamondmm.com

Multimedia Computer Solutions
400 Union Ave., Unit 4
Haskell, NJ 07420
(201) 839-3300
http://www.intac.com/~mcs

Philips Professional Products
One Philips Dr.
Knoxville, TN 37914
(423) 541-5762
http://www.philipspro.com

Presentation Products Inc.
10349 Heritage Park Dr., #4
Santa Fe Springs, CA 90670-3776
(800) 722-6444
http://www.presproducts.com

Toray Marketing & Sales, Inc.
1875 S. Grant St., suite 720
San Mateo, CA 94402
(415) 341-7152
http://www.toray.com

Valiant International Multimedia Corp.
55 Ruta Court
S. Hackensack, NJ 07606
(201) 229-9800
http://www.valiantimc.com/

CH 4: Manufacturers of DVD Drives

Fidelity International Technology
215 Campus Plaza, Raritan Center
Edison, NJ 08837
(908) 417-2230
http://www.ourworld.compuse
rve.com/homepages/fiti

Multimedia Computer Solutions
400 Union Ave., Unit 4
Haskell, NJ 07420
(201) 839-3300
http://www.intac.com/~mcs

Panasonic Broadcast & Television Systems
1 Panasonic Way
Secaucus, NJ 07094
(800) 524-0864

Pioneer New Media Technologies
2265 E. 220th St.
Long Beach, CA 90810

Chapter 5: Videodiscs in the Library

CH 5: Major Videodisc Hardware Producers

Panasonic Communications Company
1 Panasonic Way
Secaucus, NY 07094
(800) 524-0864 or (800) 528-8601

Pioneer New Media
2265 E. 220th St.
Long Beach, CA 90810
(800) LASER-ON

Sony Education Systems
3 Paragon Dr., S-115
Montvale, NJ 07645
(800) 472-SONY

CH 5: Sources of Authoring Software and Products Mentioned in the Chapter

Authorware Professional
Macromedia, Inc.
600 Townsend St.
San Francisco, CA 94103
(800) 945-4051
http://www.macromedia.com

Bar'n'Coder
Pioneer Corp.
2265 E. 220th St.
Long Beach, CA 90810
(800) LASER-ON

Digital Chisel
Pierian Spring Software
5200 S.W. Macadam Av., Suite 250
Portland, OR 97201
(800) 472-8578

Encyclopedia of Animals
Optical Data Corporation
30 Technology Drive
Warren, NJ 07059
(800) 524-2481

HyperCard withVideo Tool Kit
Claris Corporation
5201 Patrick Henry Drive
Box 58168
Santa Clara, CA 95052
(800) 544-8554

HyperStudio
Roger Wagner Publishers
1050 Pioneer Way
El Cajon, CA 92020
(800) 448-9797

HyperWriter
Ntergaid
2490 Black Rock Turnpike, Suite 337
Fairfield, CT 06430
(800) 254-9737

IconAuthor
AimTech Corp.
20 Trafalgar Sq.
Nashua, NH 03063
(800) 289-2884

Instant Replay Pro
Instant Replay Corp.
8290 N.W. 27th St., #605
Miami, FL 33122
(800) 749-8779

LessonMaker
Optical Data Corporation
30 Technology Drive
Warren, NY 07059
(800) 524-2481

LinkWay/LinkWay Live!
EduQuest
P.O. Box 2150
Atlanta, GA 30055
(800) IBM-4EDU

LINX Test Factory
Warren-Forthought
1212 N. Velasco
Angleton, TX 77515
(409) 849-1239

Literature Navigator
Sunburst
101 Castleton St.
Pleasantville, NY 10570
(800) 321-7511

The Living Textbook
Optical Data Corporation
30 Technology Drive
Warren, NJ 07059
(800) 524-2481

Media Developer
Lenel Systems
290 Woodcliff Office Park
Fairport, NY 174450
(716) 248-9720

MediaScript
Network Tech
1275 Danner Dr.
Aurora, OH 44202
(216) 562-7070
http://www.newtek.com

Multimedia Toolbook
Asymetrix
110 110th Avenue North
Belleview, WA 98004
(800) 448-6543

TutorTech
Techware Corporation
P.O. Box 151085
Altamonte Springs, FL 32715
(800) 347-3224

Visual Almanac
Apple Computer, Inc.
1 Infinite Loop
Cupertino, CA 95014
(800) SOS-APPL

Voyager VideoStack
Voyager Company
578 Broadway, Suite 406
New York, NY 10012
(800) 446-2001

Chapter 6: Local Area Networks

CH 6: Periodicals

Intranet Journal
http://www./brill.com/intranet/
index.html

INTRAnet News
Publications Resource Group
PO Box 765
North Adams, MA 01247
(413) 664-6185

Network Magazine
Miller Freeman
600 Harrison St.
San Francisco, CA 94167
(415) 905-2200
http://www.lanmag.com

LAN Technology
Henry Hold
411 Borel Ave., Ste 100
San Mateo, CA 94402
(415) 358-9500

Network Computing
CMP Publications
600 Community Dr.
Manhasset, NY 11030
(516) 562-5000

Network World
161 Worcester Rd., 5th Fl.
P.O. Box 9172
Framingham, MA 01701-9172
(800) 622-1108
Note: Free to qualified individuals
http://www.nwfusion.com

CH 6: Sources of Network Products

Apple Computer
One Infinite Loop
Cupertino, CA 95014
(408) 996-1010 or (800) 538-9696
Products: AppleTalk, LocalTalk,
AppleShare, System 7, Apple
Workgroup Server 95, Newton
eMate 300.
http://www.apple.com

Artisoft, Inc
2202 N. Forbes Blvd.
Tucson, AZ 85745
(800) 233-5564, (602) 670-7145
Product: LANtastic, LANtastic for
Windows
http://www.artisoft.com

Banyan Systems, Inc.
120 Flanders Road
Westboro, MA 01581
(800) 222-6926
Product: VINES, VINES for UNIX
http://www.banyan.com

Bay Networks
Santa Clara, CA
(800) 231-4213
http://www.baynetworks.com

Compaq
Houston, TX
(800) 888-3224
http://www.compaq.com

Digital Equipment Corp.
Main St.
Maynard, MA 01754-2571
(508) 493-5111
http://www.digital.com
Products: Wireless LAN products

Farallon Communications
2470 Mariners Square Loop
Alameda, CA 94501
(800) 814-5000
http://www.farallon.com
Product: Apple networks, fast
Ethernet for Mac

IBM
4111 Northside Parkway
Atlanta, GA 30327
(800) 3IBMOS2 or (800) 426-2468
Products: LAN Server, Token Ring,
wireless LAN
http://www.ibm.com

Logicraft Information Systems, Inc.
22 Cotton Road
Nashua, NH 03063-9977.
Products: CD-ROM networking
systems including **LAN CD**

Lucent Technologies
211 Mt.
Basking Ridge, NJ 07920
http://www.lucent.com
Products: Wireless LANs

Meridian Data, Inc.
5615 Scotts Valley Drive
Scotts Valley, CA 95066
(800) 767-2537
http://www.meridian-data.com
Products: CD-ROM networking
systems

Micro Design International, Inc.
6985 University Boulevard
Winter Park, FL 32792
(800) 228-0891
http://www.mdi.com
Products: SCSI Express

Microsoft Corp.
One Microsoft Way
Redmond, WA 98052-6399
(800) 426-9400
Products: LAN Manager, Windows
for Workgroups, Windows NT.
Http://www.microsoft.com

Novell, Inc.
122 East 1700 South
Provo, UT 84606-6194
(800) NETWARE
Products: NetWare, NewWare Lite
http://www.novell.com

Ornetix Network Products
1885 Lundy Avenue, Suite 200
San Jose , CA 95131
(800) 965-6650
http://ornetix.com

Standard Microsystems Corp.
Hauppauge, NY
(800) 762-4968
http://www.smc.com

Sun Microsystems
2550 Garcia Ave.
Mountain View, CA 94043-1100
(415)960-1300
http://www.sun.com

Todd Enterprises
65 East Bethpage Rd.
Plainview, NY
(800) 643-4351
http://www.toddent.com
Products: OPTI-NET networking
software

*CH 6: Network Resources
on the Internet*

Apple Network Information
http://ed.info.apple.com/education/
products/netadmin.html

BugNet Web site (bug problems on
networks)
http://www.bugnet.com/~bugnet

**Macintosh start up and
maintenance disks updates**
ftp.support.apple.com/pub/apple_sw_
updates/US/Macintosh/System%20
Software/System_7.5_Update_1.0/

Beginners guide to networking
http://w3.fwn.rug.nl/itgeheer/nwdoc/
netware_info/NetWare_introduction
.html

CD-ROM LAN Internet Listserv
CDROMLAN@IDBSU.IDBSU.EDU
List owner is Dan Lester

**Complete conflict compendium for
Macintosh software conflicts**
http://www/quillse rv.com/www/c3/
c3.html

Ethernet Page
http://wwwhost.ots.utexas.edu/
ethernet/ethernet-home.html

**Future of Networking Technologies
for Learning**
http://inet.ed.gov/Technology/Futures/
index.html

**List of frequently asked questions
about Windows 95 and networking**
http://mercury.cs.uregina.ca/links/faq/
comp.os.ms-windows.networking.
win95/
and http://www.clearlight.com/
~visanu/win95.html

**Basic network information and
links**
http://sunsite.unc.edu.cisco

**Network Administrator's
Handbook**
http://tampico.cso.uiuc.edu/nas/nash/
nash.html

Network Buyer's Guide
http://www.sresearch.com

Network Vocabulary
http://toucan.iecs.fcu.edu.tw/doc/
vocabulary/voc.html

Novell's Network Primer
http://www.novell.com/manuals/
primer.html

**Texas guidelines for hooking a LAN
to the Internet**
http://www.tenet.edu/tenet-info/
connect/intro.html

Wireless LAN Alliance
http://www.wlana.com

CH 6: Intranet Resources

The Complete Intranet Resource
http://www.lochnet.com/client/smart/
intranet

The Intranet Handbook Page
http://www.ntg-inter.com/ntg/
intra_hb/handbk.htm

Intranet Resource Center
http://www.infoweb.com.au/
intralnk.htm

Chapter 7: Computer Telecommunication

*CH 7: Professional
Organizations*

Consortium for School Networking
(CoSN)
P.O. Box 65193
1555 Connecticut Ave., N.W. Suite 200
Washington, CD 20035-5193
(202) 446-6296
http://cosn.org

**Coalition for Networked
Information** (CNI)
21 NW Dupont Circle
Washington, DC 20036
(202) 296-5098

Electronic Frontier Foundation
1550 Bryant St., Suite 725
San Francisco, CA 94103
(415) 668-7171

Internet Society
12020 Sunrise Valley Dr., Suite 210
Reston, VA 22091
(800) 468-9507

Society for Electronic Access
P.O. Box 7081
New York, NY 10116-7081
(212) 592-3801

CH 7: Periodicals

+online User
14 Princeton Ave.
P.O. Box 17507
Covington, KY 41017
(603) 331-6345

Boardwatch Magazine
8500 W. Bowles Ave., Suite 210
Littleton, CO 80123
(800) 933-6038

Connect: The Journal of Computer Networking
3Com Corp
5400 Bayfront Plaza
Santa Clara, CA 95052-8145
(800) NET-3com
http://www.3com.//gg

Database : The Magazine of Electronic Database Review
90 Great Oak Dr.
P.O. Box 43
Springboro, OH 45066
http://www.onlineinc.com/database

International Telephony
55 E. Jackson Blvd., Suite 1100
Chicago, IL 60604-4105
(312) 922-2435

Northwest Report
Northwest Regional Educational
Laboratory
101 Southwest Main Street
Suite 500
Portland, OR 97204
(503) 248-6800
Note: Free newsletter

Online: *The magazine of online information systems*
11 Tamarack Lane
Weston, CT 06798
(203) 263-4759

Searcher
Information Today
143 Old Marlton Pike
Medford, N.J. 08055
(609) 654-6266

Telecommunications Magazine
685 Canton St.
Norwood, MA 02062
(617) 769-1923
http://www.telecoms-mag.com/
tcs.html

Telephony
1 IBM Plaza, Suite 2300
Chicago, IL 60611
(312) 595-1080

CH 7: Communications Software

(Note: Some of these are shareware or freeware and can be found on electronic BBS or Internet)

ClarisWorks (Mac)
Claris Corp.
5201 Patrick Henry Dr.
Box 58168
Santa Clara, CA 95052
(800) 544-8554
http://www.claris.com

Laplink
Traveling Software
18702 N. Creek Pkwy
Bothell, WA 98011
(800) 343-8080
http://www.travsoft.com

Crosstalk
Attachmate Corporation
3617 131st Avenue, SE
Bellevue, WA 98006
(800) 348-3221

Eudora Pro
Aualcomm
(800) 238-8672
http://www.eudora.com

FirstClass
SoftArc
(905) 415-7000
http://www.softarc.com

Hayes Smartcomm (IBM)
Hayes Microcomputer Products
P.O. Box 105203
Atlanta, GA 30348
(800) HAYES-28
http://www.hayes.com

Microphone II (Mac)
Software Ventures
2907 Claremont Avenue
Berkeley, VA 98052-6399
(703) 709-5500

ProComm Plus (IBM)
Datastorm Technologies
3212 Lemone Industrial Boulevard
Columbia, MO 65201
(800) 315-3282

Pronto97
CommTouch Software
(800) 638-6824
http://www.commtouch.com

Quarterdeck Mail
StarNine Technologies
(510) 649-4949
 http://www.starnine.com

QuickMail Pro
CE Software
(800) 523-7638
http://www.cesoft.com

Quick Link II
Smith Micro Software, Inc.
P.O. Box 7137
Huntington Beach, CA 92615

White Knight (Mac)
Free Soft Company
105 McKinley Road
Beaver Falls, PA 15010
(412) 846-2700

Z-Mail Pro
NetManage
(408) 973-7171
http://www.netmanage.com

CH 7: Modem Suppliers
(Top five suppliers as listed by *PC World*, January 1997)

Diamond Multimedia
(800) 727-8772
http://www.diamondmm.com

Hayes Communications
(770) 840-9200
http://www.hayes.com

Motorola
(800) 342-3266
http://www.mot.com

U.S. Robotics
(800) 877-2677
http://www.usr.com

CH 7: Emoticons

A list of e-mail emoticons is maintained on the following:
http://www.utopiasw.demon.co.uk/
emoticon.htm

http://www.eastern.k12.nj.us/students/
emoticons.html

CH 7: DSVD Modems

Hayes Microcomputer Products
(770) 840-9200
http://www.hayes.com
Product: Accura Fax/Modem with DSVD

Interplay Productions
(800) 969-4263
http://www.interplay.com
Product: Descent II

CH 7: Telephony Resources

Aztech Labs
(800) 886-8859
http://www.aztech.com.sg/
Product: Audio Telephony 2000

Clearwave Communications
(800) 414-9283
http://www.clearwave.com
Product: Intellect ID, Intellect IQ

Prometheus Products
(800) 477-3473
http://www/netusa.com/pcsoft/library/
p_902.htm
Product: Cyber Phone

Reveal Computer Products
(800) 738-3251
http://www2.pcy.mci.net/marketplace/
reveal/
Product: VM100, VM500, Decathlon
XL, PM800

SoftTalk
(617) 433-0800
http://www.softtalk.com/
Product: Phonetastic

Spectrum Signal Processing
(800) 667-0018
http://www.spectrumsignal.bc.ca
Product: Envoy II, V.34 Office F/X

*CH 7: ISDN Encyclopedia
Online*

http://alumni.caltech.edu/dank/isdn

*CH 7: Fax on Demand Numbers
for Technology Suppliers*

The following companies supply
information through fax-on-demand
systems.

Acer
(800) 554-2494

Apple
(800) 767-2775

AT&T
(800) 272-5300

Banyan
(800) 932-9226

Canon
(800) 520-4345

Compaq
(800) 345-1518

Dell
(800) 624-9896

Eastman Kodak
(800) 242-2424 ext. 33

Gateway 2000
(800) 846-2301

Hewlett Packard
(800) 333-1917

IBM
(800) 765-4747

Intel
(800) 525-3019

Lotus
(800) 346-3508

Microsoft
Operating systems & hardware
(800) 936-4200
Desktop & home products
(800) 936-4100

Mitsubishi
Printer
(800) 634-4309
Monitor
(800) 937-2094

Motorola
(800) 221-4380

Novell
(800) 228-9960

Samsung
(800) 229-2239

Sony
(800) 776-3449

Sharp
(800) 512-2086

Tandy
(800) 323-6586

Texas Instruments
(800) 848-3927

Zenith
(800) 227-3360

*CH 7: Commercial Online
Services*

America Online
(800) 887-6364
http://www.aol.com

Compuserve
(800) 524-3388 x664
http://www.compuserve.com

Concentric Network Corporation
(800) 939-4262

Delphi
(800) 695-4005

Microsoft Network
(800) 373-3676
http://www.msn.com

Prodigy
(800) 213-0992
http://www.prodigy.com

CH 7: Educational Networks

America Tomorrow
P.O. Box 2310
West Bethesda, MD 20827-2310
(800) 456-8881

AT&T Learning Network
400 Interpace Parkway
Parsippany, NY 07054
(800) 809-1097

National Geographic Kids Network
P.O. Box 10768
Des Moines, IA 50340
(800) 368-2728

Scholastic Network
2931 East McCarty Street
Jefferson City, MO 65101
http://scholastic.com

CH 7: State Computer Networks

A list of computer networks can be
found at:
http:/129.180.87.4/studentsPapers/
Craig/unindex.htm

California
California Online Resources for
Education
California Dept. Of Education
http://www.cde.ca.gov/pg2teach.html

Florida
Florida Information Resource
Network
Florida Educational Center
B1-14 325 W. Gaines St.
Tallahassee, FL 32399
(904) 487-8586
http://www.firn.edu/index.html

Georgia
Georgia EduNET
Regional Teacher Educational Center,
CBX 034
School of Education
Georgia College
Milledgeville, GA 31061-0490
(912) 453-5121

Kansas/Missouri
KC ShareNet
Pan-Educational Institute
10922 Winner Road
Independence, MO 64052
(816) 461-0201

Michigan
Merit MichNet
2901 Hubbard, Pod G.
Ann Arbor, MI 48109-2016
(313) 936-3000

North Dakota
SENDIT - North Dakota's k-12
Telecom Network
Box 5164
NDSU Computer Center
Fargo, ND 58105
(701) 237-8109

Texas
TENET - the Texas Education
Network
Texas Education Agency
1701 North Congress Ave., Room
4159
Austin, TX 78701
(512) 463-9091

Virginia
Virginia's PEN (Public Education
Network)
Virginia Department of Education
P.O. Box 6-Q
Richmond, VA 23216
(804) 225-2921

CH 7: Online Database Services

Dow Jones News/Retrieval
Dow Jones Interactive Publishing
P.O. Box 300
Princeton, NJ 08543-0300
(800) 522-3567
http://bis.dowjones.com

**ERIC Clearinghouse on
Information & Technology**
4-194 Center for Science & Technology
Syracuse University
Syracuse, NY 13244-4100
(800) 464-9107
http://ericir.syr.edu/ithome

Knight-Ridder Information
Worldwide Headquarters
2440 W. El Camino Real
Mountain View, CA 94040
(800) 334-5634
http://www.krinfo.com/

Lexis-Nexis
Mead Data Central, Inc
9443 Springboro Pike
Miamisburg, OH 45342
(800) 227-4908

Wilsonline
H. W. Wilson Company
950 University Avenue
Bronx, NY 10452
(800) 367-6770
http://www.hwwilson.com

CH 7: Free E-Mail

Juno Online Services
(800) 654-5866
signup@juno.com
http://www.juno.com

CH 7: Resources for Videoconferencing

Apple Corp.
Cupertino, CA
(800) 898-2775
Product: *Apple VideoPhone Kit,
QuickTime Videoconferencing*

CineCom Corp.
(703) 680-4733
http://www.cinecom.com
Product: *CineVideo/Direct*

Compression Labs
(408) 435-3000
Product: *Cameo*

Connectix
San Mateo, CA
(800) 751-7558
http://www.connectix.com
Product: *QuickCam*

Creative Labs
(408) 428-6600
Product: ShareVision PC 3000

Fiber & Wireless
Torrance, CA
(310) 787-7097
http://www.fiberwire.com
Product: *Mediafone* software

RSI Systems
Edina, MN
(800) 496-4304
Product: *Meet-Me* (ISDN), *Eris*

Shark Multimedia
Santa Clara, CA
(800) 800-3321
http://www.sharkmm.com
Product: *SeeQuest*

VIC Hi-Tech Corp.
(310) 643-5193
http://www.vic-corp.com
Product: *Global Phone*

VideoLabs Inc.
(800) 467-7157
http://www.flexcam.com
Product: *FlexCam VC*

White Pine
(800) 241-7463
http://www.cuse eme.com
Product: *CU-SeeME, Enhanced
CU-SeeME for Windows*
Demo available at http://goliath.
wpine.com/cuseeme.htm
(Try also the original at Cornell:
http://cu-seeme.cornell.edu)

Xirlink
San Jose , CA
(408) 324-2100
http://www.xirlink.com
Product: *Visionlink Video Phone*

CH 7: Miscellaneous Resources

E-mail encryption software
PGP
Prety Good Privacy, Inc.
(800) 536-2664
http://www.pgp.com

If you get "junk" E-mail
Respond to the postmaster at the e-mail site by writing to "postmaster @" and the address from which the e-mail was sent.

Surveys about state networking
http://www.tenet.edu/snp/states.html

Search software
SearchWare
P.O. Box 9182
Calabasa, CA 91372-9182
(800) 243-2541

Easynet
Telebase Systems Inc.
134 N. Narberth Ave.
Narberth, PA 19072
(800) 220-9553

CU-seeMe Event Guide on the Internet
http://www-personal.umich.edu/~johnlaue/cuse eme/default.htm

Chapter 8: Internet and the World Wide Web

CH 8: Periodicals

Boardwatch Magazine: Guide to Internet Access and the World Wide Web
8500 W. Bowles Ave., Suite 210
Littleton, CO 80123
(800) 933-6038
http://www.boardwatch.com

Classroom Connect
1866 Colonial Village Lane
PO Box 10488
Lancaster, PA 17605-0488
(800) 638-1639
http://www.classroom.net

Net Guide Directory
Hoover's Inc. (Distributor)
1033 La Posada Dr.
Austin, TX 78752
(800) 486-8666
http://www.hoovers.com

Online-Offline; Themes & Resources
Rock Hill Press
14 Rock Hill Road
Bala Cynwyd, PA 19004
(888) ROCK HILL
http://www.rockhillpress.com

CH 8: Internet Providers

National

America Online
(800) 827-6364

AT&T
(800) 967-5363

Concentric
(800) 939-4262

Compuserve
(800) 848-8199

Earthlink Network Totalaccess
(800) 395-8425

MCI Internet
(800) 550-0927

Microsoft Network
(800) 386-5550

Netcom
(800) 638-2661

Prodigy
(800) 776-3449

PSINet, Inc.
(800) 827-7482

SpryNet
(800) 777-9638

UUNET Technologies
(800) 488-6383

CH 8: Browsers

Internet Explorer
Microsoft
(800) 426-9400
http://www.microsoft.com

Netscape Navigator
Netscape Communications Corp.
(800) 638-7483
http://home.netscape.com

CH 8: Search Engines and Search Utilities

A Business Compass
http://www.abcompass.com

All-in-One
http://www.albany.net/allinone

Alta Vista
http://altavista.digital.com

CyberHound
http://www.thomson.com/cyberhound/

Excite
http://www.excite.com

E-Z Find at the River
http://www.theriver.com/TheRiver/Explore/ezfind.html

Galaxy
http://galaxy.einet.net

Hotbot
http://www.hotbot.com

Infoseek
http://guide.infoseek.com

Internet Sleuth
http://www.isleuth.com/

Lycos
http://www.lycos.com

MetaCrawler
http://www.metacrawler.com

Metasearch
http://metase arch.com

OpenText
http://www.opentext.net/

Search.com
http://www.se arch.com

Webcrawler
http://www.webcrawler.com

Yahoo!
http://www.yahoo.com

CH 8: Internet Special Directories

Argus Clearinghouse
http://www.clearinghouse .net

CyberDewey
http://ivory.lm.com/~mundie/
CyberDewey/CyberDewey.html

Internet Public Library
http://ipl.sils.umich.edu/ref/

Lycos Sites by Subject
http://a2z.lycos.com/index.html

CH 8: Lists of Listservs

List of listservs
http://tile.net/listse rv/

Listservs for librarians
http://www.netstrider.com/library/
listse rvs/

send e-mail to:
listse rv@listse rv.net
In the body of the message, type "list global" This will generate a several-hundred page list. To narrow the search, type a keyword after global: "list global/*insert a keyword*"

CH 8: Publicly Accessible Mailing Lists

http://www.neosoft.com/internet/
paml/bysub.html

CH 8: LM_NET

To subscribe send the following in the body of your e-mail message SUBSCRIBE LM_NET firstname lastname. Send it to: listserv@
listserv.syr.edu

LM_NET archives
Gopher to: ericir.syr.edu   Port 70

Telnet to: ericir.syr.edu
Login: gopher. Then: AskERIC
Education Listservs Archives
LM_NET
Web: gopher://ericir.syr.edu:70/11/
Listservs.LM_NET
http://ericir.syr.edu/lm_net

CH 8: Acceptable Use Policies - Samples on the Internet

Bellingham Public Schools
http://www.bham.wednet.edu/
policies.htm

Critiquing Acceptable Use Policies
http://www.io.com/~kinnaman/
aupessay.html

K-12 Acceptable Use Policies
http://www.erehwon.com/k12aup/

Legal analysis of AUPs
http://www.erehwon.com/k12aup/
legal_analysis.html

Northwestern University facts on AUPs
http://typhoon.covis.nwu.edu:80/
AUP-archive/CoVis_AUP.html

Stafford County Schools
(inc. Web guidelines)
http://pen1.pen.k12.va.us/Anthology/
Div/Stafford/tech/tech.html
(Note, the number one follows the first "pen.")

Virginia
(inc. Web links to other AUPs)
http://www.pen.k12.va.us/go/VDOE/
Technology/AUP/home.shtml

CH 8: Offline Browsers

FlashSite
InContext Systems
(888) 819-2500

HotCargo Express
DocuMagix
San Jose , CA
(800) 362-8624
http://www.documagix.com

Smart Bookmarks
First Floor Inc.
Mountain View, CA
(800) 639-6387
http://www.firstfloor.com

WebBuddy
DataViz, Inc.
55 Corporate Drive
Trumbull, CT 06611
(800) 733-0030
http://www.dataviz.com

Web Retriever
Folio Corp
5072 North 300 West
Provo, UT 84604-5652
(801) 229-6700
http://www.Folio.com

WebClip
PaperClip Software
Three University Plaza, Suite 600
Hackensack, NJ 07601
(800) 929-3503
http://www.paperclip.com

WebEx for Windows 95
Traveling Software
18702 North Creek Parkway
Bothell, WA 98011
(800) 343-8080
http://www.travsoft.com

WebMirror Personal
MobilWare Corp
Plano, TX
(214) 509-8200
http://www.mobileware.com

WebWhacker
ForeFront
1330 Post Oak Blvd., Suite 1300
Houston, TX 77056
(800) 475-5831
http://www.ffg.com

CH 8: Web Ratings

NetShepherd Ratings
http://www.netshepherd.com/

PICS Standard Information from W3
http://www.w3.org/pub/WWW/PICS/

RSACiRatings
http://www.rsac.org/

CH 8: Web Filter Software

Cyber Patrol
Microsystems Software
600 Worcester Road
Framingham, MA 01702
(800) 828-2608
http://www.microsys.com

Cybersitter
Solid Oak Software
P.O. Box 6826
Santa Barbara, CA 93160
(800) 388-2761
http://www.solidoak.com

InterGo with Kinderguard
InterGo Communications
(972) 424-7882
http://www.intergo.com

Net Nanny
Software International Inc.
(800) 340-7177
http://www.netnanny.com

CH 8: Monitoring Software

ZooWorks PE
Hitachi Software
(800) 619-2100

CH 8: Links for Guiding Children Through Cyberspace

Carolyn Caywood
http://www6.pilot.infi.net/~carolyn/guide.html

CH 8: Disconnect Software

Dagar Software Corp.
(800) 687-1966

CH 8: Web Site Authoring Software

Adobe Pagemill
Adobe Systems, Inc
(800) 833-6687
http://www.adobe.com

Corel Web.Designer
Corel Corp.
Ottawa, Ontario, Canada K1Z8R7
(613) 728-8200
http://www.corel.com

Front Page
Microsoft Corp.
Redmond, WA
(800) 426-9400
http://www.microsoft.com

Claris Home Page
Claris Corp
(800) 3-CLARIS
http://www.claris.com

HotDog Professional
Sausage Software
(800) 711-6030
http://www.sausage.com

HoTMetaL Pro
SoftQuad
Toronto, Ontario, Canada
(800) 387-2777
http://www.sq.com

HTML Assistant Pro
Brooklyn North Software Works
(800) 349-1422
http://www.brooknorth.com

School Version of Web Workshop
Sunburst Communications
(800) 321-7511
http://www.nysunburst.com

Web Workshop
Vividus
(888) 4VIVIDUS
http://www.vividus.com

Webmaster
Wentworth Worldwide Media
http://www.wentworth.com

WebPublisher
Asymetrix Corp.
(800) 448-6543

WebWeaver
Miracle Software
http://www.MiracleInc.com

CH 8: Web Sites to Help You Design a Web Site

HTML Reference Page
http://www.oz.net/~dylan/

Java Boutique
http://www.j-g.com/java/

Killer Websites
http:www.killersites.com

Sharon's World
http://www.aceofspace.com/sharonworld/sharon.htm

Web Page Construction
http://www.ism.net/~rvaught/html.html

Yale Web Style Manual
http://info.med.yale.edu/caim/nmanual/

CH 8: Web Server Software

Internet Information Server
Microsoft
(800) 426-9400
http://www.microsoft.com

Netscape Enterprise Server
Netscape
(415) 937-3777
http://www.netscape.com

WebSite Pro
O'Reilly & Associates
(707) 829-0515
http://www.software.ora.com

WebSTAR
Quarterdeck
(800) 525-2580
http://www.starnine.com

CH 8: Web Sites Especially for SLMSs

AASL
http://www.ala.org/aasl

AT&T Toll-Free 800 Directory
http://www.tollfree.att.net:80/index.html

Banned Books Online
http://www.cs.cmu.edu/Web/People/spok/banned-books.html

BookWire Index
http://www.bookwire.com

Brittanica's Lives
http://www.eb.com/lives/cal.htm

Canadian Teacher-Librarian's Resource Page
http://www.inforamp.net/~abrown

Children's Literature Guide
http://www.ucalgary.ca/~dkbrown/index.html

Computer Dictionary Online
http://wombat.doc.ic.ac.uk

Copyright Information
http://web.capco.com/capco/QA Copyright.html
http://fairuse .stanford.edu/

Education Technology WWW Virtual Library
http://tecfa.unige.ch/info-edu-comp.html

Electronic Resources for Youth Services
http://www.ccn.cs.dal.ca/~aa331/childlit.html

Embassy Page
http://www.embpage.org

Encarta Schoolhouse
http://encarta.msn.com/sch

Encyclopedia Mythica
http://www.pantheon.org/myth

Evaluating a Web site
http://www.science.widener.edu/~withers/webeval.htm

Federal Government Information
http://www.fedworld.gov

Galaxy
(Contains directory of school library media centers)
http://galaxy.einet.net/galaxy/Reference/Libraries/School.html

ICONnect Home Page
http://www.ala.org/ICONN/index.html

Internet Public Library
http://ipl.sils.umich.edu

Knowledge Adventure Online
http://www.adventure.com

Librarian's Online Internet Directory
http://www.libsonline.com

Library of Congress
http://www.loc.gov/

My Virtual Reference Desk
http://www.refdesk.com

Publisher's Catalogs Home Page
http://www.lights.com/publisher

School Librarian Links
http://www.yab.com/~cyberian

School Librarian Web Pages
http://wombat.cusd.chico.k12.ca.us/~pmilbury/lib.html

School Librarians on the Web, a Directory
http://www.voicenet.com/~bertland/libs.html#top

School Library Hotspots
http://www.mbnet.mb.ca/~mstimson/text/hotspots.html

U.S. Dept. Of Education Online Library
http://www.ed.gov/Technology

U.S. Postal Zip Code Information
http://www.usps.gov/ncsc/

Virtual Library for Information Technology
http://agora.unige.ch/tecfa/edutech/welcome_frame.html

CH 8: Web Sites for Educators

American School Directory
http://www.cfe.com

AskERIC
http://ericir.syr.edu

Bellingham, Washington staff development
http://www.bham.wednet.edu/literacy.htm

Busy Teachers K-12 Web
http://www.ceismc.gatech.edu/BusyT/

Cap Web, a Guide to the U.S. Congress
http://policy.net/capweb/congress.html

Citation Guide for Internet Sources: History and Humanities
http://www.ume.maine.edu/~polisci/cit-bib.htm

Daily Reviews of Mac and PC Software
http://www.cooltool.com

Education Resource List
http://www.state.wi.us/agencies/dpi/www.ed_lib.html

Educational Internet Resources
http://hub.terc.edu

Educational News Resources
http://www.bc.edu/bc_org/avp/soe/cihe/direct2/Ed.News.html

ERIC Documents Online
http://edrs.com

Federal Communications Commission
http://www.fcc.gov./learnet

GLOBE
http://www.globe.gov

Global SchoolNet Foundation
http://gsn.org

Global Schoolhouse
http://k12.cnidr.org/gsh/gshwelcome.html

HotList of K-12 Internet School Sites
http://rrnet.com/~gleason/k12.html

How to Cite Internet Sources
http://www.cgrg.ohio-state.edu/interface/W96/page.html

Interactive Teacher Online
http://www.interactiveteacher.com

Kathy Schrock's Guide for Educators
http://www.capecod.net/schrockguide/

Mars information
http://cmex-www.arc.nasa.gov/

Media Awareness Network
(Canadian)
http://www.schoolnet.ca/medianet

Mr. Moore's Library and Information Seeking Page
http://www.col.k12.me.us/bjh/203a/BJHS203a.html

Science information: EurekAlert
http://www.eurekalert.org/E-lert/current/mainpage.shtml

SchooolNet
http://k12.school.net/home.html

School Net Navigator
http://school.net/go/go.g_na_us.html

SchoolSites
http://www.schoolsite.com

Teaching with Technology
http://www.wam.umd.edu/~mlhall/teaching.html

Virtual Classroom
http://www.enmu.edu/virtual/virt.html

Web66 - Schools on the Web
http://web66.coled.umn.edu

WebEd Curriculum Links
http://badger.state.wi.us/agencies/dpi/
www/WebEd.html

World Wide Words (how to cite
sources)
http://www.clever.net/se lf/index/htm

CH 8: Online Projects for Kids

Adventure Online
http://www.adventureonline.com

CyberKids
http://www.mtlake.com/mtlake/
CyberKids/CyberKids.html

Cyberspace Middle School
http://www.scri.fsu.edu/~dennis/
CMS.html

Electronic Schoolhouse
http://town.pvt.k12.ca.us/Collabora-
tions/e-school/e-school.html

Global SchoolNet
http://gsn.org

**Intercultural E-Mail Classroom
Connections Projects**
http://www.stolaf.edu/network/iecc

**International Education and
Resource Network**
http://www.iearn.org/iearn

**Internet Scout Report for Students
by Students**
http://wwwscout.cs.wisc.edu/scout/
report/index.html

KIDLINK/KIDPROJ
http://www.kidlink.org/KIDPROJ

KidsConnect
se nd e-mail to:
AskKC@iconnect.syr.edu

**Quest, NASA K-12 Internet Initia-
tive Page**
http://quest.arc.nasa.gov

NASA SpaceLink
http://www.spacelink.msfc.nasa.gov

CH 8: News sites

Free from PointCast
http://www.pointcast.com

Free from *AfterDark*
http://www.berksys.com

C NET
http://www.cnet.com

CNN
http://www.cnn.com

iGuide
http://www.iguide.com

New York Times
http://www.nytimes.com

Point NOW
http://www.point.com.com/now

Time-Warner (Pathfinder)
http://pathfinder.com

CH 8: Internet Conferencing Software

Apple VideoPhoneLite
Apple
(408) 996-1010
http://qtc.quicktime.apple.com

CineVideo/Direct
Cinecom
(703) 680-4733
http://www.cinecom.com

eye2eye
SEMS America
(213) 628-9940
http://www.semsamerica.com

Internet Video Phone
Intel
(503) 696-8080
http://www.intel.com

NetMeeting
Microsoft
(800) 936-5900
http://www.microsoft.com/netmeeting

VideoPhone
Connectix
(800) 950-5880
http://www.connectix.com

CH 8: Internet and Privacy

**Center for Democracy and
Technology**
http://www.cdt.org

Cookie Cutter (software)
http://www.shareware.com (Apple)
http://www.pgp.com (Windows)

Electronic Frontier Foundation
http://www.eff.org

Electronic Privacy Information
http://www.epic.org

TRUSTe
http://www.truste.org

Web Site Anonymizer
http://www.anonymizer.com

CH 8: Internet and Television

WebTV Network
http://www.webtv.net

CH 8: Miscellaneous Sites:

Calafia Consulting
(Guide to the major search engines)
http://se archenginewatch.com/
major.htm

Java
http://java.sun.com

KidsConnect
(answers to kid's questions by school
library media specialists)
send e-mail to:
askKC@iconnect.syr.edu

**McKinsey report on the National
Information Infrastructure including networking costs**
http://www.benton.org/Library/
KickStart/

**Public Library Internet Filters
Resource**
http://sunsite.berkeley.edu/PubLib/
pubref.htm

Review of ISPs
http://www.cnet.com/Content/
Reviews/Compare/ISP/

Spider's Apprentice
(overview of search engines)
http://www.monash.com/spidap.html

Telephony on the Internet
http://www.scholastic.com/EL (click
on Emerging Technologies)

Telephony Consortium
http://rpcp.mit.edu/itel/

**Telephony via. Jack Decker's Audio
and Video**
http://www.novagate.com/~jack/
audiovid.html

Urban legends
http://www.urbanlegends.com/

Chapter 9: Distance Learning: Television and Beyond

CH 9: Periodicals

American Journal of Distance Education
American Center for the Study of
Distance Education
College of Education, Rackley Bldg.
The Pennsylvania State University
University Park, PA 16802

Cabel in the Classroom Magazine
141 Portland St., Suite 7100
Cambridge, MA 02139
(800) 516-2225

CPB Teacher's Digest
with *PBS Teacher Connex*
141 Portland St., Suite 7100
Cambridge, MA 02139
(617) 494-4997
http://www.cpb.org

Distance Educator
Saba & Associates
San Diego, CA
(619) 461-0625
http://www.distance-educator.com

*ED, Education at a Distance
Magazine*
United States Distance Learning
Association
Box 5106
San Ramon, CA 94583
(510) 606-5150
http://www.usdla.org

Education Satlink
2100 I-70 Dr., Southwest
Columbia, MO 65203-4685
(800) 243-3376

ONSAT
Triple D. Publishing
1300 S. Dekalb St.
P.O. Box 2347
Shelby, NC 28152
(704) 482-9673
http://tripled.com

Satellite Orbit
CommTek Publishing
8330 Boone Blvd., Suite 600
Vienna, VA 22180
(800) 234-4220

Satellite TV Week
Fortuna Communications
140 S. Fortuna Blvd.
Fortuna, CA 95540

CH 9: Television Networks and Other Services

Arts & Entertainment Network
c/o Danielle Jackson
P.O. Box 1610
Grand Central Station
New York, NY 10163-1610
(212) 210-9780
http://www.aetv.com

Black Entertainment Television
BET on Learning
1 BET Plaxa
1900 W. Place NE
Washington, DC 20018
(800) 229-2388
http://www.betnetworks.com

C-SPAN in the Classroom
C-SPAN
400 N. Capitol St., NW, Suite 650
Washington, DC 20001
(800) 523-7586 (educators line)
http://www.c-span.org

Cable in the Classroom
1900 North Beauregard St., Suite 108
Alexandria, VA 22311
(703) 845-1400
(800) 743-5355 - educator hotline
http://www.ciconline.com

Cable News Network (CNN)
1 CNN Center
Box 105366
Atlanta, GA 30348-5366
(800) 344-6219
http://www.cnn.com/newsroom
http://www.learning.turner.com

The Discovery Channel
7700 Wisconsin Avenue
Bethesda, MD 20814-3522
(800) 321-1832
http://school.discovery.com

Distance Education Clearinghouse
University of Wisconsin\Madison
http://www.uwex.edu/disted/
home.html
Note: excellent links to distance
learning providers

Distance Learning Listserv
To subscribe send the following
message: SUB DEOS-L
yourfirstname yourlastname
to: listserv@psuvm.psu.edu

**Family & Community Critical
Viewing Project**
1724 Massachusetts Ave., NW
Washington, DC 20036
(202) 775-3629
(800) 452-6351 for free video

Ingenius (Ingenius X*Change)
Formerly Epress Information Services
4 Inverness Court East
Inglewood, CO 80112
(800) 772-6397
users list and archives
http://frit.web.aol.com/mld/produc-
tion/yiad3ld6.htm

KIDSNET
6856 Eastern Ave., NW
Suite 208
Washington, DC 20012
(202) 291-1400

Knowledge TV
9697 E. Mineral Avenue
Englewood, CO 80155
(800) 777-MIND
http://www.jec.edu

The Learning Channel
7700 Wisconsin Avenue
Bethesda, MD 20814-3522
(800) 321-1832
http://school.discovery.com

Public Broadcasting Service
PBS Elementary/Secondary
Service
1320 Braddock Place
Alexandria, VA 22314
(703) 739-5402
http://www.pbs.org
http://www.pbs.org/tconnex (teacher's connection)

The Weather Channel (TWC)
Educational Services
300 Interstate North
Atlanta, GA 30339
(800) 471-5544
http://www.weather.com/weather

CH 9: Distance Learning Networks

Access Wisconsin
2801 International Lane, Suite 200
Madison, WI 53704
(800) 800-4818
http://www.info@accesswis.com

AETN (Arkansas Educational Telecomunications Network)
(800) 662-2386
(Http://www.aetn.org/

Central Education Telecommunications Network (CETN)
2100 Crystal Drive
One Crystal Park, Suite 1100
Arlington, VA 22202
(703) 979-8686

CCET - University of Alabama
P.O. Box 870167
Tuscaloosa, AL 35487-0167
(800) 477-8151

Distance Learning Associates
190 West Washington Ave.
Pearl River, NY
(800) 786-6614

Educational Communication Center
Bob Dole Hall
Kansas State University
Manhattan, KS 66506
(800) 533-6036
http://www.ksu.edu/ecc/

Educational Satellite Network (Missouri)
Star Schools Clearinghouse
2100 I-79 Drive, Southwest
Columbia, Missouri 65203
(800) 243-3376

Fairfax (VA) County Public Schools
Educational Programs
Chapel Square Media Center
4414 Holborn Ave.,
Annandale, VA 22003
(800) 233-3277

IDEANET
2121 5th Ave.
Seattle, WA
(800) 440-4332

Iowa Educational Telecommunications Network
Iowa Public Television
P.O. Box 6450
Johnston, Iowa 50131
(515) 242-3100

Kentucky Network
600 Cooper Dr.
Kexington, KY 40502
(606) 258-7260

Massachusetts Corp. for Educational Television
One Kendall Square, Bldg 1500
Cambridge, MA 02139-1562
(617) 252-5700 se t. 717

Michigan Information Technology Network
(516) 336-1321

National School Network Exchange
http://nsn.bbn.com
service: Net Pals, a student mentoring project

Oregon ED-NET
7140 SW Macadam Ave., Suite 260
Portland, OR 97216
(503) 293-1992

Prince William Network
Box 389
Manassas, VA 22110
(800) 609-2680

Satellite Education Resources
Consortium
P.O. Box 50008
Columbia, SC 29250
(800) 476-5001
http://www.scsn.net/~serc

Satellite Telecommunications Educational Programming
East 4022 Broadway
Spokane, WA 99202
(509) 536-2150

TEAMS Distance Learning
9300 Imperial Highway
Downey, CA 90242-2890
(310) 639-7797
http://teams.lacoe.edu

Texas Education Telecommunications Network (TETN)
Texas Education Agency
Division of Instructional Technology
(512) 463-9401
http://www.tea.state.tx.us/technology/tetn/index.html

United Star Distance Learning Consortium
Star Schools Project
Education Service Center, Region 20
1314 Hines Ave.
San Antonio, TX 78208-1899

Virginia Satellite Education Network
P.O. Box 2120
Richmond, VA 23218-2120
(800) 544-7120

CH 9: Miscellaneous Tips and Hints

For help with VCR problems:
http://bradley.bradley.edu/~fil/vcr.html

Distance Education at a Glance Internet Site
http://www.uidaho.edu/evo/distglan.html

Distance Learning Demonstration Projects
http://www.visc.vt.edu/succeed/distance.html

Distance Learning Clearinghouse
http://www.uwex.edu/disted/home.html

Chapter 10: Video and Computers

CH 10: Periodicals

Camcorder & Computer Video
4800 Market St
Ventura, CA 93003-7783
(805) 644-3824

DV: Digital Video
411 Borel Ave., Suite 100
San Mateo, CA 94401
(888) 776-7002
http://www.dv.com

InterActivity:Tools + Techniques for Interactive Media Developers
411 Borel Ave., Suite 100
San Mateo, CA 94402
(415) 358-9500
http://www.eyemedia.com

PC Presentations
417 Bridgeport Ave.
Milford, CT 06460-4105
(203) 877-1927
http://www.cadavision.com/nolimits/pcpp.html

Video Toaster User
Miller Freeman, Inc.
600 Harrison St.
San Francisco, CA 94107
(800) 274-2430

Videomaker
Videomaker, Inc.
920 Main St.
P.O. Box 4591
Chio, CA 95927
(800) 284-3226
http://www.videomaker.com

CH 10: Digital Cameras

Agfa ePhoto 307
Agfa
(201) 440-2500
htto://www.agfahome.com

Apple QuickTake
Apple Computer
1 Infinite Loop
Cupertino, CA 95014
(800) 776-2333
http://www.info.apple.com/qtake

Canon PowerShot 600
Canon Computer
(800) 848-4123
http://www.ccsi.canon.com
http://www.usa.canon.com

Casio QV-10 and **Casio CV-30**
Casio
570 Mt. Pleasant Ave.
P.O. Box 7000
Dover, NJ 07801
(201) 361-5400
http://www.casio~usa.com

Chinon ES-3000 and **Chinon ES-1000**
Chinon America
615 Hawaii Ave.
Torrance, CA 90503
(800) 932-0374

Dycam CD-10
Dycam, Inc.
9414 Eton Ave.
Chatsworth, CA 91311
(800) 883-9226
http://www.dycam.com

Epson
(800) 463-7766
http://www.epson.com

Fuji DS-7
Fuji
(800) 378-3854
http://www.fujifilm.com

Kodak DC40 and **Kodak CD-50**
Eastman Kodak
343 State St.
Rochester, NY 14650-1139
(800) 235-6325
http://www.kodak.com

Minolta
(800) 825-4000
http://www.minolta.com

Nikon
(800) 526-4566
http://www.nikonusa.com

Olympus D-200L
Olympus
(800) 622-6372
http://www.olympusamerica.com

Polaroid PDC-2000/40
Polaroid
(800) 816-2611
http://www.polaroid.com

Ricoh RDC-2
Ricoh
(800) 225-1899
http://www.ricoh.com

Sony
(800) 352-7669
http://www.sony.com

CH 10: Internet Sites for Images (check copyright!)

http://www.mccannas.com

http://www.uky.edu/Artsourse / artsource-home.html

http://www.bizcafe.com/freegrfx.html

CH 10: Digital Camcorders

Hitachi America
(800) 241-6588
http://www.hitachi.com

JVC
41 Slater Dr.
Elmwood Park, NJ 07407
(800) 582-5825
http://www.jvc.ca/jvc

Panasonic
Matsushita Corp.
One Panasonic Way
Seacaucus, NJ 07094
(800) 524-0864
http://www.panasonic.com

Sony
One Sony Dr.
Park Ridge, NJ 07656
(201) 930-1000
http://www.sony.com

CH 10: Real-time Nonlinear Video Editing Systems

Avid
(800) 949-2843
http://www.avid.com
Product: MCXpress

NewTek
(800) 862-7837
http://www.newtek.com
Product: Video Toaster Flyer

Panasonic
(800) 528-8601
http://www.panasonic.com
Product: PostBox 2.0

CH 10: Video Editing, Composing, Processing Software

Digital Video Producer
Asymetrix
110 110th Ave., NE
Bellevue, WA 98004
(800) 448-6543
http://www.asymetrix.com

Director
Macromedia
600 Townsend St.
San Francisco, CA 94103
(800) 326-2128
http://www.macromedia.com

Lumiere
Corel
1600 Carling Ave.
Ottawa, Ontario K1Z 8R7 Canada
(800) 772-6735
http://www.corel.com

Media Studio Pro
Ulead Systems
970 West 190th St., Suite 520
Torrance, CA 90502
(800) 858-5323
http://www.ulead.com

Premiere
Adobe Systems, Inc.
1585 Charleston Rd.
Mountain View, CA 94039
(800) 642-3623
http://www.adobe.com

Razor Professional
In:Sync Corp.
6106 MacArthur Blvd.
Bethesda, MD 20816
(800) 864-7272
http://in-sync.com

Video Action Pro
Star Media
1163 East Ogden Ave., Suite 705-364
Naperville, IL 60563
(800) 775-3314
http://www.videoaction.com

VideoShop
Strata
2 W. St. George Blvd., Suite 2100
St. George, UT 84770
(800) 678-7282
http://www.strata3d.com

CH 10: Sources of Other Products Mentioned in the Chapter

Cinepak
Radius
(800) 966-7360
http://www.radius.com

ComputerEyes
Digital Vision Inc.
270 Bridge St.
Dedham, MA 02026
(617) 329-5400

Corel Photo-Paint
Corel Corp.
(800) 772-6735

Indeo Video Capture Board
Intel
http://www.intel.com/imaging

Logitech
6505 Kaiser Dr.
Fremont, CA 94555
(800) 231-7717
http://www.logitech.com

PhotoEnhancer
Picture Works Technology
(800) 303-5400

PhotoMotion
IBM Multimedia Division
4111 Northside Parkway
Atlanta, GA 30327
(404) 238-3139

Photoshop and *Photoshop Delux*
Adobe, Inc.
(800) 833-6687

Picture Publisher (and *PhotoMagic*)
Micrografx
(800) 676-3110

Producer
Passport Designs
100 Stone Pine Rd.
Half Moon Bay, CA 94019
(415) 349-8090

*QuickTime and QuickTime
Media Layer*
QuickTime Starter Kit
Apple Computer Inc.
20525 Mariani Ave.
Cupertino, CA 95014
(408) 996-1010
download a copy to QuickTime VR
for Windows from:
http://qtvr.quicktime.apple.com

Reed Magic
Sigma Designs
(510) 770-0100

Slide Shop
Scholastic Software
2931 E. McCarty Street
P.O. Box 7502
Jefferson City, MO 65102

Snappy, Video Shapshot
Play, Inc.
2890 Kilgore Rd.
Rancho Cordova, CA 95670-6132
(800) 306.PLAY
http://www.play.com

VCR Companion
Broderbund Software
500 Redwood Blvd.
Novato, CA 94928-6121
(800) 521-6263
http://www.broderbund.com

Video for Windows
Microsoft Corp.
Redmond, Washington
(800) 426-9400

Video-fusion
VideoFusion Ltd.
1722 Indian Wood Circle, Suite H
Maumee, OH 43537
(419) 891-1090

VideoShop
Avid Technology
222 Third St.
Suite 1320
Cambridge, MA 02142

VideoSpigot for Windows
Creative Labs
1902 McCarthy Blvd
Miltpitas, CA 92035
(408) 428-6600

CH 10: Miscellaneous Video Resources

Indeo Video Codec information from Intel
http://www.intel.com/pc-supp/multimed/indeo

Shareware and freeware including 3-D tools
http://www.sgi.com/Fun/fun.html

Sample 3-D with VRML and Java
http://www.construct.net

According to *Multimedia World* it's "the center of the universe for VRML"
http://rose bud.sdsc.edu.vrml

Chapter 11: Multimedia Presentation Systems and Hypermedia

CH 11: Associations

International Interactive Communications Society (IICS)
10160 SW Nimbus Ave., Suite F2
Portland, OR 97223
(503) 620-3604

Interactive Multimedia Association (IMA)
48 Maryland Ave., Suite 202
Annapolis, MD 21401
(410) 626-1380

Multimedia PC Marketing Council (MPC)
Subsidiary of the Software Publishers Association
1730 M NW Suite 700
Washington, DC 20036
(202) 452-1600

CH 11: Periodicals

HyperNEXUS: Journal of Hypermedia and Multimedia Studies
Special Interest Group for Computer Science
2801 W. Bancroft SM344
Toldeo, OH 43606

Journal of Artificial Intelligence in Education
Advancement of Computing in Education
P.O. Box 72
Leetsdale, PA 15056-0072

Journal of Educational Multimedia and Hypermedia
Advancement of Computing in Education
Box 2966
Charlottesville, VA 22902-2966
(804) 973-3987
http://www/aace.org

Multimedia Monitor
Future Systems, Inc.
P.O. Box 26
Falls Church, VA 22040-0026
800) 323-3472

Multimedia World
501 Second Street
San Francisco, CA 94107
(415) 281-8650
http://www.mmworld.com

NewMedia
HyperMedia Communications
901 Mariner's Island Blvd.
Suite 365
San Mateo, CA 94404
(415) 573-5170
Note: Has annual multimedia tool guide issue

CH 11: Sources of Presentation Software and Related Programs

ASAP WordPower
Software Publishing Corp.
Santa Clara, CA
(408) 986-8000
http://www.spco.com

Astound
Astound, Inc.
Santa Clara, CA
(408) 982-0298
http://www.goldisk.com

Corel Presentations
Corel Corp
Ottawa, Ontario, Canada
(613) 728-8200
http://www.corel.com

Digital Chisel
Pierian Spring
5200 S.W. Macadam Ave., Suite 570
Portland, OR 97201
(800) 856-8350
http://www.perian.com

Director 5
Macromedia, Inc.
San Francisco, CA
(415) 626-2000
ttp://www.macromedia.com

Express Presenter
Spinnaker Software Corp.
201 Broadway
Cambridge, MA 02139
(800) 826-0706

Freelance Graphics for Windows
Lotus Development Corp.
Cambridge, MA
(617) 577-8500
http://www.lotus.com

Harvard Graphics for Windows
Software Publishing Corp.
Santa Clara, CA
(408) 986-8000
http://www.spco.com

HyperCard
Claris Corporation
5201 Patrick Henry Drive
Box 58168
Santa Clara, CA 95052
(800) 544-8554

HyperStudio
Roger Wagner Publishers
1050 Pioneer Way
El Cajon, CA 92020
(800) 497-3778
http://www.hyperstudio.com

Incredible Toon Machine
Sierra On-Line Inc.
(800) 757-7707

Kidpix/KidPix Companion
Broderbund Corp
Box 6121 500 Redwood Blvd.
Novato, CA 94948-6125
(800) 521-6263

Kid's Studio
Storm Software
(800) 787-2983

LinkWay/LinkWay Live!
EduQuest
P.O. Box 2150
Atlanta, GA 30055
(800) 426-9402

Mammals: A Multimedia Encyclopedia
National Geographic Society
(800) 342-4460

Morph
Gryphon Software Corp.
(800) 795-0981

Multimedia Assessment Tool
Touch Media
1555 Palm Beach Lakes Blvd.
West Palm Beach, FL 33401
(800) 482-8682

Multimedia ToolBook
Asymetrix Corp.
110 110th Ave. N.E., Suite 717
Bellevue, WA 98004
(800) 448-6543
http://www.asymetrix.com

Multimedia Workshop
Davidson & Associates
(800) 545-7677

Nickelodeon Director's Lab
Viacom New Media
(212) 258-6000

Persuasion
Adobe Systems, Inc.
Mountain View, CA
(800) 833-6687
http://www.adobe.com

Plus
Spinnaker Software Corp.
201 Broadway
Cambridge, MA 02139
(800) 826-0706

PowerPoint
Microsoft Corp.
One Microsoft Way
Redmond, WA 98052
(800) 426-9400
http://www.microsoft.com

Tutor Tech
Techware Corp.
P.O. Box 151085
Altamonte Springs, FL 32715-1085
(800) 34-REAse

Video Jam
Electronic Arts Kids
(800) 245-4525

WordPerfect Presentations
Corel
(800) 222-2808
http://wordperfect.com

CH 11: Performing Rights Permissions for Music

ASCAP (Association of Composers, Authors, and Publishers)
7920 Sunset Blvd., Suite 300
Los Angeles, CA 90046
(213) 883-1000 (LA)
(212) 595-3050 (NY)

BMI (Broadcast Music Inc.)
8730 Sunset Blvd., 3rd Floor
Los Angeles, CA 90069
(310) 659-9109 (LA)
(212) 586-2000 (NY)

CH 11: Miscellaneous Multimedia Resources

Online samples of stock media for productions:
http://www.eyemedia.com

Chapter 12: Technology Staff Development for Teachers

CH 12: Periodicals

The Journal of Staff Development
National Staff Development Council
P.O. Box 240
Oxford, OH 45056
(513) 523-6029

CH 12: Associations

AASL/ICONnect
http://www.ala.org/ICONN/
index.html

ASCD
Association for Supervision and Curriculum Development
Alexandria, VA
(800) 933-ASCD
http://www.ascd.org

ISTE
http://www.iste.org

LITA (Library and Information Technology Association)
http://www.lita.org/

CH 12: Staff Development Sources on the Internet

Apple Education Staff Development
http://ed.info.apple.com/education/
staff

BCK2SKOL
http://web.scd.sc.edu/bck2skol/
bck2skol.html

Eisenhower National Clearinghouse
http://www.enc.org

ICONnect Home Page
http://www.ala.org/ICONN/
index.html

Intel Teacher Literacy
http://www.intel.com/intel/educate/

ISTE (International Society for Technology in Education)
http://www.iste.org/standards/
found.htm

Roadmap96 Archives
http://www.gnofn.org/whs1/educa-tion/teacher/rdmap96/remap96.html

Winona Middle School
http:/wms.luminet.net

Appendix A
Searching ERIC

Basic Tips for Searching the ERIC Database

Wherever you choose to run a computer search of the ERIC database, the result of the search will be an annotated bibliography of journal (EJ) and document (ED) literature on your topic. There are a few important tips to keep in mind to ensure that your search meets your needs.

Find the best way to access the ERIC *database*

You can now use ERIC from your personal computer, at university libraries, at many public and professional libraries, and through contacting the ERIC Clearinghouses. Before you decide where to search ERIC, ask these questions:

1. How much will it cost? You may have free or inexpensive access to ERIC. If not, you may have to pay for connect time on some computer systems or order a search through a search service.

2. How much of the ERIC database is available? Some services provide access to the entire ERIC database, which goes back to 1966; others may allow you to search only the last 5 or 10 years of ERIC. If this is important to you, find out how much of ERIC is available before choosing a search system.

3. How long will it take? Turnaround time can vary from a few minutes, if you have direct access to ERIC on a personal computer, to several days or longer if you have to order a search that someone else will run for you.

4. How much flexibility does the search system offer? Many different software systems are used to search ERIC. Some menu-driven search systems make it easy for a first-time user, but may limit opportunities to make changes to the search question. If you try searching ERIC and feel you cannot locate exactly what you are looking for, ask your librarian for help or call an ERIC Clearinghouse.

Use the Thesaurus of ERIC Descriptors

Every one of the more than 850,000 articles and documents in the ERIC database has been given subject indexing terms called *descriptors*. Before you run an ERIC search, it is important to take a few minutes to find the ERIC descriptors that best capture your topic.

For example, articles and documents about the development of children's social skills would be indexed under the descriptor *interpersonal competence*. The ERIC descriptor for children at risk is *at risk persons*. When you search for information about high school students, you can use the descriptor *high school students* but would miss a lot of material if you did not also use the descriptor *secondary education*.

Locations that offer ERIC searches should have reference copies of the *Thesaurus of ERIC Descriptors*, and some search systems allow access to the Thesaurus while running your search.

If you cannot locate a copy of the *Thesaurus of ERIC Descriptors*, call the ERIC Clearinghouse that covers your subject and ask for help with the search strategy.

Know your ANDs and ORs

Although the software used to search ERIC will depend on which system is used, all searching is based on Boolean logic: the computer creates sets of information based on the way you tell it to combine subject terms.

For example, to find out how computer networks and e-mail can be used to improve high school students' writing, you could use the Thesaurus to find these subject descriptors: *computer networks, high school students*, and *writing skills*.

If you want to find records that are indexed under all of these concepts, you would use the AND command to tell the computer to find the intersection of these three subsets.

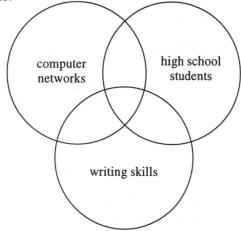

If more information on this topic is needed, use the Thesaurus to locate additional relevant descriptors and add them to your concept sets by using the OR operator. When the OR command is used, documents and articles indexed with either descriptor are searched and combined in a set.

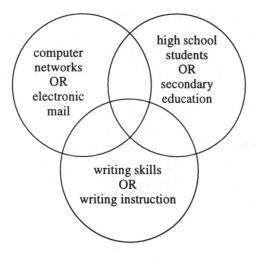

Plan Your Search Strategy

To plan your ERIC search, follow these steps:

1. Write the topic in your own words;

2. Divide the search into major concepts; and

3. Use the *Thesaurus of ERIC Descriptors* to locate the subject descriptors for each concept of the topic.

Here's an example of how a search topic/question can be turned into an ERIC search strategy:

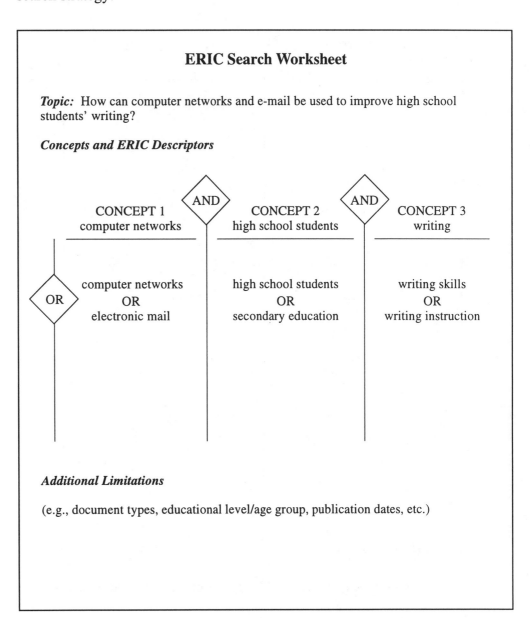

ERIC Search Worksheet

Topic: How can computer networks and e-mail be used to improve high school students' writing?

Concepts and ERIC Descriptors

| CONCEPT 1 | AND | CONCEPT 2 | AND | CONCEPT 3 |
| computer networks | | high school students | | writing |

computer networks
OR
electronic mail

high school students
OR
secondary education

writing skills
OR
writing instruction

Additional Limitations

(e.g., document types, educational level/age group, publication dates, etc.)

You can use the blank ERIC Search Worksheet on page 378 to plan your ERIC search.

ERIC Search Worksheet

Topic

Concepts and ERIC Descriptors

CONCEPT 1   AND   CONCEPT 2   AND   CONCEPT 3

OR

Additional Limitations

(e.g., document types, educational level/age group, publication dates, etc.)

Vendors of ERICOnline Services and CD-ROM Products

Online Vendors

Data-Star/Dialog
Plaza Suite
114 Jermyn Street
London SW1Y 6HJ
Telephone: +44 71 930 7646
Fax: +44 71 930 2581

Knight-Ridder Information, Inc.
2440 El Camino Road
Mountain View, CA 94040
Toll Free: 800-334-2564
Telephone: 415-254-7000
Fax: 415-254-8123

OCLC
(Online Computer Library Center)
6565 Frantz Road
Dublin, OH 43017-0702
Toll Free: 800-848-5878
Telephone: 614-764-6000
Fax: 614-764-6096

Ovid Technologies
333 Seventh Avenue, Fourth floor
New York, NY 10001
Toll Free: 800-950-2035
Telephone: 212-563-3006
Fax: 212-563-3784

CD-ROM Vendors

EBSCO Publishers
83 Pine Street
P.O. Box 2250
Peabody, MA 01960-7250
Toll Free: 800-653-2726
Telephone: 508-535-8500
Fax: 508-535-8523

ERIC Processing and Reference
Facility
1301 Piccard Drive, Suite 300
Rockville, MD 20850-4305
Toll Free: 800-799-3742
Telephone: 301-258-5500
Fax: 301-948-3695

Kline Publishing, Inc. (KPI)
635 Zaqueros Avenue
Sunnyvale, CA 94086
Telephone: 408-720-8321
Fax: 408-522-9806

Knight-Ridder Information, Inc.
(Address at left)

National Information Services
Corporation (NISC)
Wyman Towers, Suite 6
3100 St. Paul Street
Baltimore, MD 21218
Telephone: 410-243-0797
Fax: 410-243-0982

Oryx Press
4041 North Central Avenue, Suite 700
Phoenix, AZ 85012-3397
Toll Free: 800-279-ORYX (6799)
Telephone: 602-265-2651
Fax: 800-279-4663; 602-265-6250

SilverPlatter Information, Inc.
100 River Ridge Drive
Norwood, MA 02062-5026
Toll Free: 800-343-0064
Telephone: 617-769-2599
Fax: 617-769-8763

ERIC: Tips for Teachers

If you're a teacher, you owe it to yourself and your students to learn about ERIC. ERIC is a personable acronym for the Educational Resources Information System, the largest education database in the world. Today's ERIC database continues to be your best source for searching the education literature, but the new ERIC has much more!

The ERIC Database

At the heart of ERIC is the largest education database in the world—containing more than 900,000 records of journal articles, research reports, curriculum and teaching guides, conference papers, and books. Each year, approximately 30,000 new records are added. Whether your interests include the latest teaching methods, curriculum, or research, start by searching ERIC.

ERIC Now Offers You:

- toll-free numbers that put you in touch with subject-specific clearinghouses
- more than 1,800 two-page, research synthesis publications: in print and electronic formats
- a 48-hour turnaround, electronic question-answering service
- access from your personal computer to the database and ERIC-sponsored Gopher and World Wide Web (WWW) sites
- hundreds of lesson plans you can access and download to your computer
- document ordering via fax or toll-free phone call

You can probably search the ERIC database at your university library. If you have a computer with a modem, you may be able to access ERIC on your library's online system or on the Internet.

If you need help locating the best way for you to access ERIC, call ACCESS ERIC Monday-Friday at 1-800-LET-ERIC.

ERIC on the Internet

If you have a computer with a modem, and have Internet e-mail, gopher, or WWW access, you can tap into a vast array of ERIC information. For questions about education, child development and care, parenting, learning, teaching, information technology, and other related topics, e-mail askeric@ericir.syr.edu.

More than a dozen ERIC Components host gopher and WWW sites. For general information about ERIC and links to all ERIC Internet sites, start with the systemwide sites: gopher: aspensys.aspensys.com:74/11/eric or URL: http://www.aspensys.com/eric2/welcome.html.

You can also use the Internet to connect to sites that offer free public access to the ERIC database. For a list of public Internet access points to the ERIC database and step-by-step login instructions, e-mail ericdb@aspensys.com.

ERIC on Commercial Services

Commercial networks such as America Online and CompuServe feature ERIC information including Digests, Parent Brochures, articles from *The ERIC Review*, bibliographies, and more. For help finding ERIC on these networks, contact ACCESS ERIC at 1-800-LET ERIC.

ERIC on CD-ROM

If your computer has a CD-ROM drive and you have frequent need for searches of the education literature, a subscription to the ERIC database is now available for as little as $100 per year. For information, call the ERIC Processing and Reference Facility at 1-800-799-ERIC.

ERIC Digests online

ERIC is your source when you need a brief overview of the latest research on topics like:

- inclusion of students with disabilities in regular classrooms
- increasing the school involvement of Hispanic parents
- authentic writing assessment
- trends in K-12 social studies

These and more than 1,800 other topics are available as ERIC Digests, and new titles are produced each year. Digests are often in question-answer format and always include a list of additional resources for more information.

You can search and locate the complete text of ERIC Digests on the CD-ROM versions of the ERIC database (available at hundreds of university libraries) and on the Internet. You can also contact the ERIC Clearinghouse that covers your topic and ask for its latest Digest list.

Don't Forget ERIC When You Get to the Classroom

A large percentage of the information requests to ERIC last year came from classroom teachers. Every week close to 500 teachers send questions to AskERIC's e-mail address. Electronic networks for teachers in Texas, New York, Massachusetts, Washington, Florida, Missouri, and other states feature ERIC on their menu systems, as do a number of regional and school district networks. If you're on a network, ERIC is likely to be there now or soon.

Give ERIC a Call!

Toll-free phone numbers put you within easy reach of ERIC information specialists. Staff provide ERIC publications, answer questions about ERIC, help you locate hard-to-find documents, and refer you to other information sources. It is best to call an ERIC Clearinghouse if you have a subject-specific question.

For information about ERIC, call:

ACCESS ERIC for general ERIC information............................ 800-LET-ERIC

EDRS to order an ERIC document.. 800-443-ERIC

ERIC Processing and Reference Facility...................................... 800-799-ERIC
    to purchase the ERIC Database or ask
    technical questions:

Call the ERIC Clearinghouse with your subject-specific education questions:

Adult, Career, and Vocational Education......................................800-848-4815

Assessment and Evaluation 800-464-3742

Community Colleges 800-832-8256

Counseling and Student Services 800-414-9769

Disabilities and Gifted Education 800-328-0272

Educational Management 800-438-8841

Elementary and Early Childhood Education 800-583-4135

Higher Education 800-773-3742

Information & Technology 800-464-9107

Language and Linguistics 800-276-9834

Reading, English, and Communication 800-759-4723

Rural Education and Small Schools 800-624-9120

Science, Mathematics, and Environmental Education 800-276-0462

Social Studies/Social Science Education.....................................800-266-3815

Teaching and Teacher Education 800-822-9229

Urban Education 800-601-4868

Adjunct ERIC Clearinghouses

Art Education...800-266-3815

Chapter 1 (Compensatory Education) 800-456-2380

Child Care 800-616-2242

Clinical Schools 800-822-9229

Consumer Education...800-336-6423

ESL Literacy Education..202-429-9292, x200

Law-Related Education 800-266-3815

Test Collection 609-734-5737

U.S.-Japan Studies 800-266-3815

ERIC: Tips for Teachers from *All About ERIC* was written by Lynn Smarte, Project Director, ACCESS ERIC, 1600 Research Boulevard, Rockville, Maryland, 1-800-LET-ERIC. The text is in the public domain.

Appendix B
Fair Use Guidelines for Educational Multimedia*

Table of Contents

1. Introduction

1.1 Preamble

Fair use is a legal principle that provides certain limitations on the exclusive rights** of copyright holders. The purpose of these guidelines is to provide guidance on the application of fair use principles by educators, scholars, and students who develop multimedia projects using portions of copyrighted works under fair use rather than by seeking authorization for noncommercial educational uses. These guidelines apply only to fair use in the context of copyright and to no other rights.

There is no simple test to determine what is fair use. Section 107 of the Copyright Act*** sets forth the four fair use factors which should be considered in each instance, based on the particular facts of a given case, to determine whether a use is a "fair use": (1) the purpose and character of use, including whether such use is of a commercial nature or is for nonprofit educational purposes, (2) the nature of the copyrighted work, (3) the amount and substantiality of the portion used in relation to the copyrighted work as a whole, and (4) the effect of the use upon the potential market for or value of the copyrighted work.

While only the courts can authoritatively determine whether a particular use is fair use, these guidelines represent the participants'**** consensus of conditions under which fair use should generally apply and examples of when permission is required. Uses that exceed these guidelines may or may not be fair use. The participants also agree that the more one exceeds these guidelines, the greater the risk that fair use does not apply.

---

*These Guidelines shall not be read to supersede other preexisting education fair use guidelines that deal with the Copyright Act of 1976.
**See Section 106 of the Copyright Act.
***Copyright Act of 1976, as amended, is codified at 17 U.S.C. Sec. 101 et seq.
****The names of the various organizations participating in this dialog appear at the end of these guidelines and clearly indicate the variety of interest groups involved, both from the standpoint of the users of copyrighted material and also from the standpoint of copyright owners.

The limitations and conditions set forth in these guidelines do not apply to works in the public domain — such as U.S. Government works or works on which copyright has expired for which there are no copyright restrictions — or to works for which the individual or institution has obtained permission for the particular use. Also, license agreements may govern the uses of some works and users should refer to the applicable license terms for guidance.

The participants who developed these guidelines met for an extended period of time, and the result represents their collective understanding in this complex area. Because digital technology is in a dynamic phase, there may come a time when it is necessary to review the guidelines. Nothing in these guidelines shall be construed to apply to the fair use privilege in any context outside of educational and scholarly uses of educational multimedia programs.

This Preamble is an integral part of these guidelines and should be included whenever the guidelines are reprinted or adopted by organizations and educational institutions. Users are encouraged to reproduce and distribute these guidelines freely without permission; no copyright protection of these guidelines is claimed by any person or entity.

1.2 Background

These guidelines clarify the application of fair use of copyrighted works as teaching methods are adapted to new learning environments. Educators have traditionally brought copyrighted books, videos, slides, sound recordings and other media into the classroom, along with accompanying projection and playback equipment. Multimedia creators integrated these individual instructional resources with their own original works in a meaningful way, providing compact educational tools that allow great flexibility in teaching and learning. Material is stored so that it may be retrieved in a nonlinear fashion, depending on the needs or interests of learners. Educators can use multimedia projects to respond spontaneously to students' questions by referring quickly to relevant portions. In addition, students can use multimedia projects to pursue independent study according to their needs or at a pace appropriate to their capabilities. Educators and students want guidance about the application of fair use principles when creating their own multimedia projects to meet specific instructional objectives.

1.3 Applicability of These Guidelines

(Certain basic terms used throughout these guidelines are identified in bold and defined in this section)

These guidelines apply to the use, without permission, of portions of lawfully acquired copyrighted works in educational multimedia projects which are created by educators or students as part of a systematic learning activity by nonprofit educational institutions. **Educational multimedia projects** created under these guidelines incorporate students' or educators' original material, such as course notes or commentary, together with various copyrighted media formats including, but not limited to, motion media, music, text material, graphics, illustrations, photographs and digital software which are combined into an integrated presentation. **Educational institutions** are defined as nonprofit organizations whose primary focus is supporting research and instructional activities of educators and students for noncommercial purposes.

For the purposes of these guidelines, **educators** include faculty, teachers, instructors and others who engage in scholarly, research and instructional activities for educational institutions. The copyrighted works used under these guidelines are **lawfully acquired** if obtained by the institution or individual through lawful means such as purchase, gift or license agreement but not pirated copies. Educational multimedia projects which incorporate portions of copyrighted works under these guidelines may be used only for **educational purposes** in systematic learning activities including use in connection with non-commercial curriculum-based learning and teaching activities by educators to students enrolled in courses at nonprofit educational institutions or otherwise permitted under Section 3. While these guidelines refer to the creation and use of educational multimedia projects, readers are advised that in some circumstances other fair use guidelines such as those for off-air taping may be relevant.

2. Preparation of Educational Multimedia Projects Using Portions of Copyrighted Works

These uses are subject to the Portion Limitations listed in Section 4. They should include proper attribution and citation as defined in Section 6.2.

2.1 By Students
Students may incorporate portions of lawfully acquired copyrighted works when producing their own educational multimedia projects for a specific course.

2.2 By Educators for Curriculum-Based Instruction
Educators may incorporate portions of lawfully acquired copyrighted works when producing their own educational multimedia projects for their own teaching tools in support of curriculum-based instructional activities at educational institutions.

3. Permitted Uses of Educational Media Projects Created Under These Guidelines

Uses of educational multimedia projects created under these guidelines are subject to the Time, Portion, Copying and Distribution Limitations listed in Section 4.

3.1 Student Use
Students may perform and display their own educational multimedia projects created under Section 2 of these guidelines for educational uses in the course for which they were created and may use them in their own portfolios as examples of their academic work for later personal uses such as job and graduate school interviews.

3.2 Educator Use for Curriculum-Based Instruction:

Educators may perform and display their own educational multimedia projects created under Section 2 for curriculum-based instruction to students in the following situations:

3.2.1 for face-to-face instruction.

3.2.2 assigned to students for directed self study.

3.2.3 for remote instruction to students enrolled in curriculum-based courses and located at remote sites, provided over the educational institution's secure electronic network in real-time, or for after class review or directed self-study, provided there are technological limitations on access to the network and educational multimedia project (such as a password or PIN) and provided further that the technology prevents the making of copies of copyrighted material.

If the educational institution's network or technology used to access the educational multimedia project created under Section 2 of these guidelines cannot prevent duplication of copyrighted material, students or educators may use the multimedia educational projects over an otherwise secure network for a period of only 15 days after its initial real-time remote use in the course of instruction or 15 days after its assignment for directed self-study. After that period, one of the two use copies of the educational multimedia project may be placed on reserve in a learning resource center, library or similar facility for on-site use by students enrolled in the course. Students shall be advised that they are not permitted to make their own copies of the educational multimedia project.

3.3 Educator Use for Peer Conferences

Educators may perform or display their own educational multimedia projects created under Section 2 of these guidelines in presentations to their peers, for example, at workshops and conferences.

3.4 Educator Use for Professional Portfolio

Educators may retain educational multimedia projects created under Section 2 of these guidelines in their personal portfolios for later personal uses such as tenure review or job interviews.

4. Limitations – Time, Portion, Copying and Distribution

The preparation of educational multimedia projects incorporating copyrighted works under Section 2, and the use of such projects under Section 3, are subject to the limitations noted below.

4.1 Time Limitations

Educators may use their educational multimedia projects created for educational purposes under Section 2 of these guidelines for teaching courses, for a period of up to two years after the first instructional use with a class. Use beyond that time period, even for educational purposes, requires permission for each copyrighted portion incorporated in the production. Students may use their educational multimedia projects as noted in Section 3.1.

4.2 Portion Limitations

Portion limitations mean the amount of a copyrighted work can reasonably be used in educational multimedia projects under these guidelines regardless of the original medium from which the copyrighted works are taken. In the aggregate means the total amount of copyrighted material from a single copyrighted work that is permitted to be used in an educational multimedia project without permission under these guidelines. These limitations apply cumulatively to each educator's or student's multimedia project(s) for the same academic semester, cycle or term. All students should be instructed about the reasons for copyright protection and the need to follow these guidelines. It is understood, however, that students in kindergarten through grade six may not be able to adhere rigidly to the portion limitations in this section in their independent development of educational multimedia projects. In any event, each such project retained under Sections 3.1 and 4.3 should comply with the portion limitations in this section.

4.2.1 Motion Media

Up to 10% or 3 minutes, whichever is less, in the aggregate of a copyrighted motion media work may be reproduced or otherwise incorporated as part of an educational multimedia project created under Section 2 of these guidelines.

4.2.2 Text Materials

Up to 10% or 1000 words, whichever is less, in the aggregate of a copyrighted work consisting of text material may be reproduced or otherwise incorporated as part of an educational multimedia project created under Section 2 of these guidelines. An entire poem of less than 250 words may be used, but no more than three poems by one poet, or five poems by different poets from any anthology may be used. For poems of greater length, 250 words may be used but no more than three excerpts by a poet, or five excerpts by different poets from a single anthology may be used.

4.2.3 Music, Lyrics, and Music Video

Up to 10%, but in no event more than 30 seconds, of the music and lyrics from an individual musical work (or in the aggregate of extracts from an individual work), whether the musical work is embodied in copies, or audio or audiovisual works, may be reproduced or otherwise incorporated as a part of a multimedia project created under Section 2. Any alterations to a musical work shall not change the basic melody or the fundamental character of the work.

4.2.4 Illustrations and Photographs

The reproduction or incorporation of photographs and illustrations is more difficult to define with regard to fair use because fair use usually precludes the use of an entire work. Under these guidelines a photograph or illustration may be used in its entirety but no more than 5 images by an artist or photographer may be reproduced or otherwise incorporated as part of an educational multi-media project created under Section 2. When using photographs and illustrations from a published collective work, not more than 10% or 15 images, whichever is less, may be reproduced or otherwise incorporated as part of an educational multimedia project created under Section 2.

4.2.5 Numerical Data Sets

Up to 10% or 2500 fields or cell entries, whichever is less, from a copyrighted database or data table may be reproduced or otherwise incorporated as part of an educational multimedia project created under Section 2 of these guidelines. A field entry is defined as a specific item of information, such as a name or Social Security number, in a record of a database file. A cell entry is defined as the intersection where a row and a column meet on a spreadsheet.

4.3 Copying and Distribution Limitations

Only a limited number of copies, including the original, may be made of an educator's educational multimedia project. For all of the uses permitted by Section 3, there may be no more than two use copies, only one of which may be placed on reserve as described in Section 3.23.

An additional copy may be made for preservation purposes but may only be used or copied to replace a use copy that has been lost, stolen, or damaged. In the case of a jointly created educational multimedia project, each principal creator may retain one copy but only for the purposes described in Sections 3.3 and 3.4 for educators and in Section 3.1 for students.

5. Examples of When Permission is Required

5.1 Using Multimedia Projects for Non-Educational or Commercial Purposes

Educators and students must seek individual permissions (licenses) before using copyrighted works in educational multimedia projects for commercial reproduction and distribution.

5.2 Duplication of Multimedia Projects Beyond Limitations Listed In These Guidelines

Even for educational uses, educators and students must seek individual permissions for all copyrighted works incorporated in their personally-created educational multimedia projects before replicating or distributing beyond the limitations listed in Section 4.3

5.3 Distribution of Multimedia Projects Beyond Limitations Listed In These Guidelines

Educators and students may not use their personally-created educational multimedia projects over electronic networks, except for uses as described in Section 3.2.3, without obtaining permissions for all copyrighted works incorporated in the program.

6. Important Reminders

6.1 Caution In Downloading Material from the Internet

Educators and students are advised to exercise caution in using digital material downloaded from the Internet in producing their own educational multimedia projects, because there is a mix of works protected by copyright and works in the public domain on the network. Access to works on the Internet does not automatically mean that these can be reproduced and reused without permission or royalty payment and, furthermore, some copyrighted works may have been posted to the Internet without authorization of the copyright holder.

6.2 Attribution and Acknowledgment

Educators and students are reminded to credit the sources and display the copyright notice © and copyright ownership information if this is shown in the original source, for all works incorporated as part of educational multimedia projects prepared by educators and students, including those prepared under fair use. Crediting the source must adequately identify the source of the work, giving a full bibliographic description where available (including author, title. publisher, and place and date of publication). The copyright ownership information includes the copyright notice (©, year of first publication and name of the copyright holder).

The credit and copyright notice information may be combined and shown in a separate section of the educational multimedia project (e.g. credit section) except for images incorporated into the project for the uses described in Section 3.2.3. In such cases, the copyright notice and the name of the creator of the image must be incorporated into the image when, and to the extent, such information is reasonably available; credit and copyright notice information is considered "incorporated" if it is attached to the image file and appears on the screen when the image is viewed.. In those cases when displaying source credits and copyright ownership information on the screen with the image would be mutually exclusive with an instructional objective (e.g. during examinations in which the source credits and/or copyright information would be relevant to the examination questions), those images may be displayed without such information being simultaneously displayed on the screen. In such cases, this information should be linked to the image in a manner compatible with such instructional objectives.

6.3 Notice of Use Restrictions

Educators and students are advised that they must include on the opening screen of their multimedia project and any accompanying print material a notice that certain materials are included under the fair use exemption of the U.S. Copyright Law and have been prepared according to the educational multimedia fair use guidelines and are restricted from further use.

6.4 Future Uses Beyond Fair Use

Educators and students are advised to note that if there is a possibility that their own educational multimedia project incorporating copyrighted works under fair use could later result in broader dissemination, whether or not as commercial product, it is strongly recommended that they take steps to obtain permissions during the development process for all copyrighted portions rather than waiting until after completion of the project.

6.5 Integrity of Copyrighted Works

Educators and students may make alterations in the portions of the copyrighted works they incorporate as part of an educational multimedia project only if the alterations support specific instructional objectives. Educators and students are advised to note that alterations have been made.

6.6 Reproduction or Decompilation of Copyrighted Computer Programs

Educators and students should be aware that reproduction or decompilation of copyrighted computer programs and portions thereof, for example the transfer of underlying code or control mechanisms, even for educational uses, are outside the scope of these guidelines.

6.7 Licenses and Contracts

Educators and students should determine whether specific copyrighted works, or other data or information, are subject to a license or contract. Fair use and these guidelines shall not preempt or supersede licenses and contractual obligations

Appendix A

1. Organizations Endorsing These Guidelines

Agency for Instructional Technology (AIT)
American Associations of Community Colleges (AACC)
American Society of Journalists and Authors (ASJA)
American Society of Media Photographers, Inc. (ASMP)
American Society of Composers, Authors and Publishers (ASCAP)
Association for Educational Communications and Technology (AECT)
Association for Information Media and Equipment (AIME)
Association of American Publishers (AAP)
Association of American Colleges and Universities (AAC&U)
Association of American University Presses, Inc. (AAUP)
Broadcast Music, Inc. (BMI)
Consortium of College and University Media Centers (CCUMC)
Instructional Telecommunications Council (ITC)
Maricopa Community Colleges/Phoenix
Motion Picture Association of America (MPAA)
Music Publishers' Association of the United States (MPA)
Software Publishers Association (SPA)

2. Individual Companies and Institutions Endorsing These Guidelines

Houghton Mifflin
McGraw-Hill
Time Warner, Inc.